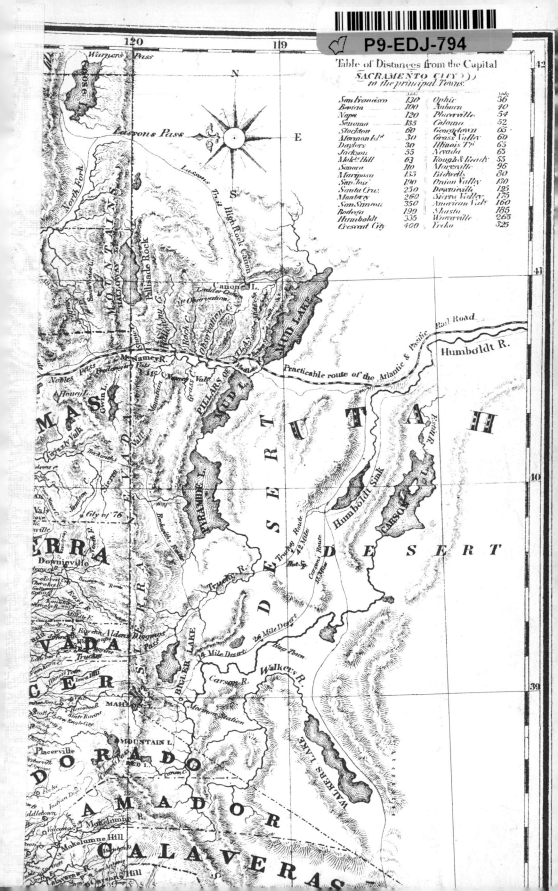

Table of Distances from the Capital
SACRAMENTO CITY
to the principal Towns.

	Miles		Miles
San Francisco	130	Ophir	36
Benicia	100	Auburn	40
Napa	120	Placerville	54
Sonoma	135	Coloma	52
Stockton	60	Georgetown	65
Mormon Isl.d	30	Grass Valley	60
Daylors	30	Illinois Tn	65
Jackson	55	Nevada	65
Mok.s Hill	63	Rough & Ready	55
Sonora	110	Marysville	96
Mariposa	155	Bidwells	80
San Jose	190	Onion Valley	130
Santa Cruz	250	Downieville	125
Monterey	260	Sierra Valley	175
San Simeon	350	American Vals	160
Bodega	199	Shasta	185
Humboldt	335	Weaverville	265
Crescent City	400	Yreka	325

Scenes of

WONDER &
CURIOSITY

JAMES MASON HUTCHINGS, miner, traveler, publisher of the *California Magazine*, "Father of Yosemite": A Taber portrait of the grand old man, *circa* 1900.
—Courtesy California Historical Society

SCENES OF

Wonder & Curiosity

from

HUTCHINGS'
CALIFORNIA
MAGAZINE

1856-1861

Edited by R. R. Olmsted

*Embellished by three hundred engravings
of California life and scenery*

Faithfully Reproduced by the Publishers

Howell-North

Berkeley, Califo

Published by Howell-North Books
1050 Parker Street, Berkeley 10, California

PREFACE

The five volumes of *Hutchings' California Magazine*, published between 1856 and 1861, are at once a mine for the historian and a delight to the curious. The editor of *this* volume, a most curious historian, has lost many hours over the past years, when, turning *Hutchings'* pages in search of that specific comment or drawing which will advance the project of the moment, he has been seduced from the narrow path of scholarship by an intriguing illustrated essay on the method of coining gold at the San Francisco mint, the trials of winter in the Sierra mines, the museum at the What Cheer house, the prospects of the honey bee in California . . . before he finds that which he seeks: a description of the Sacramento River salmon fishery, or the Farallone Islands egg industry.

James Mason Hutchings certainly did not intend his magazine only for the piratical eyes of the historian. He sought to both divert and instruct a wide and literate audience. He succeeded often, and where he did he has lost nothing through the passage of a century. The lucid and detailed sketches of life, nature, and institutions to be found in the pages of *Hutchings' Magazine* comprise a vivid portrait of California in the golden 'fifties.

The artist who created this portrait was thoroughly in love with his subject. J. M. Hutchings was no literary carpetbagger, nor was he an editor and publisher with the instincts of an accountant. He sought to promote California, what he saw as best in California, not to any narrow end, but for its own sake. His magazine with its many expensive illustrations was by far the most ambitious and costly publication among its contemporaries in California. Hutchings appears to have sold it to the subscribers at cost, for he could pay his contributors nothing, and in five years he cleared only the price of a suit of clothes from its profits. When ill health — possibly aggravated by a subscription list which promised economy rather than improvement in his magazine — drove him to sell out to the publishers of the *California Mountaineer*, the quality of the effort he had put into his magazine quickly became apparent. The *California Magazine and Mountaineer* started off a good cut below Hutchings' worst and from there rapidly slipped into the "literary" steerage-class that Hutchings so detested.

Hutchings stated quite clearly his views as to the editor's responsibility to his public when he wrote, in answer to a suggestion that the purpose of a magazine was to enable a reader to throw his time away pleasantly,

> We have an idea that the general reading public of California and particularly the mining population have been underrated, that they have not been given credit for the real degree of intelligence and good taste which they possess. A great many

V

persons suppose that the only literature for the mines is of the "yellow kivered" description; but we must differ from them, differ from them not only in opinion but in practice. We have an abiding faith that the people want solid information and a sober, common-sense view of topics of interest — and we shall endeavor, as far as in our power lies, to supply them.

That "solid information" James Hutchings was well prepared to supply. California was his subject; he knew it very well indeed. Born in England in 1824, he had come to the United States as a youth and was employed in a New Orleans business house when news of the great California gold strike swept the nation. He crossed the plains and mountains in '49, arriving in Placerville in October. He served more than an apprenticeship in the mines: he made his "pile" and lost it in the failure of a San Francisco bank, thus gaining invaluable first-hand experience with two major California institutions. He later had little to say about banks in his magazine, but he identified himself strongly with the miners, portraying their life and problems, and ever holding "the industrious miner" the best of the state's citizens.

Back in the mines, Hutchings again struck it rich — with his initial publishing venture. "The Miner's Ten Commandments," an illustrated letter-sheet he brought out in 1853, proved a best-seller of monumental proportions. Its success may have kindled the idea of a California magazine; in any event Hutchings became an inveterate tourist, gathering material and sketches throughout 1854 and 1855 which later appeared in the first volume of the magazine. He took a cameraman (daguerreian in those years) with him whenever possible, that the engravers might work from a perfectly accurate original. In 1854 he put out a letter-sheet depicting one of the Big Trees; in 1855 he led the first tourist party into Yosemite.

On the Yosemite trip he took with him Thomas Ayres to make sketches, as the daguerrotype equipment was too bulky for such a pioneer journey. After Hutchings began publication of the magazine, in 1856, he relied heavily on Arthur and Charles Nahl, the best of California's early artists, for drawings. The result was an illustrated magazine which could compare favorably with the *Harper's* or *Leslie's* of the day. We will neither support nor deny the statements of readers in Europe or "back in the States" that *Hutchings'* was the best of the illustrated magazines published in the whole world — but *Hutchings'* was most certainly an effort which California was not again prepared to match.

After James Hutchings retired from his magazine in 1861 he struck out with characteristic energy upon a new career. March of '62 found him struggling through the snows to discover whether or not Yosemite Valley was habitable in winter. (Conceivably with the consent of his physician: in that buoyant era the imposition of astonishing hardship was thought certain to subdue any but the most stubborn *malaise*.) Later in the season he brought his wife to the valley; he built a house; then he bought the primitive "Upper Hotel," renaming it "Hutchings' House." Already the leading publicist of Yosemite, he became a full-time prophet. He published a guide to Yosemite in 1877, *The Heart of the Sierras* in 1886,

Yosemite Valley and the Big Trees in 1894. He met death at the entrance to his beloved valley on October 31, 1902, when his team shied at a bear — or a rock, or a shadow — bolted, and threw him headlong onto the rocks beside the road.

THIS VOLUME

In the first number of the fifth volume of his magazine J. M. Hutchings (as introductory to an appeal for more subscribers) recounted an exchange with a friend, who, on seeing the newly bound fourth volume, remarked,

> "After all, there is a large amount of labor in writing, collecting and correcting five hundred and seventy-six pages of California matter, in such a volume as this!"

> "Which," we continued, "multiplied by four, gives two thousand three hundred and four pages, and includes nearly five hundred characteristic engravings of California life and scenery."

> "But," he continued, "I don't see where you could obtain so much interesting material."

In explaining what criteria we used in reducing such a mass of material to rather small compass we would fasten upon the use of the word "interesting" by Hutchings' friend as well as his own reference to "California life and scenery." They were both really talking about the informative articles dealing with California — which comprise far less than the total number of pages in a magazine that carried a large amount of fiction, poetry and editorial matter. Above all, they both most probably had in mind the longer and more lavishly illustrated articles which give the essential character to the magazine.

This volume contains the majority of these major illustrated articles on California. We have chosen what we felt would be most informative — or sometimes most curious or amusing — to the modern reader. A disproportionate number of these articles Hutchings placed in the favored "lead" position, indicating that he liked them, too. Some good articles dealing with Mexico, Central America, or other places outside of California have been left out, as has some California material which has been recently and fully treated elsewhere (*e. g.*, the Pony Express).

The articles are reprinted as they originally appeared, the page size increased slightly in the interests of readability. The reproduction of this work was made possible through the kind cooperation of Donald Coney, Librarian of the University of California; Dr. James Hart, Dr. Robert Becker, and Dr. John Barr Tompkins of the Bancroft Library; and James de T. Abajian of the California Historical Society.

ROGER R. OLMSTED

San Francisco
June, 1962

CONTENTS

PART IV

ODDS AND ENDS

Published Monthly.   Price 25 Cents.

HUTCHINGS'
CALIFORNIA
MAGAZINE

Nº. 16....OCTOBER, 1857.

PUBLISHED BY HUTCHINGS & ROSENFIELD,
146 MONTGOMERY STREET, second door north of Clay,... SAN FRANCISCO.
Postage pre-paid, ONE CENT to any part of the United States.

HUTCHINGS'
CALIFORNIA MAGAZINE.

No. I.—JULY, 1856.—Vol. I.

OUR INTRODUCTORY.

I N D READER, this is the first of our greeting and acquaintance. We hope, with your approval, to spend many pleasant hours in company with each other. It is our hope, as it will be our aim, to make our monthly visit to your fireside as welcome as the cheerful countenance and social converse of some dear old friend, who just drops in, in a friendly way, to spend the evening.

We wish to picture California, and California life : to portray its beautiful scenery and curiosities ; to speak of its mineral and agricultural products ; to tell of its wonderful resources and commercial advantages ; and to give utterance to the inner life and experience of its people, in their aspirations, hopes, disappointments and successes—the lights and shadows of daily life.

Whatever is noble, manly, useful, intellectual, amusing and refining, we shall welcome to our columns.

It will ever be our pride and pleasure to be on the side of virtue, morality, religion and progress.

We shall admit nothing that is partizan in politics or sectarian in religion ; but, claiming the right to please ourselves, we shall accord to the reader the same privilege.

Whatever we believe to be for the permanent prosperity of California, we shall fearlessly advocate, in any way that suits us.

We have no expectation of pleasing every one ; nor, that perfection will be written upon every page of its contents, for the simple reason that we are human ; but we shall do our best, continually, and those who do not like the magazine are not required to —buy it.

We have commenced its publication with the hope of filling a void—humbly it may be—in the wants of California, and the intelligent reader will see at a glance that the costly manner in which it is gotten up, and the price at which it is sold, the publishers rely upon a wide circulation for their pecuniary reward ; but they are confident that altho' placed within the reach of those who could only take *one* per month, that others will be tempted to *take a dozen*.

Therefore, placing ourselves in the hands of a generous public, we make our bow, and introduce to your kindly notice the first number of HUTCHINGS' CALIFORNIA MAGAZINE.

PART I

In and About SAN FRANCISCO

CHINESE — MALE AND FEMALE

This commingling of men of all creeds, and conditions, from all quarters of the world, with one common object — that of improving their condition — and who, more or less, have been dependent upon each other in its accomplishment, has given a commendable and cosmopolitan spirit of liberality towards each other — more perhaps than in any other land. . . .

IN AND ABOUT SAN FRANCISCO

When J. M. Hutchings wrote that his magazine would be on the side of virtue, morality, religion, and progress, and that he would admit nothing partisan in politics, he meant it. Nowhere is this editorial restraint more apparent than in what he saw fit to publish about San Francisco, that stronghold of vice, immorality, and partisanship. The first number of *Hutchings'* appeared at the height of the Vigilance excitement, the last when the City, and the whole state, was inflamed with the passions engendered by the onset of deadly war between the North and South. Hutchings allotted few pages to these momentous events, though he was a stout supporter of Vigilance and Union. His sentiments were most strongly expressed through the verse of his contributors, as in Carrie D.'s "The Vigilance Call":

The Ballot-box is naught to thee, 'tis wrested from thy power,
Thy fathers purchased it with blood and left it as thy dower;
But villains of the darkest dye, have wrested it from thee,
And now stand up a freeman, or forever bend the knee.

and Edward Pollock's "Disunion":

— our banner of blue
Has STRIPES for the traitors, as STARS for the true.
And the sun shall not shine on the men that shall see
Dismember'd or conquer'd the FLAG of the FREE.

Such verses are about as sensational as any material Hutchings allowed in his magazine (unless he was dealing with Brigham Young). He generally sought to instruct, or at least divert, his readers. The exposure of social evils he ordinarily eschewed, preferring to promote what seemed to him to further the public welfare. Hence, we find him boosting the Mechanic's Fairs, the public school system, the museum and library of the What Cheer House—San Francisco's leading temperance institution.

Above all, the combination of the off-beat and the instructive, preferably in conjunction with a glorious outing, J. M. Hutchings found most worthy of full-scale treatment. All of the major illustrated articles dealing with San Francisco are included in this volume. Hutchings' tastes and purposes are evident in this selection. Here are the mint and the post office — but not the Pacific Mail Steamship Company; here are the life and scenes of the Sacramento and the Farallones — but not Montgomery Street. Yet *because* he looked for a side of San Francisco life that was out of the controversial or sensational he gives us a picture hard to find in any other source.

HUTCHINGS'

CALIFORNIA MAGAZINE.

| Vol. IV. | JULY, 1859. | No. 1. |

FROM SAN FRANCISCO TO SACRAMENTO CITY.

SCENE AT THE MOUTH OF OLD SACRAMENTO RIVER.

MANY of our readers are aware that the great navigable highway for at least three-fourths of the inland commerce and passenger transit of the State, lies through the northern end of the bay of San Francisco, from thence past the southern shore of the bays of San Pablo and Suisun, and up the Sacramento river to Sacramento city. To illustrate the beautiful scenes upon this route we find it next to impossible to obtain faithful and reliable sketches from the deck of a swiftly moving steamboat, that generally makes the upward trip (123 miles,) within ten hours, about seven of which, even in summer, are by night. To obviate this difficulty, the writer, in company with two others, engaged a sailing craft of about five tons burthen, and deposited thereon our precious lives, (without even taking the precaution of having them insured) a limited but assorted cargo of general stores, cooking apparatus, bedding, and other sundries, then gave our canvas to the breeze, and were off.

As one of our party, in addition to being an excellent draughtsman, was familiar with the mysteries of navigation, and the other with the duties appertaining to the office of a *chef de cuisine*, we all considered that our prospects of securing the end at which we aimed were indeed flattering; while the comfort and pleasure we endured would more than counterbalance all the risks that were undertaken, and at the same time allow us the opportunity of sailing when and where we pleased, for all the sketches and enjoyment that we wanted.

Inasmuch as the course of our voyage, by mutual consent, lay around several islands and among numerous sloughs and lagoons of the Sacramento, as well as on the principal streams, occupying some eight days, and as much of our time was consumed among the beaver-trappers and salmon-fishers and curers on the above named waters, we shall not now recount our personal experiences and adventures, but reserve these subjects for a future and more suitable occasion, and take the reader, with his or her consent, by the far more pleasant and expeditious route of steamboat navigation.

There probably is not a more exciting and bustling scene of business activity in any part of the world, than can be witnessed on almost any day, Sunday excepted, at Jackson street wharf, San Francisco, at a few minutes before 4 o'clock P. M. Men and women are hurrying to and fro; drays, carriages, express-wagons and horsemen, dash past you with as much rapidity and earnestness as though they were the bearers of a reprieve to some condemned criminal whose last moment of life had nearly expired, and by its speedy delivery thought they could save him from the scaffold. Indeed one would suppose by the apparent recklessness of driving and riding through the crowd, that numerous limbs would be broken, and carriages made into pieces as small as mince meat; but yet to your surprise nothing of the kind occurs, for on arriving at the smallest real obstacle to their progress, animals are suddenly reined in, with a promptness that astonishes you.

On these occasions, too, there is almost sure to be one or more intentional passengers that arrive just too late to get aboard, and who in their excitement often throw an overcoat or valise on the boat, or overboard, but neglect to embrace the only opportune moment to get on board themselves, and are consequently left behind, as these boats are always punctual to their time of starting.

Supposing that we have been more fortunate, by securing our passage and stateroom in good time, please to put on your overcoat, as it is always cool in the evening on the bay, and let us take a cosy seat together, and while the black volumes of smoke are rolling from the tops of the funnels, and the boat is shooting past this

THE STEAMBOATS ANTELOPE AND BRAGDON AT JACKSON STREET
WHARF, SAN FRANCISCO.

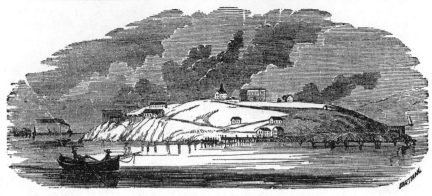

ALCATRACES ISLAND.

wharf, and that vessel now lying at anchor in the bay or in full sail upon her voyage, or while numerous nervous people are troubled about their baggage and asking the porter all sorts of questions, let us have a quiet chat together, upon the scenes we may witness on our trip, and the historical facts connected with the early navigation of this beautiful route to the interior.

The first sailing vessel that made the voyage from San Francisco to where Sacramento city now stands, was the schooner Isabella, chartered by Capt. John A. Sutter, about the 5th of August, 1839; and owing to the numerous intricate outlets of the Sacramento river, he was eight days in discovering its main channel; and when about ten miles below where Sacramento city now stands, two hundred armed and hostile Indians intercepted his progress.

These however, he succeeded in conciliating, and was then allowed to proceed on his voyage accompanied by two of the natives. Other sail vessels of course followed at different times, in the wake of the pioneer schooner "Isabella," but as we are now more interested in steam navigation we shall not mention them more length.

The first steamboat that ever plowed the waters of the Sacramento, from San Francisco, was the "Sitka," a Russian built, stern wheel vessel, about sixty feet in length by seventeen in breadth, owned by Capt. Leidesdorff, (the former owner of most of the Folsom property,) and she reached what was then known as Sutter's Embarcadero, now Sacramento city, in the summer of 1847.

The next was a stern wheel steam scow named the "Lady Washington," built at Sutter's Embarcadero, in Sept., 1849, and was owned by Simmons, Hutchinson & Co., and Smith, Bensley & Co., of that place, was run upon the upper rivers, and was the pioneer steam vessel above the mouth of the American river. The first trip was to where Coloma now stands; but unfortunately on her return trip she struck a snag and sunk, but was afterwards raised, refitted, and named the Ohio.

The next was a side-wheel steamer that was sent out on board ships from New York, put together in Sacramento city, there named the "Sacramento," and was run between Sacramento city and New York, on the Pacific, (a city of great pretensions, that was located near the mouth of the San Joaquin, but long since defunct,) and there connected with a line of schooners from San Francisco. This vessel was owned and commanded by Capt. John Van Pelt.

A small craft called the "Mint," was the next steamboat, and ran on this route through from San Francisco to Sacramento.

The large propeller McKim, of about 400 tons burthen, was the next in rotation, and made her trip from New Orleans, through the straits of Magellan to San Francisco, in 1849, and took her first trip up the Sacramento, in the latter part of Oct. of that year.

By far the most beautiful, most commodious, most comfortable, and at the same time, the most successful steamboat that ever run on the Sacramento river, was the "Senator," of 500 tons burthen. She made the voyage around Cape Horn, and arrived here on the 27th of Oct., 1849, and her first trip up to Sacramento city Nov. 5th, following. Her rates of fare were $25 per passenger up, and $30 down; Meals $2, each; Stateroom $10; Freight per ton from $40 to $50.

During the first year on that route her net profits exceeded $60,000 per month; and ever since she has been a very profitable boat for her owners. The number of her passengers was generally about three hundred, and her freight about from two hundred to three hundred tons.

The next was a stern-wheel steamboat called the "Lawrence," 108 feet in length by 18 feet in width. She was brought out by a New Bedford company and put up at New York on the Pacific; and when finished, she was sent to Stockton about the latter part of Nov., 1849, and was the first steamboat that ever sailed for or arrived at that city. In December following she was taken to Sacramento and there sold, when her new owners sent her up the Feather river to Marysville, in command of Capt. Chadwick, and she was the first steamboat that ever ascended that river.

The "Linda," a stern-wheel steamer, was the next, owned by a company of which Mark Brummagem was one of the principal members. She ran between Sacramento

city and Marysville. Freight on the Lawrence and Linda was from 8 to 10 cents per pound; drinks 50 cents each.

THE first steamboat that ever ascended the Sacramento river as far as Tehama was the "Jack Hayes," commanded by Capt Mosely, in May, 1850. She was first named the Commodore Jones, but being lengthened and otherwise changed, she lost her identity and her name at the same time.

The "Gold Hunter," commanded by Capt. Branham, now the U. S. surveying schooner Active, was put on about this time, but soon withdrawn.

The "Capt. Sutter," a small stern wheel boat, although only the second boat to Stockton, was the first to make regular trips from San Francisco to that city, and

RED (OR TREASURE) ROCK.

succeeded the "Lawrence." She was put up by Capt. James Blair, of the U. S. Navy, and was more successful in proportion to her size than the Senator on the other route; and cleared not less than $200,000 for her owners the first year.

We might mention *en passant*, to illustrate the large profits made by steamboats at that early day, that the Lawrence made a trip from Sacramento city to Lassen's Ranch, and received 30 cents per pound for freight on her entire cargo.

The following list of the various steamboats that have from time to time been running on this route, occasionally changing to some other, or been laid up, is as complete as we could make it, and we think will include nearly the whole that have ever been upon it:—

THE TWO SISTERS.

STERN WHEEL.
(*High Pressure,*)
Young America,
Goodman Castle,
Gov. Dana,
Shasta,
Plumas,
Gazelle,
Cleopatra,
Belle,
Gem,
Capt. Sutter,
Pike,
Orient,
Fashion,
Nevada,
Daniel Moir,
Kennebec,
Marysville,
Clara,
Medea,
James Blair,
Enterprise,
Lawrence,
Latona,
Maria,
Pearl,
Etna,
Sam Soule,
Swan,
San Joaquin,
Tehama,
Fire Fly,
Kangaroo,

SIDE WHEEL.
(*High Pressure.*)
Urilda,
Camanche,
J. Bragdon,
H. J. Clay,
American Eagle,
Helen Hensley,
Anna Abernethy,
Willamette,
Eclipse,
Queen City,
Kate Kearny,
Express,
Caleb Cope,
Sagamore,
Mariposa,
W. E. Robinson,
Gov. Dana, No. 2,
Sophia,
Union, (*Iron Vessel*)
Cornelia,
C. M. Webber,
(*Low Pressure.*)
Senator,
New World,
Confidence,
W. G. Hunt,
Antelope,
Thomas Hunt,
Surprise,
Goliah,
El Dorado,
Gold Hunter,
(*now Active.*)

PROPELLERS.
McKim,   Hartford,
Gen. Warren,   Eudora,
Commodore Preble,   Major Tompkins,
          Chesapeake.

While we have thus been gossiping about steamboats, we have arrived off Alcatraces or Pelican Island. This we see is just opposite the Golden Gate, and about half way between San Francisco and Angel Island. It commands the entrance to the great bay of San Francisco, and is but three and a half miles from Fort Point.

This island is 140 feet in height above low tide, 450 feet in width, and 1650 feet in length, somewhat irregular in shape; and fortified on all sides. The large building on its summit, about the centre or crest of the island, is a defensive barrack or citadel, three stories high, and in time of peace will accommodate about 200 men, and in time of war at least three times that number. It is not only a shelter for the men, and will withstand a respectable cannonade, but from the top a murderous fire could be poured upon its assailants at all parts of the island, and from whence every point of it is visible. There is a belt of fortifications encircling the island, consisting of a series of Barbette batteries, mounting altogether about 94 guns, 24, 42, 68, and 132 pounders.

The first building that you notice after landing at the wharf is a massive brick and stone guard house, shot and shell proof, well protected by a heavy gate and draw-bridge, and has three embrasures for 24 pound howitzers that command the approach from the wharf. The top of this, like the barracks, is flat, for the use and protection of riflemen. Other guardhouses of similar construction are built at different points, between which there are long lines of parapets sufficiently high to preclude the possibility of an escalade, and back of which are circular platforms for mounting guns of the heaviest caliber, some of which weigh from 9,000 to 10,000 pounds. In addition to these there are three bomb-proof magazines, each of which will hold 10,000 lbs of powder. On the south-eastern side of the island is a large furnace for the

STRAITS OF CARQUINEZ.

purpose of heating cannon balls; and other similar contrivances are in course of construction.

Unfortunately there is no natural supply of water on the island, so that all of that element which is used there is taken from Saucelito. In the basement of the barracks is a cistern capable of holding 50,000 gallons of water, a portion of which can be supplied from the roof of that building in the rainy season.

Appropriations have been made for the fortification of this island to the amount of $896,000, and about $100,000 more will complete them. From 40 to 200 men have been employed upon these works since their commencement in 1853.

At the south-eastern end of the island is a fog bell of about the same weight as that at Fort Point, and which is regulated to strike by machinery once in about every fifteen seconds.

The whole of the works on this island are under the skillful superintendance of Lieut. McPherson, who very kindly ex-

plained to us the strength and purposes of the different fortifications made.

The lighthouse at the south of the barracks contains a Fresnel lantern of the third order, and which can be seen on a clear night some twelve miles outside the heads, and is of great service in suggesting the course of a vessel when entering the bay.

Yet, as we are sailing on at considerable speed across the entrance to the Bay, towards Angel Island, we must not linger here, not even in imagination; especially as we can now look out through the far famed Golden Gate and towards the golden hinged hope of many who with lingering eyes have longed to look upon it and to enter through its charmed portals to this land of gold. How many too have longed and hoped for years to pass it once again, on their way out to the endeared and loving hearts that wait to welcome them at that dear spot they still call Home! God bless them.

Now the vessel is in full sail, and steam-

BENICIA, MARTINEZ, AND MONTE DIABLO.

ships, that are entering the heads, as well as those within that are tacking now on this stretch and now on that to make way out against the strong northwest breeze that blows in at the Golden Gate for three eighths of the year, are fast being lost to sight, and we are just abreast of Angel Island and but five miles from the city of San Francisco. This Island was granted by Gov. Alvarado to Antonio M. Asio, by order of the Government of Mexico, in 1837; and by him sold to its present owners in 1853. As it contains some 800 acres of excellent land it is by far the largest and most valuable of any in the Bay of San Francisco; and the green wild oats that grow to its very summit in early spring, but ripened now, give excellent pasturage to stock of all kinds; while the natural springs at different points afford abundance of water at all seasons. At the present time there are about 500 sheep roaming over its fertile hills. A large portion of the land is susceptible of cultivation for grain and vegetables.

From the inexhaustible quarries of hard blue and brown sandstone that here abound, have been taken nearly all of the stone used in the foundations of the numerous buildings in San Francisco.— The extensive fortifications at Alcatraces Island, Fort Point, and other places, have been faced with it; and the extensive Government works at Mare Island have been principally built with stone from these quarries, and many thousands of tons will yet be required from the same source before the fortifications and other Government works are completed. Clay is also found in abundance, and of an excellent quality for making bricks.

In 1856 this Island was surveyed by the U. S. Engineers, for the purpose of locating sites for two 24 gun batteries, which are in the line of fortifications required before our Bay may be considered as fortified. The most important of these

SCENE AT THE JUNCTION OF OLD RIVER AND STEAMBOAT SLOUGH.

batteries will be on the north-west point of the Island, and will command Raccoon Straits; and until this is built, our Navy Yard at Mare Island, and even the city of San Francisco itself cannot be considered safe, as through these Straits ships of war could easily pass, if by means of the heavy fog that so frequently hangs over the entrance to the bay, or other cause, they once passed Fort Point in safety. But let us pass on to Red Rock.

This singular looking island was formerly called Treasure or Golden Rock in old charts, from some traditionary report being circulated of some large treasure having been once carried there by early Spanish navigators. In charts of recent date however, it is sometimes called Molate Island, but is now more generally known as Red Rock, from its general color.

There are several strata of rock, of different colors, if rock it can be called, one of which is very fine and resembles an article sometimes found upon a lady's toilet-table—of course in earlier days— known as rouge-powder. Besides this there are several stratas of a species of clay or colored pigment, of from four to twelve inches in thickness, and of various colors. Upon the beach numerous small red pebbles, very much resembling cornelian, are found. There can be but little wonder it should be called "Red Rock" by plain matter-of-fact people like ourselves. It is covered with wild oats to its summit, on which is planted a flag-staff and cannon. Some four years ago its locater and owner, Mr. Selim E. Woodworth, took about half a dozen tame rabbits over to it, from San Francisco, and now there are several hundred.

As Mr. W., before becoming a benedict, made this his place of residence, he partially graded its apparently inaccessible sides; and at different points planted several ornamental trees. A small bachelor's cabin stands near the water's edge, and as this affords the means of cooking fish and sundry other dishes, its owner and a small party of friends pay it an occasional visit for fishing and general recreation. Several sheep roam about on the island, and as they like rabbits never drink water, they do not feel the loss of that which nature has here failed to supply.

But on, on we sail, and pass Maria Island and also two low rocks called the Two Sisters, and after shooting by Point San Pablo, we enter the large bay of that name ; charmed as we are with fine table and grazing lands on our right at the foot of the Contra Costa range of hills.

Just before entering the Straits of Carquinez, that connects the bays of San Pablo and Suisun, on our left we get a glimpse of the Government works at Mare Island, and the town of Vallejo; but as we shall probably have something to say about these points at some future time, we will now take a look at the straits. As the stranger approaches these for the first time, he makes up his mind that the vessel on which he stands is out of her course and is certainly running towards a bluff, and will soon be in trouble if she does not change her course, but as he advances and the entrance to this narrow channel becomes visible, he then concludes that a few moments ago he entertained a very foolish idea.

Now however the bell of the steamboat and a porter both announce that we are coming near Benicia, and that those who intend disembarking here had better have their baggage and their ticket in readiness. One would suppose as the boat nears the wharf that she is going to run "right into it," but soon she moves gracefully round and is made fast; but while those ashore and those aboard are eagerly scanning each other, to see if there is any familiar face to which to give the nod of recognition, or the cordial waving of the hand in friendly greeting, we will take our seats and say a word or two about this city.

Benicia was founded in the fall of 1847 by the late Thomas O. Larkin, and Roland Semple (who was also the originator and editor of the first California newspaper published at Monterey, Aug. 15th, 1846, entitled "The Californian,") upon land donated them for the purpose by Gen. M. G. Vallejo, and named in honor of the General's estimable lady.

In 1848 a number of families took up their residence here. During the fall of that year a public school was established, and which has been continued uninterruptedly to the present. In the ensuing spring a Presbyterian church was organized, and has continued under its original pastor, to the present time.

The peculiarly favorable position of Benicia recommended it at an early day as a suitable place for the general military headquarters of the U. S., upon the Pacific. Being alike convenient of access both to the sea-board and interior, and far enough from the coast to be secure against sudden assault in time of war, it was seen that no more favorable position could be selected, as adapted to all contingencies. These views met the approval of the General Government; and according-

VIEW FIVE MILES ABOVE STEAMBOAT SLOUGH.

ly extensive storehouses were built, military posts established; and arrangements made for erecting here the principal arsenal on the Pacific coast.

There already are erected barracks for the soldiers, and officers' quarters; two magazines capable of holding from 6,000 to 7,000 barrels of gun-powder of 100 lbs. each; two storehouses filled with gun-carriages, cannon, ball, and several hundred stand of small arms, besides workshops, &c.

About one hundred men are now employed, under the superintendance of Capt F. D. Calender, in the construction of an Arsenal 200 feet in length by 60 feet in width, and three stories in height, suitably provided with towers, loop-holes, windows, &c. Besides this a large citadel is in course of erection. $225,000 have already been appropriated to these works, and they will most probably require as much more before the whole is completed.

Here too are ten highly and curiously ornamented bronze cannon, six 8 pounders and four 4 pounders, that were brought originally from old Spain, and taken at Fort Point during our war with Mexico.

The following names and dates are inscribed on some of them, besides coats of arms, &c.

"San Martin, Ano. D. 1684."
"Poder, Ano. D. 1693."
"San Francisco, Ano. D. 1673."
"San Domengo, Ano. D. 1679."
"San Pedro, Ano. D. 1628."

As the barracks are merely a depot for the reception and transmission of troops, it is difficult to say how many soldiers are quartered here at any one time.

There are numerous other interesting places about Benicia, one of which is the extensive works of the Pacific Mail Steamship Company, where all the repairs to their vessels are made, coal deposited, &c., &c.

In 1853 Benicia was chosen the capital of the State by our peripatetic Legislature, and continued to hold that position for about a year, when it was taken to Sacramento, where it still (for a wonder) remains.

And, though last, by no means the least important feature of Benicia, is the widely known and deservedly flourishing boarding school for young ladies, the Benicia seminary, under the charge of

CHURCH ON THE RIVER, NINE MILES ABOVE
STEAMBOAT SLOUGH.

New York on the Pacific, we arrive at the west end of a large, low tule flat lying between the San Joaquin and the Sacramento, named Sherman's Island, and here we enter the Sacramento river. The Montezuma hills seen on our right, and a few stunted trees on the left, are the only objects in the landscape to relieve the eye by contrast with the low tule swamp, until we approach the new and flourishing little settlement of Rio Vista, just opposite the mouth of the "old Sacramento river," or more properly speaking, the principal branch of the stream.

Miss Mary Atkins, founded in 1852, and in which several young ladies have taken graduating honors. Next to this is the collegiate school for young gentlemen under the superintendence of Mr. Flatt, and which was established in 1853. Next to this is the college of Notre Dame for the education of Catholic children.— These, united to the excellent sentiments of the people, make Benicia a favorite place of residence for families.

Nearly opposite to Benicia and distant only three miles is the pretty agricultural village of Martinez, the county-seat of Contra Costa county. A week among the live-oaks, gardens, and farms in and around this lovely spot, will convince the most skeptical that there are few more beautiful places in any part of the State. A steam ferry boat runs across the straits between this place and Benicia every hour in the day. The Stockton boat always touches here both going and returning.

But now we must hurry on our way, as the steamboat is by this time passing the different islands in the bay of Suisun, named as follows:— Preston Island, King's, Simmons', Davis', Washington, Knox's and Jones' Islands; and passing

This village is just about half-way between Benicia and Sacramento, and bids fair to be a place of some importance eventually, as arrangements are now being made to open a road past here, and between Suisun and Vacca Valleys and Stockton. From Mr. C. A. Kirkpatrick, the obliging post-master there, we are favored with the following table of distances :—

		Miles.
From San Francisco to Benicia....		30
Benicia to New York,.................,		20 "
" to mouth of San Joaquin,		21 "
" to mouth of Sac. River,...		26 "
" Montezuma,....................		27 "
" Lone Tree Island,............		29 "
" Twin Houses,.................		32 "
" Seven Mile Slough,.........		39 "
" Wood Island, [2 M. Long.]		40 "
" Rio Vista,.....................		41 "
" Mouth of old Sac. River,		42 "
" Mouth Cache creek slough,		46 "
" Hog's Back,...................		48 "
" Beaver Slough,..............		52 "
" Mouth Steamboat slough,		54 "
" Mouth of Sutter slough,...		54 "
" Head of Sutter slough,....		55 "
[one mile long.]		
" Head Steamboat slough, and junction with the main Sacramento river, [5 miles long.]		59 "
From Benicia to Randall's Island [2 miles long.]		61 "
From Benicia to Sac. city,........		90

THE LEVEE AT SACRAMENTO, FROM WASHINGTON, YOLO COUNTY.

As we have seen, six miles above the mouth of the old river, is the far famed " Hog's Back." This is formed by the settling of the sediment which comes down, caused by a widening of the stream, and a decrease in the fall of the river. It extends for about three hundred yards in length; and at the lowest stage of water is about five feet from the surface, and at the highest point eleven feet six inches. Being affected by the tides, and as they are exactly at the same point every two weeks, during the fall season of the year for two or three days at each low tide, a detention of heavily freighted vessels of from one to four hours will then take place. Persons when descending the river, as the steamboat generally leaves Sacramento city at 2 o'clock, P. M., have an opportunity of knowing when they arrive at the Hogs Back by seeing the mast of a vessel with the lower cross-trees upon it, and sometimes a portion of her bulwarks. This vessel was named the Charleston, and was freighted principally with quartz machinery, a portion of which being for the Gold Hill Quartz Co., at Grass Valley, she had discharged, but the owners of another and larger portion of it not being found, she was returning with it to San Francisco, but having stuck upon this sand bank at a very low stage of the water, she careened over and was swamped. Several attempts have since been made to take out the machinery, but as yet it has defied all attempts, and being filled with sand it will be a very difficult task for any one to perform, and the reward be but a poor one, inasmuch as it cannot be in any other than a spoiled condition from rust and other causes.

There is a little steam scow called the Gipsey, that plies between the various ranches and gardens on the river, and Sacramento city, taking vegetables, grain flour &c., up to the city, and returning with groceries, dry goods, papers, &c.—

By this means she has created quite a snug little business for herself and become an indispensable visitor to the residents on the river.

Sacramento City is at length in view, but we have gossiped so much by the way, that we have not the space left to devote to the subject which we should wish to give to a place holding the second rank on the Pacific coast, and possessing as many objects of interest as does our sister City of the Plains. We shall, therefore, defer all remarks until some future number, when we intend to give an elaborate description of the capital of our Golden State.

In conclusion, we would say to those who wish to escape for a brief season the confinement of city life, and enjoy a summer's ramble, we could not recommend a tour which can be made with so much ease, and is so generally calculated to please every variety of tastes, as a trip on the bay and river. The tourist who merely journeys for amusement—the individual desirous of beholding the unbounded resources of our state, and the artist, will each find much to gratify the desires which induced them to travel.

The scenery as you steam up the river is in no slight degree picturesque. Here and there, as you turn with the sudden windings of the stream, you come upon the little boats of fishermen, and sloops, with their sails furled like the folded wings of a sea-bird, waiting for the wind. The improvements of the husbandman are everywhere seen along the shores.— Cottages half hidden among the drooping branches of the sycamores, out-houses, haystacks, orchards, and gardens, with their product of squashes and cabbages piled in huge heaps, give a cheerful domestic character to the scene. The landscape is diversified by the gnarled oaks, with vines clinging about them for support, and their branches covered with dark masses of mistletoe. Far away the snow-capped Sierras, with a black belt of pines at their base, and nearer the mist-draped Coast Range, rise on the view. Along the plains are here and there seen clumps of trees—a sure indication of water; and occasionally the charred trunk of some blasted tree lifts its bare branches toward heaven in solitary grandeur. During the seasons when the immense tracts of tules which cover the low lands are on fire, the conflagration lends a wild and peculiar beauty to the Scenes on the Bay and River.

THE ENGLISHMAN.

"AROUND THE BAY," IN THE SEASON OF FLOWERS.

THE Rev. T. Starr King in a letter to an eastern journal, written last July, thus describes the "flowers by the acre, flowers by the square mile," which paint our bay-hills from bases to tops in the spring season:

In the early part of May, a week after my arrival in California, I was invited by a very intelligent gentleman in San Francisco, to take a seat in his carriage for a "drive around the bay." This means around the Bay of San Francisco, which extends southerly about fifty miles from the Golden Gate, where the tides of the Pacific force their way inland. The bay is, therefore, a large salt-water lake, about eight miles broad and six times as long. It is undotted with islands, and lies placid in the embrace of some of the richest lands of California. In making the tour around it, we drive down along the narrow county of San Mateo, whose hills divide the dreamy bay from the billows of the Pacific, then across the county of Santa Clara, and up, on the eastern side, through Alameda county to Oakland, where the ferry-boat returns us to the metropolis of wind and fog, whose climate in summer is exhaustively stated in the phrase, "gust and dust."

Early in May is the true time to make this excursion, for then the country is at the height of its brief bloom. California has often been compared with Palestine and Syria for scenery. The passages in the Psalms and the New Testament which describe the fleeting beauty of the flowers and the grass, are certainly applicable here. "For the sun is no sooner risen with a burning heat, than it withereth the grass, and the flower thereof falleth, and the grace of the fashion of it perisheth." Indeed, there is no grass, properly speaking, native to the landscape. The green of early May on the uncultivated plains and slopes is mostly that of the wild oats. As the summer sun rises, and the rains cease, they ripen into a golden tinge, which, at a distance, is the hue of sand, and their seed drops into the parched and crackling ground for new crops when the rain returns. By the middle of June all the wild fields that are destitute of trees, look sandy with this harvest of indigenous and self-sowed grain; and it is only in May that the plains and hill-sides which the plowshare has not broken are clad in their vesture of embroidered green.

But the beauty is as captivating as it is evanescent. Some travelers have written of the marvelous effect of the air of California on the spirits. Bayard Taylor tells us that, on this very drive, he felt in breathing the air like Julius Cæsar, Milo of Crotona and General Jackson rolled into one. I cannot honestly say that the vivifying quality was any greater than I have experienced in the Pinkham woods, or the forests of Mount Adams, or on the heights of Randolph. Oxygen is oxygen, and will General Jacksonize a man as quickly in Coos county, New Hampshire, as when it blows over the coast range of California, fresh from the Pacific. But there was a great exhileration in the first acquaintance with the scenery of a strange land, especially when made in a luxurious carriage and with the accompaniment of pleasant companions and a very spirited team.

The first thing that arrested attention after leaving the sandy shores of San Francisco was the flowers. Early in May, in New England, people *hunt* for flowers. A bunch of violets, or a sprig or two of brilliant color, intermixed with green, is a sufficient trophy of a tramp that chills you, damps your feet, and possibly leaves the seed of consumption. Here they have flowers in May, not shy, but rampant, as if nothing else had the right to be; flowers by the acre, flowers by the square mile, flowers as the visible carpet of an immense mountain wall. You can gather them in clumps, a dozen varieties at one pull. You can fill a bushel-basket in five minutes. You can reap them into mounds. And the colors are as charming as the numbers are profuse. Yellow, purple, violet, pink and pied, are spread around you, now in separate level masses, now two or three combined in a swelling knoll, now intermixed in gorgeous confusion. Imagine yourself looking across a hundred acres of wild meadow, stretching to the base of hills nearly two thousand feet high—the whole expanse swarming with little straw-colored wild sun-flowers, orange poppies, squadrons of purple beauties, battalions of pink—and then the mountain, unbroken by a tree or a rock, glowing with the investiture of all these hues, softened and kneaded by distance. This is what I saw on the road to San Mateo. The orange and purple seemed to predominate in the mountain robe. But on the lower slopes, and reaching midway its height, was a strange sprinkling of blue, gathered here and there into intenser stripes, and running now and then into sharp points, as if over the general basis of purple, orange and yellow, there had fallen a violet snow, which lay tenderly around the base, but in a few places on the side had been blown into drifts and points.

The wild poppy of California, in May, is the most fascinating of all the flowers. It does not have a striped or spotty leaf, but is stained with a color which is a compromise between a tea-rose and an orange, and is as delicately flushed and graduated in hue as a perfect rose. I never tire in studying their color, in masses or singly. While driving to San Mateo, we came upon little clumps of them, springing out of the rocks on the edge of the road that overhangs the bay, and their vivid orange, upheld on graceful stems, and contrasted with the grey stones and the blue of the bay, gave me a joy which comes up as fresh while I write as when I saw it first. Another piece of cheer intrudes itself between my eyes and the paper, and insists that a note shall be made of it. I mean a California black-bird, perched on a mustard stalk ten feet high. The wild mustard grows luxuri-antly on the lands at the foot of the bay. It is a great trouble to the farmers, for if the cows eat even a little of it—and they seem to like it for seasoning—it gives a pungent flavor to the milk and makes the butter bite. But a field of it in bril-liant yellow is decidedly a pleasing con-diment to the general feast of colors. And when a blackbird with a large spot of scarlet on each wing flutters over a tall spear of it and then alights with a cheery twitter, one has a picture before him which gives two-fold delight by mak-him repeat the couplet of Holmes—

The crack-brained bobolink courts his crazy mate,
Poised on a bulrush tipsy with his weight.

If I quote wrongly, may the genial and always accurate Professor forgive me. I repeat from memory, and must wait till the *Mameluke* arrives from Boston with my books, before I can verify a dozen passages of his, which the Californian scenery sets to music again in my brain. And yet the old Californians, "forty-nine-ers," sigh when you speak in praise of the May-luxuriance around the bay. They say that the glory is over now. "Ichabod" is written on the landscape. They rode over the same districts when there were no roads, or ranches, or fen-ces, between San Francisco and San José, and when the horses wallowed and gal loped through an ocean of floral splendor. The visitor cannot help noticing, when he leaves the base of the mountains, and comes to the farms, how civilization has tamed the land. The barley and wheat, and bearded sweeps of simple green, look cool and unromantic in contrast with the

natural coat of many colors which the unploughed districts wear. The brindled leopard has taken the hue of the cat. It is only when, here and there, we come upon a garden, and see the blaze of roses which bloom the year through, that we see how superior art is to nature.

THE HYBRID.

To the Homeward Bound.— Something to Remember.—Before going East be sure to subscribe for

𝔥𝔲𝔱𝔠𝔥𝔦𝔫𝔤𝔰' 𝔠𝔞𝔩𝔦𝔣𝔬𝔯𝔫𝔦𝔞 𝔪𝔞𝔤𝔞𝔷𝔦𝔫𝔢.

OUR CHOWDER PARTY.

READER, if you feel morose, or ill-natured: if you believe that life is one vast workshop, and "every man and woman merely workers," whose duties to themselves and to the world they live in, consist in any number of hours faithfully devoted to their daily tasks, we respectfully invite you to pass on—you don't belong to us ; and cannot, on any pretence whatever, form part of, or accompany, our party—our chowder party—not even in imagination. If you are such, again we say, " pass on."

Our little company, though earnest workers in such daily avocations as circumstances or duty indicates, are also believers in that pleasing truth—written by every ray of glorious sun-light on each flower-covered hill, and sung in every breath by bird or breeze—that everything created is, or should be ministers of good to man to make him happier; and that only they whose hearts are shut against the gladdening lessons these should teach, are its untruthful readers.

You could see in every face that Care (always an unpleasant and uninvited guest on such occasions) was absent from the company—perhaps had lost his way, or fell, like many of his victims, through the chinks or trap-holes of the wharves. The light in every eye, the smile on every lip, gives answer before you question, " Thank you, I am jolly ! How are you ?" We venture to say that could the good-natured reader have seen our happy group stowed away so cosily in the cabin of the " Restless," among plethoric baskets of inner-man comforts, a huge black pot, fish-lines and general stores, he would have wished to have formed a part of that group.

Presently the anchor was weighed, the sails set, and our trim and taut little craft, in command of Capt. Moody, was gliding over—it scarcely seemed to be running through—the waters of the bay. First we must visit the wreck of the steamship " Granada," lying in Fatality Bay, just below Fort Point. Here could be found plenty of fish for " the chowder," but the swell having raised a stomachic objection to a thorough enjoyment of the Waltonic amusement on the part of some of the ladies, the wreck was hurriedly inspected, and the yacht "put about."

From Fort Point we darted across the channel to Raccoon Straits, at great speed, and anchored in a small bay near Saucelito. Here, to our discomfiture, we found that the finny tribes seemed to have been notified of our intent, for they manifested their disfavor at the part we intentionally had assigned them in the " chowder party " by becoming *non est inventus*.

It is true we enjoyed the trip, the pleasant company, the good-humored jokes, the good things (luckily) provided; but for that " chowder" upon which our imaginations (not our appetites) had feasted, where was it ? " Who ever knew a chowder party to catch fish enough for any single person—and here were eighteen ?" " Did any one know why this should be an exception ? " " We ought to have bought fish enough before sailing." These and other pertinent queries were received with hearty laughter. It was true that we had caught no fish ; it was equally true that a chowder could not very well be made without them ; but how were we to help ourselves ? " Aye, that was the question !"

At this juncture a small boy, with a large head and a long slice of bread-and-butter, cleared his mouth and his throat by gulping down the bread-and-butter amalgamation to make way for the remark, " Plenty—fish—down—down—by the—big—dock—yonder." Fine boy, that; excellent boy; hoped he personally

MAKING THE CHOWDER.

would be as great a comfort to his mother as his remark was to us. Should his prophecy be fulfilled, why, there were other prognostications that had previously been indulged in that would not be ; if we could obtain a chowder, after all, who would not exult in our good luck ?

A little before sunset fish after fish were taken in, (in a double sense) and an abundance for a large chowder bucketed, when the question arose, shall we go ashore and make an evening of it, or take them home ? The moon already gave assurance that she would light us homeward, and decided our unanimous vote in favor of chowder.

To tell the care and safety with which we were all landed by our excellent captain ; the delight manifest in our success ; the speed with which the wood was gathered, and the fire lighted ; the readiness with which men cleaned the fish, pared the potatoes, or peeled the onions ; and how the ladies—God bless them—resolved themselves into a chowder-and-tea manufacturing committee : or, to relate how young lassies ran races on the beach with young and elderly gentlemen, and beat them ; and how this one measured his length on the beach, and the others— didn't ; or how —— made love to ——, &c., lie beyond the province of this narrative to confess, as we remember the *maestro's* maxim, that " good boys and girls never tell tales out of school." Suffice it to say that there never was such a chowder ; that Boston, Nantucket, and other celebrated concoctions of this kind, could not be brought into favorable comparison with our " California chowder "; that our appetites, although capacious, (and it is with no ordinary satisfaction that we write the fact,) found the contents of the large black pot fully equal thereto. If the reader will be kind enough to take a full look at the engraving, (from a sketch by our first officer,) he or she will see at a glance how beautifully picturesque was our situation.

But the voyage home was a fitting close to the pleasures of the day. The bright moon without a cloud; the fresh breeze; the graceful, bird-like buoyancy and swiftness of the yacht; the songs sung, as our little craft sped onward, homeward; the kindly feelings and sentiments exchanged; and, although last, not least, the grateful hearts we each possessed towards Captain Moody, our first officer, to whom we were so much indebted for the day's enjoyment, and who, besides being a pleasant gentleman, knew his duty as a seaman, and did it well.

LIBRARY OF THE WHAT CHEER HOUSE, SAN FRANCISCO.

A LIBRARY in a public hotel has presented itself to us as such a novelty, that we have sent our memory on an expedition of exploration among all the hotels with which we are familiar, both north and south, east and west, and over parts of Europe, and the report on its return is, "Nothing of the kind to be found."

It would seem that the physical wants and comforts of the public have been the only ones deemed worthy of consideration. The enterprising proprietor of the What Cheer House, Mr. R. B. Woodward, has inaugurated a new era in his hotel department, by including the intellectual, and has thus set an example we hope to see followed in all parts of the world.

It was a happy thought. Hotels are mainly for the accommodation and entertainment of the traveling public, who are not supposed to be able to carry but a very limited number of books with them. There is often much leisure, especially on wet or unpleasant days, which intelligent strangers wish to employ to advantage.

If they have to traverse the streets in search of intellectual occupation, especially when weary, it becomes an unpleasant task. Besides, to walk upon the highways of a strange city, and feel that every face looked into is that of a stranger, often creates a loneliness in social minds that is very oppressive. Indeed, we know of no solitude as unpleasant as that upon the crowded paths of life, where the living tide is perpetually drifting past, leaving you unknown and uncared for in some little eddy, alone. To have some quiet corner, into which to retire and commune with yourself, or with some favorite author, is a great relief. This is provided for in the library of the What Cheer House; and, we repeat, it was a happy idea. There can be no greater proof of this, than the fact that the Library Room, although large, is the best patronized and the most crowded of any in this extensive establishment.

The sketch from which our engraving was made, was taken early in the morning, and yet it will be seen that already the room was well filled with attentive readers. On either side are files of newspapers from all parts of California, and the principal ones of the Eastern States and Europe. On the south side and western end is the library, which contains between two and three thousand volumes, on almost every variety of subject. There are about one hundred volumes on farming, bee-raising, gardening, vine-growing, stock-raising, horticulture, etc., etc.; and some one hundred and fifty works on biography, including those of the most remarkable men and women of the present and past ages. The classics are not forgotten, as there are translations of the principal scholarly productions of the ancients. There are nearly four hundred volumes of the best fictitious works, including several from Dickens, Irving, Scott, Cooper, Miss Bremer, Marryat, Thackeray, Hawthorne, and

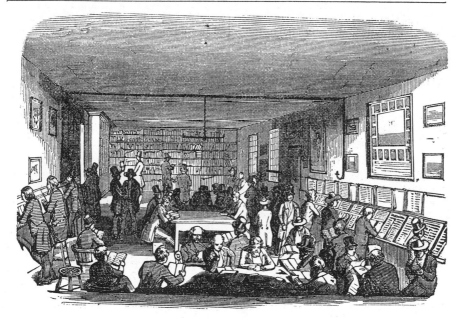

THE LIBRARY AT THE WHAT CHEER HOUSE.

others; and about one hundred and fifty fine historical works. Then there are many excellent selections from poetical and dramatic authors; a large collection of books on voyages and travels, besides a large and choice variety of practical, miscellaneous, religious, and other works.

We think that the good taste of the purchaser is apparent in almost every volume; for we do not often find a better selection in libraries of much greater pretensions. This, moreover, is free to all the patrons of the house, as is also the museum, of which we gave an account in a former number.

It is with no ordinary pleasure that we record the above interesting facts; and we feel proud that such a public convenience has been established. Whenever others shall follow so excellent an example, we assure them we shall take great pleasure in "making a note of it."

FLOWERS.—The most humble abode is made pleasant to the sight of all persons of good taste and refined feelings, when it exhibits flowers in its surroundings, or plants peeping out of the windows. Flowers are a luxury that the poorest may enjoy—the most common are among the most beautiful—and a few seeds sown in the garden patch, however small it may be, or in a pot or a box, will in a short time gladden the heart of the sower, and all who look upon them, in the spirit of love, with a beauty and fragrance too exquisite for description.

THE LOVE FOR A SISTER.—Some one has appropriately said that there is something lovely in the name of sister—its utterance rarely failing to call up the affections of the heart. The thoughts that circle round it are all beautiful and pure. Passion has no place with its associations. The hopes and fears of love, those strong emotions, powerful enough to shatter and extinguish life itself, find no home there. The bride is the star, the talisman of the heart, the diamond above all price, bright and blazing in the noonday sun; a sister the gem of milder light, calm as the mellow moon, and set in a coronet of pearls.

THE VIGILANCE CALL.

Away, away to duty, no longer linger now,
Merchant leave the counting-room, Farmer leave the plow;
   Miner drop the heavy pick, Trader leave thy wares,
Artizan, Mechanic, now, assume your country's cares;
   The Ballot-box is naught to thee, 'tis wrested from thy power,
Thy fathers purchased it with blood, and left it as thy dower;
   But villains of the darkest dye, have wrested it from thee,
And now stand up a freeman, or forever bend the knee.

Who fill thy posts of honor? are they honest men and free?
Will they ever be found faithful to thy country or to thee?
   Are they men of sterling wisdom? elected by one voice?
The best men in the nation? the people's only choice?
   Blush now to own the truth, and hang thy head with shame,
Thy rulers have been rowdies—and disgraced to thee thy name,
   Loafers bribed by hireling gold—knaves of a foreign shore,
Murderers, convicts, bullies—how I blush to name them o'er.

Freeman be up and doing, thy country calls for thee,
No longer look discouraged, no longer bend the knee;
   Dare to assert thy rights—fight for them if ye must,
And yield not till your life's blood is mingled with the dust;
   Upon the pine-clad mountain, deep in the fertile vale,
Is heard the infant orphan's cry, the widow's bitter wail:
   And villains of the darkest dye would take thy life from thee,
But rise up *now* a freeman, or forever bend the knee.

Then husbands, fathers, brothers, sons, ALL vigilant be now,
For curs'd is he who would look back with hand upon the plow;
   The work of reformation has scarcely yet begun,
Then shrink not back from duty, till faithfully 'tis done;
   The FUTURE of this golden west is now within thy hands,
Wilt thou give it noble freedom? or succumb to knavish bands:
   Wives, mothers, sisters, daughters are pleading now for thee,
So now stand up a freeman, or forever bend the knee.

Then away, away to duty, 'tis woman bids thee go,
Though her soul is full of sadness—her heart with deepest woe;
   Oh! 'tis a fearful thing we know—we've thought it o'er and o'er,
Yet, though we love *thee* dearly, we love *thy honor* more.
   Then come to us thou nobly brave, we'll gird thy armor on,
And then go kneel in prayer, till the battle's lost or won:
   Yes, women will thy armor bring, and gird it on to thee,
Then stand up *now*, a *freeman*, or *forever* bend the knee!

San Francisco, May, 1856.   CARRIE D.

HUTCHINGS'

CALIFORNIA MAGAZINE.

| Vol. II. | JANUARY, 1858. | No. 7. |

THE STEAMER HAS ARRIVED.

THE HISTORY OF A LETTER.

Language is incapable of expressing the thrill of feeling which passes through the mind, when, from the outer telegraph station at Point Lobos, a telegram announces in San Francisco that "the mail steamer —— is in sight, — miles outside the heads." To almost all "expectation is on tip-toe," and the welcome intelligence is rapidly passed from lip to lip, and recorded on the various bulletin boards of the city, that the "—— steamer is telegraphed." After an hour or more of suspense, the loud boom-oom-oom-o-o-o-o-o-m of the steamer's gun reverberates through the city, and announces that she is passing between Alcatraz Island and Telegraph Hill, and will soon be at her berth alongside the wharf.

Almost simultaneously with the sound of the steamer's gun, the newsboys are shouting the "arrival of the steamer," and the "New York Herald," "New York Tribune," "Fourteen days later news from the Eastern States." Meanwhile, all the news depots are crowded with eager applicants for the latest news; and, in order to obtain it as early as possible, small boats have been in waiting off Meiggs' Wharf, to receive the bundles of "express" newspapers thrown them

from the steamer as she passed; and the moment these boats reach the dock, fast horses, which have also been kept in waiting, speedily carry the bundles to the city.

Carriages and other vehicles now begin to rumble and clatter through the streets, in the direction of the steamer's wharf; men commence walking towards the post office, or gather in groups upon the sidewalks, to learn or discuss the latest news. Interest and excitement seem to become general.

On the dock, awaiting the delivery of the mail-bags, mail wagons and drays are standing; and as fast as the mail matter is taken from the vessel, it is removed to the post office.

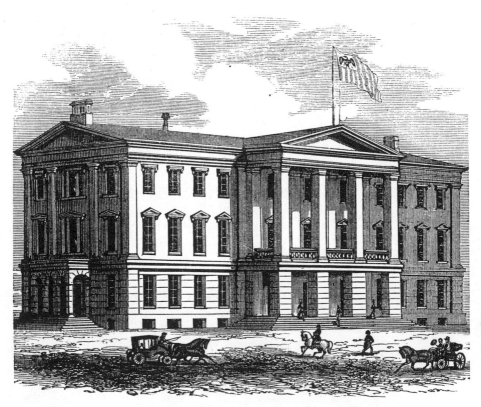

SAN FRANCISCO POST OFFICE AND CUSTOM HOUSE.

While the loaded wagons and drays, with mail matter, are hastening to the general delivery, and the passengers who have just arrived are seeking the various hotels, in carriages or on foot, after hiring a porter to carry their baggage, or

DISTRIBUTING THE MAILS.

becoming their own for the time being; let us, while all this is going on, make our way to the post office, there to see what we can.

Men we find are hurrying to and fro, and gathering in front of their letter-boxes; some, with the doors open, are waiting to see when the first letter finds its way there, that they may not lose one moment before the contents are enjoyed.

At the various windows—alphabetically arranged, with about as many letters to each window as, in all probability will make the number of applicants at each about equal—men are congregating in single file, forming long and crooked lines, and patiently awaiting the time when the little window will be opened, from which the treasured letter from some dear and absent one is expected. Who can tell the hope and fear, the joy and sorrow, the love and (perhaps) hate, the good and evil, that occupy the minds of those who thus stand watching and waiting for the little missives.

Further on, too, at the end of the building, and apart from the rest, is the ladies' window; and here stand a row of ladies and gentlemen, waiting as patiently as at the others. The gentlemen, who form part of the line, do so to obtain letters for their wife, or sister, or perhaps sweetheart, or other lady friend; and, if they are there first, they invariably give precedence to the ladies, no matter how many may come, or how long they may be thus detained.

At the centre of the building, mail-bags are being carried in from the mail wagons and drays, one after the other, to the number of from two to three hundred and upwards; we wonder how, out of that mass of apparent confusion, order will be restored; or how, in the course of a few hours, thirty-five thousand letters and newspapers will be properly arranged for distribution to the various boxes and delivery windows. Have patience, and we shall see.

Before entering the post office with the reader, we wish most sincerely to express our thanks to Mr. Charles L. Weller, the Postmaster, Mr. John Ferguson, his assistant, and the other gentlemen belonging to this department, for the courtesy and promptness with which they placed the various and interesting particulars concerning this important branch of the public service, at our command.

While the mail-bags are being examined, to ascertain their contents, whether letters or papers, for San Francisco or the interior cities, let us read over the rules of the office, for our especial entertainment:

RULES AND REGULATIONS.

I.—General office hours from 8 A. M. to 5 P. M., Sunday excepted, on which day the office will be kept open from 9 to 10 A. M.

II.—The mailing clerks will be at their posts at 6 A. M., the box clerk at $6\frac{1}{2}$ A. M., and all other clerks and employés at $7\frac{1}{2}$ A. M.

III.—No clerk will absent himself from the office during office hours, without the knowledge and consent of the Postmaster, or, in his absence, the Assistant Postmaster.

IV.—Courtesy and forbearance, and a spirit of accommodation, being requisite to efficient services, they should be extended to everybody with whom clerks may have business intercourse.

V.—Memory must not be trusted to, but when an applicant presents himself for a letter or paper, thorough search must be made in the appropriate place, and care will be taken to let the applicant see the search made.

VI.—When an applicant shall exhibit a disposition to aggravate, or insult, or even abuse, he should be met with forbearance and gentlemanly conduct, recollecting that the contact is of a business nature only, and that personalities should be adjourned to outside the office entirely. If a clerk fail to satisfy an applicant, let him be referred to the Postmaster.

VII.—Angry or excited discussions upon any subject must not be indulged in during office hours.

VIII.—Clerks will not carry from the office, letters for their outside friends and acquaintances, nor receive letters from such out of the office for mailing.

IX.—Each clerk will confine his delivery of letters to his own alcove, except when he may be acting as a relief for the time being.

X.—None other than delivery clerks will disarrange, handle, or deliver letters, at any alcove, at any time.

XI.—If application be made for letters inside the office, when deliveries are not open, the applicant will in all cases be referred to the Postmaster or his assistant.

XII.—No person except sworn clerks and employés must be permitted to handle mail matter, or come within reach thereof.

XIII.—During any absence of the Postmaster, his whole authority over the internal affairs of the office rests with his assistant, and that officer will be respected accordingly.

Now the scene around us is becoming interesting. The bustle and exciting life that first presented itself on the outside, by the arrival of the mail-bags, seems to have extended within; for on all sides great activity—systematic activity—is the order of the time. It appears that the Postmaster, on the arrival of each steamer, engages a corps of from fifteen to twenty-five extra assistant clerks, in order to facilitate more rapidly the distribution of the mail; and these, with the regular force, are all busy in the departments assigned them.

While all this is going on in one department, the mail-bags containing packages of newspapers for the different newspaper firms in the city, are being opened, checked, and removed, in another. Every part of the office is literally alive with active business; slow coaches would be at an immense discount here at all times, especially when the mail has just arrived, and when it is about to depart.

The bags containing the letter mail for distribution in San Francisco, are rapidly selected from the others, and passed to the "examining table," where they are opened, and the contents compared with the "post bill" which accompanies them; after which they are deposited in "alphabetical cases" in the following manner: A letter, for instance, addressed "John Adams," is placed under the division A; those addressed "Timothy Brown," under division B; and so forth, to the end of the alphabet. From thence they are taken to the different alcoves, to which they belong alphabetically, and where each delivery clerk has cards placed, upon which is written the name of every box-holder, commencing with letters belonging to his alcove, with the number of the box; and, as each letter is examined, it is marked with the box number to which it belongs; it is then sent out to be placed in a case, and distributed according to number, thus: Letters from 1 to 100 are placed in one division; from 100 to 200 in another; and so on, to the highest corresponding number of the box; and from this case they are taken by clerks to the boxes of the parties to whom they are addressed. If it is not a box letter, it is put up in its proper place in the alcove for general delivery, which is generally opened immediately the whole of the letters are assorted and arranged.

THE NEWSPAPER DISTRIBUTING TABLE.

This being a distributing post office, and the only one on the Pacific coast, a great amount of mail matter is sent here for distribution to other points. Newspapers for the interior, and for Oregon and Washington Territories, are taken to the newspaper distributing table, rapidly to be distributed in accordance with their address. Bags of newspaper matter are made up for Sacramento, Marysville, Benicia, Shasta, Stockton, Columbia, Martinez, Petaluma, and other places; and all newspapers addressed to points in these respective districts, are placed in those bags.

At the same time, another division of the forces is engaged in assorting the letters addressed to offices on this coast other than San Francisco. To facilitate this, a letter-case, with apartments for all the offices in this State and Oregon and Washington Territories, respectively labelled, is used, in which are placed all letters for those points, and mailed as usual.

The following Table will give the name, day of arrival, and number of days out from New York to San Francisco, of each Steamer, from August 31st, 1854, to December 16th, 1857 ; also, the number of bags of mail matter brought to the San Francisco Post Office:

NAME OF STEAMER.	DATE OF ARRIVAL.	TIME FROM N. Y.	NUMBER OF MAIL BAGS.	NAME OF STEAMER.	DATE OF ARRIVAL.	TIME FROM N. Y.	NUMBER OF MAIL BAGS.
Sonora, ...	Aug. 21, 1854	26	315	Golden Gate,....	April 13, 1856	24	339
California,......	Sept. 19, "	29	323	J. L. Stephens,	May 1, "	27	348
J. L. Stephens,	Oct. 2, "	27	293	Golden Age,...	May 22, "	31	329
Golden Age,...	Oct. 16, "	26	303	Sonora, ...	June 1, "	26	298
Sonora, ...	Nov. 1, "	27	291	Golden Gate,...	June 15, "	25	354
Golden Gate,...	Nov. 13, "	24	292	J. L. Stephens,	July 1, "	26	336
J. L. Stephens,	Dec. 1, "	25	317	Golden Age,...	July 14, "	25	331
Golden Age,...	Dec. 14, "	24	296	Sonora, ...	July 29, "	24	318
Sonora, ...	Dec. 30, "	25	268	J. L. Stephens,	Aug. 14, "	24	313
J. L. Stephens,	Jan. 13, 1855	24	249	Golden Age,...	Aug. 28, "	23	337
Golden Age,...	Jan. 29, "	24	277	Sonora, ...	Sept. 16, "	27	359
Oregon, ...	Feb. 17, "	28	317	J. L. Stephens,	Sept. 29, "	24	309
Sonora, ...	March 2, "	25	286	Golden Age,...	Oct. 14, "	24	299
J. L. Stephens,	March 17, "	25	266	Sonora, ...	Nov. 1, "	26	296
Golden Age,...	March 28, "	23	295	Golden Gate,...	Nov. 14, "	24	277
Golden Gate,...	April 12, "	23	317	Golden Age,...	Dec. 1, "	26	321
Sonora, ...	May 1, "	26	333	Sonora, ...	Dec. 16, "	26	302
J. L. Stephens,	May 16, "	26	300	J. L. Stephens,	Dec. 30, "	25	290
Golden Gate,...	May 30, "	25	274	Golden Gate,...	Jan. 15, 1857	26	307
Sonora, ...	June 16, "	26	306	Sonora, ...	Jan. 30, "	25	286
Golden Age,...	June 30, "	25	242	J. L. Stephens,	Feb. 14, "	25	267
J. L. Stephens,	July 13, "	23	268	Golden Gate,...	March 2 "	25	342
Golden Gate,...	July 28, "	23	303	Sonora, ...	March 17, "	25	295
Sonora, ...	Aug. 18, "	29	326	J. L. Stephens,	March 29, "	24	282
J. L. Stephens,	Sept. 1, "	26	294	Golden Age,...	April 12, "	23	327
Golden Age,...	Sept. 12, "	23	314	Golden Gate,...	April 29, "	23	357
Panama, ...	Oct. 2, "	26	257	J. L. Stephens,	May 15, "	25	310
Golden Gate,...	Oct. 16, "	26	234	Golden Age,...	May 29, "	24	318
Sonora, ...	Oct. 29, "	24	279	Golden Gate,...	June 15, "	26	316
J. L. Stephens,	Nov. 14, "	25	323	Sonora, ...	June 30, "	25	319
Golden Age,...	Nov. 29, "	24	291	J. L. Stephens,	July 15, "	25	295
Sonora, ...	Dec. 15, "	25	316	Golden Age,...	July 31, "	25	294
J. L. Stephens,	Jan. 1, 1856	27	322	Sonora, ...	Aug. 14, "	25	295
Oregon, ...	Jan. 12, "	*	37	J. L. Stephens,	Aug. 30, "	25	295
Golden Age,...	Jan. 15, "	26	289	Golden Age,...	Sept. 14, "	25	306
Sonora, ...	Jan. 30, "	25	274	Sonora, ...	Oct. 1, "	26	318
Golden Gate,...	Feb. 14. "	24	301	Panama, ...	Oct. 22, "	31	294
J. L. Stephens,	March 1, "	25	295	J. L. Stephens,	Nov. 2, "	26	290
Golden Age,...	March 14, "	23	278	Golden Age,...	Nov. 17, "	28	315
Sonora, ...	March 28, "	23	322	Sonora, ...	Nov. 30, "	25	276
Oregon,..........	April 12, "	*	22	Golden Gate,...	Dec. 16, "	26	344

* Only from Panama.

Now, hoping that the reader has received very interesting correspondence from his friends, and digested the contents, let us see what is done with those large piles of bags that are as yet unopened. Some we see are marked "Sacramento Dis.," others "Stockton Dis.," others Marysville, Placerville, Nevada, Sonora, or some other "Dis." in the interior ; and are placed upon the mail wagons, conveyed to the steamboats plying nearest to those places, and sent away as speedily as it is possible for them to be. No unnecessary delay is allowed to detain them, nor are they in the general bustle, by any means lost sight of. One

ALCOVE OF THE GENERAL DELIVERY.

would suppose that Argus, with his hundred eyes, would find opportunity fully to employ them all, were he post-master at such a time as this. Every part is worked by system which experience has so far perfected; and this is the secret why so much is accomplished in so short a time. Those who ever feel desirous of complaining of delay, might do well to remember how matters went some four or six years ago.

Supposing that the mail which has arrived is all distributed, we should like the reader's company to see how the letter and newspaper mails are made up for Eastern conveyance and distribution.

Of course we take it for granted that you have written your letter; and which, being prepaid *in stamps* if it is for any portion of our Union, and *in money* if for foreign distribution, has found its way into the "drop basket" within the office. From this they are first taken to the "facing up table," that they may all be "faced" with the address before you: they are then conveyed to the "sorting case," for the purpose of weighing and ascertaining that the full amount of postage due on each letter is paid: after this is satisfac-

torily settled, they are passed to the "stamping-block," that the office-stamp, with the date of mailing, may be imprinted upon them: they are then placed in the "distributing case," that they may receive proper distribution according to their address. The letters are now ready to be entered upon the "post-bill"—similar to the one received with the letter-mail on the arrival of the steamer at this port—which is done in this wise: say, for instance, the mail is now made up for "New York Distribution," which includes all letters addressed to the following places: New York State, Rhode Island, Connecticut, eastern and northern counties of New Jersey, northern counties of Pennsylvania and Ohio, Michigan, and Lower Canada. Letters thus addressed are laid upon the "mailing table," when all letters of the same rate of postage are placed together, and their number and rate of postage is entered on the "post-bill." After this is done, they are put up in convenient-sized packages (gener-

THE DROP BASKET.

ally about eighty letters in one package) and stamped "New York Dis." They are then put in a mail-bag labeled "N. Y. Dis.," and are then ready to be dispatched over their route of destination. The same process is adopted in the making up of all the mails to every portion of the Union; and all this is done with the view of securing dispatch, and avoiding unnecessary labor and consequent delay.

Register of Departure of the Mails for the Atlantic States, via Panama, &c.; names of the Steamers, date of sailing, and number of bags of mail matter:

NAME OF STEAMER.	DATE OF DEPARTURE.		NO. BAGS MAIL MATTER.	NAME OF STEAMER.	DATE OF DEPARTURE.		NO. BAGS MAIL MATTER.
John L. Stephens,	Sept. 1,	1854.	108	John L. Stephens,	May 21,	1856.	129
Panama,	Sept. 16,	"	89	Golden Age,	June 5,	"	149
Sonora,	Sept. 30,	"	101	Sonora,	June 20,	"	150
Golden Gate,	Oct. 16,	"	116	John L. Stephens,	July 5,	"	142
John L. Stephens,	Nov. 1,	"	100	Golden Age,	July 21,	"	147
Golden Age,	Nov. 16,	"	114	Sonora,	Aug. 5,	"	121
Sonora,	Dec. 1,	"	91	John L. Stephens,	Aug 20,	"	141
John L. Stephens,	Dec. 16,	"	93	Golden Age,	Sept. 5,	"	140
Golden Age,	Jan. 1,	1855.	107	Sonora,	Sept. 20,	"	114
Sonora,	Jan. 16,	"	98	Golden Gate,	Oct. 6,	"	129
John L. Stephens,	Feb. 1,	"	108	Golden Age,	Oct. 20,	"	113
Golden Age,	Feb. 16,	"	99	Sonora,	Nov. 5,	"	115
Golden Gate,	March 1,	"	102	John L. Stephens,	Nov. 20,	"	122
Sonora,	March 16,	"	85	Golden Gate,	Dec. 5,	"	99
John L. Stephens,	March 31,	"	95	Sonora,	Dec. 20,	"	112
Golden Age,	April 17,	"	103	John L. Stephens,	Jan. 5,	1857.	120
Golden Gate,	May 1,	"	89	Golden Gate,	Jan. 20,	"	96
Sonora,	May 16,	"	80	Sonora,	Feb. 5,	"	121
John L. Stephens,	June 1,	"	100	John L. Stephens,	Feb. 20,	"	119
Golden Gate,	June 16,	"	102	Golden Age,	March 5,	"	103
Sonora,	June 30,	"	92	Golden Gate,	March 20,	"	119
John L. Stephens,	July 16,	"	97	Golden Gate,	March 23,	"	6
Golden Age,	Aug. 1,	"	95	John L. Stephens,	April 6,	"	115
Golden Gate,	Aug. 18,	"	94	Golden Age,	April 20,	"	102
Oregon,	Sept. 5,	"	93	Golden Gate,	May 5,	"	122
Sonora,	Sept. 20,	"	96	John L. Stephens,	June 1,	"	116
John L. Stephens,	Oct. 5,	"	82	Sonora,	May 20,	"	104
Golden Age,	Oct. 20,	"	95	Golden Age,	June 20,	"	96
Sonora,	Nov. 5,	"	93	Sonora,	July 4,	"	109
John L. Stephens,	Nov. 20,	"	96	John L. Stephens,	July 20,	"	108
Golden Age,	Dec. 5,	"	101	Golden Age,	Aug. 5.	"	121
Sonora,	Dec. 20,	"	113	Sonora,	Aug. 20,	"	102
Golden Gate,	Jan. 5,	1856.	89	California,	Sept. 5,	"	112
John L. Stephens,	Jan. 21,	"	125	John L. Stephens,	Sept. 21,	"	109
Golden Age,	Feb. 5,	"	101	Golden Gate,	Oct. 5,	"	91
Sonora,	Feb. 20,	"	106	Golden Age,	Oct. 11,	"	23
Golden Gate,	March 5,	"	95	Sonora,	Oct. 20,	"	96
John L. Stephens,	March 20,	"	107	Golden Gate,	Nov. 5,	"	125
Golden Age,	April 5,	"	126	John L. Stephens,	Nov. 20,	"	110
Sonora,	April 21,	"	116	Golden Age,	Dec. 5,	"	110
Golden Gate,	May 5,	"	92	Golden Gate,	Dec. 21,	"	94

RATES OF FOREIGN POSTAGE ON LETTERS.

(PER ½ OUNCE.)

SOUTH PACIFIC.—Eucador, Bolivia, and Chili, 34 cents; Peru, 22; Panama, 20 cents; and Mexico, 10 cents. Spain, 78 cents; West Indies (not British), Cuba excepted, 44 cents; Cuba, 20 cents; West Indies (British), 20 cents. Payment required for all the above.

Great Britain, 29 cents; Canada and Provinces, 15 cents; France, 15 cents per

"RATING" THE LETTERS.

quarter oz.; Germany, 30 cents; Russia, 37 cents; Norway, 46 cents; Sweden, 42 cents; Italy, 33 cents; Switzerland, 35 cents; Holland, 26 cents; Austria 30 cents; and Prussia, 30 cents. For the above, prepayment is optional.

All ship letters, prepaid, are one cent.

The number of stamps and envelops sold monthly at the San Francisco Post Office will about average—of one cent stamps, 45,000; three cents, 27,000; ten cents, 32,000; twelve cents, 500. Of stamped envelops, three cents, 120,000, (of which Wells, Fargo & Co. use nearly 100,000 per month); six cents, 500; ten cents, 12,000. This statement, it should be remembered, is principally for the city of San Francisco alone; inasmuch as the principal interior offices obtain their supplies of stamps and envelops direct from the General Post Office, Washington.

The U. S. postage on letters for each half ounce is, if under three thousand miles, three cents; over three thousand miles, ten cents. For newspapers the postage is one cent to any part of the U. S. Magazines not exceeding one and a half ounces one half cent; not exceeding

"STAMPING" THE LETTERS.

MAKING UP OF THE MAILS.

three ounces, one cent; over three ounces, one and a half cent.

On newspapers sent to foreign places, the following are the rates of postage: To the West Indies, 6 cents; South Pacific Coast, 6; German States, Denmark, Holland, Prussia, Russia, Sweden, Norway, Switzerland, and Italy, 6 cents; Great Britain and France, 2 cents; British North American Provinces, 1 cent.

———

SCHEDULE OF MAIL DEPARTURES FROM SAN FRANCISCO POST OFFICE.—Atlantic States, via Panama, 5th and 20th of every month.

San Diego and Salt Lake, 3d and 18th of every month.

Oregon and Washington Territories, taking mails also for the Northern Coast, 1st and 21st of every month.

San Jose, 8 A. M. every day.

Northern Mail via Sacramento, 4 P. M. every day, Sundays excepted.

Southern and Eastern Mail via Stockton, 4 P. M. every day, Sundays excepted.

Mails are kept open until ten minutes before the hour of departure, except for the Atlantic, in which case thirty minutes before the time of departure is required for closing the mails; though it would be better for the convenience of the Post Office, as well as for the safety of the correspondence, if letters were mailed during the night previous.

Ship Mails are despatched by every opportunity for the Sandwich Islands, Society Islands, Australia, and China. Postage on letters to all parts of the Pacific, by ship, to be prepaid.

———

DEAD LETTERS. — Letters technically termed "dead," are such as have been advertised, and have remained on hand three months; including letters refused; letters for foreign countries which can not be forwarded without pre-payment of postage; letters not addressed, or so badly directed that their destinations can not be ascertained; and letters addressed to places which are not Post Offices. All the dead letters are returned to San Francisco at the middle or end of each Post Office quarter, which is on the last day of March, June, September, and December. Refused and dropped letters are not advertised. Every dead letter, before its return to San Francisco, is stamped or postmarked on the sealed side, with the name of the office and the date of its return.

THE PUBLIC SCHOOLS OF SAN FRANCISCO.

A good system of public schools is essential to the existence of a republican form of government.

Public schools are not peculiar to the United States; but the American free schools differ very materially from those of European nations. There, they are designed for those who are too poor to pay private tuition, and the children of the rich never darken their doors; here, the wealthiest and most aristocratic make no apology for sending their children to the free schools, which public opinion pronounces the best in discipline and training, and most in accordance with our republican institutions.

A system like ours is too great a *leveller* to be encouraged by a titled aristocracy.

The American system of free schools was nurtured and sustained by the liberty-loving, God-serving Puritans of Massachusetts Bay, and wherever the sons of New England have settled, they have carried it with them as a household god. Across a mighty continent, stretching further and further west, the little school houses have taken up their line of march, until, pouring over the slopes of the Sierra Nevada, they rest, with the weary emigrants, on the golden shores of the Pacific; and, to-day, the schools of San Francisco will compare not unfavorably with those of Boston—the great radiating point of the system on the Atlantic coast.

The school department owns two fine buildings — the Union Street and Denman — the other schools are mostly held in inferior rented rooms. Those teachers, who, like the present Superintendent, and ex-Superintendent Mr. Pelton, taught in the "shanties" of early times, would consider them comparatively comfortable, but compared with the palaces of eastern cities, they are inadequate, ill-ventilated and unsightly. In other respects our schools will generally compare pretty favorably with eastern ones, though irregularity and change of pupils, render it impossible to advance classes with the same degree of accuracy as in more stationary communities. Neither is there the same strict discipline here as in eastern city schools; children are under less rigid home-government, and consequently more difficult to govern at school. And the system of running at large, from one school to another, over the whole city, is destructive to school government. In some respects, our schools are undoubtedly in advance of the less progressive ones of older States.

There is less of the *forcing* system,—less of overtaxed brain and precocious development. The school room is made a pleasanter place. More attention is given to physical training. The hours of study are fewer, though at present too long. A return to the hours of two years ago—from 10 A. M. to three o'clock P. M.—would be far better, and more acceptable to a vast majority of parents.

Many of the schools are well provided with gymnastic apparatus, and in some, the classes are regularly drilled in gymnastic feats on the "horizontal bar," "parallels," "ladders," and with "clubs," "dumb-bells" and "rods." Two years ago, on a visit to the schools of Boston and New York, we found none of the schools so provided; we doubt if any now are. The muscular development given to the boys, the love of athletic exercises and manly sports, will be worth quite as much to their future life, as the mental culture and book knowledge there imparted. The boy needs strong muscles to fight his way in the world ;—coop him up in close rooms, leave his muscles flabby and soft, and no amount of book-feed will make a manly man of him.

In some of the schools calisthenic exercises are as regularly given as the daily recitations; and the girls are deriving incalculable benefit from the daily drill. Erect forms, well developed chests, grace of movement, and ease of carriage are the results.

Dancing is also very generally a part of school recreation; what would the staid old Puritans have said at the thought of it? No harm seems to result, however.

The annual May parties are quite a feature of the schools, giving a vast amount of enjoyment to smiling faces and twinkling feet, and real delight, and a merry time, to friends and parents—not Puritanical, but social. Singing receives a good degree of attention, but should receive still more.

Music is an essential element in the education of girls. It is vastly more important for a young lady, in the social circle, to know how to sing, than to comprehend all the mysteries even of cube root, square root, algebra and geometry. "A gentle voice is a pleasant thing in woman."

We think the course of study in the grammar schools might be slightly modified for the better. One half the time in all the schools is devoted to arithmetic—the grand hobby of American teachers, and Yankee ones, in particular—while penmanship, drawing, and spelling receive comparatively little attention. The *crack* classes are the *arithmetic* classes, and the merits of a whole school not unfrequently rise or fall with exploits of the great first class in arithmetic, on "examination day." Arithmetic is well enough in its place, but the sky is not a black-board, nor are mountains all made of chalk; children have other faculties than that of *calculation*, which can better be exercised on something else. Is it not quite as important that a boy of fifteen should write a neat, well-spelled letter, as to give the analysis for dividing one fraction by another, or, "to ex-plain the reason of the rule for extracting cube root"? Might not the girls learn the elements of botany, eat a few less figures, and admire flowers a little more? Could not the boys, who devote two hours a day, for three years, to arithmetic, spare a little of that time to learn enough of Natural History to tell the difference between a hippopotamus and a rhinoceros; or a condor and a gray eagle; or a fish and a quadruped?

Ought not both boys and girls to learn enough of Physiology and Hygienne, to understand and obey the common laws of health? Ought not a boy of fifteen, leaving a grammar school, to know how to keep a commom, plain, working man's account book? Practical men would say, that all these things were quite as important as complicated problems in arithmetic, or complex analysis in grammar?

A natural system of teaching little children would train them to use their senses for gaining a knowledge of common things around them; yet most of the primary room teaching still consists in "learning how to read and spell." In this respect, our primary schools are a quarter of a century behind the European. It is now an exploded notion that education consists in learning how to "read, and spell, and cypher." Education is development—the harmonious development of all the faculties of man's nature. The perceptive and expansive faculties, and training, as well as the reasoning and reflective.

The physical nature should be cared for; and the *soul* needs expansion quite as much as either mind or body. The best teachers are not those who can cram the most mathematics into the heads of pupils; or hitch on the longest trains of pondrous verbatim recitations to the crack teams of "smart" classes, but those who can win the love, and touch the hearts, and awaken the sympathies, and move the souls of unfolding manhood and womanhood. Feeling, affection, and sympathy are better teachers than cold, reasoning intellect.

The *truest* teaching is something intangible—an electric fire, which cannot be set down in figures and percentages, by examining committees. A teacher with a great heart is better than one with a great head. It will always be so, while children have *souls* as well as *brains*.

Many of our best female teachers never pass " brilliant " examinations ; their column of " percentage" is always low, but a great woman's heart, womanly tact, love, and kindness which are all set down as "zero " in the column of " percentage," if expressed in figures—as if such a thing were possible—would place them far up in the scale. A week in the school-room is a better test than forty columns of "percentages."

The truest teaching, that which influences manner, stamps the character, electrifies the heart, cannot be reduced to a mathematical system ; it is superior to " rules and regulations." It needs neither " reviews" nor regulations forbidding them. It will not be limited to so many pages of arithmetic, or grammar, or geography. It is the intangible Aurora which plays over the sky of the school, until one gorgeous glow rests upon the firmament of heavenly faces. Bunglers may think that a school is a complicated mechanism of wheels and pivots — a weekly clock, which the teacher has only to "wind up " and then watch its running—but in truth, each individual unit of humanity is a living harp, ready to breathe forth harmonious tones, if touched with the light fingers of a master hand. Would you have the teacher an organ grinder or a harpist?

On the whole, the present condition of our schools is encouraging. The teachers, as a body, are enthusiastic and progressive. The present Superintendent is a man in every way fitted for his position.

Five years a teacher in our schools, rough-hewing the elements into symmetry, few understand their wants so well as he. He has no " crotchets " in teaching ; no particular hobbies ; no fine spun theories of attenuated transcendental instruction, or homœopathic dilutions of milk-and-water " reforms." There is much work for him to do, and we shall be much mistaken if he does not do it, and do it well.

The "nativities " of the pupils illustrate the cosmopolitan character of our population. Every State in the Union is represented, every nation of Europe but four—Spain, Portugal, Greece and Turkey. Asia gives us the "Mongolians," and even Africa sends us a return wave of civilization. All the islands of the Pacific yield us their mite of humanity, and " off Cape Horn " and the Atlantic, swell the rising generation. What a composite race will result from this strange mixture of nationalities ? Of the States, it will be seen that New York leads the list, but Massachusetts is more largely represented in proportion to population. Here are the statistics:

Born in		Born in	
Maine	168	Louisiana	334
New Hampshire,	55	Texas	30
Vermont	17	Wisconsin	19
Massachusetts,	726	Michigan	40
Rhode Island	48	Ohio	70
Connecticut	45	Kentucky	39
New York	1468	Tennessee	19
New Jersey	102	Arkansas	11
Pennsylvania	230	Missouri	84
Delaware	10	Iowa	10
Maryland	72	Illinois	57
Virginia	29	Indiana	10
North Carolina,	5	Minnesota	6
South Carolina,	8	Oregon	5
Georgia	14	California	1010
Florida	6	Utah	1
Alabama	17	Dist. Columbia,	18
Mississippi	29	Wash. Territory,	1

Nationaltity.		Nationality.	
England	150	Panama	5
Scotland	35	Chili	59
Ireland	72	Peru	3
Canada	53	Brazil	1
Australia	191	Mexico	47
France	57	Van D. Land	5
Germany	149	New Zealand	16
Austria	14	Sandwich Isls	13
Prussia	15	Madeira Isls	1
Russia	8	Prince Edward,	2
Switzerland	6	West Indies	2
Holland	1	China	29
Italy	7	Africa	1
Denmark	1	Off Cape Horn,	
Belgium	4	voyage to Cal.	7
Sweden	1	Pacific Ocean	1
South America	19	Atlantic Ocean,	1

By the Annual Report of the City Superintendent, for the year ending November 1st, 1859, to the State Superintendent, the number of pupils attending the public schools, is as follows: —

	Total No. of Pupils registered.	Average daily attendance.	No. of Teachers.
Rincon School	912	470	11
Denman	445	225	6
Powell Street	506	231	6
Union Street	937	338	10
Spring Valley	246	126	4
Mission Dolores	152	80	2
Market Street	489	212	5
Hyde Street	364	165	4
Sutter St. Intermediate	268	137	3
Sutter St. Primary	512	179	4
Greenwich Street	341	153	4
Wash'ton St. Primary	361	151	4
Mission St. Primary	257	82	2
Evening School	91	38	2
Chinese School	32	21	1
Colored School	100	39	1
High School	139	97	3
Total	6152	2704	72

The whole number of pupils registered is 6152: deduct from this total 600 promoted from one department to another and registered twice; also, 600 more who have changed schools, there will remain 4952, an approximation to the exact number. The returns by this census indicate 4865 in attendance at the public schools. For this large number, the average daily attendance is only 2704—being 55 per cent. of the whole number. This does not indicate the irregular attendance of children, but only shows the floating character of the population. The number belonging to school at any one time is about two-thirds of the whole number registered for the year, which would give 66 per cent. for regularity of attendance.

In 1854, the number of pupils was 1803; in 1855, 2081; in 1857, 2823; in 1858, 5283, all subject to the same deductions as the returns for 1859.

To teach these schools, seventy-two teachers are employed — fifteen gentlemen and fifty-seven ladies; also a teacher of foreign languages in the High School, and a general teacher of singing.

Their salaries are as follows: —
Principal of High School $250 per month.
Teacher of Natural Sciences $240 per mo.
Assistant, lady $125 per month.
Principals of Grammar, $200 per month;
Female Prin. Prim. & Inter. $105 per mo.
Assistants $85 per month.

But the teachers are seldom employed ten months, and the average annual salaries would be about ten per cent. discount on the above rates.

A PARENT who sends his son into the world uneducated, and without skill in any art or science, does as great injury to mankind as to his own family: he defrauds the community of a useful citizen, and bequeaths to it a nuisance.

LIFE is what we make it. Let us call back images of joy and gladness, rather than those of grief and care. The latter may sometimes be our guests to sup and dine, but let them never be permitted to lodge with us.

HUTCHINGS'

CALIFORNIA MAGAZINE.

No. II.—AUGUST, 1856.—Vol. I.

SOUTH-EAST VIEW OF THE FARRALONE ISLANDS.

THE FARALLONE ISLANDS.

—

This is the name of a small group of rocky islands, lying in the Pacific Ocean, about twenty-seven miles west of the Golden Gate, and thirty-five miles from San Francisco. These islands have become of some importance, and of considerable interest, on account of the vast quantity of eggs that are there annually gathered, for the California market; these eggs having become an almost indispensable article of spring and summer consumption, to many persons.

By the courtesy of the Farallone Egg Company, through their President, Captain Richardson, the schooner Louise, Captain Harlow, was placed at our service, for the purpose of visiting them; and, in company with a small party of friends, we were soon upon the deep green brine, plowing our way to these "Isles of the Ocean."

To the dwellers of an inland city, there is music in the ever restless waves, as they murmur and break upon the shore; but, to sail upon the broad heaving bosom of the ocean, gives an impression of profoundness and majesty that, by contrast, becomes a source of peaceful pleasure; as *change* becomes *rest* to the weary. There is a vastness, around, above, beneath you, as wave after wave, and swell after swell, lifts your tiny vessel upon its seething surface, as though it were a feather—a floating atom upon the broad expanse of waters. Then, to look into its shadowy depth, and feel the sublime language of the Psalmist: "O Lord, how manifold are thy works! in wisdom hast Thou made them all: the earth is full of thy riches. So is this great and wide sea, wherein are things creeping innumerable, both small and great beasts. There go the ships. *There* is that leviathan, whom Thou hast made to play therein. These wait all upon Thee: that Thou mayest give them their meat in due season. Thou openest thy hand, they are filled with good. Thou hidest thy face, they are troubled." "They that go down to the sea in ships, that do business in great waters: these see the works of the Lord, and his wonders in the deep. For He commandeth, and raiseth the stormy wind, which lifteth up the waves thereof." "They mount up to the heavens; they go down again to the depths. He maketh the storm a calm, so that the waves thereof are still."

"Oh, that men would praise the Lord for his goodness, for his wonderful works to the children of men!"

Bright and beautiful slept the morning, as a light breeze, blowing gently from the mountains, filled our sails, and sped us on our way. Object after object became distant and less, as we left them far, far behind us.

"Yonder blows a whale!" cries one.

"Where?"

"Just off our larboard bow."

"Oh! I see it—but——"

"But! what's the matter?"

"Oh! I feel so seasick."

"Well, never mind that; look up, and don't think about it."

"Oh—I can't—I must——"

Reader, were you ever seasick? If your experience enables you to answer in the affirmative, you will sympathise somewhat with the poor subject of it. Yonder may be this beauty, and that wonder, but a

ARE ENCHANTED WITH THE DELIGHTFUL PROSPECT OFF THE BAR.

SEA LIONS

HE THINKS HE WILL TAKE A YOUNG CALF HOME, BUT ITS PARENTS RAISE OBJECTIONS.

" don't-care*ishness* " comes over you, and if all the remarkable scenes in creation were just before you, " I don't care " is written upon the face, as you beseechingly seem to say : " *Pray* don't trouble me—*my hands are full*." Whales, sea gulls, porpoises, and even the white, foamy spray, that is curling over Duxbury Reef, are alike unheeded.

" How are you now ? " kindly asked our good natured Captain, of the one and the other.

" Ah ! thank you ; I am better."

" Here, take a cup of nice hot coffee."

" No ; I thank you."

The mere mention of anything to eat or to drink is only the signal for a renewal of the sickness.

" Thank goodness ! I feel better," says one, after a long spell of sickness and quiet.

" So do I," says another ; and, just as the " Farallones " are in sight, fortunately, all are better.

Now the air is literally filled with birds—birds floating above us, and birds all around us, like bees that are swarming ;—we thought the whole group of islands must have been deserted, and that they had poured down in myriads, on purpose to intercept our landing, or " bluff us off ;" but, as the dark weather beaten furrows, and the wave washed chasms, and the wind swept masses of rock, rose more defined and distinct before us, as we approached, we concluded that they must have abandoned the undertaking—for upon every peak sat a bird, and in every hollow a thousand ; but, looking around us again, the number, apparently, had increased, rather than diminished ; and, the more there seemed to be upon the islands, the greater the increase round about us — so that we concluded *our fears* to be entirely unfounded !

The anchor is dropped in a mass of floating foam, on the southeast, and sheltered side of the islands, and, in a small boat, we reach the shore ; thankful, after this short voyage to feel our feet standing firmly on *terra firma*.

Looking at the wonders on every side, we were astonished that we had heard so little about them; and, that a group of islands like these, should lie within a few hours sail of San Francisco, yet not be the resort of nearly every seeker of pleasure, and every lover of the wonderful.

It is like one vast menagerie. Upon the rocks adjacent to the sea, repose in easy indifference, thousands—yes, thousands—of *sea lions* (one species of the seal,) that weigh from *two to five thousand pounds each.* As these made the loudest noise, and to us were the most curious, we paid them the first visit. When we were within a few yards of them, the majority took to the water, while two or three of the oldest and largest remained upon the rock, "standing guard" over the young calves, that were either at play with each other, or asleep at their side. As we advanced, these masses of "blubber" moved slowly and clumsily towards us, with their mouths open, and showing two large tusks, that were standing out from their lower jaw, by which they gave us to understand that we had better not disturb the repose of the juvenile "lions," nor approach too near; or, we might receive more harm than we intended, or wished. But the moment we threw at them a stone, they would scamper off and leave the young lions to the mercy of their enemies. We advanced and took hold of one, to try if the sight of their young being taken away would tempt them to come to the rescue; but, although they roared, and kept swimming close to the rock, they evidently thought their own safety of the most importance. One old warrior, whose head and front bore scars of many a hard fought battle—for they fight fearfully, among themselves—could not be driven from the field; and neither rocks, nor shouting moved him in the least, except to meet the enemy, as he doubtless considered us.

All of these animals are very jealous of their particular rock, where, in the sun, they take their *siesta*; and, although we remained upon some of these spots for a considerable length of time, while their usual tenants were swimming in the sea, and perhaps had become somewhat uneasy, they were not allowed to land on the territory of another.

AN OBJECTION RAISED TO COOKING BEANS ON DISPUTED TERRITORY.

Most of these young seals are of a dark mouse color, but the old ones are of a light and brightish brown about the head, and gradually become darker towards the extremities, and which are about the same color as the young calves. Most of the male and the young female seals leave these islands during the months of October or November—and generally all go at once—returning in April or May, the following spring; while the older females remain here nearly alone, throughout the winter—a rather ungallant proceeding on the part of the males.

There are several different kinds of seal that pay a short visit here, at different seasons of the year.

The Russians formerly visited these islands, for the purpose of obtaining oil, and skins, and several places can be yet seen where the skins were stretched and dried.

The Murre, or Foolish Guillemot.

The birds, which are by far the most numerous, and on account of their eggs, the most important, are the *Murre*, or *Foolish Guillemot*, which are found here in myriads,

surmounting every rocky peak, and occupying every small and partially level spot upon the islands. Here it lays its egg, upon the bare rock, and never leaves it, unless driven off, until it is hatched; the male taking its turn, at incubation, with the female—although the latter is most assiduous. One reason why this may be the case, perhaps, is from the fact that the *Gull* is watching every opportunity to steal its egg, and eat it. The "eggers" say that when they are on their way to any part of the island, the Gulls call to each other, and hover around until the Murre is disturbed by them, and, before they can pick up the egg, the Gull sweeps down upon it, and carries it off.

When the young are old enough to emigrate, the Murres take them away in the night, lest the Gulls should eat them; and, as soon as the young reach the water, they swim at once. Some idea may be formed of the number of these birds, by tne Farralone Egg Company having, since 1850, brought to the San Francisco market between three and four millions of eggs.

On this coast these birds are numerous, in certain localities, from Panama to the Russian Possessions. On the Atlantic, they are found from Boston to the coast of Labrador; differing but very little in color, shape or size.

It is a clumsy bird, almost helpless on land, but is at home on the sea, and is an excellent swimmer and diver, and is very strong in the wings. Their eggs are unaccountably large, for the size of the bird, and "afford excellent food, being highly nutritive and palatable — whether boiled, roasted, poached, or in omelets." No two eggs are in color alike.

The bird of most varied and beautiful plumage, on the islands, is the *Mormon cirrhatus*, or *Tufted Puffin;* and, although they are rather numerous on this coast, they are very scarce elsewhere.

In addition to the *Murre*, *Puffin* and *Gull*, already mentioned, there are *Pigeons*, *Hawks*, *Shag*, *Coots*, &c., which visit here during the summer, but — with the exception of the *Gull* and *Shag* — do not remain through the winter. The *horned billed Guillemot* has been seen & caught here, but it is exceedingly rare.

Now, with the reader's permission, we will leave the birds and animals—at least if we can —and take a walk up to the light-

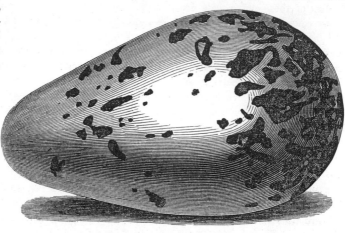

THE MURRE'S EGG—FULL SIZE.

house, at the top of the island, three hundred and fifty-seven feet above the sea. A good pathway has been made, so that we can ascend with ease. If you find that we have not left the birds, nor the birds left us, but that, at every step we take, we disturb some, and pass others, and that thou-

THE TUFTED PUFFIN.

sands are flying all around us, never mind—when we reach the top we shall forget them, at least for a few moments, to strain our eyes in looking towards the horizon, and seeking to catch a glimpse of some distant object. Yonder, some eight miles distant, are the "North Farralones," a very small group of rocks, and not exceeding three acres in extent—but, like this, they are covered with birds.

Now let us enter the lighthouse, and, under the guidance of Mr. Wines, the superintendent, we shall find our time well spent in looking at the best lighthouse on the Pacific coast. Everything is bright and clean, its machinery in beautiful order, and working as regular in its movements as a chronometer.

The wind blows fresh outside, and secretly you hope the lighthouse will not blow over before you get out. Here, too, you can see the shape of the island upon which you stand, mapped out upon the sea below.

Let us descend, wend our way to the "West End," and pass through the living masses of birds, that stand, like regiments of white breasted miniature soldiers, on every hand ;—and it might be well to take the precautionary measure of closing our ears to the perpetual roaring, and loud moaning, of the *sea lions*, for their noise is almost deafening. A caravan of wild beasts is nothing, in noise, to these.

Let us be careful, too, in every step that we take, or we shall place our foot upon a nest of young *Gulls*, or break eggs by the dozen, for they are everywhere around us. We soon reach the side of the "Jordan," as a small inlet is called, and across which we can step at low tide, but which is thirty feet wide at high water. To cross it, however, a rope and pulley is your mode of conveyance; so hold tight by your hands, and you'll soon get across. Safely over, let us make our way for a glimpse of the *West End View, looking East.*

VIEW FROM WEST END, LOOKING EAST.

This is a wild and beautiful scene. The sharp pointed rocks are standing boldly out against the sky, and covered with birds and sea lions. A heavy surf is rolling in, with thundering hoarseness, and as the wild waters break upon the shore, they resemble the low booming sound of distant thunder; while the white spray curls over, and falls with a hissing splash upon the rocks, and then returns again to its native brine; while, swimming in the boiling sea, amid the foam and rocks, just peering above the water, are the heads of scores of sea lions. Let us watch them for a moment. Here comes one noble looking old fellow, who rises from the water, and works his way, slowly and clumsily, towards the young which lie high and dry, sleeping in the sun, or are engaged lazily scratching themselves with their hind claws; and, although we are very near them, they lie quite unconcerned, and innocent of danger. Not so the old *gentleman*, who has just taken his position before us, as sentry. Experience has doubtless taught him that such looking animals as we are behave no better than we should do, and he knows it!

There are water-washed caves, and deep fissures, between the rocks, just at our right; and, in the distance, is a large arch, not less than sixty feet in height, its top and sides completely covered with birds. Through the arch you can see a ship which is just passing.

Now let us go to the "Big Rookery," lying on the northwest side of the island.

This locality derives its name from the island here, forming a hollow, well protected from the winds, and being less abrupt than other places, is on that account a favorite resort of myriads of sea fowl, who make this their place of abode and where vast numbers of young are raised. If you walk amongst them, thousands immediately rise, and for a few moments darken the air as though a heavy cloud had just crossed and obscured the sun light upon your path. But few persons who have not seen them can realize the vast numbers that make this their home, and which are here, there

VIEW FROM THE BIG ROOKERY, LOOKING EAST.

and everywhere, flying, sitting and even swimming upon the boiling and white topped surge among the seals.

Here, as elsewhere, there are thousands of seals, some are suckling their calves, some are lazily sleeping in the sun, others are fishing, some are quarreling, others are disputing possession, and yonder, just before us, two large and fierce old fellows are engaged in direful combat with each other —now the long tusks of the one are moving upwards to try to make an entrance beneath the jaw of the other—now they are below—now there is a scattering among the swimming group that have merely been looking on to see the sport, for the largest has just come up amongst them, and they are afraid of him. Now appears his antagonist, his eyes rolling with maddened frenzy, they again meet,—now under, now over— fierce wages the war, hard goes the battle, but at last the owner of the head, already covered with scales, has conquered, and his discomfitted enemy makes his way to the nearest rock, and there lies panting and bleeding, but he may not rest here, for the owner of that claim is at home and has possession, and without any sympathy for his suffering and unfortunate brother, he orders him off, although " only a squatter," and he again takes to the sea in search of other quarters.

From this point we get an excellent view of the lighthouse, and the residence of the keepers. Everywhere there is beauty, wildness, sublimity. Let us not linger too long here, although weeks could be profitably spent in looking at the wonders around us, but let us take a hasty glance at the *View from the North Landing.*

Here there is a fine estuary, where, with a little improvement, small schooners can enter at any season of the year ; and where the oil and other supplies are landed, for the lighthouse. Like the other views, it is singular and wild—each eminence covered with birds, each sea-washed rock occupied by seals, and the air almost darkened by

VIEW FROM THE NORTH LANDING, LOOKING NORTH.

the sea gulls, skimming backward and forward, like swallows, and by the rapid and apparently difficult flight of the murres.

From this point we can get an excellent view of the *North Farallones*, that, in the dim and shadowy distance, are looming up their dull peaks just above the restless and swelling waves. From the sugar loaf shaped peak, and the singularly high arch, and bold rugged outlines of the other rocks, this view has become a favorite one with the " eggers."

Upon these islands, of three hundred and fifty acres, there is not a single tree or shrub to relieve the eye, by contrast, or give change to the barrenness of the landscape. A few weeds and sprigs of wild mustard are the only signs of vegetable life to be seen upon them. To those who reside here, it must be monotonous and dull; but, to those who *visit* it, there is a variety of wild wonders, that amply repays them for their trouble.

Some Italian fishermen having supplied our cook with excellent fish, let us hasten aboard and make sail for home.

Before saying " good bye " to our kind entertainers, and again leaving tnem to the solitary loneliness of a " life near the sea," we will congratulate them upon their useful employment, and ask them to remember the comforting joy they must give to the tempest-tossed mariner, who sees, in the " light afar," the welcome sentinel, ever standing near the gate of entrance to the long wished and hoped for port, where, for a time, in enjoyment and rest, he can recover from the hardships, and forget the perils, of the sea.

On our left, and but a few yards from shore, is an isle, called *Seal Rock*, and where the sea lions have possession, and are waving their lubberly bodies to and fro, upon its very summit; and from whence the echoes of their low howling moans are heard across the sea, long after distance has hidden them from our sight.

After a pleasant run of five hours, without any seasickness, we were again walking the streets of San Francisco, abundantly satisfied that our trip was exceedingly pleasant and instructive.

VIEW OF THE PAVILION.

Our Social Chair.

HENEVER a Social Chair is out of the humor to be sociable, or rather to write confidentially and sociably, what a huge blessing is it to find that some kind-hearted and jocular friend —for friend such an one always proves—to write us like our correspondent "Weeper." Mr. Weeper, who seems to have been to the S. F. Mechanics' Pavilion, and having had the temerity (!) to take his wife with him, thus discourses thereon:

Dear Hutchings: Have you been to the Mechanics' Pavilion, I mean to the great Fair of the Industrial resources of the State? If you have'nt, don't you go—or at least if you do, (and I suppose that all of your profession ought to go,) be sure and not take your wife with you—if you have a wife—for if you do, unless you are richer than editors have the reputation of being, you will rue the day.

I had heard such great praise of the thousand and upwards of curious and beautiful articles on exhibition, and says I to my wife, "Lizzie, suppose we go to the 'Fair' this evening; what say you?" "I should like it very much, Tim," said she; and as soon as twilight began to deepen into night I deposited our "50 cents each" on the palm of the pleasant looking door-keeper, and we soon found ourselves introduced to the wonders there exhibited. "Bless me," says she, "Tim, what is that beautifully bright and odd-looking thing on that platform?" "Oh! my love," I replied, "that is a California marine engine." "Where was it caught?!' "Caught!" I inquired with a look of surprise—"do you suppose it to be some kind of reptile?" "No; but I do take it to be some kind of animal, for didn't you say it was 'a marine Indian?'" After I had explained how Mr. Donahue, a skillful machinist on First street, had manufactured it for a steamboat as large as the *Chrysopolis*, now running on the Sacramento river, and that it was not only of California manufacture, but the first of the kind ever built here, she remarked that "it would make a very curious and uncommon ornament for our garden!"

"Yes, my love," I replied, "I will buy it for that purpose!"

Scarcely had that remark been concluded and we were walking up towards the engine, than a flood of light and a sizzling and hissing sound at our right, attracted us to a long row of lamps—coal oil lamps—of all sizes and styles; and near them a small kitchenfull of cooking stoves—not your common wood or coal consuming articles—but some of a new style that stand as well on a table in a bed-room, as in a kitchen, and cook anything, from a cup of coffee to an extensive and elaborate dinner; and without ashes, dust, soot, or any similar abomination. "Ah!" Lizzie began to whisper in my ear, when Mr. Dietz had finished his explanation, "that is just what *we* want, Tim; you'll buy me one of those." "The lamps or the stoves?" "Oh! the stoves, of course; you know we have several lamps; and if the stoves—the Æra vapor stoves, is the name, I believe—they seem to be called, if they are as good as the lamps and as economical and cleanly, I wouldn't be without one for the world." "I'll buy you one."

Then we looked at the time-piece with a brass flower on the top, that opened its petals every hour, and disclosed to view a little bird, which fluttered its tiny wings and sung a merry tune, and was again covered up as before,—and I was to buy that also.

Then—Tucker's magnificent "Railroad-set" of silver; the 2,200-pound cheese, for the What Cheer House; some fine and large California-made blankets—all these were to be bought for us. But, thank goodness, when examining the fine quality of California-made paper from the Pioneer Mills, I was to speak to *you*, to buy *that* for the Magazine, to have it printed on California paper.

Perhaps you think that this ended the chapter of wants! Oh! dear no. Hank's & Packard's California prepared oil and water colors were to be purchased to make some paintings of the Yosemite Valley. Then a washing-machine—and no doubt a sewing and a knitting machine also, but we had the good fortune to have one of the former already. Then, I was to buy the beautiful little model sloop "Mermaid"—just to take a sail in on Sundays, New Years, Thanksgiving Days and Fourth of July. Then, that beautiful carriage was to be bought, (not the new steam fire-engine.)

Next we were to get some Redwood and have a new parlor-set of furniture made of that, or of the Madrone, chiefly because these looked well, were well polished, and Californian. (My wife is the most enthusiastic Californian you could become acquainted with)—and she threatens me with—"she don't know what," if I don't introduce you to her; but if I were to tell you all that she says about you and the Magazine, you would be as proud as I am jealous.

Next, as we wandered through the picture gallery, we were to have Nahl's beautiful and life-like sketches, and Butman's paintings, and Neal's India-ink portrait, Eastman's and Loomis' pencilings and water-color drawings, with nearly the whole of the wondrous and pretty articles in Kohler's case, etcetera, etcetera, etcetera.

So that after carefully estimating the cost of that visit, if I were to buy all the articles wanted, it would amount to the insignificant sum of $197,428 39, and you know the old maxim about figures.

I will just add that if you are familiar with the homely proverb, "A nod's as good as a wink to a blind horse," no more will be necessary for me to say but that I remain as ever,

Your Sincere Admonisher,

TIMOTHY WEEPER.

P. S.—I ought perhaps to mention that I couldn't excuse myself from purchasing, at her entreaty, the four volumes of your Magazine, as nicely bound as those on exhibition in the Fair, although I have taken the numbers from the beginning and intend so to do for many years to come, simply because it is just what it professes to be— a *California Magazine.*

PAVILION OF THE FIRST CALIFORNIA INDUSTRIAL EXHIBITION, UNDER THE AUSPICES OF THE MECHANICS' INSTITUTE, SAN FRANCISCO, OPENED
SEPTEMBER 7TH, 1857.

HUTCHINGS'

CALIFORNIA MAGAZINE.

VOL. IV.   JUNE, 1860.   No. 12.

SALMON FISHERY ON THE SACRAMENTO RIVER.

BY C. A. KIRKPATRICK.

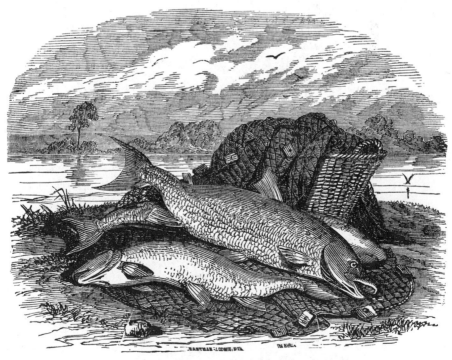

GROUP OF SALMON FROM THE SACRAMENTO RIVER.

MANY of the Pioneers of California, if they are not already aware of the fact, will be sorry to learn that the Salmon fish are fast disappearing from our waters—that is, upon all the streams upon which mining is carried on to any extent, and, in fact, we may say from all the streams of importance.

This may be attributed to three causes. First, the mining operations, by which the water is carried by ditches and flumes for miles out of its channel, and, when it again finds its natural course, it would scarcely be true to call such a muddy mass, *water*.

This being the case on all the tributaries, the fountain being impure the whole stream is polluted, and our beautiful and highly palatable fish, scorning to "live, move, and have their being" in such an impure element, are seeking other realms, where their native element is not made so unpleasant by man's search for gold.

FISHERMAN'S HUT ON THE SACRAMENTO.

How well does the writer remember the good old days of '49, when he wished for no better mirror than the crystal waters of the "Rio de los Americanos," Mokelumnes, or Los Mariposas, and how the pure water sparkled and flashed from the shining sides of the merry fishes, as they hurried to their mountain retreats, to spend the "season" at the "Springs," or returned to the busy scenes of their old ocean home, the crowded capital of all Fishdom—where stand in all their original splendor, the palaces of the real "Codfish Aristocracy."

The second cause for the disappearance of the Salmon, is the navigation of the rivers, which has been shown in their leaving the Hudson, Connecticut, and other streams of the Eastern States, where they were once plentiful, and where the first cause spoken of did not exist.

The third cause is the immense destruction of the fish, which has been going on for the last ten years. Just note the recession.

In the year 1849, we had no trouble whatever in procuring all the salmon we wished, by just constructing a rude barb or spear of this kind ——————o— }— wade out a few steps, and literally pick up all we desired.

In 1851, we could observe a great decrease, and since that time the fish have been gradually retreating beyond their pursuing destroyers, until, like the "poor Indian," they are being driven westward into the sea.

But, before taking the final "plunge," they seem to have turned at bay in one part of the Sacramento river, and here they are eagerly caught. Rio Vista is now the principal shipping point for the Salmon. This town is situated about forty-five miles below the city of Sacramento, and below the outlets of all the large sloughs, or at least two of the largest, Steamboat and Cache Creek sloughs—unite with the main, or old Sacramento river, just above this place; making the stream here about one-third of

NIGHT SCENE ON THE OLD SACRAMENTO RIVER.

a mile wide. The reader will see that being upon the main river, so near its outlet into Suisun bay, not over twenty miles, and so far from the mining region, that there is a clearer and larger body of water than can be found any where else on the river. It is to this place that the fish now resort.

The Salmon are taken in this manner:

First, however, we will speak of the means, then the process:

Nets are constructed of stout shoe-thread, first made into skeins, then twist-ed into a cord about the size of common twine, after the fashion of making ropes. It is then, with a wooden needle, manu-factured into a web of open net work from 780 to 1200 feet, or 130 to 200 fathoms long, and 15 feet wide. On both sides of the net are small ropes, to which it is fastened. On the rope designated for the upper side, are placed, at intervals of five or six feet, pieces of cork or light wood, for the purpose of buoys; while on the other line, bits of lead are fastened to sink the net in the water. Now attach to one end of the upper line a small buoy, painted any dark color which can be easily distinguished, and at the other end make fast a line fifteen or twenty feet long, for the fisherman to hold, while his net floats, and the net is complete.

Whitehall boats are those most gener-ally used in this branch of State industry, and which are from nineteen to twenty-two feet in length of keel, and from four to five feet breadth of beam; this size and style being considered the best.

Now, the next thing wanted, is two fearless men; one to manage the boat, and the other to cast the net.

The net is then stowed in the after part of the boat, and everything made ready for a *haul*. Being at what is called the head of the *drift*, one of the men takes his place in the stern of the boat, and while the rower pulls across the stream, the net is thrown over the stern. Thus is formed a barrier or net work almost the entire width of the stream, and to the depth of fifteen or twenty feet.

The *drift* is the distance on the river which is passed after casting the net, and floating with the tide until it is drawn into the boat. This passage, and the drawing in of the net, completes the process of catching the salmon.

In coming in contact with the net, the head of the fish passes far enough through the meshes, or openings, to allow the strong threads of the net to fall back of and under the gill, and thus, they are unable to escape, and are effectually *caught in the net* and drawn into the boat.

During the year 1852, there were probably as many fish caught in that part of the Sacramento river before alluded to, as at any time previous, and more than at any time since. Two men with one net and boat having caught as many as three hundred fish in the course of one night; the night being the best time to take them, on account of their being unable to see and avoid the net.

The fish which are caught in the spring, are much larger and nicer than those caught during the summer months; the former being really a bright *salmon color*, and the texture of the flesh firm and solid, while the latter, in appearance, might properly be called salmon color faded, and the flesh soft and unpalatable. This difference is no doubt owing to the temperature and composition of the water in which the fish may be sojourning; the cold, salt sea water hardening and coloring the flesh, while the warm, fresh river water tends to soften and bleach.

PAYING OUT THE SEINE.

HAULING IN THE SEINE.

In regard to the habits of this fish, but little seems to be known. They seem to be gregarious in their nature, traveling in herds, or as the fishermen call it "*schools*." They do not love a very cold climate, as is indicated by their not ascending the rivers on the northern coast, except in very limited numbers, until the month of July. In those streams where the current is very rapid, their rate of speed is supposed to be five or six miles an hour; but where the current is eddying and slow, not more than two miles an hour. It has been also ascertained that they will stop for two or three days in deep, still water; no doubt to rest and feed, as they choose such places where food can be easily procured.

There seems to be quite a difference in the size, flavor, and habits of the Salmon, as found in the Sacramento, Columbia and Frazer rivers; those of the Sacramento, being larger, more juicy and oily, and brighter colored. They are, however, more abundant in the North, and about half the average weight; the average of the former being fifteen pounds.

Although early in the spring some are caught in the North quite as large as any caught in the Sacramento, weighing from fifty to sixty pounds.

In the gulf of Georgia, and Bellingham Bay, and on the Columbia, Frazer and Lumna rivers, the salmon are taken by thousands; while we of the Sacramento, only get them by hundreds. One boat, last season, on the Fraser river, in one month, caught 13,860.

There is also one peculiarity with the fish of the North. Every second or third year there are but few salmon in those waters, their places being taken by a fish called the *Hone*, which come in great numbers, equal if not greater than the salmon. The two fish never come in any considerable numbers together.

In regard to the manner and power of reproduction of these fish, we shall not even present a supposition. Suffice it to say, that in portions of Frazer river—mentioning but one which they frequent—the water is so filled with their eggs as to render it unfit for use, and the air becomes tainted with the effluvia a total of 22,500 fish' or 337,500 pounds; the greater part of these are shipped, and used fresh in San Francisco. But this number forms but a small proportion of what are caught, the principal part being retained and salted, or smoked, or otherwise prepared for shipment to various parts of the world— many finding their way to Australia, and the Islands of the Pacific, as well as to New York, and other domestic ports on the Atlantic seaboard.

During the last summer, a new process, which had been for some time maturing, was at last brought to perfection, for putting up in a neat, portable style, the fish, all ready for the table, and capable of being transported to any climate, retaining all its original sweetness and flavor.

INDIAN SPEARING SALMON.

of their decomposition. From this statement let the reader form his own conclusion in regard to the probable number of fish which might have been hatched, provided they had not been *bad eggs!*

But as this article is growing too lengthy, we will close it with a few words relating to the business of taking the salmon, and its importance as one of the resources of the Pacific coast.

From facts obtained from the obliging freight clerks of the C. S. N. Co.'s boats, we learn that from the principal shipping port of the Sacramento river, Rio Vista, there are an average of 150 fish, or 2,250 pounds, sent each day to market, for five months of the year, making

There are many other facts and subjects connected with this business which might be of interest to many; and if such should be found to be the case, the subject may, at some future time, be renewed.

But few persons who have ever walked the streets of any English city can forget the cry of "Pickled Salmon! Salmon, Oh! Fresh Pickled Salmon," from a pair of stentorian lungs: and the method of preserving those delicious fish on the Sacramento, very much resembles that adopted by the most celebrated, and best, of the English preserving houses.

THE WRECK OF THE STEAMER GRANADA.

THE engraving represents the position and appearance of the ill-fated Steamer Granada, which was wrecked upon the rocks at Fort Point on the night of October 13th. The drawing was made a week after the disaster, and was taken from the door of the light-house at the Fort. The bluffs are seen on the left and the line of Point Lobos beyond. The strained appearance of the vessel, or the sinking of the bow and stern, called in nautical parlance "hogging," is as fairly represented as could be in a view from the bow.

The Granada was—we can already speak of it in the past tense—was a vessel of about 1400 tons, six years old, and had been running in the line between Aspinwall and Havana. She was one of two vessels, the Moses Taylor being the other, purchased by Marshall O. Roberts and intended for the Pacific side of the new line between San Francisco and the Atlantic States by the way of Tehuantepec. She left New York on her way hither on July 14th last, came through the Straits of Magellan, and after 14,000 miles of ocean voyage, without an accident, was wrecked upon endeavoring to enter her harbor of destination.

She had taken on board a pilot before passing Point Lobos, and it was doubtless owing to his rashness that the vessel was lost. He attempted to bring her in at evening and during a very heavy fog. A short time before the vessel struck, he had ordered a full head of steam to be turned on; and the ship was going at full speed, when breakers were observed at her bow. The order was given to reverse the engines, but it was too late; she was already firmly imbedded in the sand and on the rocks—and there she remained. There was no freight and no passengers on board but a son of Mr. Roberts. There was no loss of life. Strenuous attempts with steam-tugs and by pumping were made to save the steamer, but all failed ; and the wreck was dismasted. It was sold at auction "for the benefit of whom it might concern" on October 18th for $9,400; and measures were immediately taken to remove the engines, boilers and other valuable parts.

The rocky shore where the wreck lies has become famous for wrecks. It is the same where several previous ones took place, among them the Jenny Lind and Golden Fleece ; the Chateau Palmer only a few years ago, and the General Cushing. The ship Euterpe went ashore there a few months since, but was fortunately recovered.

THE MUSEUM AT THE WHAT CHEER HOUSE.

IT is not a little strange that the most extensive and in many respects the best Museum in California, should be due to the private enterprise of a smart Yankee, and be a mere adjunct or addition to an extensive hotel. There are in various quarters of the city and State, cabinets of minerals, and Indian curiosities; the Academy of Natural Sciences has a rich collection of minerals; the Odd Fellows have a collection of curiosities ; various private gentlemen have valuable collections of ores, shells, insects, eggs and other objects of scientific interest ; but for variety and all that goes to make up a museum, no collection in the State can compare with the museum of R. B. Woodward's What Cheer House, on Sacramento street. The proprietor, finding that his house was the best patronized in the State, seems to have come to the conclusion that he would make a little world in itself out of it; and accordingly established an extensive and well-chosen library for the use of the patrons of the house—and, from several visits to the place, we believe we can say with truth that no Library in the State is more extensively and better read than the What Cheer Library. It is arranged on two sides of the reading room, and seldom can any one enter it without finding the large apartment entirely blocked up with readers. Lodgers, and particularly lodgers from the country who are waiting for conveyance out of the city, have much time on their hands; and here the soberer and better classes find amusement and instruction. Though Mr. Woodward reaps his own profit from his library, we are not altogether certain but that he is entitled to the name of being a public benefactor with this reading room of his.

The Museum was established last summer with much the same objects as the Library, that is to say, as a part of the House, and for the amusement of its patrons, though everybody, who takes interest in seeing it, has access. It consists of a large apartment forty-five feet long by fourteen wide, with an entrance through the Library and Reading Room. It contains large cases of preserved birds and animals, filling up one entire side of the room, and including almost all the noted birds of California. They were collected by F. Gruber, the taxidermist; and the arrangement of them by him is very tasteful and appropriate. They are, as well as could be possible under the circumstances, represented in their natural positions, and in various instances we are taught a portion of their Natural History by the surroundings in the case. The Hawk with the Sparrow in his claw occupies a dry limb, apparently removed from all sympathy with the rest of the feathered creation. The Woodpecker seems to be rapping on the dead branch; the Thrush to be luxuriating among the berries. The Quail rambles among the stubble, and the Cranes and Herons seem stalking among the shallows.

The spirited engraving at the head of this article represents a general view of the Museum, the birds and animals being ranged along the right side, the Indian curiosities on the left; the eggs in front and the minerals, shells and insects in the rear. We shall have occasion hereafter to give a number of the various objects of interest in detail and with special drawings, and particularly some of the most remarkable of the Californian birds and antiquities; but for the present let it suffice to call attention to the Museum as a whole, give it the proper credit for being the best one in the State, and state, as a matter of general information, what is to be seen in it.

There are six hundred specimens of birds, including species from every part of the world. Among them are Eagles, Vultures, Hawks, Owls, Nighthawks, Falcons, Crows, Magpies, Jays, Cuckoos, Woodpeckers, Creepers, Kingfishers, Thrushes, Orioles, Starlings, Sparrows, Finches, Warblers, Crossbills, Cardinals, Larks, Wrens, Buntings, Parrots, Cockatoos, Trojans, Birds of Paradise, Pigeons, Doves, Toucans, Satin Birds, Hummingbirds, Nightingales, Sun Birds, Snipes, Woodcocks, Rails, Avosets, Plovers, Coots, Bustards, Grouse, Quails, Pheasants, Guinea Hens, Snow Grouse, Gold and Silver Pheasants, Albatrosses, Sea Gulls, Terns, Petrels, Auks, Tufted Puffins, Horn-bill Guillemots, Oyster Catchers, Murres, Sea Pigeons, Cormorants, Cranes, Herons, Egrets, Bitterns, Grebes, Swans, Pelicans, Geese, Ducks, and Divers.

There are twenty five specimens of preserved animals, including the Deer, Armadillo, Black Hare, Mountain Pole-Cat, White and Norway Rat, Red and

Grey Squirrel, Ground Squirrel, Gopher, White-bellied, Northern and Yellow-cheeked Weasel, Mole and Dog.

The collection of Eggs comprises 1200 specimens from the largest Ostrich to the smallest Humming-bird's eggs. They were collected and arranged by J. L. Jungerman.

Of Indian Curiosities there are war and fishing implements, and weapons from the South Sea Islands, Sandwich Islands and North West coast; Idols, Spears, Bows and Arrows, Dresses, Gourds, War clubs, Fish nets, Boats, Drums, Pipes, Oars, Ornaments, Belts, Blankets and Fish hooks.

There is a large collection of old and rare Coins, chiefly copper and brass, going back even to the times of the Romans; also Medals, Indian Wampum, Beads, Cowries and other currency.

The cabinet of Shells was chiefly procured from Dr. Frick, and embraces marine specimens from many localities of the Pacific Ocean. A complete collection of the rare and beautiful terrestrial shells from the Sandwich Islands, collected by himself and containing many new species, described by him in a catalogue, which is to be found with the collection. To these must also be added all the fluviatile shells found in the same Islands, as well as the Society and Friendly Islands.

The Cabinet of Minerals is devoted chiefly to Californian specimens, and contains a little of almost everything of interest in this line on the Pacific coast.

The Alcoholic Preparations embrace specimens of the Pilot Fish, Shark, Rattle Snake, Black Snake, Coral Snake, Pilot Snake, Whip Snake, Striped Snake, Copper Snake, Horney Ants from Arizonia, Lizzards, Polyps, Tape-worms, a four-legged Chicken, Snails, and Horned Frogs.

There is a large collection of Butterflies and other insects, Australian, European and American.

Some other curiosities are scattered around, among them an excrescence from a Whale's nose, tusks of the Walrus and Wild boar, Seal and Sea-lion skins, and horns of the Elk, Deer and Mountain Sheep.

It may be said of the Museum as a whole, what has been said of the Library, that it has constant visitors and is always a popular quarter for the patrons of the What Cheer House. It is well known that no bar-room or gaming table is to be found about the establishment; but instead of the vicious and dangerous pleasures of dissipation, there is abundant invitation to the higher, more refined and more respectable pleasures of the well-stocked cabinet and well selected and well filled shelves.

THE GREAT KNIGHT'S FERRY DIAMOND.—A late number of the San Joaquin *Republican* tells a story which would serve excellently as the foundation of a romance. Upon such a basis a Bocaccio would have raised a splendid structure in the way of a tale. The story goes, that a party of miners were working a claim with sluice and hydraulic pipe and hose, at a point called Buena Vista, nearly opposite Knight's Ferry. One night about dark, the pipeman saw an object which he had washed out of the bank, lie glittering in the pile of dirt and stones, that was about to be passed through the sluice. The gleams from it lit up all the space in the vicinity, and caused much astonishment to the hardy workmen. The pipeman picked it up and moved along to show it to one of his comrades, but accidentally dropped it into the sluice, and it was borne down by the torrent of water into the mass of stones and dirt known as "tailings." A company of Spiritualists at Knight's Ferry are trying to discover the present locality of the jewel, which is represented to be larger than the Koh-i-noor.

HUTCHINGS'
CALIFORNIA MAGAZINE.

VOL. I.   OCTOBER, 1856.   NO. IV.

FRONT VIEW OF THE SAN FRANCISCO BRANCH MINT.

COINING MONEY,
AT THE SAN FRANCISCO BRANCH MINT.

On the north side of Commercial street, between Montgomery and Kearny, there stands a dark, heavy looking building, with heavy iron bars, and heavy iron shutters, to windows and doors; and high above, standing on, and just peering over a heavy cornice, there is a large American eagle; looking down into the building, as if he meant to see, and take notes, of all that is going on within, "and print 'em too." At his back there is a small forest of chimney stacks, from which various kinds of smoke, and different colored fumes, are issuing. This building is the Branch Mint of San Francisco.

On the pavement, in front, stands a number of odd looking, square boxes, containing bottles with glass necks rising above the top, and in which are the various kinds of acid used in the manufacture of gold and silver coin within.

In the street can be seen drays and wagons with men unloading supplies of various kinds for the Mint; express wagons with packages of the precious metal from all parts of the mines; men going up ·with carpet sacks hanging heavily on their hand, all desirous of having their gold dust converted into coin.

At the entrance door a man is sitting whose business it is to inquire your business whenever you present yourself for admission; and, if it is tolerably clear to him that you have no intention of obtaining a hatful of gold without a proper certificate; and more, that you have business dealings with Uncle Sam-

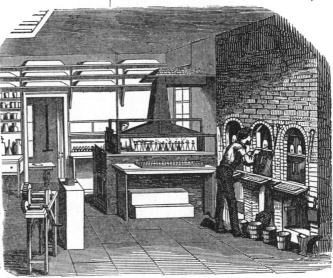

ASSAYING THE "CHIPS."

uel; or, at least, wish to see how gold and silver is made into coin; why, it is probable that you may be allowed to pass:

By the kindness of Mr. Lott, the Superintendent of the Mint, and the courtesy of the officers of the different departments, every facility was offered us for obtaining sketches, and all the necessary information concerning the *modus operandi* of coining, cheerfully given in all its branches.

To make the subject as plain as possible, we will suppose that the reader has just placed a bag of gold at the Treasurer's counter, for the purpose of having it coined. Here the Receiving Clerk takes it, and after accurately weighing it, hands to the depositor a certificate for the gross weight of gold dust received, before melting. It is then sent to the *Melting Room*, where it is put into a black-lead crucible, melted, (each deposit is melted by itself,) and run into a " bar." A "chip," weighing about a tenth of an ounce, is then taken from each · end of the bar, at opposite corners,—one from the top, the other from the bottom side. These chips are then taken to the *Assay Room* where they are carefully analyzed, by chemical process, and the exact amount of gold, silver, and other metals contained in each chip, accurately ascertained. The Assayer then reports to the Treasurer the exact proportion of gold, silver, and other metals, found in the chips. The standard fineness of the whole bar is then determined, and the value of the deposit ascertained ; it then awaits, in the Treasurer's Office, the orders of the depositor. When it is withdrawn, the depositor presents his certificate to the Superintendent's Clerk, who issues a warrant upon the Treasurer for the nett value of the deposit; and, upon the payment of this warrant, in coin, or bar, the Treasurer delivers the Mint memorandum, which contains the weight of the deposit before and after melting, fineness, nett value, &c., &c.

To facilitate business and prevent delay, a large amount of coin is always kept on hand, so that depositors are not

MAKING THE GRANULATIONS.

required to wait until the gold dust taken in, is coined; but the moment its value is ascertained from the Assayer, the value is promptly paid the depositor: this is a great public convenience.

Now with the reader's permission let us see the gold bars accurately weighed in the Treasurer's Office; and let us carefully watch the many and interesting processes through which they must pass while being converted into coin.

On leaving the Treasurer's hands they are first sent to the *Melting Room*— where, as California gold contains from three to twelve per cent. of silver, it

becomes necessary in order to extract it, to alloy the gold with about twice its weight of silver; and thereby destroy the affinity of the gold for the silver, this enables the acid to act upon the silver. For this purpose, the gold and silver are melted together; and, while in a hot and fluid state, is poured gradually into cold water, where it forms into small thin pieces somewhat resembling the common pop-corn in appearance, and these are called " granulations." The *Granulations* are then conveyed from the *Melting Room* to the *Refining Room;* where they are placed in porcelain pots, that are standing in vats lined with lead. Nitric Acid is then poured in upon the granulations, in about the proportion of two and a half pounds of acid, to one of gold; and, after the porcelain pots are thus filled sufficiently, the shutters, by which they are surrounded, are fixed closely down, and the granulations and acids boiled by steam for six hours, by which process the silver and all the base metals are dissolved, while the gold lies upon the bottom untouched. The bright orange colored vapor that we see issuing from the top of one of the chimneys of the Mint is generated from this process. After boiling, the solution is drawn out of the pots by means of a gold syphon, (worth over two thousand dollars) into small tubs; it is then carried and emptied into a large tub or vat, twelve feet in diameter and six feet in depth—where a stream of salt water is poured upon it, which precipitates the *nitrate of silver* contained in solution, and it becomes *chloride of silver.* The chloride is then run out of the vat into large filters, where it is washed until the water es-

DRAWING OFF THE ACID FROM THE PORCELAIN POTS.

caping from the filter is perfectly free from the acid. The chloride of silver is then taken out of the filter and placed in a "reducing vat" where it is mixed with *granulated zinc* and water: oil of vitriol is then poured in upon it, where by the action of the oil of vitriol upon the zinc and the water, *hydrogen gas* is generated; which, combining with the *chlorine* of the *chloride of silver* forms *muriatic acid*, and leaves pure metalic silver, in fine powder, at the bottom of the reducing vat.

The silver is then taken out, and again washed carefully for the purpose of removing the acid, and the chloride of zinc that has been formed by the action of zinc upon the chloride of silver while in the reducing vat.

After the silver is thus thoroughly washed, it is placed in a hydraulic press, and subjected to the enormous pressure of twelve thousand pounds to the square inch, and the water nearly all forced out of it, leaving a compact, circular cake of silver, about ten inches in width, by three in thickness. These cakes are then placed on a drying-pan, and the remaining moisture dried out. The silver is now ready for melting, and making into coin; or, for use in the granulating process.

Now, if you please, let us return to the porcelain pots, and notice what becomes of the *gold* left in the bottom. This is now subjected to another boiling process of six hours, in fresh nitric acid in about the same proportion as before, during which time it is frequently stirred, to enable the acid to permeate the whole of the gold in the pot.

After this second boiling the acid is baled out (and saved for the first boiling process) and the contents of the porcelain pots emptied into a filter, where it is well washed with hot water, prepared expressly for this purpose, and the remaining nitrate of silver is entirely washed out, leaving nothing but pure gold. The water is now pressed out in the same manner as it was from the silver, and the cakes locked up in a drying furnace for about three hours, when they are taken out and are ready for melting.

Let us now go to the *Melting Room.* There we find men moving about among "crucibles," "shoe" and "ingot-moulds," and what not, in front of the furnace, and as they lift back the cover, and the bright light breaks upon the eyes; down in the white heat we can see the crucible, ready to receive the precious metal. The gold is then put into it, with a sufficient amount of copper to reduce the standard of 1000 to 903. The gold is then run off into what are technically called

whether it is now of the fineness required.

These ingots of standard gold, each weighing about sixty ounces, of which there are from thirty-six to forty in one "melt" are then "pickled," which, being interpreted, means, to heat them red-hot and immerse them in sulphuric acid water, which cleans and partially anneals them. They are then delivered by the Melter and Refiner to the Treasurer, who weighs them accurately and then delivers them to the *Coiner.*

The ingots thus delivered, for twenty dollar pieces, are about 12 inches in length, about 1 inch and 7-16ths in

RUNNING THE GOLD INTO INGOTS.

"shoe-moulds." The bar thus run is termed "toughened bar." It is again assayed, for the purpose of knowing the exact amount of copper to be added to reduce it to 900–1000, or the United States' standard fineness of coin. It is then again melted and reduced to the above standard; after which it is run into "ingot-moulds," and is again assayed, to determine

width, and about 1-2 an inch in thickness; yet for every different sized coin the width varies to suit.

They are now removed to the *Rolling Room* where the ingots pass thirteen consecutive times through the rollers, and at each time decrease in thickness, and increase in length, until they are about three feet six inches long: they are then taken to the *Annealing*

ROLLING AND CUTTING ROOM.

Room, enclosed in long copper tubes, and securely sealed to prevent oxidation or loss of the metal. They are now placed in the annealing furnace, where, after remaining for about forty-five minutes in sealed tubes, they are taken out and cooled in clear water. The " strips " of gold are now ready for rolling to the finished thickness and are re-taken to the *Rolling Room* for that purpose ; and are afterwards re-turned to the *Annealing Room* and sub-jected again to a red hot heat for forty-five minutes, and again cooled as before.

These " strips" are now carried to the *Drawing* and *Cutting Room*, where they are first pointed ; then heated, by steam ; then ' greased, " with wax and tallow ; and are then ready for the draw-bench. The point of the strip is then inserted in the " draw-jaw" and the whole strip is drawn through the " jaw" which reduces it exactly to the required thickness for coining. The strips thus gauged are then taken to the " cutting press," where, from the end of each strip a " proof-piece" is " punched " and accurately weighed ; and, if found correct is punched into "blanks" or " planchets" at the rate of about one hundred and eighty per minute. Should any of the strips be found too heavy, they are re-drawn through the " draw-jaw." If too light, they are laid aside to be regulated, by what is technically termed the "doctor" —a process by which the strip is made concave, before the planchets are cut out, and which gives them the re-quired weight. This is an improve-ment only in use in the San Francisco Branch Mint and is, we believe, the invention of Mr. Eckfeldt, the Coiner ; and by which some thirteen thousand dollars in light strips are saved from re-melting every day. Simple as the fact appears, it prevents the melting of about four millions of dollars per an-num, and is doubtless, a great saving to the public.

After the blanks or planchets are

cut out, the strips are bent in a convenient shape for re-melting, and are sent to the Coiner's Office to be weighed, preparatory to making up his account for the day, and which, with the planchets, must make up the gross amount received in the morning from the Treasurer.

They are afterwards delivered to the Treasurer, by whom they are again weighed and then sent to the Melter and Refiner to be again cast into ingots.

The planchets are then carried from the cutting-press to the *Cleaning Room* where they are boiled in very strong for re-melting ; and those which are too heavy are reduced, by filing, to the standard weight. All the planchets thus adjusted, are then re-taken to the Coiner's Office, and, with the filings and light planchets, are carefully weighed, and that weight must tally with the gross amount of the planchets delivered to the Adjustors during the day.

The work of "adjusting" is performed by females of whom from ten to fifteen are employed, according to the amount of labor to be accomplished.

From the adjusting room the planchets are taken to the *Milling Room*, where they are dropped into a tube,

ADJUSTING ROOM.

soap-suds, from which they are taken and dried in a pan, heated by steam, and then conveyed to the Coiner's Office to be weighed. After which, they are sent to the *Adjusting Room* where each piece is separately weighed, and those found too light, are condemned belonging to the "milling machine," and by means of a revolving circular steel plate, with a groove in the edge, and a corresponding groove in a segment of a circle, the planchets are borne rapidly round, horizontally, by which process the edges are thickened, and the diameter of the planchet accurately adjusted to fit the collar of the

MILLING THE PLANCHETS.

"coining press." After "milling" they are returned to the Coiner's office and again weighed, to ascertain if the weight is correct.

They are then sent to the *Annealing Room*, where they are put into square cast-iron boxes, with double covers, carefully cemented with fire-clay, and placed in the annealing furnace, where they are subjected to a red heat for about an hour, when they are taken out and poured into a "pickle" containing diluted sulphuric acid. By this process they are softened and cleansed; and after they are rinsed with hot water they are well dried in saw-dust heated by steam, taken out and returned to the Coiner's office, where they are again weighed, and afterwards carried to the *Coining Room*, to be "stamped." This process is performed by dropping the planchets into the tube in front of the machine, from

whence they are carried by "feeders" to the "collar," into which they are dropped upon the lower die : the head die then descends, and by its immense power displaces every particle of gold in the planchet, and gives the impression upon both sides of the coin and the fluting on the edge, at the same moment. At every motion, the "feeders" not only take a planchet to the collar, but at the same time push the coin, previously struck, and now perfect, from the lower die, which rises and falls for the purpose at each revolution of the wheel, from whence the coin slides into a box underneath.

From the Coining Room they are again taken to the Coiner's office where they are weighed, counted and delivered to the Treasurer for payment to depositors.

There is one piece always taken out of about every sixty thousand dollars, coined into double-eagles, and a similar amount from smaller coins, which are

CLEANING THE PLANCHETS.

sent to Philadelphia, and carefully preserved for examination at the "judg-

STAMPING INTO COIN.

ment day," as it is curiously and expressively called, which takes place annually at Philadelphia, under the superintendence of commissioners appointed by the U. S. government.

We are surprised at the aggregate amount of coin produced in so short a time, in such a small and very inconvenient building; for, it seemed to us that every man was more or less in the others' way; and wherever the fault may lie, we think it of very questionable economy, that requires a remedy without delay.

The following statement, kindly furnished us by the officers, will show the large amount of

COINAGE AT THE U. S. BRANCH MINT, *From its Commencement up to September 15th, 1856.*

Gold Coinage for 1854.

Double Eagles..	$2,829,360	00
Eagles..........	1,238,260	00
Half Eagles.....	1,340	00
Quarter Eagles.	615	00
Gold Dollars....	14,632	00
	$4,084,207	00
Bars..........................	$5,631,151	43
Total.....................	$9,715,358	43

Silver Coinage - None.

1855.

Double Eagles.	$17,643,500	00
Eagles.........	90,000	00
Half Eagles....	305,000	00
Three Dollar Pieces	19,800	00
	$18,058,300	00
Bars	3,359,377	43
	$21,417,677	43

Silver Coinage.

Half Dollars.......	$64,975	00
Quarter Dollars...	99,100	00
	$164,075	00

Total Coinage, 1855.....$21,581,752 43

1856.

Double Eagles.	$19,395,000	00
Eagles.........	600,000	00
Half Eagles....	455,500	00
Quarter Eagles.	122,800	00
Three Dollar Pieces	73,500	00
Gold Dollars...	24,600	00
	$20,671,400	00
Bars..........................	3,047,001	28
	$23,718,401	28

Silver Coinage.

Half Dolllars.....	$105,500	00
Quarter Dollars...	71,500	00
	$177,000	00

Total Coinage, 1856.....$23,895,401 28

RECAPITULATION.

1854..................................	$9,715,358	43
1855..................................	$21,581,752	43
1856..................................	$23,895,401	28
Total...........................	$55,192,512	14

AN OMNIBUS RIDE.

Jump in—only a shilling from North Beach to Rincon Point—the whole length of the city : twelve tickets for a dollar. Gentlemen, jump in—make way for the ladies—and, bless me! do crowd closer for the babies. One, two, three, four! actually seven of these dear little humanities. Here we go, right through Stockton Street. Four years ago this was one long level of mud in the rainy season—not such a luxury as an omnibus thought of.— Tramp went the pedestrian the length and breadth thereof, thankful for side-walks. But now note the handsome private residences, the neat flower gardens, the fruit stands, the elegant stores in Virginia Block, the display in the windows both sides the way—dry goods, toys, stationery, tin ware, &c., &c.

But let us get in at the starting point. Leaving the promenade which makes Meiggs' wharf so pleasant of a summer morning, we step into one of the coaches, which are ready every eight minutes, according to the advertisement ; run along Powell street a few squares, catching glimpses here and there of the greatest variety of architecture in the residences, and remarking upon the neatness of those recently erected ; thence down a square into Stockton street, where the attention is distracted between the outside prospect and the protection of one's own limbs from the fearful thumping into divers holes which the ponderous vehicle encounters every few minutes.

Steady now—we have passed the worst part, and there is the State Marine Hospital,—quite a respectable amount of brick and mortar, patched at the rear with appurtenances of lumber, and which in its time has used up more "appropriations" than would comfortably have supported three times the number of sick within its walls. It is at present in the hands of the Sisters of Mercy.

There! make room for the lady in hoops! only a shilling for all that whalebone ! so now—let out the thin spare man, he fears suffocation—and the nervous gentleman too wants to alight; that baby has whooping cough, and annoys him. Poor bachelor! he cannot begin to comprehend infantile graces, and he votes the whole race a bore ; while glancing satirically at the lady, he observes to his friend, the spare man, " Poor little sufferer, how it *hoops*."

Rows of pretty cottages on one side the street—handsome brick buildings on the other—and at the corner of Stockton and Washington, a private garden laid out with exquisite taste and neatness. A refreshing fountain sends its spray over the blossoms of the sweet roses and verbena, while the graceful malva trees stand sentinel at the gateway. Only a passing glance, however, for the turn is accomplished, and down Washington street to Montgomery is generally a pretty rapid descent.

That is a family market near the corner of Washington—quite convenient these —the nicest of vegetables, the best of meats, procurable at market prices. We up-towners could scarcely dispense with them. Past the Plaza—how well I remember that formerly as a receptacle for old clothes, cast off boots and shoes, cans, bottles, crockery ware, skeleton specimens of the feline race— dogs who had had their day—rats whose race was run, and various other abominations ; but a treasure heap to the rag pickers, or bottle venders, who in those days were not. But now the Plaza has been smoothed into shape, and if the green things within its borders are perfected by sun and rain, it may yet flourish into grace and beauty.

Montgomery street—look down the long avenue. Where can be found more substantial edifices ? more elegant stores ? a gayer promenade ? Handsomely dressed ladies—gentlemen of business—gentlemen of leisure—mechanics—laborers—children—thronging the side-walks ; glitter, and show, and wealth in the windows ; equipages, omnibusses, horsemen, in the streets.

Hundreds of human beings passing and repassing in an hour, and from almost every nation under heaven.

The Frenchman with his "bon soir" greets you; the Spaniard and Italian, the Chinese, German, Mexican. The rose, the thistle, and shamrock have each their representatives, and beside these many others born in remote regions are congregated in this great thoroughfare of cities.

Past the fancifully arranged drug stores; past the tempting exhibitions of jewelry; past the attractive displays of dry goods, book and stationery establishments, banking houses, express buildings, lawyers' offices, and here we are, turning into Second street. Whirling by the Metropolitan market, we drive down as far as Folsom street, and observe that the neat cottages in this part of the city have a more rural aspect than those in locations nearer to business. A tree is seen here and there, and vines clamber over the porches, and droop over the windows. At the corner of Second and Folsom a garden in luxurious bloom refreshes the sight, and the questioning stranger in the 'bus is informed that the house and grounds were formerly owned, and were the residence of the late Captain Folsom, whose remains now lie in Lone Mountain Cemetery.

Adjoining this, on Folsom street, is another stately private residence— another lovely garden, where luxuriant flower growths may be seen at almost any season of the year. Nearly opposite is Hawthorne street. Ah! what associations of "Seven Gabled Houses" are connected with that name. But the eye rests upon none such—only a line of pretty cottages are peeped at ere we are driven past into Third street.

Another long avenue—grocery, dry goods, fruit, market—ever-recurring reminders that humanity has numberless wants, and that, for a golden boon, the supply is always equal to the demand. There are few handsome residences on Third, but many comfortable looking ones.

South Park—a passenger stops.— There is a homelike appearance in this solitary row of uniform houses, charming to one who recalls images of long streets, whose "white marble steps" have no parallel in San Francisco. But beyond us is Rincon Point—and in view of the blue waters, the omnibus stops. Nurses and babies alight, and the inquiring passenger strolls, where? Perhaps I may tell you in my next.

H. L. N.

———

TO THE HOMEWARD BOUND.— SOMETHING TO REMEMBER.—Before going East be sure to subscribe for

Hutchings' California Magazine.

———

THE ITALIAN.

THE PIONEER STEAM FIRE-ENGINE.

[*Photographed by W. Watkins.*]

WE present above an illustration of the new Steam Fire-Engine, which has been imported from New York, by Wethered & Tiffany of this city. It is now in the hands of Monumental Engine Company, No. 6, and will be purchased by them, provided that on trial it prove satisfactory. We have had the cut made from a photographic view taken while the engine was on parade, on the occasion of the Tenth Anniversary of Monumental Fire Company, No. 6, which took place September 12th.

The annexed notice of the Engine in question, taken from the *Scientific American*, gives a description of it: It was built, says that journal, by Messrs. Lee & Larned, of New York, at the Novelty Iron Works. These engines are fitted to be drawn by hand, being intended especially for the use of engine and hose companies; so that villages and small cities may now avail themselves of the superior and untiring power of steam, for fire-engine purposes, with no change in existing organizations, and without the expense of a horse establishment. The engine from which the view is taken was on duty for several months, in the hands of the Valley Forge Hose Company, stationed in Thirty-seventh street, New York, and it rendered signal service on several occasions. It is about ten feet in length, exclusive of the pole, and weighs 3,700 pounds; which weight, we understand, will be reduced at least 200 pounds in engines of the same style to be hereafter built. Having large wheels and sensitive springs, it runs as easily as an ordinary fire-engine of 500 or 600 pounds less weight, and easier than the average of first-class hand engines. Its best single stream, for distance, is one inch diameter; for quantity, $1\frac{1}{8}$; but for ordinary fire duty, it will handle, with good effect, *two* one-inch streams, drawing its own water. This it did, for ten consecutive hours at a fire on the ship *John J. Boyd*, in January last.

The steam power is derived from one of Lee & Larned's patent annular boilers, of 125 feet of heating surface, with which steam can be raised to working pressure, in from six to eight minutes. The pump, which is of brass, and highly finished, is Cary's patent rotary, driven by a single reciprocating engine, of 7 inches bore and 8½ inches stroke, with a pair of light balance wheels to carry it over the centers. It is intended to make from 200 to 400 revolutions per minute. A flange-disk, cast on the pump shell, makes one of the heads of the steam cylinder; the two, thus combined, forming a steam pump, of novel form and unequaled simplicity and compactness; occupying, indeed, so small a space (only 27 inches in length), that they are hardly seen in the engraving. The piston rod, passing out through the opposite head, acts on a cross-head of such length as to allow a connecting rod from each end of it to pass the cylinder and take hold of cranks on the pump shaft. The valve movement is obtained by means of a rockshaft, actuated by an eccentric rod from the main shaft. The boiler is supplied from an independent feed pump, but has also a connection with the main pump, which may be used at pleasure. The carriage frame is, in front, simply a horizontal bed plate of iron, of less than a foot in breadth, expanding, behind, into a ring, to the inside of which is bolted an upright open cylinder of thin, but stiff, sheet-iron, strengthened at the bottom by an angle-iron ring, the whole forming at once a seat and a casing for the boiler, which is placed within it. This end of the bed or frame is hung on platform springs, arranged like those of an omnibus, by means of tension rods and braces, taking hold of

the angle-iron ring. The center of weight is directly over the hinder axle, which opens into a hoop allowing the boiler to hang within it. The springs are plates of steel, one or more to each, of uniform thickness, but tapering in width from the middle towards either end. In front, two springs of this form are used, placed one above the other, in line with and directly under the bed, receiving the weight of the machinery at the middle or widest part. These serve the two-fold purpose of spring and reach, taking hold in front, by means of forked ends, on swivel-boxes at each end of a short vertical shaft, forming a universal joint with the front axle; giving thus a single point of front suspension, annihilating the tendency of the bed to wring and twist under its load in traveling over rough roads, saving all the weight of metal needed under the ordinary arrangement to counteract that tendency and secure the necessary stiffness, protecting the machinery perfectly against the concussions of travel, and dispensing with the complication and friction of a fifth wheel.

These engines are built of several different sizes; the one we have described being the smallest. The next size larger, weighing 5,200 pounds, is also a hand engine (though either can be fitted to be drawn by a horse or horses, if required), and being of proportionally greater power, it is to be preferred where the condition of the streets is favorable, in respect to surface and grades, and the company is strong enough in numbers to manage it. This engine throws a 1¼-inch stream 260 feet, a 1⅜-inch 228 feet, and for fire duty not unfrequently plays a 1½-inch stream with great effect. The Manhattan engine, which, in the hands of Manhattan Company, No. 8, of New York, did such admirable service at the severe fires of the last winter, and which was, according to the estimate of competent authorities, the means of saving property to the amount of at least a hundred times its cost, is of this size.

GRAMMAR SCHOOL BUILDING, POWELL STREET, SAN FRANCISCO.

PUBLIC GRAMMAR SCHOOL BUILD-ING IN SAN FRANCISCO.

FROM the report of the Superin-tendent of Common Schools we glean the following. The edi-fice, an engraving of which may be seen on page 485 of this magazine, is located on Powell near Clay street. The contract for its erection was awarded to Mr. H. L. King, in September, 1859, but for want of funds, its completion was delayed until the seventeenth of last De-cember—when it was dedicated with ap-propriate and imposing ceremonies. The halls were crowded with many of the old pioneers in the cause of education, to celebrate the completion of this edifice, as the crowning success of our system of public instruction.

The exercises were instructive and in-teresting, and will long be remembered by those present, with many pleasing as-sociations. The address of the Rev. T.

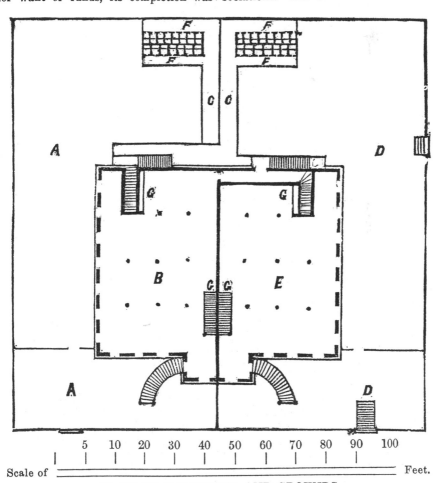

Scale of Feet.

PLAN OF BASEMENT AND GROUNDS.

A A, Girls Yards.
D D, Boys Yards.
E, Boys Basement.
B, Girls Basement.

C C, Covered passages to Water Closets.
F F F F, Water Closets.
G G G G, Lavatories.

Starr King was a brilliant effort, which was received with the highest approbation.

The building is a neat, two story edifice, designed by Victor Hoffman, Architect. The main portion is 32 by 88 feet, with two wings, 17⅓ by 32¾ feet, making the whole front on Powell street 69⅔, The wings and front are constructed of brick, covered with mastic, in imitation of red freestone.

On the first floor there are two recitation rooms in the wings, 17 by 32 feet, one of which is occupied by the Teacher of Modern Languages, and the other, when required, will be used by the Second Assistant. The main building is divided into two separate halls for calisthenic and gymnastic exercises for the boys and girls. The wings of the second story form two recitation rooms of the same size as those on the first floor, for the Teacher of Natural Sciences, and the First Assistant. The principal building is divided into two large halls of entrance, and a general session room, 30 by 64 feet, which is surrounded with an open corridor, overlooking the city, presenting an extended and beautiful view of the surrounding country. There is, also, a teacher's room in the attic, which, by means of folding doors, communicates with, and overlooks the session room. The rooms are neatly furnished with the most approved modern style of furniture, arranged according to Woodcock's diagonal system. The building, as at present arranged, will accommodate 120 scholars; but if required, there could be another session room fitted up on the first floor, which would, also, seat the same number of pupils.

As the plan of this building was remodeled from Dr. Boring's church, it is not, therefore, claimed as a perfect pattern of modern school architecture. It is constructed of brick and wood, and in its general design and arrangement, it is convenient, tasty and well adapted to the present wants of the school. The contract price for the building and furniture was $14,772. The lot, grading and bulkhead walls cost $12,575, which will swell the whole amount to $27,347.

BANCROFT'S
HAND–BOOK OF MINING

FOR THE PACIFIC STATES.

THE above is the title of a new and highly interesting work by John S. Hittell, a book that must prove itself invaluable to those unacquainted with mining, and who are about to undertake that business.

Much valuable time is lost by people for want of the information needful to enable them intelligently to direct their labors, a lack that this book is better calculated, perhaps, than any other known work, to obviate, to the miners of this coast—as it is written with especial reference to these latitudes. We predict that the practical utility and general interest of the work will secure for it a general success.

TIME is like a ship which never anchors; while I am on board, I had better do those things that may profit me at my landing than practice such as shall cause my commitment when I come ashore. Whatsoever I do, I would think what will become of it when it is done. If good, I will go on to finish it; if bad, I will either leave off where I am, or not undertake it at all. Vice, like an unthrift, sells away the inheritance, while it is but in reversion; but virtue, husbanding all things well, is a purchaser.

To be humble to superiors, is duty, to equals, is courtesy; to inferiors, is nobleness; and to all, safety; it being a virtue that, for all her lowliness, commandeth those souls it stoops to.

HUTCHINGS'

CALIFORNIA MAGAZINE.

Vol. III.   JUNE, 1859.   No. 12.

A JAUNT OF RECREATION,

FROM SAN FRANCISCO, BY THE MISSION DOLORES, TO THE OCEAN HOUSE
AND SEAL ROCK; RETURNING BY FORT POINT AND THE PRESIDIO.

SOUTH VIEW OF FORT POINT AND THE GOLDEN GATE.
[*From a Photograph by Hamilton & Co. San Francisco.*]

Out of a population of from sixty-five to seventy thousand persons—the number estimated to be in San Francisco at the present time—it is to be expected that for health, change, business or recreation, a large proportion, at convenient seasons, will make a flying visit to localities of interest that can be easily and cheaply reached, beyond the suburbs of the city. Of these, one of the most interesting and pleasant is that from San Francisco by the Mission Dolores to the Ocean House, and Seal Rock; returning by Fort Point and the Presidio. Upon this interesting jaunt we hope to have the pleasure of the reader's company; for it is almost always more agreeable to visit such scenes in good companionship than to go alone.

As these places are visited by all classes of persons, whose means and tastes widely differ, it is not for us to say whether it is better to go on horseback, or in a buggy; by a public omnibus, or a private carriage; or, on that very primitive, somewhat independent, but not always the most popular conveyance, technically denominated "a-foot." We must confess, however, that inasmuch as our physical and mental organization are both capable of enduring a large amount of comfort, as well as pleasure, our predilections decidedly incline to the former. Yet, to those who, to be suited, would choose even the latter, we can most conscientiously affirm that "we have no objection!" This point, then, being duly conceded, with the reader's consent, we will set out at once on our jaunt, each one by the conveyance that pleases him best.

Let us now thread our way among the numerous vehicles and foot-passengers that crowd the various thoroughfares of the city, to Third street, at which point we can take one of three routes to the Mission Dolores; namely: by the Old Mission road, Folsom street, or Brannan street, but either of the former is now by far the best. The Old Mission road, as its name would indicate, was the first made road to that point; although in 1849 and 1850, we had to thread our way among the low sand hills, and across little valleys, by a very circuitous and laborious route. In 1851, this road was graded and planked; but as the planks wore rapidly away, it was found to be very expensive to keep it in repair.— Within the past year, it has been macad-

amized nearly its entire length, and now is almost as good as the far famed Shell road, between New Orleans and Lake Pontchartrain.

It is difficult to give the actual amount of travel on either of these roads, as much of this is regulated by the state of the weather; yet the following will give an approximate estimate:

On the Old Mission road, an omnibus passes and repasses fourteen times daily, with from 1 to 30 passengers, and will average 12 each way; leaving the Plaza on the even hour, from 7 o'clock, A. M., to 8 P. M. The San Jose stage, which leaves the Plaza at 8 A. M., and the Ocean House omnibus, which leaves the Plaza at 10 A. M., passes and repasses daily; the Overland Mail stage, *via* Los Angeles, which leaves the Plaza every Monday and Friday, at noon; is due, returning on the same day, but it generally arrives three or four days before time; Dorlin's express runs twice a day to the Mission and back; in addition to these, there are 5 water carts, 10 milk, 12 meat, 18 bread, 40 vegetable, and from 20 to 30 express, or parcel wagons, daily. On the 24th ult., there were 34 horsemen, 66 double horse, and 177 single horse vehicles, such as carriages, buggies, sulkies, &c., in addition to those above mentioned.

On the Folsom street plank road, an omnibus passes and repasses twelve times daily, with an average of 12 passengers, each way, leaving the Plaza on the half hour. There are also, 40 milk, 20 vegetable, 20 lumber, liquor, bread, and meat wagons, of single and double horse; and about 80 buggies, single and double; besides foot passengers. On Sundays, no less than 40 omnibusses, and from 150 to 200 buggies, pass and repass, besides from 1 to 3,000 people, a large proportion of whom are bound for Russ' Gardens.

With this preliminary explanation, and the reader's consent, as we cannot very conveniently journey together on both

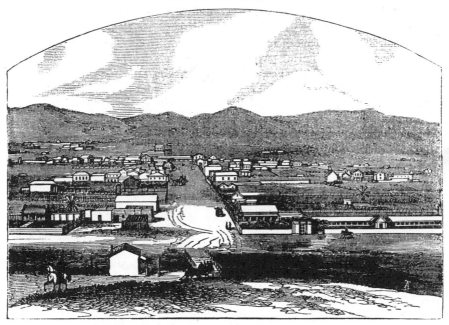

VIEW OF THE MISSION DOLORES, FROM THE POTRERO.

[*From a Photograph by Hamilton & Co.*]

roads, we will take that which, of the two, is rather the most pleasant, namely, the Folsom street. The sides of this road, like those of the other, are adorned with private residences, and well cultivated gardens and nurseries; among the latter, the first which attracts the traveler's attention, is the "Golden Gate Nursery;" then the "United States;" then "Sonntag's;" and at the corner of Folsom and Centre, the "Commercial Nursery."— But after passing the former of these, and before arriving at the latter, a large building to the south attracts our attention; that is the French Hospital. Next is the celebrated Russ' Gardens," a popular resort for Germans, especially on Sundays. Here let us digress for a moment, to relate a somewhat amusing conversation that took place on California street, between the servant of a friend, and a German woman whose husband makes a comfortable living by mending boots and shoes, in a little wooden house on the side walk.

German woman, to Irish servant:

"Bridget, why don't you get married, and live in a comfortable house of your own?"

"Faith, and I don't see that ye's very comfortable ye'self, for ye's slaving ye'self from Monthay marning until Satharday nite, washing clothes for other peoples, while ye'r husban' is mending boots and shoes, in that box, on the side walk."

"O yes, but what of that; you know we must all work for a living; and besides, I and my husband are very happy the whole of the week, for if I wash clothes, and he mends old boots and shoes, from Monday morning until Saturday night, *we always go to Russ' Gardens on Sunday's!*"

Now, if this does not preach a sermon on contentment, it is of no use our trying. So we may as well pass on to say, that the next object that attracts our attention, is the black volumes of smoke, that roll from the chimney-top of the San Francisco Sugar Refinery. In this refinery, some 4,200 tons of sugar, is refined annually, consuming about 1,600 tons of coal, 400 tons of bones, (for making ivory or bone black for filtering purposes,) 1,300,000 staves, 1,100,000 hoops, and 200,000 heads for barrels and kegs.— Within, there are about 60 men employed; and without, from 75 to 80 more, in getting of staves, hoops, heads, making barrels, freighting, teaming, &c.

But we must now pass on, and as quickly as possible, for two reasons; reason first, the hog-ranches by the road side are not as fragrant as the roses in Sonntag's nursery; and reason second will appear when we arrive at Center st., and, turning to the right, cross the bridge over Mission Creek, and on the new San Bruno turnpike, turn to get a general view of the Mission, that may enable us to forget reason first.

The beautiful green hills, and pretty houses that here dot the landscape; with the fine nurseries in the foreground, will explain why the Mission Fathers chose this fertile and well watered valley in preference to the bleak and comparatively barren Lagoon for their semi-religious and semi-philanthropic object.

In the hollow, some three hundred yards below the Nightingale hotel, is the Willows, a shady retreat for pleasure seekers and parties; from which spot let us now go at once to the Mission.

Now we have arrived at the quaint, old-fashioned, tile-covered adobe church, and buildings attached; part of which is still in use by the Mission, and a part is converted into saloons and a store. This edifice was erected in 1775-'76, and was completed and dedicated, August 1st, 1776; and was formerly called San Francisco, in honor of the patron saint, St. Francis, the name given to the Bay by its discoverer, Junipero Serra, in October, 1769.

While the church buildings were in course of erection, the Fathers had great difficulty in keeping the Indians who performed most of the labor at work. The earthy clay, of which the adobes were made, had to be prepared by the Indians, who, after water had been thrown upon it, jumped in and trampled it with their feet, but soon growing tired, they would keep working only so long as the Fathers kept singing.

The visitor will notice a number of old adobe buildings scattered here and there, in different directions; these were erected for the use of the Indians; one part being used for boys, and the other for girls, and in which they resided until they were about seventeen years of age, when they were allowed to marry; after which other apartments were assigned them, more in accordance with their condition.

As late as 1849, there were two large boilers in the buildings back of the church; and as meat was almost the only article of food, an ox was killed and boiled wholesale, at which time the Indians would gather around and eat until they were satisfied. Of course, most of our readers are aware that Catholics are not allowed to eat meat on a Friday, but owing to this being the only article of diet to the Indians and native Californians, around the Mission, they were not required to abstain from it, even on that day.

According to Mr. Forbes, a very careful and accurate writer, who published a work in 1835, entitled the "History of Lower and Upper California," the number of black cattle belonging to this Mission in 1831, was 5,610; horses, 470; mules, 40; while only 233 fanegas (a fanega is about 2½ bushels) of wheat; 70 of Indian corn; and 40 of small beans, were raised altogether. At that time, however, the missions had lost much of their former glory; for in 1825, only six years before, that of Dolores, alone, is said to have had 76,000 head of cattle; 950 tame horses; 2,000 breeding mares;

THE OLD MISSION CHURCH AND BUILDINGS, BUILT IN 1776.
[*From a Photograph by Hamilton & Co.*]

84 stud, of choice breed; 820 mules; 79,000 sheep; 2,000 hogs; and 456 yoke of working oxen; and raised 18,000 bushels of wheat and barley. Besides, in 1802, according to Baron Humboldt, there were of males, in this Mission, 433; of females, 381; total, 814. And yet, according to Mr. Forbes, in 1831, there were but 124 males, and 85 females; and now, there are—none. Truly, "the glory has departed."

At that time, the Indians and native Californians, for many miles around, would congregate at the Mission Dolores, about three times a year, bringing with them cattle enough to kill while they remained, which was generally about a week, and have a good holiday time with each other.

Before the discovery of gold it was the custom here to keep a tabular record of all the men, women and children; members of the church; marriages, births and deaths; the number of live stock; and amount of produce in all their business details: but since then everything has changed for the worse. Even the lands devoted to, and set apart for, the use of the Mission, have nearly all been squatted upon, so that now but a few hundred varas remain intact; and as to where the stock of all kinds have gone, "deponent saith not."

It is quite a pleasurable curiosity to examine the old Spanish manuscript books, still extant at this mission, and look upon their sheep-skin covered lids, and buckskin clasps. Besides these there are about six hundred printed volumes, in Spanish, on religious subjects; but being in a foreign language they are seldom or never read.

At the present time the only uses to which this Mission is devoted is to give public instruction in the Catholic religion, the education of some seventeen pupils; the burial of the dead; and an occasional marriage. Of the last named, about eighteen have taken place within the past four years.

The great point of attraction here to visitors from the city, is its quiet green graveyard; and but for its being so negligently tended and slovenly kept would be one of the prettiest places near the city. In this last peaceful home, from June 1st, 1858 to May 20th, 1859, the following will show how many have been laid—June, (1858) 52; July, 67; August 55; September, 55; October, 65; November, 57; December, 56; January, (1859) 35; February, 45; March, 38; April, 33; May, up to the 20th, 28.

It seems as though we could never weary in looking upon these interesting scenes; but as we have fart e to go; and we trust, many more to look upon, let us again set out on our jaunt, and visit this spot at our leisure.

Between the Mission Dolores and the Ocean House there are no objects of striking interest, except, perhaps the San Francisco Industrial School, recently erected for the benefit of depraved juveniles, situated near the top of the ridge we are gently ascending, about six miles from the city and three from the ocean. About this school we shall have something to say at a future time.

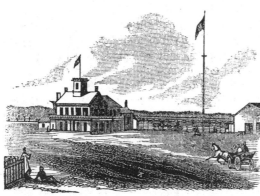

THE OCEAN HOUSE.

Upon reaching the top of this ridge you perceive that we get a glimpse of the Pacific ocean; and shortly afterwards find ourselves comfortably seated in one of the parlors of the Ocean House, where, while our animals are resting, let us say that this house is about eight and one fourth miles from San Francisco, and was erected in 1855 by Messrs. Lovett and Green; when, if report speaks the truth, they were just beginning to reap the reward of their labors they were cheated out of it.

From this point we have a commanding view of the surrounding country. The hill in front of us, and at the back of the Industrial school, contains a quarry of the finest of sandstone, and which, were there but a railroad upon which to convey it to the city, could be delivered there at from two to three dollars per ton. South is the Lake House, and Rockaway House, at the east end of lake Merced, but the latter is now used only as a private residence. From this point, too, an excellent view of the ocean is obtained, where the ships and steamers are plainly visible.

One would scarcely suppose that here, where the winds sweep over the lands with such fury, that stock of all kinds flourish better than in many of the favored inland valleys, yet such is the fact; for owing to the dense masses of heavy fog-clouds that roll in from the ocean the verdure is perpetual, while in other localities it is parched up. The gardens around produce from fifty-five to one hundred sacks of potatoes to the acre, although the soil is very light and sandy. Besides, vegetables are taken to the San Francisco market from this section, at an earlier time than from that of any other part of the State.

About two miles north of the Ocean House, is a lake, known as the Laguna Honda, at which a distressing accident occurred in 1855, as the reader will call to memory, when two ladies and their two children were all drowned together, under the following circumstances. In the back part of a carriage, built in the rockaway style, were seated Mrs. Opeinhimer and Mrs. Urzney, each lady holding a child. On the front seat were two servants, a man and woman, the former of whom was driving. Having taken the road up the Rock House ravine, instead of that to the Ocean House, they arrived at the edge of the lake, above named, and the road not being wide enough to admit their carriage, they drove into the water a little, on the edge of the lake. They could have passed here in safety, but unfortunately, the wheel struck a stump,

THE DRIVE ALONG THE BEACH TOWARDS SEAL ROCK.

and by some unexplainable means, the horse was thrown round, and he fell into deep water; when the carriage was immediately turned upside down, and the forepart striking the water, was forced down upon the two ladies and their children, shutting them completely in, and they sunk to rise no more. The servants being left free, in the front of the carriage, succeeded in reaching the shore, and were saved.

Snugly ensconsed beneath the hill, about half a mile from the Ocean House, and within a quarter of a mile of the sea, is the Beach House. This was first built on the shore, near the edge of a small lake that we pass, but the high tides flowing in, washed away its foundations, and compelled the alternative of their removing it at once, or of allowing the sea to do it for them; and as the owners considered themselves the best carpenters of the two, they undertook, and succeeded, in the task—but here we are, on the beach. There is a never ceasing pleasure to a refined mind, in looking upon or listening to the hoarse murmuring roar of the sea; and an unexplainable charm in the music of its waves, as with a seething sound, they curl and gently break upon a sandy shore, during a calm; or dash in all their majesty and fury, with thundering voices upon the unheeding rocks in a storm. This is sublimity. Besides, every shell, and pebble, and marine plant, from the smallest fragment of sea-moss, to the largest weed that germinates within the caverns of the deep, has an architectural perfection and beauty, that ever attracts the wondering admiration of the thoughtful. Yet we must not now linger here, or night will overtake us.

This beach extends continuously from Seal Rock to Muscle Rock, about seven miles. Near the last named place is a soda spring, and several veins of bituminous coal; to obtain which shafts have been sunk to the depth of 124 feet, in which the coal was found to grow better as they descended; but like many similar enterprises, when means to work it failed, it was abandoned. Other minerals are also found in this chain of hills.

Having had our ride along the beach as

far as Seal Rock, and watched the movements, and listened to the loud shrill voices the sea-lions, let us take up the sand-bank south of the old Seal Rock House, (now tenantless,) and we shall find the road from the Fort, as sandy and as heavy as we could desire it; yet, with the consolation that we can endure it, if the horses are able, until we reach Fort Point.

When this was first taken and occupied by American troops belonging to Col. Stephenson's battalion, under Maj. Hardie, in March, 1847, they found a circular battery of 10 iron guns, 16 pounders, mounted upon the hill just above the present works, and which was allowed to remain until a better one was ready to occupy its place.

VIEW OF THE PRESIDIO.
[From a Photograph by Hamilton & Co.]

The present beautiful and substantial structure was commenced in 1854, and is now nearly completed. It is four tiers in height, the topmost of which is 64 feet above low tide; and is capable of mounting 150 guns, including the battery at the back, of 42, 64, and 128 pounders; and during an engagement, can accommodate 2,400 men. There have been appropriations made, including the last, of $1,800,000. The greatest number of men employed at any one time was 200; now there are about 80.

The Lighthouse adjoining the Fort, can be seen for from 10 to 12 miles, and is an important addition to the mercantile interests of California, although we regret to say, it is only of the fifth order, and known as the "Fresnel Light," and is

the smallest on the coast; the lanthorn is 52 feet above level. Two men are employed to attend it. Connected with this is a Fog Bell, weighing 1,100 pounds, and worked by machinery, that strikes every ten seconds, for five taps; then has an intermission of thirty-four seconds, and recommences the ten-second strike. This is kept constantly running during foggy weather.

In the small bay south of the Fort, have been two wrecks, the Chateau Palmer, May 1st, 1856, and the Gen. Cushing, Oct. 9th, 1858; both outward bound, and partially freighted.

Between Fort Point and (the celebrated political hobby) Lime Point, is the world-famed Golden Gate, or entrance to the Bay of San Francisco. This is one mile and seventeen yards wide. The tide here varies about seven feet.

From this interesting spot, and on our way to the city, we pass the Presidio. This is a military post that was established shortly after the arrival of the first missionaries, mainly for their protection; and was originally occupied by Spanish troops, and afterwards by Mexican, until March, 1847; when it was taken by the United States; at which time the whole force of the enemy was a single corporal. At this time also there were two old Spanish brass field-pieces found here; and two more near the beach about where the end of Battery street, San Francisco, now is, and from which that street derived its name.

The original buildings were constructed in a quadrangular form; these having fallen into decay, but three remain, two of which at the present are used as store rooms. At the close of the war, this post was occupied by a company of dragoons, who were relieved by a company of the 3rd Artillery, under Capt. Keyes, who kept it continuously for ten years. Its present garrison consists of two companies of the 6th Infantry, numbering about 180, officers and men.

SAMUEL BRANNAN'S BANK.

DEPOSITS SECURED BY

FOUR HUNDRED AND FIFTY THOUSAND DOLLARS

OF PRODUCTIVE REAL ESTATE,

IN TRUST FOR THEIR REDEMPTION.

THE UNDERSIGNED has established in the City of San Francisco a BANK, under the above name, style and title. The object is to furnish a safe place of deposit to all classes of the community, especially to FARMERS, MINERS and MECHANICS. For the accomplishment of this object there has been conveyed to

COMPETENT AND RELIABLE TRUSTEES.

PRODUCTIVE REAL ESTATE,

AMOUNTING TO NOT LESS THAN

Four Hundred and Fifty Thousand Dollars.

Certificates of Deposit will be issued for any amount, from Five Dollars upwards, but no Certificate will be issued bearing interest for a less sum than One Hundred Dollars, nor for a shorter time than six months. The interest paid upon these Certificates will be at the rate of three per cent. per annum.

All Moneys Loaned will be upon First Class Securities,

but borrowers will be required to pay all the expenses of searching titles, drawing mortgages and other papers; the right reserved to the Bank to say who shall search the titles, draw the papers, and the manner in which they shall be drawn.

GOLD DUST will be received and deposited at the United States Mint, or any Assay Office, for assay, and the depositors of the same charged the usual market rates for so doing.

FOREIGN AND DOMESTIC EXCHANGE purchased and forwarded, charging usual commissions in such cases; but no Exchange will be forwarded, without funds or ample satisfactory security in hand.

THE BANK IS SITUATED IN THE

CITY OF SAN FRANCISCO,

On the Northeast Corner of MONTGOMERY and CALIFORNIA STREETS,

And will be open daily, (Sundays and Holidays excepted,) from 9 A. M. until 4 P. M.; on every Saturday evening from 7 to 9 o'clock, and on the night previous to the sailing of the steamers from 7 o'clock until 11 P. M.

SAMUEL BRANNAN.

San Francisco, October 31st, 1857.

MERCHANT.

Advertising is all the go,
Our goods are selling very low,
If you will only call and try,
You cannot fail of us to buy.

MINER.

We Miners have no ti me to spare
To look for what we eat and wear;
Just let us know the cheapest place—
We pay the cash, not run our face.

We advertise to let you know
Of whom to buy, and where to go.

PRIZE POEM.

My Maiden Muse her magic lyre
  Has strung again, that all
May list with pleasure to the strains
  She sings of QUINCY HALL.

The fount of Helicon would dry,
  And Washoe's rivers fall,
Were all the waters used for ink
  Describing QUINCY HALL.

The greatest Clothing Mart on earth
  Where mortals all should call,
Be it remembered has been found
  To be our QUINCY HALL.

Davis & Bowers, Proprietors,
  Can fit the short and tall,
The fat and lean, the rich and poor,
  Who go to QUINCY HALL.

No fortune will these people take,
  Whether 'tis great or small,
For they have all that they can do
  Each day at QUINCY HALL.

So all the needy persons should
  With all the wealthy call,
As well as everybody else,
  And buy at **QUINCY HALL,**

The Largest Clothing Emporium on the Pacific Coast,

149 & 151 Washington St., Montgomery Block,

SAN FRANCISCO.

STENCIL PLATES

CUT TO ORDER, at TEN CENTS A LETTER, at the Stereotype Foundry, 159 Jackson Street, near Montgomery.

A. KELLOGG.

FRENCH ACADEMY

— FOR —

LADIES & GENTLEMEN,

Corner of Jackson and Mason Sts.,

SAN FRANCISCO.

French School for both sexes and all ages. All the ordinary and higher branches taught.

PROF. J. MIBIELLE, *Principal.*

DR. BOWEN'S

CELEBRATED

BLOOD PURIFIER,

COMPOSED of the Extracts of Sarsaparilla, Yellow Dock, Dandelion, and Stylingia.
  This medicine has cured more cases of Scrofula, Rheumatism, Liver complaint, &c., than any other medicine offered to the public. It also cures all Eruptions on the skin.

For sale wholesale and retail, at

PHILADELPHIA DRUG STORE,

Corner Clay and Kearny Sts. . . . . Price $1, in quart bottles.

**If you ADVERTISE, you'll find
That you will never run behind.**

MECHANIC.

Our clothes and provisions we earn with our hands,
So we must buy our goods very low;
We do not depend on houses or lands—
Now tell us the best place to go.

SAILOR.

We bring you goods from ev'ry clime,
To suit all classes and all time;
Let people know what you've for sale,
You'll sure succeed, and never fail.

PART II
THE GOLD COUNTRY

THE MINER

. . . he turns the river from its ancient bed, and hangs it, for miles together, in wooden flumes upon the mountain's side, or throws it from hill to hill, in aqueducts that tremble at their own airy height; or he pumps a river dry, and takes its golden bottom out.

THE GOLD COUNTRY

James Mason Hutchings was first of all a miner. He crossed the plains to make his fortune in the mines, and his personal experience in working his claims left in him a firm faith in both the miners and mining in California. He made his first "strike" in the publishing field in Placerville, where he worked as a columnist and general assistant to the editor of the *Herald,* and to the miners of the state, more than to any other group, he addressed the *California Magazine.*

J. S. Hittell, who was an occasional contributor to *Hutchings',* has described the period which roughly coincides with the life-span of *Hutchings' Magazine* as "the golden era in decline." While Hutchings was tramping up and down California with his artists and photographers, gathering materials for his projected magazine, the mines annually gave up less treasure, the speculators of San Francisco went under in disastrous bank failures, and the tide of immigration was closely matched by a flood of disappointed Argonauts returning to their distant homes. The first number of *Hutchings' California Magazine* (July, 1856) circulated among a public somewhat sobered in the three years since the publication of Hutchings' "The Miner's Ten Commandments."

California was still free-wheeling, to be sure, but it had been learned that the vehicle had brakes and that guidance of some sort was desirable. The facts of political and economic life were bringing forth some glimmerings of civic and business responsibility. The People's Party was on its way in at San Francisco; the "Know Nothings" were on their way out at Sacramento. Thousands of prospective miners still tramped the mountains with pick and wash pan, but thousands of others lived a vastly more settled life than they had in the glorious days of '49 and '50. Cooperative effort and investment in bringing water to the placers or sinking shafts to the quartz promoted the attitudes of the businessman rather than the adventurer.

Hutchings' views were well calculated to suit the changing temper of the times. He addressed himself to the more responsible element among the miners, and since he believed in them he told them what they wanted to hear. He told them what was interesting about themselves and their state. He was a *Californian* now, his far-off "home" a point of origin rather than destination. An increasing number of his readers were coming to feel the same way.

HUTCHINGS'

CALIFORNIA MAGAZINE.

Vol. V.   SEPTEMBER, 1860.   No. 3.

THE   DEPARTURE.

THE WIND, with low moans, stirred the tops of the pines,
    That grew at the foot of a forest-crowned hill;
Then it swooped, like a bird, to sing 'mong the vines,
    With beauty embowering a rude cabin.   Still,

Like an airy-winged sprite on a mission of love,
    There it hovered, and sung, that its music might trend
To soothe one lone inmate, with notes like a dove,
    Or, what is far dearer, the voice of a friend.

And oh! who can tell but such sounds came to cheer
    The suffering one, on his hard pine-leaf bed,
As he talked with the loved ones, in spirit so near,
    Whose bodies were absent—perchance with the dead.

Some bright guardian angels perhaps were allied,
    And these were their voices to welcome him home;
For he stretched out his arms to embrace them, and died
    With a smile, and the words, "God bless you, I come."

As the broad hand of day clutched the curtain of night,
    And rolled up the darkness as though 'twere a scroll,
A kind neighbor entered—appalled with affright,
    Gasped faintly, "What! dead! In peace rest thy soul!"

Aye, rest thee. No more shall thy spirit be sad,
    That thy wearying toil 'neath the summer sun's ray
Or the chill winter's rain, went unblessed, to make glad
    Thine own yearning heart, or the loved far away.

While the cold dew of death lay unwiped on his brow,
    A calm and sweet smile told the peace of his end;
The sighs of the mourners rose high, as a vow
    That those thus bereaved should not e'er want a friend.

In a dark, shady glade on the side of a hill
    That was then draped by clouds in a mantle of rain,
In the deep grave they laid him, all solemn and still,
    And the winds murmured o'er him a mournful refrain.

MINING FOR GOLD IN CALIFORNIA.

The reader, no doubt, well remembers the peculiar impressions which the first tidings of the discovery of gold in California produced upon his mind. How in every possible way the imagination industriously endeavored to picture the exhilarating scenes which surrounded, and the pleasurable excitement which attended the enviable employment of digging for gold. What lucky fellows they must be, who, untrammeled by the common-place constraint of ordinary business, could, with their own hands, take the precious metal from the earth, and in a few brief months, perhaps, by their own labor, become the fortunate possessors of sufficient wealth to make a whole lifetime happy for themselves and family, as well as useful to others.

What enchanting visions of the good to be accomplished—of the pleasures to be

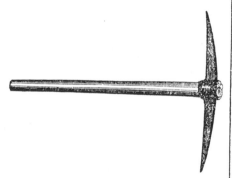

PICK.

enjoyed—of the greatness to be achieved,—or the triumphs to be won, influenced his decision and turned his thoughts and footsteps towards the Land of Gold.

No wonder that his impressions were somewhat vague, and his knowledge limited and indefinite; as but little was then known of the country, manner of living, the labor required, or methods in use for working the mines. Even to this day, with all that has been written, and all the pictorial illustrations which have been published, those who have not actually visited the mines, have but a very incorrect conception

of what they are, or how they are worked. We therefore believe that the reader—be he ever so familiar with everything apper-

PAN AND SCOOP.

taining to mining and mining life—will be the better pleased should our description of each and every method and implement be simple, and easy to be understood.

After the discovery of gold, by James W. Marshall, at Sutter's Mill, on the South Fork of the American River, near Coloma, in the early spring of 1848, altho' the forests and glens were almost untrodden, and their stillness unbroken, except by wild animals, and Indians; the "Prospector,"

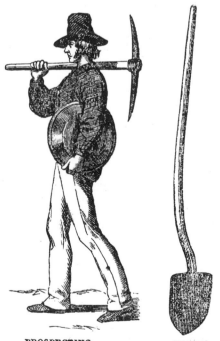

PROSPECTING.   SHOVEL.

with his pick or shovel upon his shoulder, his pan in his hand, and his knife and trusty revolver in his belt around his waist, began to wander among the hills, and up the ravines and gulches "prospecting" for gold.

In 1849 and 1850 it was very common for small companies of men to start on a prospecting excursion, with several days' provisions, cooking utensils, blankets, tools, and fire-arms, at their backs ; and with this small mule-load, climb the most rugged and difficult mountains ; descend and cross the most rocky and dangerous cañons ; endure fatigue and hardship ; and brave privation and peril almost entirely unknown at the present time.

Sometimes it is true an animal might be taken for that purpose ; but, if his neck was not broken, he was almost invariably the cause of more anxiety and trouble than of comfort ; as men would often have to travel over snow, into which an animal would sink ; and cross an impetuous mountain stream upon a small pine, which, of course, no animal would ever attempt ; and could he have been induced to enter the stream for the purpose of fording it, the force of the rushing water would have tripped him off his feet and dashed him to pieces upon the rocks: so that the company's course had to be entirely changed, or the enterprise abandoned.

At that period the precious metal was supposed to be found only in rivers, cañons, gulches, or ravines ; and, as the latter were the readiest prospected, and the easiest worked, and often paid very well ; they offered the most tempting inducement to the prospector ; and consequently, were the first places sought after and tested by him.

Having arrived at a spot which looked inviting, and which he thought would "pay," down would go his pan and pick, or shovel, and after removing some of the loose earth or stones which were lying on the top, he would commence making a small hole (generally about the size of his hat !) in the lowest part of the ravine, from whence a panful of dirt would be taken, and washed ; and, if found to be rich, a "claim" or "claims" would be immediately staked off, and a notice put up which generally read as follows :

"*We, the undersigned, claim fifteen feet square* (or other quantity mentioned) *commencing at this stake, and running up this ravine to the oak tree with a notch in it.*

(*Signed.*)   *PETER SNIGGINS*
          JEREMIAH TURTLE."

As somewhat illustrative of this rule among miners, we may mention that a short time ago, a stalwart son of the "Emerald Isle," was prospecting a ravine near Forbestown, having obtained a dollar to the pan, and considering it a pretty good prospect, he concluded to "take up a claim" there ; but just as he was exulting over his good fortune, he espied a "notice" upon an old stump with the ominous words written thereon : " *We, the undersigned, claim, &c., &c., having duly recorded the same.*" "Ow the divil," he exclaimed, "how came ye there now ?" But as the notice returned him no answer, and as he saw some men working but a few yards below, he went to them with the inquiry—"I say Misther, who ouns thim claims ?"

"We do," replied one.

"Be gorrah thin ye hav no right to thim."

"Oh yes, we have a right to them, as we took them up, and recorded them, and have been working upon them all summer."

"Recarded thim ! Ow the divil recard ye's ! sure there's not an owld stoomp within five miles of Forbestown but what has a notice plasthered all over it as big as a winder, with 'Recarded' in mighty fine letters all over the paper, from the top to the bottom. To the divil with ye's and the recarder too—the baist !" With this generous wish and benediction, he walked away muttering—"The divil 'recard' ye's."

If, however, a good prospect was not obtained in the first panful of auriferous dirt, a second was seldom attempted by the prospector of 1848.

Before leaving him, let us see how his

panful of dirt is washed—as the process of "panning out" is precisely the same now as it was then, and is an indispensable accompaniament to every method of gold mining.

Having placed his pan by the edge of a pool or stream, he takes hold of the sides with both hands, and squatting down lowers it into the water, then, with a kind of oscillating and slightly rotary motion, he moves it about beneath the surface for a few moments, then, after drawing it to the edge of the pool, he throws out the largest of the stones, and assists to dissolve the dirt by rubbing it between his hands; the washing is then repeated; and, while the muddy water and sand are floated out of the pan into the pool, the gold, if there is any, settles gradually to the bottom of the pan and is there saved.

If a little only of very fine gold was found, it was called in miner's phraseology "finding the color," and if from ten to twenty-five cents were found to the pan, it was called "a good prospect." Now, however, with improved modes of mining, and less extravagant expectations, from *one* to *three* cents is pronounced "good pay dirt."

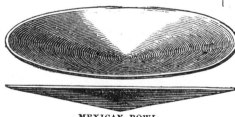

MEXICAN BOWL.

The Mexicans and Chilians use almost exclusively the *batea*, or broad wooden bowl shown in the engraving above, instead of the pan.

Next to the *pan* and bowl as implements for the more speedy separation of gold from the earth, the *cradle* or *rocker* holds an important place; from the fact that it was the first appliance, superior to the pan used with effect in all parts of the mines. I s size and weight rendering it portable, it

was easily transferred from place to place, and even now is much in use as a prospecting implement upon a scale more extended than can well be executed with the pan.

Our description of the cradle or rocker is this: an oblong box from three to three and a half feet in length, eighteen to twenty-two inches in width, and about nine inches in depth at the upper end, with a bar across the middle; one end of the box is left open or has no end board. There is no cover to the box or cradle; but a separate box, sieve, or hopper, is made to fit into and occupy the half of the cradle furthest from the open or lower end; this hopper is about four inches in depth; the bottom is of sheet iron, perforated with holes about three-eighths or half an inch in diameter, and one and a half inches apart.

Under the hopper and sloping downward toward the upper end of the cradle, is the *slide* or *apron*. This apron being somewhat hollow or concave on its upper side, and covered with canvass, retains much of the fine gold that falls upon it.

Rockers are attached to the under side of the whole, quite similar to those of a child's cradle; near the middle an upright handle is attached, by which motion is given to it.

The hopper being nearly filled with auriferous earth, the operator being seated by its side, while rocking the cradle with one hand, he dips and pours on water with the other, from an adjacent pool or rivulet, using a half gallon tin dipper for the purpose.

The water dissolving the earth, it falls through the sieve upon the sloping apron, which conveys it to the upper end of the bottom of the cradle. On this bottom, about the center, is a "riffle-bar" placed crosswise, and one a little deeper at the lower end; and while the lighter sand and dirt passes over them with the water, the gold, by its greater weight, is retained by them, and thus kept from passing out at the lower end.

THE CRADLE AND MANNER OF USING IT.

The coarse stones and gravel remaining in the hopper after the water runs clear are then thrown out, the hopper replaced and refilled, and the process repeated. As often as is necessary, the apron, riffle-bars, and bottom are cleaned of the sand and gold that has concentrated upon them; the larger portion of the fine gold, being generally found upon the canvass of the apron.

The cradle, though still extensively used by the Chinese throughout the mines, has given way among Americans, and the more enterprising class of miners, to more summary methods for separating the gold from the pay-dirt; its use being superseded by far more efficient implements; and among them, as next in importance to the cradle, was introduced the "Long-Tom."

THE LONG TOM.

It was not long after the pan and cradle were in general use, that it became apparent that some more expeditious mode was required for washing the gold from large quantities of earth. Men were not satisfied with the slow, one man system, the use of pan or cradle; but something must be done, some invention made of an implement by the use of which the united efforts of individuals, as companies, could be made available and profitable.

To supply this want, the wits and ingenuity of the earlier miners soon brought out the "long tom," exceedingly primitive in its first inception and form it is true, but proving so effective in its operations, it was soon greatly improved upon, and at length became the indispensable implement in the hands of companies of from three to five men in prosecuting their gold washing operations.

From the primitive toms, which were but troughs hollowed out from the half trunks of pine trees, they soon assumed the proportions and shape of the neatly constructed tom of sawed lumber and sheet iron of the present day.

The tom varies much in size, depending on the number of men intending to use it. It is an oblong box or trough about twelve feet in length, open at the top and usually at both ends; but always at the lower end. It is about eight inches in depth, and at the upper end from one foot to two feet in width; but increasing to nearly double that width at the middle, from thence its sides are parallel to the lower end. The bottom of this broad portion for a distance of from three to six feet from the end, is made of strong, perforated sheet iron, in every respect similar to the sieve or hopper of the cradle, but of much heavier iron. The tom is not straight upon its bottom the whole length; but the sheet iron portion is turned upward as it approaches the lower end, so that the depth of the tom is diminished at that end to less than three inches. The object of this is that the water may all pass through the seive or tom-iron without running over the top.

Under this perforated iron portion is placed a riffle box, similar in principle to the bottom of a cradle; but larger, and alike with the tom, always to remain stationary or immovable while in use.

MINING WITH THE LONG TOM.

The tom is now placed in a proper position, having reference to the dirt to be washed, generally as near the ground as possible to admit of the "tailings" passing off freely. The riffle box is first fixed in proper position, then the iron-bottomed portion of the tom placed over it, with its open or narrow end several inches the highest. Water is now let on, either in open troughs of wood, or through canvass hose, which by its force, carries the dirt when put in, down the tom; and while two or more men are employed shoveling the dirt into the tom at the upper end, one man at the side of the lower end, with hoe or shovel in hand, receives the dirt as brought down by the water; and after being violently stirred and moved about upon the perforated iron bottom until all has passed through it that will, the residue of stones and coarse gravel is thrown out by the shovel.

The manner of saving the gold by the riffle box, is precisely the same in principle as that of the cradle, with this advantage over it; that the falling of streams of water through the tom iron serve to keep the sand upon the bottom of the riffle box stirred up and loose, permitting the gold the more easily to reach the bottom, where it is retained by the riffle bars; while the lighter matter, sand and pebbles, pass off with the water and is called "tailings."

Sometimes thirty or fifty feet or more of sluice boxes are attached to the tom at the upper end, and the dirt is shoveled in along the whole length, to be carried down to the tom by the force of the water, there to receive its final stirring up.

Toms are particularly adapted to nearly level grounds, or where there is not sufficient fall to admit of the still more efficient mode of gold washing with sluices.

SLUICING.

This is a mode of mining particularly adapted to those localities where it becomes desirable to wash large quantities of dirt,

SLUICING.

GROUND SLUICING.

and where the descent is sufficient to operate advantageously.

To get at a proper understanding of this method of mining, seems to require a description of the "sluice box." This is merely an open trough, usually made of three inch boards—a bottom, and two sides; twelve or fourteen feet in length, and from twelve inches to forty in width, and sawed purposely for this use, two inches wider at one end than at the other. The sides of these troughs are secured from spreading by cleats nailed across the top; and from splitting at the bottom, by similar cleats on the under side.

A continuous line of these troughs or "sluice boxes," the smaller and lower end of each, inserted for three or four inches into the larger end of the next one below, form the "sluice," and being placed upon the ground or other supports, with a proper descent; the dirt, by whatever mode is adopted to remove it thereto, and into the sluice, either by shoveling, or the power of the hydraulic as hereafter described, is, by the force of a larger body of water than is usually used in tomming, conveyed through a continuous line of from fifty to several hundred feet in length, and when the de-

scent is sufficient, the whole mass of dirt, from the finest particles, to stones and boulders of four or five inches in diameter, go rattling down by their own gravity and the force of the water, the entire length of the sluice.

Where the descent is not quite sufficient for this, forks and shovels are used along the sluices to loosen up and finally to throw out such of the larger stones and rocks as the water cannot force through them; as shown in the engraving.

There are different appliances attached to the bottoms of these sluices, inside, for the purpose of saving or catching the gold in its passage down the sluice, such as riffles of a great variety of pattern, and false bottoms, perforated or split in pieces, the interstices of which are admirably adapted to the saving of fine gold.

These sluices are sometimes "run," as it is termed, for many days together before "cleaning up;" when this is done the false bottoms or riffles are removed, the sluices "washed down," and the gold secured by being carefully swept down the whole length of the sluice into a pan, to be more thoroughly cleaned by "panning out."

This is doubtless of all others the most expeditious mode of mining or separating the gold from the dirt that has yet been discovered, and where it can be adopted is doubtless the best.

GROUND SLUICING.

Among the more important operations connected with gold mining upon an extensive scale, is "ground sluicing." Localities are often found in which the largest portion of the gold lies upon, or near the "bed rock;" above which may rest a depth of earth of many feet, containing no gold, or so small a quantity compared with the mass of dirt, that it would not pay either to wash in sluices or for the expense of re

moval in any other way than by ground sluicing.

The principle of the operation is this; a bank of earth is selected which it is desired to reduce or wash away, down to the pay dirt; a stream of water is conducted thereto, at so high a level as to command it; a small ditch is then cut along the portion to be ground sluiced, the water turned on, and then any number of hands with picks and shovels either upon the edges of the ditch or by getting directly into the stream of water, pick away and work down the banks and bottom, to be dissolved and carried away by the water, while the gold that may be contained in it, settles down without being conveyed or lost, to be finally saved by being passed through the ordinary sluice.

When the process is solely for the purpose of removing the top strata of earth in which no gold or pay dirt is found, down to that which will pay, it is called "stripping," by ground sluicing. Often however when no pay is expected from the stripping process, the miner is unexpectedly cheered by finding in the top dirt more gold than sufficient to pay all the expenses of the operation.

SINKING A SHAFT.

SINKING A SHAFT.

The mining region of California in its physical conformation is made up to a great extent of immense ridges and hills, with gulches and ravines intervening, and all underlaid by what is usually termed the "bed rock." In very many places this bed rock assumes upon its surface the form of basins deep beneath the great earth ridges, and these basins are frequently found to be exceedingly rich in their golden deposits.

To reach the bed rock in these positions, two methods are adopted; "sinking shafts" and "running tunnels."

To "sink a shaft"—a shaft being a perpendicular opening in the earth usually from four to six feet in diameter—the same means and appliances are ordinarily used as in sinking a deep well; which in fact it much resembles, except that it is seldom walled up as wells are, nor is water desired in them; but which unluckily too often occurs.

Sometimes a "streak" or strata of pay dirt is reached, before arriving at the bed rock, and is termed a "lead." When the lead is followed horizontally to the right or left from the shaft, it is termed "drifting;" and when the bed rock is reached, if operations are continued they are all done by drifting.

The pay dirt is raised to the surface by the same means that are used in sinking the shaft, the principal of which is, the windlass and bucket, or tub. Sinking shafts is often performed, solely with the view of prospecting, in the cheapest and most expeditious manner, the bed rock, before proceeding to the greater expense, but more efficient mode, of working these deep hill claims by "tunneling." But this is not always the case; for shafts are sometimes sunk upon flats, to a great depth, and the entire process of mining out all beneath, conducted through the shaft; in aid of which, steam engines are often employed.

RUNNING A TUNNEL.

TUNNELING.

Tunnels are usually commenced upon hillsides, or near the bottom of gulches and ravines and are run in nearly horizontal. Commencing at the surface upon the proper level, or what is supposed will prove to be the proper level, when the basin of the hill or pay dirt is reached, an open cut is first made into the hill, until a sufficient depth is attained to enable the tunnel to be commenced, with enough of earth or rock overhead to sustain itself in the form of an arch, or if of earth only and inclined to cave in, then to be supported by "timbering" at a height scarcely sufficient to clear a tall man's head when standing upright.

The tunnel is now commenced, and usually from five to seven feet in width. When only earth and detached stones or boulders are met with, it often becomes necessary to "timber up," as the tunnel progresses; which is done by setting strong posts about

FLUMING IN A CANON.

FLUMING OVER A GORGE.

three feet apart on each side, and opposite to each other; and these supporting a cross timber above, and on these one or more plank are laid which support the roof; sometimes the sides are necessarily planked also.

In very many instances the tunnel is "driven" by picking and blasting through solid bed-rock many hundred feet in length, requiring a great expenditure of time, labor, money, and perseverance. To convey from the tunnel, the excavated portions of rock, stones, and earth, the wheelbarrow was formerly in general use, and is even now in many places; but with the more systematic, a narrow rail-road is constructed as the work progresses, on which is run a suitable car, the bottom of the tunnel having the necessary grade to enable a loaded car to be propelled outwardly easily by man power.

When the pay dirt is reached, a division is made of the excavated portion on being brought out, into that which is, and is not, pay dirt, and as often as expedient when water is procurable, it is washed by sluicing in the usual manner.

FLUMING.

Only those who are familiar with the physical formation of the mountain and gold region of California, have anything like an adequate idea of the vast amount of labor expended, in the construction of the artificial water-courses that supply our mining canals and ditches with water from the mountain streams.

To hear of the construction of a hundred miles of mining ditch, conveys but a feeble conception of the magnitude of the enterprise, or the difficulties to be overcome. The mountain country from which the supply of water is obtained, does not consist of slope upon slope, or of successive tables of comparatively level land, and rising one above another; but from the foot hills, the mountains rise to the height of from seven to nine thousand feet, in one uninterrupted succession of immense ridges, lying in every conceivable direction and position, with intervening gorges or cañons of corresponding depth; and by this we mean, of very great depth; many of the mountain streams occupying and rushing down cañons, whose sides are almost perpendicular walls of rock, and often three thousand feet or more in height, and along which the pedestrian can only make his way for a hundred yards together, by taking to the bed of the stream.

It is from such cañons, that the water is mostly obtained for the supply of our mining canals and ditches; and it is not unusual that from three to ten miles of wooden flume is required at the upper end, before the water can be brought out of the cañon sufficiently high to oretop or command the ridges and foot hills of the lower country, in which the mines and placers are principally found.

To lift as it were, the waters from these deep cañons, or rather to convey them at a fall of from five to twenty feet to the mile, out of them, often requires many miles of flume constructed entirely of wood, because the steep sides have not, in many places, a single inch of earth in which to excavate a ditch; and even the rocky sides often so high and steep as to require the flume to be constructed upon trestle work, a hundred or more feet in height; and even in some instances actually suspended by iron work, upon the smooth face of almost overhanging rock and precipices; the workmen are let down and suspended by ropes from above, while prosecuting their arduous labors.

Then again, the flume is made to span a vast gorge sometimes, and in places supported by timber work from beneath; at others, by suspension from the sides; and in its tortuous course, running up and crossing adjacent gorges, perhaps to take in the waters of some small tributary, and then again heading for and coursing along the great main cañon, leaping as it were,

from point to point of jutting crag and cliff, till at last it reaches the more earthy side or summit of the ridge, there to be at once used for gold washing, or milling purposes, or conveyed by ditches in countless ramifications to the lower mining world; and these enterprises constitute the great fulcrum of our mining prosperity.

THE "HYDRAULIC" METHOD OF WORKING.

By far the most efficient system of mining yet known, for hill diggings, is the hydraulic; for the discovery of which California is indebted to Mr. Edward E. Matteson, formerly of Sterling, Windham County, Connecticut. Through the kindness of Mr. Cloud of Omega, Nevada County, we are enabled to present our readers with the likeness of Mr. Matteson, the discoverer, engraved from an excellent Ambrotype by Mrs. J. F. Rudolph, of Nevada.

Mr. M. first commenced the use of this method at American Hill, Nevada, in February, 1852, and such was the success attending its operation that others around him immediately began to adopt it; and it is now in general use throughout the mining districts of the State.

The large and accurate engraving on another page, from a beautiful ambrotype by Messrs. E. B. & D. H. Hendee, will give to the reader an excellent and correct idea of its manner of working and appearance.

Water being conveyed as before described, by canals and ditches, around and among the hills and mountain sides where mining is carried on, it is thence distributed from the main canal by smaller ditches to the mining claims requiring it.

Here it is run from the small ditch into a trough fixed upon tressel work, which is often technically termed the " Hydraulic Telegraph"; or, run in heavy duck hose upon the ground, to the edge of the claim, thence over the edge and down the almost perpendicular bank to the bed rock, or bottom of the claim, where it lies coiled about

EDWARD E. MATTESON.

on the rock and dirt like a huge serpent. As the upper end of the hose is much larger than the lower end, the water running in, keeps it full to the very top; and the weight of this water, escaping through a pipe attached to the lower end of the hose, in a similar manner to that of a fire engine, plays upon the bank with great force and effect, washing it rapidly away.

There are sometimes stratas of gravelly cement in the bank which are exceedingly hard and difficult to wash away, even with the immense force given by the weight of from fifty to two hundred and twenty feet of fall, which the water contained in the hose receives from above.

The most efficient manner of washing down these banks is by undermining them near the bed rock, when large masses—fre-

quently many tons in weight—"cave down" and not only break themselves to pieces by the fall, but unfortunately often bury the too venturesome miner beneath them. It is in this kind of mining so many accidents have occurred; and when we read in the newspapers of the day that Mr. so and so was badly injured—or killed—by the "caving of a bank," we may know it is generally in such places.

If the reader will please refer to the engraving he will see a stream of water running over the bank, which is often required effectually to cleanse and remove the large quantities of earth and rocks washed down by the pipe, and convey them to the sluice, down which they pass, and in which the gold is principally saved, although large amounts of the golden dust lie among the earth and stones, but a few feet from whence they were washed.

After " cleaning up" the rock and " washing down" the sluice, the precious contents are swept into a pan where they are carefully panned out. After the day's work is done the miner repairs to his cabin to build his fire, cook and eat his supper, dry his dust, and blow out the black sand.

Sometimes when a man has been covered up by the bank falling upon him, not only the stream generally used in the claim, but often the entire contents of the ditch are thus turned on, and with the assistance of every miner who knows of the accident, it is used for sluicing him out, and which is by far the speediest and best method for his deliverance.

One becomes surprised when looking at the bold defiant strength of a miner's will and purpose, and the risk he so often runs, that comparatively so few accidents of this kind occur. By care, however, this branch of mining can be conducted with the same safety as any other.

The " hydraulic process" removes and washes immense masses of earth that would otherwise be useless and its working unprofitable, thus making it not only one of the most useful and effectual, but almost an indispensable method of mining for gold in California.

RIVER MINING.

In the beds of nearly all the rivers that traverse the gold region of California, deposits of gold have been found, many of them exceedingly rich ; and large expenditures have been made in order successfully to work these " river claims."

Oftentimes the entire water of the river is turned into new channels, generally consisting of flumes of wood, built along the banks. A dam is constructed that turns the water into the flume, and being conveyed, often many hundred yards, is turned into the river bed again below. The water that remains is then pumped out, and usually, by the power obtained from wheels

acted upon by the water in its rapid passage through the flume.

The bed of the river by this means rendered dry or nearly so, the sand and gravel down to the bed-rock is then washed by either of the usual modes, with pan, cradle, tom, or sluice.

In a future number, we shall give engravings illustrative of river and quartz mining ; the latter, having within the last two years, assumed an importance that entitles it to a more extended notice and space in our columns, than can well be devoted to it in this number.

CONSOLATION.

BY ANNA M. BATES.

She went to the radiant mansions afar,
The robes of the kingdom to wear ;   [star
And I think that the angels who dwell in the
Have twined a green wreath in her hair.

Not long on our shore did the child-pilgrim
Amid all our sorrow and sin ;   [wait.
For gently they opened a beautiful gate,
And said to her soul " welcome in."

The leaves of the summer were fresh on the
        trees,
The primrose was bright in its bloom,
Waxen-like daisies were thick on the leas,
And winds were all breathing perfume ;

When suddenly over her beautiful eyes,
There closed down the fring'd lids of snow ;
The angels were singing far up in the skies,
And so she was ready to go :

Away in a lonely and beautiful vale,
We laid down our darling to rest ;
Cross'd as in prayer were the hands milky pale,
O'er the burial flowers on her breast.

The sweet golden robin goes there, and sings,
In the hush of the bright morning hours :
And a rose tree above, her soft fragrance flings,
And covers the spot with pale flowers.

Ah not with the tears that are vain ones and
        wild
Remember her earth vanished bloom,
But think that it is not the SOUL of your child
Hid in the cold clasp of the tomb :

Remember she went to her home in the sky
The robes of the kingdom to wear,
And YE when the shadows of life have gone by
May meet with the beautiful there!

HUTCHINGS'

CALIFORNIA MAGAZINE.

| VOL. II. | SEPTEMBER, 1857. | No. 3. |

RIVER MINING.
[*From a Photograph, by E. B. & D. H. Hendee.*]

RIVER MINING.

At this season of the year, when every energy of the enterprising river miner is concentrated upon the great undertaking of his arduous work, it may not be amiss to describe the manner in which the plannings of his mind, perhaps for months, or even years, are carried out.

When it becomes desirable to chain the mountain torrent, which is heedlessly rushing past, and turning it out of its natural channel, that the glittering gold, lying in the river's bed, may be transferred from thence to the buckskin purse of the miner ; he talks the matter over with some confidential and trustworthy and herd-working companions, when they mutually agree that "there is gold there — sure," if they can only get it.

The ways and means are accordingly devised; sometimes by making up a company of eight, or ten, or twenty, or any other desirable number; and as the cost will be about so much, each member of the company has to contribute his share of the amount agreed upon, as the work progresses. Should it cost less or more—generally it is the latter—the proportion is diminished, or increased by assessments according to the number of shares. At other times, a number of men who live together on the same bar, and who, being well acquainted with each other, and tolerably well informed of what the other possesses, will raise whatever timber or tools may be required, from among themselves, and "get along as well as they can, for the balance"— which often is but very indifferently—and go to work with a will to accomplish their object.

To to do this, sometimes, a race has to be dug; at others, a flume has to be built, requiring to be of sufficient capacity to take in the whole amount of water running in the river. This being done, a dam has to be constructed across the river, that shall be water-tight, or nearly so. To build this dam, very often requires that men work in the water, which is generally very cold, for, as it comes from the melting snows, it cannot be expected to be very warm; at least, before the river is very low, and men seldom wait for that — they therefore enter the river; and by rolling up large boulders into a line for building a wall, they turn the water from the one side towards the flume on the other, and when one wall is thus rudely but substantially constructed, another is built behind it; when all the light floating sand is cleaned out, that it may not be in the way of making the space water-tight between the walls; a clayey soil is then filled in and well tramped, until the dam is tight; and the water is running through the race or flume. Sometimes a tree or

log is felled across the stream, (if one can be found long enough to reach, and in the right place,) when slabs or split timbers are put in, in an inclined position, and either nailed or pinned to the log, when the whole space in front is filled up with clayey soil and fine boughs of trees until it is made water-tight.

The river now being turned into the race, wheels are erected across it; and pumps are attached by which the water still remaining in the river's bed is pumped out. Now river mining is commenced in real earnest; men begin to remove boulders, wheel out rocks, fix toms, or sluices, and take out the precious metal—if there is any. (The writer has seen as high as five thousand two hundred and twenty-seven dollars, taken out from behind a boulder, in a single pan of dirt.)

Should the fall rains be late before commencing, every opportunity is given to work out the river claims to advantage— or at least to test them sufficiently either to work or abandon them. If on the contrary—as frequently occurs—the rains should come early, the whole of the summer's labor and expense are swept away before a dollar can be taken out. Many men are thus left penniless, after the toil and hope of a long and scorching summer. Taking the losses with the gain, it is very questionable if more gold has not actually been invested in river mining, than has ever been taken out.

Some more comprehensive plan of operations than the present is much needed, before the streams can be thoroughly worked to profit and advantage. We propose a plan, to be accepted or modified, according to circumstances, which would, in our opinion, accomplish the object in question.

Water is the great want of all kinds of surface mining. To supply this want let *the whole* of the water in a river during the summer season, be conveyed in one or more flumes on one or both sides of the river, as may be most desirable, to mining

MEN ENGAGED IN WORKING OUT THE RIVER'S BED AFTER TURNING THE STREAM INTO THE FLUME.

ground; and let the dams be so constructed that the highest stage of water during the winter or spring season cannot in the least damage, much less destroy them, as at the present time.

There will be no less than eight hundred thousand dollars expended in flumes and dams on Feather river, above and within ten miles of Oroville, this present season.

Now had even twice that amount of money been invested in constructing one or more substantial flumes, above high water mark, it would have been an investment of profit, as well as permanency, from the amount of water sold for mining purposes, besides accomplishing the work of turning the river, not only for the present but for many summers to come.

Supposing that a dam be constructed to each mile of river turned (as at present);

each dam will cost, upon an average, about eight thousand dollars; in the ten miles mentioned of course there would be ten in number, making eighty thousand dollars; now should that sum be used to construct one permanent dam that should last not only for one, but for many seasons,—besides the advantages it would offer to other claim owners by not backing the water upon them, as now—it would be a piece of economy that must commend itself to the thoughtful consideration of all persons interested in river mining. Should all the companies on a single stream unite for this purpose, even though the claims in the river should fail, they would have an important and profitable interest in a flume; which, while it drained the river, would also supply the dry mining districts with water. We ask you to think the matter over and let us hear from you.

THE SUTTER CREEK FOUNDRY.
[*From an Ambrotype by Woods & Michaels.*]

The above works are situated in the town of Sutter, Amador county, and, with similar ones at Grass Valley, Nevada county, are the only works in the mining districts where all kinds of machinery, in brass and iron, are cast for quartz mining, and without the delay and expense of sending to the larger cities, as formerly.

The Miner's Song.

WORDS BY J. SWETT. **MUSIC BY JAS. C. KEMP.**

The east-ern sky is blushing red, The distant hill-top glowing, The riv-er o'er its rock-y bed In i--dle frol-ics flow-ing; 'Tis time the pick-axe and the spade Against the rocks were ring ing, And with ourselves the golden stream A song of labor sing-ing.

The mountain air is fresh and cold,
  Unclouded skies bend o'er us;
Broad placers, rich in hidden gold,
  Lie temptingly before us.
We need no Midas' magic wand,
  Nor wizard rod divining;
The pickaxe, spade and brawny hand
  Are sorcerers in mining.

When labor closes with the day,
  To simple fare returning,
We gather in a merry group
  Around the camp-fires burning,
The mountain sod our couch at night,
  The stars keep watch above us,
We think of home and fall asleep
  To dream of those who love us.

Our Social Chair.

THERE is such a place as "Deadwood" in California. A friend of ours passed through the town, the other day, but stopped long enough to witness a trial before the chief officer of the law, vulgarly called a Justice of the Peace.

The case was "Hanks *versus* Breese," and the facts were—*First*, that the parties had violated the law by playing "poker" on the Sabbath. (It is, perhaps, proper to state that the good folks of Deadwood had not seen the Supreme Court decisions.) *Second*, that Breese played very "low down," or, in other words, cheated plaintiff. *Third*, that the game broke up in a row, the parties being arrested by the Justice, who happened to be present. It was an important case. Both parties were well known, and had hosts of friends. The defendant, through his attorney, a sharp little man, demanded a jury. The people of Dead-Dog never go to trial without a jury.

The legal preliminaries having been properly arranged, the case was called. Twelve of the best men in the locality formed the jury. The attorneys were big with the event of the hour. At length an odd looking genius, named Stephen Lick, was placed on the stand by the prosecution. The case proceeded.

"You said you were present during the game between the parties. Did we so understand you, Mr. Lick?"

The witness nodded in the affirmative.

"Did you observe the progress of the game with any interest?"

"I reckon I did—licker was pendin' on it."

"What was the amount at stake, at the time the row occurred?"

"Well, the anti was two bits, and Lem. Hanks bet a haf on his little par. Then Bill he went in——"

"Never mind the details," interrupted the lawyer, impatiently, "answer my question."

"That's what I'm going to do," replied the witness, drawing a large black plug of tobacco from his pocket. "You see when Lem. dropped his haf on the pot, Bill he kivered it with a big dollar, 'cause I stood jest whar I could see that he helt a little par, too. Lem. he then tuck a drink and 'peared sort o' keerless——"

"Come, come," again interrupted the lawyer. "Tell us the amount of money at stake at the time the quarrel commenced."

"Steve," said the Judge, familiarly, "you say that when Bill Breese shoved up his dollar, Lem Hanks tuck a snifter and 'peared sort 'o keerless. *What did he do then?*"

"Why he seed Bill and lifted him two scads. Bill he 'peared a little uneasy, but raised Lem a five. Lem he tuck another drink and said the game was gettin' interestin', at the same time shaking a ten dollar piece out on the pot. Bill he then said 'Lem, you kinder suit me,' and called out 'twenty better.' Then—"

The lawyers here protested against this manner of giving evidence, but they were overruled by the Court, who asked the witness what the parties did *then*.

"Then we all tuck a small drink, and Lem spread himself. 'I see that matter of twenty dollars,' said he, 'and go you thirty better.'"

By one of the Jury.—"Will the Constable please keep order in the Court room, so that the Jury kin ketch all the words."

The witness proceeded: "Bill he then got down to scratch his foot, and when he got up he lifted Lem twenty more. Then Lem begin to look distressed, and pushed his shirt sleeves up to keep it from gettin' dirty, I spose, but cum up bime by like a man, with—"

"Stop, stop, stop," shouted one of the lawyers, whose patience was exhausted. We do not care about so much detail, but desire simply to know what amount of money is in dispute.

"Mr. Constable," followed the Judge, who was deeply interested in the witness' story, "do your duty." Then fixing his eyes upon the witness, he asked; "Steve, my boy, when Bill pungled his thirty better, *what did Lem come up with?*"

"Why Lem he lifted him a cool fifty."

The judge collapsed "Gentlemen of the jury, that's so, for *I* was thar and seen Lem do it."

By one of the Jury—"What did Bill do then?"

"Bill he tuck another look at his hand, and then got down and scratched his foot agin. When he come up, he said to me, said he, 'Steve, lend me a hundred dollars.' Says I, 'what fur?' He said, · to clean out Lem Hanks.' I said, 'it can't be did on your par of juces, for he's got bully sixes.' 'Good thing,' says he, giving me a wink. 'Kiver his pile, and and I'll call him.' I—"

"Never mind what you did," said the lawyer for the defendant, "that has nothing to do with the merits of the case."

The Judge gave the lawyer a terrible look. Then, turning to the witness, he said, "Steve, if the Court recollects herself, then you come up with the spondulicks, and Bill Breese tuck down Lem's pile."

This announcement was followed by murmurs of dissatisfaction. The attorney for the plaintiff was the first to speak.

"Now, if your Honor pleases," said he, "I would ask one question. How comes it that the defendant got that money, if he only had a pair of duces against my client's sixes?"

"Yes," chimed in several members of the jury, "how *could* that happen?"

"Bill did have juices fust—I'll swear to that," resumed the witness, "but somehow when it come to the last, he was stronger."

The lawyers, thinking he was about to continue the story to an endless length, requested him to be brief. Taking a fresh "chaw," Steve said:

"The way of it was this. When I kivered the pile, Bill called Lem. Says he, 'Lem. what have you to say fur yourself?' 'I have three of 'em,' says Lem., reaching out his arm. 'Three *what?*' says Bill. 'Nice little spots, all in the middle of the keerd,' says Lem., laying his fist on the money. 'Show 'em,' says Bill. 'Thar they be,' says Lem. 'That's clever,' says Bill, 'but they can't win this pop.' 'How so?' says Lem. puttin' his hand on his revolver. 'Cause here's *four of the same sort,*' says Bill, puttin' one hand on the money and tother on his revolver.' All I know is, Bill got the pot before he was arrested."

The lawyer for the plaintiff intended to have made a good case in relation to the manner in which defendant's hand became strengthened from a little pair of "juices" to four aces; but to do so, he would probably have been called on to explain how Lem. got his *three* "spots."

The Judge saw through the case at once. He charged the jury that if they thought there was anything wrong in a man scratching his foot during a game of poker, they could so find; but if they thought such a movement was on the square, they would also be likely to pass over the act of fumbling with shirt sleeves, committed by plaintiff.

The "charge" was followed by loud demonstrations of approval, such as yelling, throwing up hats, etc.

The jury, after being out three minutes, brought in a verdict to the effect that it was a "draw game," and the Judge thereupon dismissed the case.

HUTCHINGS'
CALIFORNIA MAGAZINE.

VOL. I.   DECEMBER, 1856.   NO. VI.

PACK TRAIN IN MOTION.

PACKING, IN THE MOUNTAINS OF CALIFORNIA.

Miners in search of the precious metal, have penetrated the vast forests, explored the deep cañons,
climbed the rocky steeps, and, eventually, many of
them have made themselves a dwelling place among
the rugged and almost inaccessible mountains of
California. Thus shut out from the cities of the
plain, packing, to them, has become an indispensable
necessity; and is not only the means of obtaining their
supplies, but, like the ever welcome expressman,
a kind of connecting link between the vallies and the
mountains.

In some of the more isolated mining localties, the arrival of a pack train, is an event of some importance, and men gather around it with as much apparent interest, as though they expected to see some dear old friend stowed away somewhere among the packs.

This necessity, has created an extensive packing business with the cities of Stockton, Marysville, Shasta, and Crescent City, but very little with Sacramento, at the present time.

We are indebted to a friend in Stockton for the following interesting information concerning the packing trade of that city.

The quantity of freight packed on mules to the counties of Calaveras, Tuolumne, Mariposa, and Tulare, from Stockton, is about two hundred tons weekly, or one fifth of the entire amount of goods weekly transported.

There are generally from forty to fifty mules in a train, mostly Mexican, each of which will carry from three hundred to three hundred and fifty pounds, and with which they will travel from twenty five to thirty five miles per day, without becoming weary.

If there is plenty of grass they seldom get anything else to eat. When fed on barley, which is generally about three months of the year—November, December, and January—it is only given once a day, and in the proportion of from seven to eight pounds per mule. They seldom drink more than once a day, in the warmest of weather. The average life of a mule is about sixteen years. The Mexican mules are tougher and stronger than American mules; for, while the latter seldom can carry more than from two hundred to two hundred and fifty pounds, the former

FASTENING ON THE PACKS.

can carry three hundred and fifty pounds, with greater ease. This fact may arise from the mules in Mexico being accustomed to packing only, and over a mountainous country; while the American mules are used only for draught. The Mexican mule, too, can carry a person forty miles per day, for ten or twelve days consecutively, over a mountainous trail; while it is very difficult for an American mule to accomplish over twenty five or thirty miles per day.

The Mexican mule can travel farther and endure more without food than any other quadruped; and with him, apparently, it makes but little difference whether fed regularly or not; still, like animals of the *biped* species, he has no objection to the best of good living. They can, however, always be kept fat with but little care, and it is but very little that is required; while the American mule, to do only half the amount of work, requires good food, regularly given, besides being well cared for otherwise. The Mexicans consider them altogether too delicate for their use. Then again, from the steady regularity of their steps, the Mexican mule is much the easier, generally, under the saddle, and a person will not often become as much fatigued from riding one a week, as he would be in riding an American mule for only three days.

The packing trade of Marysville is very extensive with Downieville, Eureka North, Morrison's Diggins, St. Louis, Pine Grove, Poker Flat, Gibsonville, Nelson's Point, American Valley, Indian Valley, and all the intermediate and surrounding places in the counties of Sierra and Plumas, giving employment to about two thousand five hundred mules, and between three and four hundred men.

From the town of Shasta, during the winter of 1854–'5, the number of mules employed in the packing trade to the various towns and mining localities north of Shasta, was one thousand eight hundred and seventy six. This does not include the animals used by indi-vidual miners; and, according to the *Shasta Courier*, of Nov. 11th, 1854, it would be safe to estimate the number at two thousand.

UNPACKING WITHOUT ASSISTANCE.

"With this data a very fair estimate of the amount of freight packed from Shasta may be formed. Each mule load will average two hundred pounds. A trip to the most remote point to which goods are taken will never occupy more than two weeks—in many instances three or four days less. It is a very moderate calculation, then, to average the trips of the entire two thousand mules at two weeks each."

"This will give a result of one hundred tons per week, as the aggregate amount of freight packed from Shasta—which, at the very low figure of five cents per pound, would yield the sum of twenty thousand dollars per trip, to the packers."

The principal places to which freight is thus transported from Shasta, are Weaverville, (or "Weaver," as it is now called,) Yreka, and the settlements around, and

IN TROUBLE.

ACCIDENTS SOMETIMES HAPPEN

Scott mountains, to those places; such as buggies, windows, boxes, barrels, bars of iron, chairs, tables, plows, &c.

In the fall of 1853, there was an iron safe, nearly three feet square, and weighing 352 pounds, transported on a very large mule, from Shasta to Weaverville, a distance of thirty-eight miles, over a rough and mountainous trail, without an accident; but, after the load was taken off, the mule lay down, and died in a few hours afterwards.

All kinds of goods, at all times, are not alike safely packed. A friend of ours, who resides in Yreka, sent, among other things, a rocking chair and looking-glass, " and when I reached there," said he, " I found that the chair back was broken, the rockers off, and one arm in two pieces; and the looking-glass was as much like a crate of broken crockery as anything *I* ever saw."

A gentleman has also informed us that in the summer of 1855, two sets of millstones were packed from Shasta to Weaverville, the largest weighing six hundred pounds. Being looked upon as an impossibility for one mule to carry, it was first tried to be "slung" between two mules, but that being impracticable, it was abandoned and packed on one. The following fact will give some idea of the expense often occasioned, as well as the immense weight sometimes packed, over a rough and mountainous country:

When the *Yreka Herald* was about to be published, a press was purchased in San Francisco, at a cost of about six hundred dollars, upon which the freight alone amounted to nine hundred dollars, making the entire cost $1,300.

between, those points. One is astonished to see the singular goods that are often packed across the Trinity and

PACK TRAIN IN A SNOW STORM.

The "bed-piece," weighing three hundred and ninety-seven pounds, which, with the *aparajoe,* ropes, &c., exceeded *four hundred and thirty* pounds, was the weight of the entire pack, placed upon a very large mule.

On descending the Scott mountain, this splendid animal slipped a little, when the pack over–balanced and threw him down the steep bank, killing him instantly.

Many a mule, in California, has breathed his last in a ravine where accident had tossed him—to be the food of wolves or coyotas.

One train was passing the steep side of a mountain, in Trinity county, when a large rock came rolling from above, and struck one of the mules in the side, frightening others off the track ; and killing one man and three mules. This can be appreciated by a glance at the engraving on the opposite page.

During the severe winter of 1852, and '53, there was a pack train snowed in, between Grass Valley and Onion Valley, and out of forty-five animals, but three were taken out alive. It is almost incredible, the amount of danger and privation, to which men who follow this business, are, sometimes, exposed.

It is truly astonishing to see with what ease and care these useful animals pack their heavy loads over deep snow, and to notice how very cautiously they cross holes where the melting snow reveals some ditch, or tree beneath ; and where some less careful animal has "put his foot in it," and, as a consequence, has sunk with his load into trouble. We have often watched them descending a snow bank when heavily packed, and have seen that as they could not step safely, they have fixed their feet and braced their limbs, and unhesitatingly slide down with perfect security, over the worst places.

There is something very pleasing and picturesque in the sight of a large pack train of mules quietly descending a hill, as each one intelligently examines the trail, and moves carefully, step by step, on the steep and dangerous declivity, as though he suspected danger to himself, or injury to the pack committed to his care.

The packing trade from Crescent City, a seaport town about three hundred miles north of San Francisco, is one of growing importance. From thence most of the goods required in Klamath, and some portions of Siskiyou and Trinity counties, are transported. There is already an extensive trade with Jacksonville, (Rogue River valley,) Illinois Valley, Sailor's Diggings, New Orleans Bar, (on the Klamath river,) and county seat of Klamath, Scott's river, Applegate creek, and several other prosperous localities in that section.

There are about one thousand five hundred mules in the packing trade at these points. It is no uncommon circumstance, to meet between twenty and thirty trains, with from twenty to seventy-five animals in each train, and all heavily laden, on your way from Jacksonville to Crescent City. The loud "hippah," "mulah," of the Mexican muleteers, sounds strangely to the ear, in the deep, and almost unbroken stillness of the forest.

It seems to us, that the Mexican sings no song, hums no tune, to break in upon the monotinous duties of his calling; but, is apparently indifferent to every kind of cheerfulness, until the labors of the day are done, and then but seldom.

A large portion of the trail lies through an immense forest of redwood trees, and which, from their large growth and numbers, are much more imposing in appearance than the mammoth tree grove of Calaveras.

The soil must be exceedingly fertile, as the leaves of the common fern grow to the height of from twelve to fifteen feet.

On the trail from Trinidad to Salmon river there is a hollow tree, measuring thirty three feet in diameter, which is the usual camping place of trains, holding all the packs for the largest, besides affording shelter and sleeping room to the packers.

The distance from Crescent City to Jacksonville is 120 miles, and generally takes packers about ten days to go through.

There is now a considerable packing trade carried on between Union—Humboldt Bay—and the mining settlements on Salmon, Eel, and Trinity rivers; also, with the town and vicinity of Weaverville.

All of these trails across the coast range of mountains, are very rough, and almost impassable during the winter, from snow in some places and mud in others.

We are indebted to Mr. Dressel, of the firm of Kuchel & Dressel, of this city, who has just returned from a sketching tour in the north, for interesting particulars concerning the above trail.

"During the Rogue River Indian War of 1853, while Capt. Limerick's command was stationed at Bates', on Grave Creek, to keep the trail clear, and guard the pack trains against the Indians, an incident occurred, which is too good to be lost, altogether, and for which we are indebted to a source nearly as good as an eye witness; especially as the night was extremely dark. As usual, a strong guard was placed around the house, for protecting the provisions, groceries, liquors, and other valuables, that were stacked in the rear. A Mr. D. was not very comfortably situated to sleep, from the fact that the night was very cold, and he had only one blanket " to go to bed to." In this dilemma he remembered that among the other good things piled up, was some good old rum, and the thought struck him that if he could only secure a bottleful, he could raise sufficient *spiritual* help, to make up

IN DANGER.

rub." He knew the risk that he should run if he were caught at it; or, if the guard, in the dark, mistook him for an Indian; but, after debating in his own mind all the advantages and disadvantages, he concluded that the advantages were in favor of taking his chances, and having the rum. Stealthily went his feet, and cautious were his movements, and as luck would have it, he succeeded not only in finding the right keg, and tapping it, but of transferring a portion of its contents to a large black bottle, with which he had " armed and equipped" himself before starting on his dangerous but *stimulating* mission. Grasping and guarding the treasure with his arm, he groped his way with cautious movements, towards his solitary blanket; but, as fate would have it, the guard was awake ! and moreover, to increase his trepidation and his danger, he shouted in a stentorian voice, " Who goes there ? "

HAS A WILL OF HIS OWN.

for the deficiency of blankets. But to get it, he thought, " aye there's the

" A friend," replied D.

"Advance, friend, and give the countersign," cried the guard in a fierce and firm tone. At this critical juncture of affairs, D's presence of mind forsook him, and he hesitated in his reply.

"Advance, friend, and give the countersign," again cried the guard, in a trembling and confused tone of voice, as he raised his rifle to a "present arms," "fire."

D. immediately, but cautiously, advanced towards the guard, and said in full, round, English,

"I've got a good bottle of rum."

"Then pass on, friend," said the guard, "but *be sure and pass this way*, and give *that* countersign, as he lowered his musket, and shared the plunder.

The business of packing is often attended with considerable danger, as well as exposure, which the following incident will illustrate.

In the summer of 1854, Mr. Robert Woods, (of the firm of Tomlinson & Woods boss packers, of Yreka,) was crossing the Scott mountain, when a shot was fired from behind a rock, which took effect in the neck of the mule he was riding; it fell instantly, scarcely giving him time to recover his feet—when, with great presence of mind, he deliberately aimed his revolver at the robber who had fired at him, and shot him; when he leaped up, exclaiming, "I am a dead man." Two other men then made their appearance, with their rifles; but, while they were seeking a secure place, behind a rock, from whence to shoot, Mr. Woods made his escape, leaving his saddle-mule, saddle-bags, aud money, (about $1,400,) behind.

Packers on the Sacramento rivertrail to Yreka, have been plundered of their whole train and cargoes, by the Indians, and their owners murdered. For two years this route was abandoned, chiefly from this cause.

The Mexicans invariably blindfold each mule, before attempting to pack him, after which he stands quietly, until the bandage is removed. A man generally rides in front of every train, for the purpose of stopping the train when anything goes wrong, and acting as a guide to the others; although in every train there is always a leader, known generally as "the bell mule;" most of the mules prefer a

ARRIVING IN THE MINES.

white one, which they unhesitatingly follow, so that when *he* starts it is the signal for the others immediately to follow.

They seldom start before nine o'clock in the morning, after which they travel until sunset without stopping, except when somthing goes wrong.

When about to camp, the almost invariable custom of packers, after removing the goods, (by which they

CAMPING SCENE BY MOONLIGHT.

alway sleep, in all kinds of weather,) is, for the mules to stand side by side, in a line, or in a hollow square, with their heads in one direction, before taking off the *aparajoes*; and then, in the morning, when the train of loose mules is driven up to camp to receive their packs, each one walks carefully up to his own *aparajoe* and blanket; which he evidently knows as well as does the packer.

An *aparajoe* is a kind of packsaddle, or pad, the covering of which is made of leather and stuffed with hair, and generally weighs from twenty-five to forty pounds. These are always used by Mexican muleteers, and are much easier for the mule than a common packsaddle.

When the toils of the day are over and the mules are peacefully feeding, comes the time of relaxation to the men, who while they are enjoying the aroma of their fine flavored cigarita, spend the evening hours telling tales of some far off, but fair señorita, or make up their bed by the packs and as soon as they have finished their supper, and lie down to sleep for the night.

HUTCHINGS'

CALIFORNIA MAGAZINE.

Vol. III.   JANUARY, 1859.   No. 7.

WINTER IN THE SIERRAS OF CALIFORNIA.

THE MINER GOING TO HIS CLAIM IN THE MORNING.

COMFORTABLY seated in an easy chair and a warm room, it is rather agreeable than otherwise to look out upon the gently-falling flakes of snow, that are seeking a hiding place among men's whiskers —kissing, without ceremony, the ruddy cheeks and ruddier lips of the buoyant-hearted lasses—or making irregular rows and heaps on hat and overcoat, ledge, and window-sill, and pavement, outside. Then after night has closed in, when the candles are lighted and the fires are renewed, to hear the well-known stamp of a welcome friend, who shakes off the snow from his garments, as the door is opened, and announces in pleasant tones, that "this is something like winter."

In the cities and towns around the Bay of San Francisco, the voice of winter speaks only in the rattling rain, as it falls upon the roof and beats against the window-pane, or in droppings from awnings; or splashings from footsteps of both man and beast—but seldom, very seldom, in the gentle whisperings of the gossamer snow.

Such sights as these, that ancient and venerable individual, so well known and so often quoted as "the oldest inhabitant," has never witnessed in San Francisco, nor in any of the towns and villages on the bays and coasts of California. But, as we ascend the Sacramento or San Joaquin rivers, the white tops of the Sierras give us the assurance that Winter —he of the hoary locks, bleak visage and stormy garments—is known well enough elsewhere.

On reaching the inland cities of Stockton, Sacramento and Marysville — the three great starting points to the Southern, middle and Northern mining districts —although some three or four degrees cooler, during the winter months, than the Bay City, snow is only occasionally seen, and never remains upon the ground longer than a few hours, at most, and generally melts as it falls. During the prevalence of a north or north-easterly wind, a little ice is sometimes formed in exposed places; but the genial warmth of the atmosphere never permits it to remain. The consequence is, that the wide plains stretching to the foot-hills are not only occasionally dotted with white (*Quercus Hindsii*) and live-oaks, (*Quercus Agrifolia*,) but are generally carpeted with a beautiful green during the three dreary months of winter, and very early in spring are covered with an endless variety of gay-colored flowers.

As we thread our way among the foot-hills, almost imperceptibly ascending, the scene gradually changes. A few inches of snow may be seen clothing the summits of the apparently barren hills, and the branches of the "fruit-bearing" or "nut pine," (*Pinus Sabiniana*,) the manzanita, (*A. glauca*,) and the California Buckeye, *Æsculus Californica*,) — now seen growing among the oaks—are laden with a fleecy covering of snow. In a few of the ravines and gulches, which now begin to furrow the landscape, miners are busy at work; and on the sides of the ravines, perhaps beneath the shade of some huge trees, stand a number of cabins, the temporary homes of the miners. Advancing, in our upward course, the hills increase to mountains ; the comparatively shallow gulches change to deep creeks and cañons ; and the roads, besides becoming more steep and difficult, are constructed on the tops and sides of nearly perpendicular mountains—especially when crossing the rivers from one mining district to another—and on either side of the dividing ridges, the snow has increased to several inches in depth, covering the mountain sides and filling the ravines with the aqueous element. Now the conical tops of the yellow pine (*Pinus Ponderosa*) are seen among, and gracefully towering above, the other trees of the forest. At this elevation we strike the great mining region of the State, and consequently in the valleys of the different streams and upon the very summits of the mountains, villages and towns become more numerous. and signs of mining industry are visible on every hand,

Let us now go into yonder ravine, at the foot of the mountain. We find that, although it is snowing on the "divide" we have crossed, it is raining al most in torrents here; but those miners we see at the sluice, or ground-sluice, or long tom, who have been waiting so long for the heavens to pour out their treasures, and for the want of which the precious metal has been slumbering untouched in its earthy vault—alas! too long—will not now leave their work, though the rain falls ever so fast and furiously. Their hearts are glad. Pictures of the gold to be taken out are presented to the hopeful imagination of the worker; and besides giving him the means to pay his little bill at the store—the owner of which, he fancies, has looked rather cool upon him lately, as he has entered it— he begins now to calculate how his wife and little ones at home, who have been waiting for a remittance, and, perhaps, have suffered some because of the delay, will feel when they see a draft for —— dollars; or may-be a sweetheart has received letters of assurance that his prospects are encouraging, and, if plenty of water can be obtained, as soon as the rainy season is over, she may look for his coming, when—well, he knows the happiness he anticipates better than you or I, reader, therefore let us leave him to his thoughts. He'd work on—rain or no rain—if there's water to work with, until Night's dark drapery makes him seek the shelter and comfort—such as it is—and rest of his cabin, and many are now made very cosy and agreeable.

Perhaps the uninitiated reader may suppose that when the miner arrives at his cabin home, at night, that his day's work is done. Not a bit of it. The one whose turn it is to cook quits work a few minutes earlier than the others, and, on arriving at the cabin, builds a fire, chops up the wood, and commences the cooking of the supper, so that when the others arrive, who have been detained in cleaning up the sluice or tom, and panning out the gold, they may find that, if the evening meal is not quite ready, there is at least a good fire, if there is no loving wife, to smile upon them, cold, weary and half-drowned, as they are.

After the wet clothes and boots are

SLUICING IN THE RAIN.

removed, and a good supper and an hour's rest makes them feel refreshed, the table is cleared, and the pan containing the proceeds of the day's labor is produced and dried, the black sand blown out, and the question put: "How much do you think there is to-night, Joe?" Putting on a wise and learned look, the party questioned, after due deliberation, pushes it into a little heap on the bottom edge of the pan, and pronounces the opinion, that he "will be very much surprised if there is not at least —— dollars." Not quite as much as that, my boy, I think," suggests another; but the first speaker sides with Joe, and the scales being produced confirm Joe's judgment to be reliable, and he remarks that he "couldn't be much mistaken on that pile: seen too much of that kind of gold in this old cabin."·

Now, too, the respective prospects of theirs and their neighbors' claims are discussed, the general news of the place talked over, a game of cards played, and a magazine (ours, of course!) or book is read, while the cook for the day mixes up the bread and puts the beans to soak for the morrow. Perhaps a neighbor drops in and relates that, during the storm last night, the old "nut pine" tree, on White Rock Flat, had fallen right across Fred Hayfield's cabin, and made Fred and the timber both fly, the former through the window and the latter in every direction, and did a smashing business in crockery and cabin-ware. Jerry Dayton, who was passing at the time, narrowly escaped being — frightened! for, hearing the roots of the old tree snapping, he checked himself rather too suddenly, and measured his length

EVENING AT THE CABIN.

on the ground, fortunately at a sufficient distance from the cabin to escape the danger of being made into smaller pieces than either his sweetheart or mother would be likely to approve of.

But let us ascend still higher, for the gold range extends nearly to the very tops of the Sierra Nevada Mountains. As we leave the valleys and cañons below, and climb the zig-zag trail to the summit above, where it was only inches at a lower altitude, it has here increased in depth to feet. Now, too, the sugar pine, (*Pinus Lambertiana*,) with its immense dimensions, gracefully-spreading boughs, chaste foliage and depending cones; the balsam fir, (*Picea grandis*,) the hardy Williamson spruce, (*Abies Williamsonii*,) with numerous others of the same extensive family; the California nutmeg tree, (*Torreya Californica*,) the arbor vitæ, (*Thuja gigantea*,) and other varieties of the same family, together with the California mountain laurel, (*Oreodaphne Californica*). These, and a vast number of hardy and graceful trees and

STORMY TIMES!

shrubs, by far too numerous even to name in this connection, grow on the great table-lands and ridges of the lofty and snow-covered summits of this magnificent range of mountains.

How often does the miner, residing on a bar or valley of a cañon or river, leave his snug and cosy hut to explore these vast forest solitudes in search of richer diggings—even in the midst of winter! Neither snow, nor rain, nor storm, deter him from his purpose. And who has not known or heard of many who have thus gone out, when the air was clear and the day was bright, and never again returned. Wandering on the surface of the snow, packed perhaps by a thaw or rain, or hardened by a frost, he has gone on until the gathering darkness of a coming storm has shut the sun from his sight and guidance, before the cabin of refuge was in sight. Alas! he is lost! Lost! None but those to whose hearts the reluctant conviction, by experience, has at last forced itself, with its paralyzing power, can fully realize the soul-harrowing feeling expressed in that one simple Saxon word, "*Lost!*" Lost on the wide expanse of snow and forest!

LOST.

Lost, with neither compass nor star to guide; without company, blankets, or food; the heavy flakes that fall and cling to him, as he clings to life, cover up the tracks of his footsteps, so that even the hope of returning by the way he came is denied to him. At last, weary with his fruitless efforts, he at first sits or lays himself down to rest, only for a few minutes; but the nightmare of care is pressing heavily on his bosom; fatigue, hunger and cold are fast weighing down his eye-lids, and he falls into the sleep which knows no waking. In vain do his cabin-mates, or relations, or friends, await his coming. Alas! he is dead!

The writer, while engaged in taking views for this magazine, was overtaken by a snow-storm on the Trinity Mountains, and, being lost and benighted, as well as weary, sat himself down to rest; just as a drowsiness was stealing over him, the neighing of his horse recalled him to consciousness, when he found that the storm had ceased for a few minutes, and in the distance a dim light was visible. He need not say that the horse saw the light, and by expressing his joy in a loud, long neigh, saved his master's life.

About three weeks before Christmas, in the winter of 1852—generally known as the "starvation winter"—Yreka was but a small town compared with what it now is; and as none of the inhabitants there contemplated the visit of any winter more severe than those they had previously known, no extra supplies were laid in. About this time snow began to fall, yet created no anxiety; but, as it continued for nearly a week without intermission, and snow upon the Yreka flats exceeded four feet in depth, men—especially those with families—began to feel anxious lest the small quantity of provisions on hand should fail before the usual pack-train had supplied their wants. Provisions were daily growing scarce, as the expected train was detained by the snow. On Christmas morning, five dollars per pound

were offered for flour, with which to mix a Christmas plum pudding, but none could be bought at any price. Such articles of consumption as could be found in camp rose in prices enormously. Beef —the steaks of which, on account of being so poor and tough, were denominated "sheet-iron steaks"—was 60 cents per pound; salt (only 1½ ℔s. in camp) was sixteen dollars per pound, and other articles proportionably high. None could go out—none could come in. At length several persons, apprehensive of a famine, determined to force their way out over the mountains, towards Shasta. Among them was Mr. Van Choate, our kind informant, who will relate his own story better than we can :—

About a week after Christmas, several of us determined that we would stand it no longer. As a small party had started two days before and had not yet returned, the prospects were looked upon as favorable—besides, we had the advantage of walking in their trail. We crossed over to the head of Scott Valley without much difficulty, and were surprised, on opening the door of Very's Ranch, to find that those who preceded us had made no farther progress than to this point. My first question was :

"Boys, have you any bread here?"

"No," was the bluff and somewhat surly reply, "we haven't!"

Men were strewed about upon the floor in all directions and positions; some were asleep, (for it was night,) others, not finding room to lie down, were sleeping and dozing in a sitting posture; others were quietly awaiting the luxury of lying down when their turn came. We did the best we could, and that merits no cause for boasting, although it does for thankfulness, as we at least had shelter. For that night and the day and night following, we bore our troubles as well as we could; but as provisions were getting scarce here, and the price charged was three dollars per meal, early the following morning twenty-three of us again set our faces towards Shasta, as the place of bread and refuge.

First we had to cross the Scott Mountain—one of the most dreaded in this district—and snow was already from five to nine feet in depth. Armed with a couple of axes, with our blankets at our backs, we started. Snow here — snow everywhere—but no trail anywhere. One led the van, but at every step snow came up to his middle. Others followed in his trail; but before he had travelled one hundred feet, he was thoroughly tired out, and stepped aside for another to take his place; the same result with No. 2, and so on up to the last; and thus the whole party tried it, gave out and fell back. The same process was repeated again and again, and in five hours we made just three miles; when night came, nearly five miles, altogether, were accomplished since starting in the morning.

"We are not on our right course," cried one.

"Which is the right one?" inquired another.

No one knew the course we ought to pursue. To add to our difficulties, night

ON HIS DEATHBED OF SNOW HE HAS BUT ONE LOVING AND SORROWING MOURNER.

and a snow-storm both overtook us. After delaying some little time to ascertain which of the party actually knew the course, an old packer's advice was taken, and we again started—now this way, now the other—now down the side of the mountain a little, now up. After manœuvring in this way all that night and the following day, towards evening the snowing ceased for a few minutes, and gave us an excellent view of Mount Shasta.

We now saw that we were several miles out of our course; but on we pressed and toiled for the whole of that night, and about noon on the following day reached a stream, which we could not ford. We cut down a tree that grew on the bank, to serve as a temporary bridge, by which we might gain the opposite side. In passing over, two of the party, being half frozen, slipped off the tree into the stream, and narrowly escaped drowning.

We had now been out three days and two nights, and, as the third night was fast approaching, with no friendly cabin in sight, where we could take shelter and find refreshment, the prospect looked very dark and forbidding.

" Let us camp," suggested one.

" No, no !" replied the others; " we would freeze to death before the fire was lighted !"

So on, on we toiled until midnight, when the foremost man gave a loud, exultant shout; he saw sparks issuing from a cabin nearly buried in the snow. No tongue could describe our feelings. One long, loud "hurrah !" burst from each and all, and rung over and echoed among those snow-covered mountain tops and sides. New life was infused into all of us, and we hurried briskly on; but, alas, alas ! when we reached the spot we found that it was only an old tree on fire, smouldering and burning deep down neath the snow. This was disappointment, indeed ! yet, in the shadowy distance, in bold relief, stood a cabin, not

A SNOW-BURIED CABIN IS BETTER THAN NONE.

over three hundred yards farther on. A new joy was again felt, but, like the other, was of exceedingly short duration,

for when we reached it, we found that it was not only deserted, but the roof had fallen in. On further examination, one end of the rafters was discovered to be resting on the side of the cabin, and at the farther end was a fire-place. Ah ! but you had better believe that even this gave us a feeling of joy which I can not describe. To build a fire was but the work of a few minutes, and after we had all crept beneath this welcome shelter, we counted noses, one by one, and discovered that two of the party were missing. These were found some distance from the cabin nearly frozen to death.

In "prospecting" around, one of the men found a few pounds of barley—the only eatable thing we had seen for three days. This was equally divided among us, and, while some began to eat it raw, others parched theirs in an old frying-pan, which we had found ; all were delighted—aye, overjoyed—at this most opportune discovery.

Our bodies being warmed, and our hunger somewhat appeased, we slept soundly until the middle of the following day, when, as we were pretty well aware of our position, and knew that there was a house about sixteen miles below, where we could obtain rest and refreshment, we concluded that it would be better to remain where we were till the next morning, and then push on while we had sufficient strength remaining. During the day, quite a number of others from Yreka, who had followed our trail, came up with us, and increased our party to nearly seventy.

As soon as morning light began to break, our gaunt-looking and hungry little army started in Indian file for the house before alluded to—some of us not having tasted food, with the exception of the barley, for four long days.

About nine o'clock, P. M., of this, the fifth day, the place of our deliverance was in sight. Oh! what joy thrilled every heart; for there, not only was the house to be seen, but a light moving about inside. Our little hero was ahead, and, on entering the house, he exclaimed "Have you any bread here?" "No!" was the answer; "but we have some venison." "Then I want supper for seventy men." "Supper for seventy men?" interrogated the landlord. "Yes, supper for seventy men, who have had nothing to eat for five days."

"Gammon!" *looked* the land-lord—he's crazy. By-and-by, in walked one, then another, then three or four more; all eagerly inquiring, "Have you anything to eat here?" "Yes," spoke up Mr. C., "I've or-dered supper for seventy—for all hands." But no supper seemed to be preparing.

As some forty had reached the house, and other voices were making themselves heard not very far off, the landlord concluded that Van was not mad; but that it was a fact, that there were not far, if any, from the number mentioned. Some extensive cooking was performed that night, and eating too; and, as speedily as possible, supper was announced. I should like for you to have seen us then. No allusion to "sheet-iron beef-steaks," or venison either, interfered with our appetites in the least; but what with these meats, some potatoes, and pickled beets, we made the discovery that eating had the effect of destroying a desire for more, although we thought, when we sat down, that we could eat until morning and not be satisfied.

No sooner was the inner man appeased and comforted than volunteers were mus-

tered to seek out the men we had left, frost-bitten, in our last shelter; and two of the sturdiest were selected to under-take their work of risk and love; and to whom we agreed to pay an ounce of gold per day to each, as wages, for taking care of them. When they arrived there the two frozen sufferers were nearly dead. Poor fellows, they were indeed pitiable objects. From the feet of one man fell four of his toes; and from the other a part of the heel. At length, by giving them two or three small teaspoonfulls of warm brandy, they recovered sufficiently

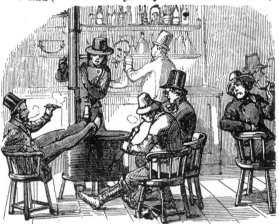

BAR-ROOM SCENE IN WINTER.

to sit up a little, while more brandy was administered in small doses, at intervals. In due time, although crippled for life, they recovered their health, and are still living and well.

After some days of relaxation and re-cuperation, another attempt to reach the settlements was crowned with success, and this heroic party placed beyond the reach of further danger.

[During the same winter—1852-'53— snow fell in Onion Valley, Sierra county, to the depth of twenty-five feet! The store of Timberman & Co. was entirely covered. It was with much labor that the roof was prevented from falling in.

The liberty-pole standing in front had to be cut down and drawn into the store for props, and the snow frequently shoveled from the roof. After a slight thaw, a few inches of the roof were bare; and, upon this spot, large numbers of wolves nightly congregated to warm their feet, fight, and howl. At this time, the people here cut a tunnel from "The Miners' Retreat" (Timberman's) to "The Golden Gate Hotel," opposite; and thus again opened communication with each other across the street. An acquaintance of ours, on Nelson creek at this time, paid eight hundred dollars for one thousand pounds of flour, for which, within a week, he was offered two thousand dollars! At St. Louis, Pine Grove, Gibsonville, and numerous other places in that vicinity; then known only as Sears' Diggings, snow was only from eighteen to twenty feet in depth; and, since that winter,

OVERTAKEN ON THE MOUNTAIN BY A SNOW-STORM.

but little, if any, over seven feet in depth, upon the level, has ever fallen in one winter.]

But the reader must not suppose that such dismal scenes form the whole of the series of winter pictures in the mining region; especially at the present time. By no means. Merry-makings, balls and social parties are beginning to relieve and warm the coldness of Winter's snowy visage; and, during the present winter, sleigh-rides with the girls—yes, with the girls! for such are *now* to be found in almost every mining town—with snow-ballings and slidings, are becoming popular pastimes in the higher mining districts. The dull, cheerless monotony endured by the sturdy sons of the pick and shovel, in earlier winters' of our State's history, is fast passing away; and, before many years have run their round, we hope that winter in the Sierras will be anticipated with pleasure rather than dreaded; and that the "making-haste-to-be-rich" feeling will have given place to that of contentment and comfort possessed.

It may seem strange to many people of the Eastern States, that in California a person may travel on several feet of snow in the morning and before noon, of the same day, be sitting down to lunch where the grass is green and wild flowers are blooming all around him. Such is winter in California.

We cannot better conclude this sketch than by giving the beautiful lines, from the Alta, of

THE LOST PREACHER.

BY MRS. E. S. CONNER.

"The Rev. Mr. Brooks perished in the snow, on Salmon Mountain, a year ago last February. A few days ago, his bones, watch, a twenty dollar gold piece, and a package of tracts, were found near a house on the north side of the mountain. He had perished almost in sight of shelter."

"Well done, thou good and faithful servant; enter thou into the joy of thy Lord."—MATT. 25.

Say, wherefore, Christian soldier, did thy faithful footsteps stray
So far from "busy haunts of men," on that lone, toilsome way?
Twas not to seek the much-loved gold, not to add "land to land,"
Nor e'en to die for science in the martyr-heroes' band;
Nor for the wealth that holy Church hath on her vassals poured,
Nor for the fame that Eloquence hath in her temple stored;
But to the lonely dweller on the mountain's dreary height,
To bear the blessed Word of God, the Gospel's gleam of light;
To say to those who live afar from book, or spire, or bell—
"Glad tidings of great joy, to man 'tis my proud task to tell!"
Hadst thou no mother watching, praying for her much-loved son?
Hadst thou no wife still hoping to behold the absent one?
Hadst thou no child still craving thy fond blessing to implore?
No friends who pined to greet thee in thine old home once more?
The winter sky shone on thee with its melancholy light;
The crisp snow neath thy footsteps sparkled falsely clear and bright;
The storm-cloud came around thee—the drifting snow fell fast—
But cheer thee, lonely traveler! Thy goal is spied at last!
Yes! with thine eyes still gazing, by the early break of day,
At that shelter unattainable, thy life-warmth passed away!
Thy course of usefulness cut off which so bravely had begun—
"Could I have died hereafter! But no! God's will be done!"
And though thy dying struggle no human eye could see,
Who knows what unseen angels were minist'ring to thee?
Alas! all search was fruitless, till eighteen months had passed;
But brothers' love hath found thee—thy fate is known at last.
The melted snow had formed a grave around the sheltered sod;
Beside it lay the precious words of prayer and love of God;
And *Time stood still* beside thee, as it will on that Great Day
When, in the Judge's presence, worlds are marshalled in array;

The rust was on the dial—the rust of death on thee—
But the immortal gem *within*, decay shall never see !
The gold still lay upon the earth, unchanged by frost or dew—
The earth, the gold will perish, but thy soul will rise anew !
Thy bones, all bare and whitened, though lifeless, have a voice,
Which whispers to the mourners—Lament not, but rejoice !
For thou hast died a soldier, in battle for thy Lord ;
Thy guerdon everlasting, proclaimeth thus His Word :
Thy " dried bones " shall be covered with righteousness on High,
For those who serve God truly have only *once* to die !
Then waken to salvation and hear these words so blest—
" Well done, thou faithful servant ; enter now into thy rest ! "

SAN FRANCISCO, Sept. 3, 1858.

THE CALIFORNIA DOG EXPRESS.

THE DOG EXPRESS IN A SNOW-STORM.

HE Dog Express, of which the foregoing wood-cut is a graphic illustration, has become a permanent "institution" in California. Prior to the year 1857, the region of Quincy, Plumas county, was almost cut off from communication with the rest of the world during several months of the wintei season, in consequence of the deep snow which formed an impassable barrier to mule travel. The only means for transporting the United States mails and express matter was by "packing" it on the shoulders of men.

This service was often very hazardous. A man might, with the aid of snow-shoes, be tolerably certain of making the trip with safety, but with an incumbrance of thirty or forty pounds of mail matter the trip was not so easy of accomplishment; particularly as the expressman would frequently be overtaken by snow storms miles distant from any habitation, and compelled to traverse deep gulches, and pick his way along steep mountain sides. The distance from Buckeye ranch in Yuba county to Quincy, the county seat of Plumas, is thirty miles. It was over this portion of the route, that Whiting & Co., of the Feather river express, employed their winter "man pack train." In the winter of 1857, Mr. J. B. Whiting undertook the Dog Express enterprise, and the plan has worked very successfully during the last four seasons. The Express runs regularly, carrying from two hundred and fifty to five hundred pounds freight according to the snow; and in ordinary times one passenger in addition to the freight may find accommodation in the sledge. When the snow is compact, the trip is easily performed in ten hours. During the storm, men are sent out on snow shoes to keep the trail open, and we believe the Dog Express never once met with interruption. The Dogs, of which four are driven to a sledge, are harnessed "á tandem." These animals are of a cross between the Alpine spaniel, or "Bernardine," and the Newfoundland—the noblest fellows of their race. The peculiar characteristics of the Bernardine dog—its almost human sagacity and untiring patience in discovering and rescuing passengers from the snow drift—are familiar to the mind of every child who has read or heard of the convent on the top of Mount St. Bernard. The Newfoundland is no less entitled to our respect and confidence. His "deeds of heroism" are also recorded in history. In his native Island, the Newfoundland is employed almost exclusively as a beast of burthen. He hauls wood all winter and fish all summer. An association of such traits of character as are found in the Bernardine and Newfoundland must be just the combination suited to the Express business, and we only wonder that enterprises similar to that of Whiting and Company have not been adopted in other portions of the State, to meet the requirements for quick dispatch in the transmission of mail matter.

There are several varieties of the dog race that seem to have been intended for the Express business in winter time.

The "Esquimaux" dog, for instance, is a splendid traveler. He will go along easily with an hundred and twenty pounds over the snow, at the rate of seven or eight miles an hour; and an instance is recorded of three of them having performed one mile in six minutes, drawing a sled weighing one hundred pounds, together with the driver.

The dog of Labrador is another peculiarly adapted to snow travel. He is very large, broad-chested, strong, active. The dog, when properly trained and cared for, is always the friend of man.

HUTCHINGS'

CALIFORNIA MAGAZINE.

VOL. I. NOVEMBER, 1856. NO. V.

MOUNTAIN SCENERY IN CALIFORNIA.

There is a wild, bold, and beautiful
magnificence in the mountain scenery
of California, that strikes the mind of
those who look upon it for the first
time, with feelings of delight and awe.
Its pine-crested hills; its deep moun-
tain-gorges; its towering and rugged
cliffs; its dark and densely-timbered
forests; its impetuous and foaming cat-
aracts; its rolling and surging streams;
its deep and shadowy cañons; its
cabin-dotted and miner-tenanted ravines; its populous and busy mining
towns; with all the diversified landscape of hill and dale, and all the variety of active mining life, and difference
in method of living and working; that,
while it pleases by its novelty, interests and charms by its mystery and
singularity.

It is our pleasing task, this month,
to place before the reader some of
those scenes, and to give a brief sketch
of each engraving. Commencing with

A MINER'S CABIN, NEAR PINE GROVE, SIERRA
COUNTY.

There is a peculiarity in the construction and appearance of cabins in

ONION VALLEY AND PILOT PEAK.

the northern part of Sierra county that is not often seen elsewhere. This consists in the roof being about twice the length of ordinary ones, with one end enclosed as a dwelling-house, the other being left open and occupied as a shed for firewood. The necessity and convenience of this arrangement will be seen at once, when we mention that snow often falls to a very great depth, completely burying up every thing. Even the ditches which supply these districts with water have to be timbered over to prevent them from being choked up.

ONION VALLEY.

During the winter of 1852 and '53, snow fell in Onion Valley to the depth of twenty-five feet, entirely covering up every building in it. Had this fallen in 1851, it would have caused an excess of suffering seldom heard of, for at that time it was supposed to be the business centre of a very large dis-

trict, and the head-quarters for Rich Bar, Hottentot, Nelson Creek, Hopkins', Dickson's, and Poor Man's Creeks. Even the towns of Gibsonville, Seventy-Six, Pine Grove, Whiskey Diggings, and several others, did their trading here. So that stores, hotels, gambling houses, &c., &c., went up with the magical rapidity of many California towns, and a population of nearly three thousand souls collected there. Fortunately, as other little towns sprung up, and trading posts were established at them, Onion Valley became gradually deserted; and, when this heavy fall of snow came, there were but about one hundred and twenty persons remaining. The few houses shown in the engraving were all that withstood the immense weight of snow —and there were no less than thirteen hotels, besides stores, and other buildings—and even to save these it became necessary to cut down the liberty poles and draw them in to use as props. We can easily imagine how much suffering, and even death, the falling buildings would have caused, had they been occupied, independent of the scarcity of provisions so severely felt that winter.

A passage was dug by the inhabitants, under the snow, from "The Miner's Retreat" to "The Golden Gate," whereby they might communicate with each other in their snow-walled prison.

A short time after the thaw had commenced, and a portion of the roof of "The Miner's Retreat" had become bare, the wolves discovered it, and paid their nightly visits, to howl, while they warmed their feet.

This is said to be the highest valley in the world that is yet settled. Now it contains only one store, one boarding-house and outbuildings for the convenience of "packers" passing through to other places.

"Pilot Peak," in the distance, "Slate Creek Mountain," and the "Downieville Buttes," are the highest points of land within a circumference of seventy miles, and are considered to be about eleven thousand feet above the sea; but their actual height, we believe, has not yet been determined.

VIEW OF NELSON POINT.

NELSON POINT Is a very romantic little settlement at the junction of Nelson Creek and the middle fork of Feather river, about ten miles north of Onion Valley. Lying as it does, just underneath the hill, as you descend from the valley, it is not seen until you are within a few yards of it.

Being upon the main pack-trail from

Gibsonville to American Valley, and the central point of trade for Nelson Creek, Rich Bar, and other places, besides being surrounded by a rich mining district, it is a town of considerable importance.

The population in the summer is about six hundred; and, in the winter, one hundred and fifty. When we were there, not very long ago, there were eight resident families, but *only one* marriageable lady! and we thought that had there even been as many as there were little fishes after feeding the multitude in the days of our Saviour—that being only a pair—we might exclaim, with wonder (and compassion), as did the unbelieving Andrew, "what are they among so many?"

At Henpeck City, about half a mile up Nelson Creek, during the summer months, there is about five hundred ounces of gold dust taken out weekly, which, with the amount bought at Nelson Point, would make the nett weekly product in this section about thirteen hundred ounces. About three and a half miles below, at the head of Rich Bar, there is a singular mountain, about two thousand feet high, in which there is a crater about eight feet in diameter at the top, and of a depth yet unascertained.

The whole of the scenery here is very singular and beautiful.

VIEW OF GIBSONVILLE.

GIBSONVILLE.

This is a prosperous mining town of about seven hundred inhabitants, situated on the "divide" between the middle fork of Feather river and the north fork of Slate creek, about four miles south of Pilot Peak, seventy miles north-northeast of Marysville.

The diggings are tolerably deep and pay regularly and well, from the surface down, although nine-tenths of the gold is found upon the rock, and is generally coarse. In the *water season*, there is about *three thousand ounces* of gold dust taken out here, *weekly*, although there is but about *one hundred and twenty ounces* taken out *weekly* in the *dry season*. We would earnestly invite the attention of the public to this fact: the GREAT WANT OF CALIFORNIA IS WATER for miners to work with.

The country around is wild and mountainous, and one vast forest of pines, firs and cedars.

About half past nine o'clock on the morning of Jan. 1st, 1855, when the inhabitants were peacefully sleeping, many were suddenly awakened by the rushing of a violent wind, almost resembling a hurricane; and, being surrounded by trees, they left their beds in haste, and with anxiety awaited the result. Mr. W. H. Alcoe and Mr. S. Snyder had kindled a fire, and just sat them down beside it, when a fir tree fell across the cabin, without doing the least injury. Mr. Lowell, hearing the trees fall all around him, became somewhat alarmed, and went out of his cabin to see where he could go for safety. He had scarcely reached the outside when a large tree fell upon the cabin and completely crushed it. One end of one of the logs struck Mr. L. on the shoulder and threw him several feet, without any further injury than a good shaking and a worse frightening.

Dr. Rutherford, wife and child, were soundly sleeping in their bed, when a large pine, almost four feet in diameter, fell across the cabin and crushed it to within about two feet of the bed. The neighbors, hearing the crash, and thinking the inmates were injured, if not killed, ran immediately to the spot, and soon received the cheering news that all were safe; as the branches of the fallen tree had blocked up and fastened the door, it was immediately broken open; and, ere they had left the building ten minutes, the tree settled entirely down to the bed.

VIEW OF KANAKA CREEK.

Several trees fell on other cabins and leveled them with the earth, yet no one was hurt.

Mr. Alcoe's cabin, unfortunately, caught fire, which destroyed all of his goods and provisions; and, as if to complete the destruction, two other trees fell upon it while it was burning.

The same wind did considerable damage on Hopkins Creek, about eight miles northeast of Gibsonville. One large tree fell upon a two-story hotel, in the bedroom of which fourteen men were sleeping, and who were precipitated into the bar-room below without ceremony, and the building was shivered to atoms; yet not a human life was taken, nor a bone broken, although eighteen hogs which were sleeping underneath the floor of the hotel were instantly killed.

KANAKA CREEK, SIERRA COUNTY.

Few who have never seen them can conceive how deep are the furrows in the face of nature in some portions of the mountain heights of California. The view before us was taken from just below the emigrant road, on the divide between Wolf and Kanaka creeks, looking west, towards Marysville, with the coast range in the distance, and gives an excellent idea of the situation of some of the mining towns that are built on the very edge of these very deep and steep canons. Here " Chips Diggings " is seen on the left bank, and " Smith's " on the right, in the great " Blue Lead " of Sierra county, and which are some of the first mining towns the emigrant reaches after crossing the Plains by way of Beckworth's Pass and Seventy-Six.

FLUMING SCENE ON SCOTT'S RIVER.

The illustration above pictures a fluming company's claim on Scott's river, Siskiyou county, just after the water of the river had been turned through the flume.

The claim, with many others on this river, proved very rich. It was no uncommon event to take from six to ten pounds of gold from a single pan of pay dirt, and a single day's labor of the company to pay from five to seven thousand dollars.

An almost incredible amount of labor and money has been invested in river mining in California; and although vast quantities of the precious metal have been produced, and men have been made rich—very rich, in a single summer, it is our conviction that, as yet, more gold has been invested in river mining than has ever been realized from it, as a whole.

Miners nevertheless hope on, and try their chances in this honorable kind of lottery—some to win, many to lose.

There is a much larger number of men at work on this river this season than on any previous one, and most of them are doing well.

The "bank" diggings pay regularly very good wages; and, were it not for the very heavy "stripping" required, men could take out a competency in a single year.

VIEW NEAR LANCHAPLANA, MOKELUMNE RIVER.

This view was taken just below the flourishing little town of Lanchaplana, on the Mokelumne river, a short distance from Winter's Bar.

The wheels shewn in the foreground of the engraving are used for the purpose of elevating water from the river, with which to wash the pay dirt that is carted from the diggings to the river for that purpose.

SCENE ON THE COSUMNES RIVER.

There are but few among the ever beautiful and picturesque scenes of California that are more pleasing to the eye than the one before us; and, when the snow is melting in the mountains, and the water of the river is high, and rushes past you with booming and impetuous haste, it is one almost of enchantment.

When the Indians first saw Chinamen at work on this river, just above this spot, there arose a dispute among them as to whether Chinamen were Indians (!) or not—one party arguing that they were an inferior kind of In-

Indians that lived far over the big water; and the other, that their eyes and general expression of the face, in no way resembled those of an Indian; consequently they could not belong to the Indian people at all. They all, however, came to one conclusion, that if Chinamen were Indians (!) they could certainly swim. This being decided upon, they soon determined to prove the fact; and, while a Chinaman was crossing a log (when the river was at its highest,) the Indians, without any further ado, quietly pushed him into the surging stream and drowned him! This at once set the question at rest; and all are now agreed that *Chinamen are not Indians!*

VIEW ON THE COSUMNES RIVER.

AN INTELLIGENT SOVEREIGN.—One of the Republican canvassers tells a hard story of an incident which came under his notice during the campaign just closed. He proposed to speak in a strong Democratic precinct in the mountains. Arriving at the place, he found two men engaged in active and violent discussion. One man was offering to bet $10 that St. Louis is the capital of the United States! Another gave vent to his opinion as follows: "The people of the north dissolve this glorious Union! Why they can't begin to do it! Just let them try it once, and the people of the south would close the port of New Orleans in a jiffy! That would at once put a stop to all the trade and commerce of the north! The northerners couldn't get out, no way!" The Republican concluded that the schoolmaster was too far away from home for him to do any good there.

LA PORTE, SIERRA COUNTY, CALIFORNIA.

HOW well do we remember the few agreable days, spent in this mining town in the winter of 1856; when snow was several feet in depth, and still falling. To sit in the cozy cabin by the large log fire, and listen to the cheerful converse of the miners, when the snow-king had driven them from their daily labors, and clogged the water ditches, was a time to be remembered. We have often thought that mining, if the claim pays well, is one of the most independent and pleasant of all occupations in the mountains—even while ad-

STREET VIEW OF LA PORTE, SIERRA COUNTY.

mitting that it is very laborious and fatiguing. But to the history.

In 1859 the *Mountain Messenger*, published at La Porte, gave a very interesting account of several mining towns in Sierra county, among which was the one here illustrated, and we know that we cannot do better than present that histtory to the reader, as there given.—

This flourishing place is pleasantly situated on the north side of Rabbit Creek, on the dividing ridge between the Yuba and Feather Rivers, about sixty-eight miles north of Marysville, and twenty miles from Downieville; and during the winter season is the highest point of the Sierra Nevadas reached by passenger trains. The altitude of La Porte is about four thousand five hundred feet above the sea level.

There is but very little definite or accurate information concerning the time of the discovery of gold in this part; but the year 1851 is generally admitted to be the time. The name of the discoverer is not now known, and probably this very important item in the town's history will ever remain among the things unchronicled.

Mr. Hackett, now a resident of Gardiner's Point, in this county, worked on Rabbit Creek in 1851, and is now the only person residing in this vicinity who was a resident at that early period.

Several stories are rumored in regard to the origin of the name by which this place was known till the year 1857; but the following has the precedence for correctness: some miners who were working, on what is now known as the West Branch, one evening were returning from their labors, when they saw a rabbit.— The sight being a rather novel one in this altitudinous region, the name RABBIT CREEK, was given to the stream; afterwards to the town—if we may dignify a few cabins by that name. In the year 1855, when a Postoffice was established, the name Rabbit Town was assumed.

The year 1851 marks an important era in the history of this town—in that year Siller's Ditch, the first brought into the place, was completed.

EVENTS IN THE YEAR 1852.

The succeeding season, 1852, is also a memorable one in the recollection of the old residents of the town. In this year the Rabbit Creek House, the first building erected in the town, was built by Mr. Eli S. Lester, still a resident of La Porte. He had commenced selling goods here in April of that year. The Lexington House, two miles south of this place, built in 1851, was at this time the head of team navigation on what was known as the Jamison route; and from the Lexington, all goods and provisions for more northern points, were packed.

In this year, the first hill diggings were opened on Rabbit Creek. The "Sailor Boys," Hillard & Co., Harrison & Co., O'Hara & Co., Hackett & Co., Brown & Co., Wagoner & Co., and Hudson & Co., opened claims on the West Branch, and E. C. Smith & Co., and Newton & Co., on the East Branch. The completion of Lester's Ditch afforded increased facilities for mining, adding considerably to the prosperity of the camp.

The latter part of the winter, '52 and 53, formed the most disagreeable season ever known in this locality. The snow averaged fifteen feet in depth, and was accompanied by very cold, boisterous weather. There may have been nearly as severe weather, as much snow, and as keen freezing since that time, but ample preparations have been made for the advent of the storm-king, and precautions which could not be taken at that early day, have contributed to make the winters much more pleasant than the one which will be remembered by the old settler, as an epoch in his life to be looked back upon with commingled feelings of joy and sadness.

Provisions this year were very scarce, and many articles not to be procured by any means, consequently high prices were demanded. Something of an idea of the prices of early times may be formed from the following list of rates:— Flour, 50 cts. per pound; pork, 65 cts.; coffee, 50 cts.; sugar, 45 cts.; butter, $1; and fresh beef—seldom to be obtained— sold for fifty cents per pound.

There were but two buildings on the present site of the town, at the close of this year; a log structure erected by Robert Bruce & Co., and Lester's building, to which we have previously alluded. But two families, Jacob Peters, wife and child, and Isaac Griffith and lady, resided here during the winter. About one hundred miners wintered on the Creek, in cabins erected near their claims, during the preceding summer.

The mines, taking into consideration the facilities for working, paid very well in 1852.

EVENTS IN THE YEAR 1853.

In the year 1853, but few improvements had been made, although the claims about were paying well.

Two stores—one kept by E. S. Lester, and the other by Mortimer Cook—carried on a fair business.

This year was a remarkable one in the history of mining in this section; being the time when hydraulic sluicing, or as it is more commonly called, "piping," was introduced. Mr. Eli Lester, (Eli Straight,) now residing in Sonoma Co., was among the first to introduce the new system of mining. The nozzle attached to the hose first used, measured but one inch in diameter.

The new manner of sluicing away the dirt was found to be a great improvement on the old method, and was generally adopted the same season. About fifty companies worked on Rabbit Creek during the water season, and as a general thing were amply rewarded for their labors.

EVENTS IN THE YEAR 1854.

During the year following, 1854, the town began to improve rapidly. More buildings were erected in the spring and summer than had been built previous to that time. Mr. Thomas Tregaskis built a dwelling house; A. Lefevre, a butcher shop; Henry Smith, a dwelling house; J. W. Perry, *alias* "Chicago," a blacksmith shop; Allen & Ball, a house; Davis & Smith, a tin shop; Everts, Davis & Co., an express office; Rigby & Co., a saw mill, on the south side of Rabbit Creek; Wells, Fargo & Co., an express and banking office.

Cutler Arnold took possession of the Rabbit Creek House in December.

Two casualities, the first that occurred here, took place this year. A man named Jenkins was killed by the falling of a tree. Another man (name unknown) was killed by the accidental discharge of a gun in his own hands. The small pox became prevalent and took away a number of victims.

In October of this year, M. D. Harlow murdered Henry Smith, in the vicinity of Rigby's mill. The circumstances of this murder are well known, and we will consequently make but a brief allusion to them. Harlow boarded at the house of Smith, who was a married man. The two men were chopping saw-logs, south of Rabbit Creek, on the 11th of October. Thomas Tregaskis, in passing the place, saw the form of Smith lying beneath a pile of brush, the head fractured in five places. Harlow, who was seated with an ax in his hand, requested Tregaskis to stop, but the latter appearing to pay no attention to his conversation, and apparently unobserving the murdered man, proceeded to town, and gave the alarm. Several persons repaired to the scene of the murder, and found Smith's corpse lying on the snow. Harlow had, in the meantime, made his escape. In about a year afterward he was arrested at San

Francisco, taken to Downieville and tried in the 14th Judicial District, before Judge Searls; H. B. Cossitt, district attorney, for the prosecution; W. S. Spear and R. H. Taylor, for the defense. He was found guilty of murder in the first degree, sentenced, and hung on the 18th of April, 1856.

EVENTS IN THE YEAR 1855.

The town continued to improve in the year 1855. Quite a number of good buildings were erected: Madame Cayote built the Hotel de France; Murray, the Kitt's Hotel, (now called the Union); Jacob Peters, a brewery and hotel; V. Bona, the El Dorado saloon; Dan Daley & Co., a bowling Alley; besides various dwellings erected in different parts of the town.

Messrs. Cook, Fuller & Buell, and Loeb, were engaged in mercantile business.

The introduction of a still greater supply of the needful water, by the Martindale ditch, formed an occasion for rejoicing among the miners.

A meeting was held in American Hall, December 22d, for the purpose of agitating the question for the division of the county, from which period the continued efforts of the citizens have their first date.

During this year, a never to be forgotten event occurred, which for a time cast a gloom over the State, from which it did not soon recover: we allude to the failure of Adams & Co. About the time the news of the failure came to this town, Mr. F. D. Everts, then agent for Adams & Co., received instructions to forward all specie on hand to the principal office at San Francisco. Many miners, merchants and others, who had made deposits, called on Mr. E., and were promptly paid, as long as a dollar remained in the office. He preferred paying the money to the honest, but too confidential depositor, to giving it to the unscrupulous, and we may add, dishonest bankers. This act of honesty on the part of Mr. Everts is well worth recording, and adds another proof to the many that our community is not destitute of men who possess integrity.

EVENTS IN THE YEAR 1856.

In 1856, Fuller & Buell erected their fire-proof brick store—*this was the first brick building built in Sierra county.* The same season H. C. Brown finished his brick store, and the same year sold goods in it.

John Conly opened a banking house, for the purpose of buying gold dust and doing a general banking business.

A man named John J. Rousch, (a soda water pedler, from the valley,) committed suicide at Kitt's Hotel, May 18th, by taking laudanum. He had been in a state of despondency for some time, and finding himself a prey to dissipation and gambling, and not having the moral strength to conquer these demons, he concluded to launch his frail life bark in the untried waters of death. Rousch left a wife and children in the Atlantic States.

On the 3rd of October, C. Stockman, better known as "Coush," was killed by a man named Betts, at the "Pontoosuc," a house of ill-fame, situated in the upper part of the town. Betts and one of the female occupants of the house were in a sleeping apartment together, when Coush knocked at the door and demanded admittance, and upon being refused he broke open the door. Some words were exchanged, whereupon Betts shot him. Immediately after the killing of Coush, Betts made his escape to Salt Lake, where he remained for several months, during which time he held an office under the Government. He afterwards returned to this State, was arrested in Oroville, taken to Gibsonville, in this county, where he was tried and acquitted.

In 1856, a number of good paying

claims were opened, several main and branch tunnels were run, and the diggings yielded a much larger amount of gold than had been taken out at any former season. Notwithstanding the depressed financial state of affairs which existed in many of the mining towns of this State, caused by the heavy failures the year previous, La Porte, or as it was then called, Rabbit Creek, felt but slightly the shock which had almost paralyzed many of its sister towns.

EVENTS IN THE YEAR 1857.

In 1857, the people, having a dislike to the name by which the town was called, held a meeting, and resolved to substitute LA PORTE for Rabbit Creek. Accordingly on the 16th of October, the name was changed, and in the language of Moore (slightly altered):

What was Rabbit then, is La Porte now.

On the 26th of April, a murder and suicide was committed, the particulars of which are still familiar to many citizens. A man named Harry Yates, an individual of rather intemperate habits, lived on the creek, and was deeply in love with a young lady named Miss Caroline Young. His demonstrations of love were not cordially received by the young woman, and being of desperate character, he resolved to either win her affections, or kill her. He went to the house of her brother-in-law, a Mr. Anderson, and immediately after his arrival, he went into a room where the girl was. He asked her to marry him, and upon being refused, drew a pistol and fired, killing her instantly. He then shot himself through the neck, lay down by the side of the murdered girl, and finding that his first attempt at self-murder had not proved effectual, he arose, put his revolver on a table, took a derringer, placed it to his head, and ended the tragedy by blowing out his brains.

EVENTS IN THE YEAR 1858.

The year 1858 was a prosperous one. The water season was as lengthy as usual, better facilities were afforded for mining than had been at any former season, and notwithstanding the Frazer river stampede, La Porte was in a healthy financial condition. Many valuable claims were opened, which though scarcely prospected, last season, amply remunerated the owners for their labors. The town rapidly improved; many valuable buildings—among others, the fireproof banking house erected by John Conly—were put up. Prominent in the improvement line, was the project—talked of years ago, but never carried out till last summer—by which the town was to be amply supplied with water. The water is brought from a spring, which is one mile from Everts, Wilson & Co's Express office, through logs which are laid below the surface. The spring is 75 or 80 feet above the level of the town, never failing, and not excelled for its purity and coldness. All the stores, and nearly all the family dwellings in the place are supplied by water which is conveyed to the buildings by hydrants. To the energy of B. W. Barns our citizens are indebted for this improvement.

MOUNTAIN MESSENGER.—In August, 1856, Myers & Head removed the *Mountain Messenger* printing establishment to this place, from Gibsonville, where the paper had formerly been published. It was published under this firm for two successive years, when A. L. Smith purchased Mr. Head's interest. Myers and Smith continued in partnership some four months, at the expiration of which time Mr. M. became sole proprietor, and continued as such until 1858, when Mr. Wm. Y. Head again became its publisher. Mr. H. continued its publication to the 1st of January, 1859, when A. T. Dewey was received into partnership; the paper appeared in new dress, machine job presses and new type were added to the office, rendering it the most complete newspaper and job printing establishment in the mining towns of this State. The paper is in a prosperous condition, and steadily increasing in circulation.

RABBIT CREEK FLUME.—This important acquisition to the mines in Rabbit Creek was located in June, 1857, by Wm. H. Reed and J. M. Barry. Work was commenced in July, and the same season the flume was finished to the bridge, a distance of 1,000 feet. The proprietors, Messrs. Reed, Underhill, Bourom and Barry, have continued the flume to the length of 2,850 feet, with a branch flume up the East Branch a distance of 1,000 feet. The intention is to run the main flume 2,500 feet farther. Dimensions of flume: 6 feet in width (below the dam), above, 5 feet, (board flume), and branch flume, 3 by 4½ feet wide.

The Rabbit Creek Flume has already proved beneficial to the miners on the Creek, and when completed cannot fail to accomplish results which must add largely to the wealth of La Porte. Many miners on Rabbit Creek will be ready to run tailings through the flume in the coming spring, and when it is completed there will be an opportunity to work one hundred valuable claims.

WATER DITCHES.—There are now four ditches coming into this place. The Martindale ditch carries forty sluice-heads of water, Feather River ditch sixty, Yankee Hill ditch twenty-five, and John C. Fall's sixty—making a total of 185 sluice heads, all of which are used during the mining season.

THE TOWN—ITS PROSPECTS.

The town now contains thirty-five business houses—has a number of wholesale establishments, which do an extensive business in selling goods to many of the miners and retail dealers in the adjoining mining camps. An extensive travel passes through La Porte, both in summer and winter, and during the former season a semi-daily line of stages runs to this place.

A brisk business season is expected as soon as water comes, and mining commences. Fifteen companies will be ready to work in a few weeks; and about three hundred miners will be at work on Rabbit Creek next season. Some of the most valuable claims in the mountains were opened last fall, and when worked, next season, a bountiful golden yield may be looked for.

SANDWICH ISLANDER.

KNIGHT'S FERRY.

W.C. BUTLER. S.F.

— 149 —

VIEW OF IOWA HILL, PLACER COUNTY, CALIFORNIA.

FOREST CITY, SIERRA COUNTY, CALIFORNIA.

HUTCHINGS'

CALIFORNIA MAGAZINE.

VOL. III.   MAY, 1859.   No. 11.

SCENES IN THE VALLEYS AND MOUNTAINS OF CALIFORNIA.

NIGHT SCENE ON THE SAN JOAQUIN RIVER—MONTE DIABLO IN THE DISTANCE.

THERE are but few persons to whom the admiration of the beautiful in nature is not an innate inspiration to a greater or less degree. With different habits of thought in different mental organizations, it may assume various forms and qualities, but the principle is the same.

To some, the graceful form or lithe movement of an animal, or the face, figure and carriage of a beautiful woman or handsome man, may be the most attractive style of beauty in existence. Others will look upon a broad meadow carpeted with flowers, or a quiet stream and placid lake, whose burnished bosom reflects the image of every object upon its margin ; and, as they watch the shadows chasing each other across it, think it the most charming of any ever witnessed: while to others, the impetuous torrent, as it dashes and foams and eddies among rocks, or rushes over a precipice, and at one bold leap breaks itself into myriads of atoms, is the embodiment of all that is grand and lovely and beautiful. Yet to others, no sight is so creative of delightful emotion as the examination of the minute and wonderful; such, for instance, as the downy petals of a flower, or the numerous scales and shades of color that blend into each other on the body of an insect or crest of a bird.

The love of everything beautiful may be possessed in an eminent degree by a single individual; but we never knew one to whom *every* form of beauty was alike inviting. Control our tastes as we may, there are some individuals whom we like in a greater degree than we do others, and often without being able to assign a reason. It is thus with the beautiful in nature; preferences for this or that particular class will exist, and often we do not know why. Yet it is well.

The engraving given on the first page of this number of the magazine will present one of those beautiful scenes that are sometimes to be witnessed in the valleys at night, from the deck of a steamboat. The serpentine course of the San Joaquin, lighted up by the moon and the tules on fire, every voyager to or from Stockton can perhaps remember. In the foreground of the picture is the boat from whence our sketch was taken. In the shadowy distance looms up Monte Diablo.

Almost every Californian has seen Monte Diablo. It is the great central landmark of the State. Whether we are walking in the streets of San Francisco; or sailing on any of our bays and navigable rivers; or riding on any of the roads in the Sacramento and San Joaquin val-

leys; or standing on the elevated ridges of the mining districts, before us, in lonely boldness, and at almost every turn, we see Monte del Diablo. Probably from its apparent omnipresence we are indebted to its singular name, *Mount of the Devil.*

Viewed from the north-west or south-east, it appears double, or with two elevations, the points of which are about three miles apart. The south-western peak is the most elevated, and is 3,760 feet above the sea.

For the purpose of properly surveying the State into a net-work of township lines, three meridians or initial points were established by the U. S. Survey, namely: Monte Diablo, Mount San Bernardino, and Mount Pierce, Humboldt County. Across the highest peaks of each of these, a "meridian line" and a "base line" were run; the latter from east to west, and the former from north to south. The boundaries of the Monte Diablo meridian include all the lands in the great Sacramento and San Joaquin valleys, between the Coast Range and the Sierras, and from the Siskiyou Mountains to the San Bernardino meridian, at the head of the Tulare Valley.

The geological formation of this mountain is what is usually termed "primitive;" surrounded by sedimentary rocks, abounding in marine shells. Near the summit there are a few quartz veins, but whether gold-bearing or not has not yet been determined. About one-third of the distance from the top, on the western slope, is a "hornblende" rock of peculiar structure, and said by some to contain gold. In the numerous spurs at the base, there is an excellent and inexhaustible supply of limestone.

At the eastern foot of the mountains, about five miles from the San Joaquin river, three veins of stove coal have been discovered; and are now being worked with good prospects of remuneration, as

MONTE DIABLO, FROM THE BANKS OF THE SLOUGH NEAR STOCKTON.

the veins grow thicker and the quality better as they proceed with their labors.

It is said that copper ore and cinnabar have both been found here, but with what truth we are unable to determine. Some Spaniards have reported that they know of some rich mineral there ; but, do not tell of what kind, and for reasons best known to themselves will neither communicate their secret to others nor work it themselves.

If the reader has no objection, we will climb the mountain — at least, in imagination—and see what further discoveries we can make.

Now, after a substantial breakfast, being provided with good horses—always make sure of the latter on any trip you may make, reader—an excellent telescope, and a liberal allowance of luncheon, let us leave Martinez at seven o'clock. For the first four miles we ride over a number of pretty and gently rolling hills, at a lively gait, and arrive at the Pacheco Valley, on the edge of which stands the flourishing little village of Pacheco. We now dash across the valley at good speed for eight miles, in a south east direction, and reach the western foot

of Diablo after a good hour's pleasant ride.

For the first mile and a half of our ascent, we have a good wagon road, built in 1852 to give easy access to a quartz lead, from which considerable rock was taken in wagons to the Bay of Suisun, and from thence shipped to San Francisco to be tested, and which was found to contain gold, but not in sufficient quantities to pay for working it; and for the next two miles, a good, plain trail, to the main summit, passing several clear springs of cold water.

From the numerous tracks of the grizzly bears that were seen at the springs we may naturally conclude that such animals have their sleeping apartments among the bunches of chaparal in the cañons yonder ; and if we should see the track makers before we return, we hope our companions will keep up their courage, and sufficient presence of mind to prevent themselves imitating Mr. Grizzly at the spring—at least not in the direction of the settlements, and leave us alone in our glory.

As you will perceive, the summit of the mountain is reached without the necessity of our dismounting; and as there are wild oats all around, and the stores of sundries provided have not been lost or left behind, suppose we rest and refresh ourselves, and allow our animals to do the same.

The sight of the glorious panorama unrolled at our feet, we need not tell you, amply repays us for our early ride. As we look around us we may easily imagine that perhaps the priests who named this mountain may have climbed it, and as they saw the wonders spread out before them, recalled to memory the following passage of holy writ:—" The devil taketh him [Jesus] up into an exceeding high mountain, and sheweth him all the kingdoms of the world, and the glory of them; and saith unto him, all these things will I give thee, if thou wilt fall down and worship me. Then saith Jesus unto him,

get thee hence, Satan &c.," *Matt. 4th, verses 8 and 9*; and from this time called it Monte del Diablo. Of course this is mere supposition, and is as likely to be wrong as it is to be right.

The Pacific Ocean; the city, and part of the bay of San Francisco; Fort Point; the Golden Gate; San Pablo and Suisun Bays; the Government works at Mare Island; Vallejo; Benicia; the valleys of Santa Clara, Petaluma, Sonoma, Napa, Sacramento and San Joaquin, with their rivers, creeks and sloughs, in all their tortuous windings; the cities of Stockton and Sacramento; and the great line of the snow-covered Sierras; with numerous villages doting the pine forests on the lower mountain range—are all spread out before you. In short, there is nothing to obstruct the sight in any direction; and

THE SULPHUR SPRING HOUSE, WITH A PORTION OF SUISUN BAY, AND MONTE DIABLO.

[*Sketched from nature, by J. A. Rankin.*]

with a good glass the steamers and vessels at anchor in the bay, and made fast at the wharves of San Francisco, are distinctly visible.

Stock may be seen grazing in all directions on the mountains. To the very summit, wild oats and chaparal alternate.

In the cañons are oak and pine trees from fifty to one hundred feet in height; and on the more exposed portions there are low trees from twenty to thirty feet in height.

In the fall season, when the wild oats and dead bushes are perfectly dry, the

SUTTER'S BUTTES, NEAR MARYSVILLE.

Indians sometimes set large portions of the surface of the mountains on fire; which, when the breeze is fresh and the night is dark, and the lurid flames leap and curl, and sway, now to this side, and now to that, the spectacle presented is magnificent beyond the power of language to express.

The "Sulphur mountain," at the foot of which is the spring and hotel, seen in the foreground of Mr. Rankin's sketch on the 484th page, is a well known local landmark, some six miles in a northwesterly direction from Benicia. Its bold, craggy top is in perfect contrast to the gently rolling hills that surround it. The waters of the spring which gush out at its base have long been known to the Indians and native Californians in this vicinity, for their medicinal properties. Judging from the numerous beds of shells to be found there—doubtless deposited by the Indians, who must have been fond of bi-

valves—it seems to have been a favorite place of resort. Be this as it may, the springs—which are slightly tepid, and of which there are two, but a few feet from each other—are highly impregnated with sulphur, soda, and other minerals; and valuable as a remedial agent in some bodily ailments. The springs were re-discovered and taken up by Milton Brockman, in 1855, and who, with others, built the present commodious hotel. If the proprietors had the taste and would take the trouble to beautify the grounds around, and then keep the hotel as it ought to be kept—which it certainly is not, now—it would become a fashionable place of resort, and very convenient to invalids from a distance.

Between the Sacramento and Feather rivers, about twelve miles west of Marysville, are "Sutter's Buttes," or, as they are sometimes called, the "Marysville Buttes." (The former, we think, should always be preferred, in honor of the illustrious California pioneer, Gen. John A. Sutter.)

This mountain towers boldly out like a large island above the plain on which it stands, to the height of 1800 feet, and is almost as great a landmark to the residents of this latitude, as Monte Diablo is to those of San Francisco. For a circumference of fifty miles, its uneven and hazy tops are visible above the belt of timber that grows in the valley and apparently girdles its base. From its shape, as much as from the scoria and other similar substances in great abundance upon and round about it, there can be but little doubt that this mountain is of volcanic origin, and of no recent date. It is moreover upon the same line as Monte Diablo and Mount Shasta. Trap, quartz, trachyte, and porphyry rocks are found at its base. Its circumference is about twenty-five miles.

Although we have tarried in the valleys a little too long, perhaps, we hope to have the pleasure of the reader's company on an excursion in the mountains, at least to a few of the localities; and in the first place pay a visit to

COLOMA,

Which is the euphonious name of one of the prettiest, and cleanest little towns in the mountains of California; and moreover of one that has the honor of being the mother of all the others! At first sight we are aware that the reader may possibly open his eyes with astonishment, and seem disposed very much to question the correctness of ascribing so large an amount of maternal fecundity, to so insignificant an object; but when we remind him that *at Coloma the first piece of California gold was discovered*, he will, we think, concede to us the parentage claimed.

It is a fact that in this beautiful valley, so pleasantly located on the south bank of the south fork of the American river,

James W. Marshall, E. Pierson, John Wimmer, W. H. Scott, A. Stephens, H. Bigler, J. Brown, Peter L. Wimmer, C. Bennett, and several others whose names we have not learned, were engaged in constructing a saw mill (seen to the left of the engraving, near the bank of the river) for Gen. John A. Sutter, when gold was discovered by Mr. Marshall, Jan. 19, 1848.

As our readers are well aware, this news was soon trumpeted abroad, and large numbers of persons flocked to the new El Dorado, (from this originated the name of the county in which Coloma is situated, and which became the county seat of El Dorado) and Coloma, from containing only a double log cabin and about eighteen persons, exclusive of Indians, became a large town with a population of between two and three thousand.

When we first became acquainted with Coloma, late in the fall of 1849, it contained several hotels, the principal of which was Winter's; and a long street of stores and dwelling houses. On the opposite or north side of the river, John T. Little formed the nucleus of a small settlement, by erecting a large hotel and other buildings. At that time the principal part of the village (as those on both sides of the river were called Coloma), on the south bank, was nearly as large as it now is, but of course was not as substancially built. Although there were some good diggings being worked near the village, and many persons were making money at mining, its principal support was from those persons who were passing through it to other places, on prospecting trips, to diggings supposed to be rich, between the south and middle forks of the American river, the principal of which were those in the vicinity of Georgetown and Oregon Cañon.

At that time meals were $2,00 each, and barley for mules sold at $1,00 per pound: other grains and hay, none.

VIEW OF COLOMA, EL DORADO COUNTY.   THE LOCALITY WHERE GOLD WAS FIRST
DISCOVERED.

From that time to the present, Coloma has experienced the ups and downs usual to most mining settlements where the population is ceaselessly changing. Nevertheless she now has a steady resident and flourishing people, who are the owners of some of the finest fruit orchards, vineyards and gardens, to be found in any of the mountain towns; and the possessors of some of the most extensive, and in many cases some of the most profitable mining claims in the State. Remunerative diggings are even found beneath the very houses of the town.

The removal of the county seat to Placerville in 1857, was a serious check to her prosperity for a time; but she is now rapidly regaining her former position. The activity seen in the long street of stores, offices and hotels, will tell their own story to the visitor. Churches and school houses; Masonic, Odd Fellows and Sons of Temperance Societies are all said to flourish here. Then, though "last yet not least," must be included among her most useful institutions, one of the best conducted newspapers in the State, "The Coloma Times," edited and published by G. O. Kies, which has our best wishes for the prosperity it so well deserves.

MARIPOSA

Is the most southerly of all the mining towns of importance in the State. Although it has suffered more, perhaps, than almost any other mining district for the want of water for mining purposes, owing to its quartz leads and rich flat, gulch, and hill diggings, it has generally been prosperous; and being the county seat, as well as the trading centre of numerous small camps around, its streets at certain seasons of the year present a very lively appearance. Two ably edited and spirited papers are issued weekly; one the "Mariposa Gazette," and the other the "Mariposa Star."

The population is about thirteen hundred, or about one seventh of the entire county.

It is here that the celebrated Fremont Grant is located.

Being an excellent starting point to the Yo-Semite valley and the Mariposa Grove of mammoth trees, it is likely to become a place famous to history and the note books of travelers. The neat, and tastefully cultivated gardens in the vicinity, give an air of freshness and home-like brightness that some other places we might mention, would do well to imitate The distance from Stockton to Mariposa is 91 miles, and the road good, upon which a line of stages is running daily.

VIEW OF MARIPOSA.

MOKELUMNE HILL.

HOWEVER much one mining town in California may be said to resemble another, generally speaking, Mokelumne Hill must certainly be considered an exception. If a stranger enters town, whether by the Stockton or Sacramento roads, the impression is almost invariably the same, "what an oddly situated and singularly constructed town this seems to be ?" This in a great measure was unavoidable as the rich diggings discovered here in the fall of 1849 created the necessity of a settlement, and as the town was located upon the most eligible spot that could be found, its builders were left but little choice in the matter; yet, standing as it does upon an elevated bench of the mountain, some eighteen hundred feet above the Mokelumne river ; its position is very commanding and picturesque, especially from the trail between Jackson and the hill

The rich gulch claims worked here in the winter of 1849 and '50 attracted a numerous population, many of whom were Mexican and Chilian. In the spring of 1851, diggings of almost fabulous richness were discovered and worked in Negro, French, and Stockton hills. From one claim on the former, of only fifteen feet square, over seventy-eight thousand dollars were taken out. Of course such profitable employment could not long remain a secret, and men began to flock there in great numbers ; but, as in many other cases, when they arrived, they found to their regret that all the good claims were taken up.

Many of our readers will call to mind the exciting scenes connected with the

MOKELUMNE HILL, CALAVERAS COUNTY.

long-to-be remembered "French War" which took place in 1851, under the following circumstances:—A Frenchman sunk a shaft on a spot which since then has been known as French Hill, and struck diggings of extraordinary richness, and which excited him to such a degree that nothing but the firing of numerous rounds of powder from an old musket could sufficiently satisfy his enthusiasm in demonstrating his joy. This very naturally called a crowd together to know what was going on: when, in hopes of being equally fortunate, several other persons, among whom were a number of Americans, staked off claims adjoining the Frenchman's. One of these persons whose name was Blankenship, having struck the same lead as the Frenchman, was not content with the product of his own claim, but must "follow the lead" into Frenchy's., When this was discovered the latter very loudly and bitterly, yet justly, complained in broken English, and a number of his countrymen flocked around him, who upon learning the facts would not allow Blankenship to remain there.

He immediately went to town and by unfair representations influenced a large party of Americans to go up with him to "clean out the Frenchmen;" when all their tents and tools were burnt, and the owners obliged to leave. Now, being discomfited, they went to Happy Valley, San Andres, and other places, and obtained reinforcements of their countrymen, who threatened to destroy the town of Mokelumne Hill, and lay violent hands upon everybody. By this time as the defenders of Blankenship had learned the true facts of the case, their enthusiasm had entirely cooled off and the Frenchman were allowed to discharge their chivalrous valor in their own way, and reinstate their countryman in his rightful claims, while the disconsolate cause of the whole, was required "to take his pick and his pan,

his shovel and his blankets, with all that he had, and go prospecting;" and it served him right.

The construction of the Mokelumne Hill Canal to the north fork of the river, in 1852, '53 and '54, at a cost of $600,000; a large proportion of which proved to be but a sorry investment to the original stockholders—attracted several thousands of miners to the vicinity, a few hundreds of whom found and worked tolerably remunerative diggings, and the others went empty away. This influx caused a comparatively large addition to the buildings and area of the settlement.

On the night of the 20th of August, 1854, the whole of this town, with the exception of a few buildings on Lafayette street, was reduced to ashes; but was speedily rebuilt, and in a much more substantial manner.

It is the county seat of Calaveras county, and the business centre of a large district, from whence miners draw most of their supplies.

Its resident population is about eleven hundred; with fewer families in proportion, perhaps, than any other town of the same size in the State. There are three churches—Methodist, Presbyterian, and Catholic—and one public school-house. A weekly paper, entitled the "Calaveras Chronicle," is here, edited and published by Mr. John Shannon; and, but for the too frequent and lengthy discussions of political questions, to the exclusion of much valuable local news, it is a faithful advocate and exponent of the interests of the county.

Mokelumne Hill being the county seat of Calaveras, and the business centre for Jesus Maria, West Point, Rich Gulch, Poison Gulch, El Dorado Cañon, Independence, Esperanza, Buckeye, Big and Middle Bar, and several other mining camps, it is destined to survive the ups and downs pertaining to mining towns in general, and will be Mokelumne Hill as long as mining is known. Besides, in addition to its hill and gulch mining, it has numerous quartz leads that are among the richest in the State. From a quarry of lava, or soft freestone, large blocks of excellent building material are easily hewn with an axe, which hardens when exposed to the atmosphere, and being unaffected by heat, could be made to supersede fire-brick. The court-house, and nearly all the fire-proof buildings in the town and vicinity, are constructed of this material.

In 1855, the flume of the Mokelumne Hill Canal was extended to Campo Seco, and other mining localities between the Calaveras and Mokelumne rivers, and supplied water to a large mining district, that before was without water, and consequently barren of results to the miner. In addition to this, large supplies of lumber are floated down the flume, from the company's saw-mills above, to the different camps upon the line of the canal.

ABBEY'S ROAD AND FERRY ACROSS THE STANISLAUS RIVER.

Those who have never crossed one of the deep cañons or rivers of the State, from one mining camp to another, in the upper mountain range, can form no idea of the difficulties and labor attending such an undertaking, especially before good stage roads were made. To the initiated we need give no description; but to others, perhaps, it is well that we should briefly describe them, that they may exercise some little sympathy for those who many times have had to per-

form the task; often, perhaps, in early mining experiences, with a sack of flour or a load of tools at their backs.

It is impossible for us to give the actual elevation of any of these mountain ridges above the beds of the streams where they are crossed, as they have not to our knowledge been measured with any pretensions to accuracy. Many persons have doubless given rough estimates of their probable height, that might perhaps approximate to correctness; but, of

FERRY SCENE ON THE COSUMNES.

course, such cannot be considered reliable authority, in the absence of actual
measurement. From the height of the
mountains that surround the great Yo-
Semite Valley, which have been measured, and are from three thousand five
hundred to four thousand five hundred
feet, we should think that from two thousand five hundred to three thousand five
hundred feet for those we are now considering would be a fair estimate. To
cross these high ridges and deep cañons
with vehicles, roads have been cut in the
sides of the mountains, from the bottom
to the top, at a low and regular grade, so
that heavily-freighted wagons, as well as
light carriages, can ascend and descend
with comparative ease and safety. At
some points excavations have been made
for the road in solid rock, and often where
the mountain side is nearly perpendicular. Of course the cost of such under-
takings is very large; but, owing to the
tolls collected, and the number of persons
and vehicles passing and re-passing, the
investment has generally proved a profitable one.

When riding in a carriage or stage on
such roads, there is generally an anxious
though perhaps silent hope that the
horses are steady and trustworthy, the
harness sound and in good order, the
running gear strong, and the coachman
not only sober, but an excellent and careful driver; lest a mishap should take us
on a sudden and undesired journey to
that land where, although many of our
acquaintances have preceded us, we are
not desirous of joining their pleasant
fellowship by such a hasty and unpre-
pared introduction.

On one occasion, a merry company of
travelers who had been to Columbia, Tuolumne County, to witness some combat-
ive entertainment—whether political or
pugilistic we are not going to state—and
on returning to Vallecito, Calaveras Co.,
via Abbey's Ferry, while descending the
hill, the driver, having imbibed a little
too freely, and formed a habit of seeing
double, mistook the side hill for the road,
and the horses, coach and passengers
were furiously hurried over the embank-
ment. Two of the horses were killed,

and a third badly injured, while the fourth escaped almost unhurt. The coach was reduced to infinitesimal fragments, and yet only one person was seriously injured. The driver escaped with scarcely a scratch; which would seem to endorse the correctness of the old adage—"A fool and a drunken man for luck." Had this accident occurred in one part of the descent, not one could have been saved to relate the story.

And although all countries may possess a fair quota, we are inclined to the belief that California endures rather more than her share, as every part of the world seems to have sent its representatives here.

LOAFERS.

TABLE MOUNTAIN FROM THE MONTEZUMA HOUSE.

TABLE MOUNTAIN FROM THE MONTEZUMA HOUSE.

The above beautiful scene of Table Mountain, Tuolumne county, is taken from the Montezuma House, about four miles below Jamestown, on the stage road between Stockton and Sonora. This very singular mountain, a few years since only admired for its curious beauty—now has a fame which is world-wide, for the immense wealth taken from beneath its dark volcanic-formed crust.

The miner, with his usual prospecting curiosity, and iron will, came to the conclusion that "there must be *gold* in *that* hill," and at once determined to know it by immediately commencing a tunnel. The company entitled to the honor of this enterprise, we believe, was the Table Mountain Tunnnel Company, near Jamestown, who, after running one tunnel for over five hundred feet, was obliged to begin another, about twenty feet lower than the first, in order to drain off the water. The second, or lower tunnel, was run nine hundred feet through solid rock before reaching gravel,

and upon which three thousand seven hundred and fifty-six days' labor were expended; besides the cost of tools, blasting powder, &c., &c.

This is another of the almost numberless instances of the unswerveing determination and perseverance of the miner, to obtain the reward so ardently desired for himself and family, and is the most expressive answer that can possibly be given to the oft repeated question—"Why does he tarry so long from his family and friends."

How very remunerative this proved but few ever heard, but sufficient was known to induce many others to follow the example, and now men are working with almost unparallelld success, from the one end of Table Mountain to the other, for a distance of over fifteen miles in length.

From its top a fine view of the surrounding country can be obtained, including the mining towns of Chinese Camp, Campo Seco, Montezuma, Belvidere, Poverty Hill, and several others, forming a panoramic view of great beauty and extent, which amply repays the visitor for his trouble in ascending it.

SUSPENSION FLUME ACROSS BRANDY GULCH.

SUSPENSION FLUME ACROSS BRANDY GULCH.

BY S——.

The engraving which we give above, from an ambrotype taken expressly for this work, represents a wire Suspension Flume, situated in the vicinity of Young's Hill, Yuba county.

The flume is intended to convey the waters of Clear Creek from the summit of one hill to that of another, across a deep ravine, called, from some mysterious cause, "Brandy Gulch." The survey was made less than twelve months ago, by D. Scott, Esq., who, by the way, has gained much reputation in this branch of science. But, independent of the great design, the mode of construction is remarkably ingenious; the flume, which is fifteen hundred feet in length, is elevated to a height of 206 feet in the air. A tower built from the bed of the ravine supports the centre, while at intervals of about a hundred feet stand tall

trees, the tops of which being cut away, contribute materially to the permanency of the structure. A cluster of small wires are secured at these points, from which is suspended the box, or flume.

Thus, by means of scarcely any perceivable agency, an artificial channel is formed, through which from four to five hundred inches of water is allowed to pass daily. It is, without doubt, a highly creditable piece of work, and reflects much credit upon its enterprising proprietors; but like the majority of newly tested projects, the originators pay dearly for their experiment, while others, of infinitely less skill and courage, reap the profits of the work. There are few experiments, of after consequence, which succeed well at first, and no important acquisition of knowledge has ever been gained but at a great sacrifice on the part of the discoverer.

Works like this, presenting themselves in every portion of the mining region of California, are the most striking evidences of the capacity for adaptation; and of which we are already sufficiently inclined to boast.

Wordsworth has somewhere said that " water is the spirit of the universe." If not so, water may at least be said to be the spirit of all our enterprise. The entire slope of the Sierra Nevadas, from the summit seaward, is pierced and traversed by artificial veins, which bring prosperity and life to every hill and plain. Water is the life-blood of the mines. When its current is diminished, or even delayed, every thing languishes — with its return, all things revive. Indeed, water has been so generally diffused, and so constantly employed, that it has been well said, "it is used for every thing but *drinking!*"

We all know that when the Roman matron was asked for her jewels, she pointed to her children ; when we are asked for ours, we may reply, less classically, but with equal truth : " Behold our ditches !"

Never, since the Roman legionry shadowed the earth with their eagles, in search of spoil — not even when Spain ravished the wealth of a world, or England devastated the Indies for its treasures — never has such a gorgeous treasury been opened to the astonished world.

But theirs was the genius of war ; ours the conquests of peace. The music of our march is the revelry of the gushing stream, and the only chains we forge are those that bind the captive water.

At a glance we see both the necessities and the advantages of application. The sheet of vapor which hangs in dreamy silence above the brow of the " Sierra," descends and gathers its misty mantle about the frail flower, which nods to the passing brook. As the morning sun melts the dewy tears, they fall into the stream and are borne along by the reckless current. On, on it glides, now struggling over rocks or craggy steeps, now dancing in the sunlight or kissing the weeping foliage which seeks to span the stream ; and now exulting in its liberty ; when, lo ! the bearded miner issues from his rude hut, and with imple-ments in hand, forthwith proceeds to chain the trembling drops. And still it struggles, but too soon the fetters are secure, and though it shrinks, yet it is urged on to its debasing destiny. All day it labors, and again night approaches, but as the tiny globulet surveys itself, how sadly changed ! Its face discolored ! the lustre of its eye is vanished ! in disgust it turns away to rest, not on the fair face of the pale flower, which cast it on the pitiless world, but to lose its identity among swarthy companions, in a neighboring pool.

Of Young's Hill, the terminus of the enterprise before described, but little may be said. It is a small village, of small importance, located some two miles north of Camptonville, and quite remote from the stage-route, as, indeed, from any point of consequence.

Mining is carried to a considerable extent in this vicinity, an accurate and comprehensive account of which branch of business will be reserved for those possessed of a more thoroughly practical knowledge or descriptive capacity.

To Messrs. Spencer & Adkinson much credit is due for promptneess, energy and enterprise. The flume, or " sluice," constructed by them, which carries the " refuse dirt " from the whole hill, is not only of inestimable value to the miners, and thereby to every other interest, but also promises to be a lucrative investment to its projectors.

The landscape views in this vicinity are, as in all portions of the State, both picturesque and grand. Truly " never need an American look beyond his own country for the sublime and beautiful in natural scenery."

There is a law—now almost forgotten—of no small importance to the human family; inasmuch as it makes everybody and his neighbor very happy. It is this—" As ye would that men should do unto you, do ye even so unto them." Now, gentle reader, what say you about giving it a trial.

HUTCHINGS'

CALIFORNIA MAGAZINE.

VOL. II.   OCTOBER, 1857.   No 4

QUARTZ MINING IN CALIFORNIA.

INSIDE OF A QUARTZ MILL AT GRASS VALLEY, NEVADA COUNTY.
[*From an Ambrotype by Woods & Michaels.*]

Quartz mining having ceased as a speculation, to become a business of profit and permanency, is again enlisting the attention and confidence of all classes to its importance. The losses and disappointments of its pioneers in the years 1851, '52, and '53, — originating, in most cases, from the excitement of its discoverers, and the inexperience of its principal owners and directors, — caused a temporary lull in the faith and enthusiasm of the public, to the great neglect of this exhaustless golden treasury: but as many of the quartz leads, then opened, proved very rich in the precious metal, they enabled their owners to make many experiments for working the quartz to advantage, by the invention and perfection of machinery for crushing the rock, and saving the gold ; and thus, while securing a personal advantage to themselves, they have been instrumental in rescuing the quartz interest in this State from the oblivion into which, doubtless, it would have sunk, for a season, had all the first attempts to make its working profitable failed.

The dearly-bought experience of the past in this branch of our State's wealth, now enables the practical worker in quartz generally to determine the quality of the rock placed before him, at a glance, and with the same accuracy and certainty as an experienced purchaser of gold-dust can decide the quality and mint value of the parcel of dust he is about to buy —or, as a merchant, by examination, knows the quality of the article offered him, and what is its market value — or, as a tailor knows the exact quality of a piece of cloth ; or a lady the materials of her dress. This becomes to the inexperienced quartz miner somewhat like the knowledge of an efficient pilot at sea, it enables him to steer his vessel clear of those rocks upon which others have gone to pieces. It may be well that this should be remembered, inasmuch as " seeing the gold " is not always a sure sign that the lead can be wrought with advantage and profit. In many of the rich-

est kinds of rock it has been almost impossible to see gold ; while in some known as pocket-lead-rock, considerable has been visible ; and yet a sufficient amount has not been taken therefrom to pay the cost of getting and crushing it.

In the best kind of leads there is often a large amount of rock which is utterly worthless ; and which has to be taken from the vein, when known to be unproductive, that workmen may be enabled to reach the paying rock, and work to advantage. It often occurs, too, that even good paying leads are not scientifically and economically worked ; and, as a consequence, do not insure a generous return to the owners, for their time and trouble.

Then again, as some good rock is soft, and other hard, it is not to be supposed that the hard can be either quarried or crushed as easily as the soft. Therefore, the amount per ton being the same, the cost of extraction is different, and the profits arising therefrom, as a matter of course, will differ in proportion.

Some persons having crushed rock that was exceedingly rich, with more pride (or self-interest) than truthfulness, reported such to be the average yield ; when, perhaps a tenth part of that amount would be nearer the net product of their mine. By these exaggerations a few years ago much disastrous speculation was fostered and encouraged ; and which, doubtless, materially retarded the development of this branch of mining. As quartz is now becoming a steady and profitable business, no respectable company attempts to exagerate the product of their lead ; but rather, like all other good business men, seek to keep their business to themselves, preferring to under than over state the yield.

As the position of a quartz lead in the mountain is generally at an angle of from twenty to fifty degrees, the most common method of working it is to sink a perpendicular shaft at a sufficient distance from the line where the vein is seen to " crop out " on the surface, and strike the angle

at the depth desired, or thereabouts. From this shaft workmen commence removing the quartz along the vein, to form a tunnel; and as the rock is removed much easier and more rapidly by beginning at the tunnel and working upwards, this plan of operation of course is adopted.

Under the guidance of Mr. Daniels, of the far-famed Allison Ranch Lead, we descended their shaft — but not before the workmen had offered and we had accepted the loan of an India rubber suit of clothing — and on reaching the bottom of it we found a considerable stream of water running in the centre of the railway, constructed along the tunnel to the shaft. This water was removed by a pump in one corner of the shaft, working by steam power, both day and night.

On, on we went, trying to keep a sure footing on the rail track, inasmuch as watertight boots even then became a very necessary accompaniment to the India-rubber clothing. Drip, drip, fell the water, not singly, but in clusters of drops and small streams, so that

QUARRYING QUARTZ AT THE VEIN.

when we arrived at the drift where the men were at work, we had a sufficient supply of water for drinking purposes (!) in the pockets of our coat. The miners who were removing the quartz from the ledge, looked more like half drowned sea-lions, than men. We did not make ourselves inquisitive enough to ask the amount of wages they received, but we came to the conclusion that they must certainly earn whatever they obtained. Stooping, or rather half lying down upon the wet rock, among fragments of quartz and props of wood, and streams of water; with pick in hand, and by a dim but waterproof lantern, giving out a very dim and watery light, just about bright enough, or rather dim enough, and watery enough, as Milton expresses it, "to make darkness visible," a man was at work, picking down the rock — the gold-bearing rock — and which, although very rich, was very rotten, and consequently not only paid well, but was easily quarried, and easily crushed; and although this rock was paying not less than three hundred and fifty dollars per ton, we could not see the first speck of gold in it, after a diligent search for that purpose.

At the bottom of the drift another man was employed to shovel the quartz into a tub standing on a railway car, and push it to the shaft, where it was drawn up and taken to the mill.

It has been a matter of much anxiety and discussion to know if the gold-bearing quartz would extend below the decomposed rock; and, if so, whether or not the rock would not become too hard and too difficult to quarry, and remove to the mill with profit. We know of but two companies in Nevada county who have mined through the decomposed rock into the *volcanic*, and these are the *Sebastopol* and *Osborne Hill*, about a couple of miles east of Grass Valley, Nevada county; both of these companies being at work in the greenstone.

We had the satisfaction of descending the Osborne Hill lead, under the guidance of Mr. Crossett, and after bumping the head against the rocky roof above, and holding on by our feet to the wet and slippery roof of rock below, on which we were descending, at an angle of forty-two degrees; now clinging to the timbers at the side; (to prevent the lubricity of our footing from taking advantage of the back part of our head, and making us to "see stars in a dark passage," from the tripping up of our heels) now winding among props, and over cast-iron pump tubes; now making our way from one side of the inclined shaft to the other, to enable us to travel as easy as possible. On, on; down, down we go, until we hear the sound of muffled voices issuing from somewhere deep down amid the darkness, and uttering something very indistinct and hard to be understood; when we again cross over to, and enter a side drift; where, in the distance, we see lights glimmering, in shadow and smoke, and hear the voices become more and more distinct, until my guide asks the question, "How does she look now, boys?" "All right—better, sir."

"Ah! that's right—there goes the supper bell, boys." Now tools are dropped and a general move was on foot for working in the bread and meat mine, as hard and as earnestly as they had worked in the quartz mine.

"Have we reached the bottom now?" we inquired. "Ah! no, we are only about one hundred and sixty feet below the surface, yet, we shall soon reach the greenstone."

Presently we reach the top of the greenstone; but, down, farther and deeper, we pass on, as before, until we reach a long tunnel, into which we enter and can stand erect.

"Is *this* the bottom?" we inquired.

"Well, nearly," was the answer; "we are now one hundred and thirty feet down in the greenstone, and three hundred feet from the out-crop of the quartz vein."

"Well, sir," we interrogated, "does the quartz rock pay you thus far down in the greenstone?"

"Yes," was the reply, "it is even better than it was above. The deeper we get, the richer the quartz becomes. We are very well satisfied with the prospect."

"Do you think that it will prove so, generally?"

"I do," was the firm and emphatic answer.

This, therefore, becomes an important fact; inasmuch as should the paying quartz end after the bottom of the decomposed rock is reached the permanency of quartz operations would be at best but very doubtful.

Now, reader, let us rest for a moment, and look around us a little—as we hope, (in imagination at least,) you have thus far accompanied us. Except from the lights in our hands all is dark, and as still almost as the tomb, with the exception of the distant creaking of a pump, and the steady dripping of some water at our elbow. Rock here, there, and everywhere. For several years men have been picking and drilling and blasting through solid rock; by day and night; in winter and in summer; led forward by the talismanic power of gold—or at least by the hope to obtain it. Hard rock, hard work, and often very hard prospects; although combined with difficulty and danger, have never for a moment daunted or dismayed them. Above ground or under; by daylight or candle light—onward—ever onward—has been their unswerving resolve—and the guiding star of hope has ever shone with cheering light upon their labors. May the reward be near.

"As it is getting rather chilly, suppose we ascend."

"All right; shall we ascend by the ladder, or by the same way that we came?" inquired our excellent guide.

"Oh, by the ladder, by all means," was the response.

Lights were then fastened on our hats; as, "in ascending we shall have need of both hands perhaps!" suggested our guide.

"What pleasure there is in seeing daylight after one has been for some time in darkness; and inhaling the cool fresh air above ground after some time spent underneath," we remarked, as we wiped the sweat from our brow, when we had reached the top.

While we cool ourselves, as we see the carts are busy in removing the gold-bearing quartz which has been taken from below, let us follow them to the mill and there see the *modus operandi* of crushing the rock and extracting the gold.

MEXICANS BREAKING THE QUARTZ.

After the quartz is emptied from the cart into the yard, the large pieces are broken by hand to about the size of a man's fist or a little smaller; they are then shoveled, with the dust and finer portions of rock, upon an inclined table or "hopper" at B, on which a small stream of water is conveyed through a pipe from

FEEDING THE MILL.

above, and by which the quartz is washed down the hopper to a solid cast-iron bedplate at H, and beneath the stampers.

The stampers at A and I being elevated by convex arms attached to a revolving shaft at K, when at the required height, fall suddenly down upon the quartz; and being shod with heavy cast-iron, which, added to the stampers, make the whole weight of a single one from six hundred to a thousand pounds, crushes the rock to powder upon which it falls.

In front of the stampers at D is a very fine seive or screen, against and through which the water, gold and pulverised quartz are constantly being splashed by the falling of the stampers; and should the rock not be pulverised sufficiently fine to pass through these discharge-screens it again falls back upon the bed-plate to receive another crushing from the stampers. If, however, it is reduced fine enough to pass through, it falls upon an apron at E, or

into an "amalgamating box" containing quicksilver, and into which a dash-board is inserted that all the water, gold, and tailings may pass *through* the quicksilver contained in the amalgamating box, to an inclined plane or blanket-table below. Across and above the apron, or amalgamating box, a small trough is fixed at O, with holes in the bottom, for the purpose of distributing clean water equally on the apron, or into the amalgamating box, and by which the pulverised rock, and gold not saved above, is washed down to the blanket-tables at F.

These tables simply consist of a flat sluice, generally about two feet in width by six inches in depth, and upon which a coarse blanket is spread for the purpose, principally, of saving the auriferous sulphurets, and which will not amalgamate with the quicksilver. Some companies, however, depend chiefly upon the apron and blankets for saving the whole of their gold, and do not use quicksilver above the blanket-tables.

The blankets are allowed to remain upon the tables from ten to thirty minutes, according to the quality of the rock being crushed; that which is rich requiring the change about every ten or fifteen minutes, and that which is poor every twenty or thirty minutes. When a change is desirable the blankets are carefully rolled up and placed in a bucket, or small tub, and carried to the "vat"—not, however, before another is spread upon the table—where they are

WASHING THE BLANKETS.

carefully washed. In order to test the quality of the rock being crushed, the contents of the blanket are frequently washed into a *batea*, or broad Mexican bowl, and prospected.

The materials contained in the blanket vats are saved in a box made for that purpose, or thrown into a heap, or taken at once to some kind of amalgamating machine—and there is scarcely a couple of mills in the State where the same process exactly is used; as each superintendent of a mill supposes that he has made some improvements in *his* mill entirely unknown or unpracticed by others; at all events he flatters himself that *he* saves more gold than his neighbor.

The processes most commonly in use are the *Rastra* and Chili mill. These we shall describe, reserving for some other numbers

THE MEXICAN RASTRA.

the various plans or improvements for saving the gold, by different persons, at different mills; inasmuch as the saving of gold is of too much importance to be lightly passed over.

One of the first used, as well as one of the most useful and most important, is the Mexican Rastra. Though rude in its construction and simple in its working, it is one of the most effectual methods of saving the gold which has yet been discovered. The Mexican method of constructing these is to lay a circular track of stone tolerably level with a low wall around the outside of the track; and in the centre a post made of a tree cut off at the required height, and generally just above a crotch or arm; another small tree is then cut in the shape required, for making a horrizontal shaft; to this is attached one or more large stones; and these being drawn around by donkey or mule power, grind the quartz to powder. Of course, as gold is the heaviest it naturally seeks the lowest places, and as quicksilver is always put in with the quartz the gold becomes amalgamated with it.

THE IMPROVED MEXICAN RASTRA;

The Mexican rastra has been improved some little in its construction and adaptation to our wants; and in many cases mule-power has been superseded by steam; but the principle remains about the same.

When the rastra is properly prepared, a "batch" of about five hundred pounds is generally emptied into one about ten feet in diameter; but the quantity is always regulated by the size of the machine. It is then ground very fine by means of the drag-stones attached to arms fixed in the perpendicular shaft, and which are generally given about eight revolutions per minute. At this rate it will require from three to four hours to grind a batch sufficiently; but this is somewhat regulated by the grit and weight of the drag-stones. About three quarters of an hour before the whole is thoroughly ground, a sufficient quantity of quicksilver is added; but the amount is regulated by the richness of the quartz in process of grinding. If, for instance, the five hundred pounds of tailings placed in the arastra is supposed to contain about three quarters of an ounce of gold, about one ounce of quicksilver is generally used — or about twenty-five per cent. more of the latter than the former. Some judgment is required in this — too much quicksilver being a disadvantage, inasmuch as the amalgam should be kept hard to make it effectual in saving the gold. Quicksilver should also be kept very free from grease, as it cannot be too clean; and should invariably be well retorted every time it is used.

About ten minutes before the grinding is finished, about sixteen buckets of water are poured into the rastra, to the quantity named, and the same motion continued, the whole appearing like muddy water. This is then baled out, or run off quickly. Five hundred pounds more of the quartz are then added, and the process repeated, adding the same portion of quicksilver to every batch.

This is kept on for one, two, three, or even four weeks, according to the richness of the quartz, or the taste and wants of the owner. The larger the amount of amalgam contained in the rastra, the more gold is there saved, in proportion, to the ton.

The amalgam is then taken out of the crevices in the bottom of the rastra, and carefully panned out, and as carefully retorted. After this, most business men melt the gold into bars or ingots, before sending it to the mint to be coined.

Before commencing to grind again, the crevices between the stones covering the floor of the rastra, about one and a half inches wide, are tightly packed and filled with clay, level with the stone.

In El Dorado County, rastras sixteen feet in diameter are used to great advantage, as more than double the amount of quartz is ground by them than by the smaller ones; but of course they require a proportionate increase in power to work them.

It should also be remembered that not less than two fifths more quartz is ground in the same rastra when worked by steam or water-power than when worked by animals, inasmuch as the speed and regularity is increased.

It should also be well remembered by every operator in quartz, that warm water is of great assistance in every thing connected with amalgam, as it will be the means of saving from ten to fifteen per

THE CHILI MILL.

cent. more gold than when it is worked with cold water — a very important kind of economy.

This mill, as used in Chili, and from whence its origin and name are derived, is nearly as simple in its construction as the rastra. It consists of a circular inclosure somewhat resembling the rastra, with the walls a little higher, and more regular; and, instead of the "drag-stones," a large stone wheel, attached to the horizontal shaft, is used for grinding the rock. Into this mill a small stream of water is constantly running, a portion of which is forced out at each revolution of the wheel. The gold is saved by means of quicksilver on the bottom of the mill, in the same manner as in the rastra.

To make this principle more subservient to the purposes of quartz mining, and better adapted to the requirements of a faster age and people, the "improved Chili

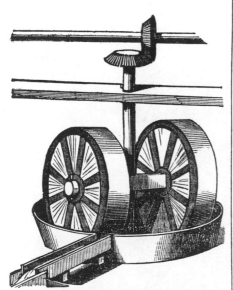

THE IMPROVED CHILI MILL.

Mill" was invented. This consists of two heavy cast-iron wheels, from three to five feet in diameter, and from ten to fifteen inches in thickness: these, revolve on an axle, moving steadily round in a cir-

cular iron basin about a foot in depth, into which the tailings from the blanket tables are conveyed, and ground to powder.

As these improved mills are generally worked by steam, the speed attained, and the work accomplished, of course very far exceeds the old process.

On the first page of the present number of the Magazine, in the foreground of the picture, will be found several small amalgamators in use at Mr. Chavanne's mill.

The methods of saving the gold which passes over the blankets in the tailings, are almost as numerous as are the mills where the quartz is crushed. The principle, however, is to allow the tailings to run down a series of inclined tables, or sluices, at the end of each of which is often placed a wood trough, or iron pan, containing quicksilver, into which they flow, when the gold falls into the quicksilver on the bottom, and is there retained; while the lighter material floats over the edge of the trough or pan into another sluice, at the end of which is another pan, where the same process is repeated. The sluices, or inclined tables, are generally fitted up with "patent riffles" across the bottom, filled with quicksilver. After the tailings have passed through the whole series of sluices they are sometimes worked through the improved Chili Mill, or other machine; but are oftener allowed to run into a large vat, from which the water flows off while the tailings settle at the bottom. These are then thrown into a heap and allowed to "rust," preparatory to other processes at some future time.

As California is one vast net-work of quartz leads, a thousandth part of which have never even been prospected; and as the bottom of a single lead has not yet been found, it is not an uncertain venture to say that this department alone is capable of giving employment to several millions of people.

MINER'S WATER SONG.

—

There is joy in the miner's camp to-night,
There is joy, and the miner's heart is light ;
  There is mirth and revelry, shouting and song,
For rain has been falling all the day long.

Hark, hark ! how it pours, pit, pit, patter, pat,
What music to miners is equal to that ?
  It comes down in earnest, we've no need to pinch,
As it falls by the bucketful—not.the short inch.

We'll have water plenty, and water to spare,
Enough for each miner to have his full share ;
  The sluice will be full, and the ditch overrun,
And the goal of our hopes will be speedily won.

Then fly round my boys, as we need not complain,
But don our best smiles tho' we work in the rain :—
  Such bountiful blessings now drop from the skies,—
The water without seems to swim to our eyes.

To wash out our gold and pay all we owe,
Makes our hearts, like the ditches, with good overflow :—
  Then hurrah, boys, hurrah ! for such rainy weather,
May ourselves, wives, and sweethearts, hurrah altogether.

CARRIE D.

May 26th, 1856.

CALIFORNIA CARTOONS.—No. II.

"TAILING OUT"—IN THE MINES.

HUTCHINGS'

CALIFORNIA MAGAZINE.

Vol. II.   NOVEMBER, 1857.   No 5.

THE DISCOVERY OF GOLD IN CALIFORNIA.

GEN. JOHN A. SUTTER.

[*From an Ambrotype by R. H. Vance.*]

THE DISCOVERY OF GOLD IN CALIFORNIA.

Ours is the age of gold,
And ours the hallowed time.—*Mellen.*

To the lovers of history, nothing can be more welcome and valuable than the unvarnished narrative of events, from the actors themselves: therefore, we feel the greater pleasure in presenting our readers with the following statements, with which we are favored: one from the good old pioneer, Gen. John August Sutter; and the other from Mr. James W. Marshall, the favored discoverer of the gold—and who, unitedly, are the fathers of *The Age of Gold.*

It was in the first part of January, 1848, when the gold was discovered at Coloma,* where I was then building a saw-mill. The contractor and builder of this mill was James W. Marshall, from New Jersey. In the fall of 1847, after the mill seat had been located, I sent up to this place Mr. P. L. Wimmer with his family, and a number of laborers, from the disbanded Mormon Battalion; and a little later I engaged Mr. Bennet from Oregon to assist Mr. Marshall in the mechanical labors of the mill. Mr. Wimmer had the team in charge, assisted by his young sons, to do the necessary teaming, and Mrs. Wimmer did the cooking for all hands.

I was very much in need of a saw-mill, to get lumber to finish my large flouring mill, of four run of stones, at Brighton, which was commenced at the same time, and was rapidly progressing; likewise for other buildings, fences, etc., for the small village of Yerba Buena, (now San Francisco.) In the City Hotel, (the only one) at the dinner table this enterprise was unkindly called "another folly of Sutter's," as my first settlement at the old fort near Sacramento City was called by a good many, "a folly of his," and they were about right in that, because I had the best chances to get some of the finest locations, near

* The Indian name and pronunciation is Cul-lu-mah, (beautiful vale,) now Americanized Coloma.

the settlements; and even well stocked rancho's had been offered to me on the most reasonable conditions; but I refused all these good offers, and preferred to explore the wilderness, and select a territory on the banks of the Sacramento. It was a rainy afternoon when Mr. Marshall arrived at my office in the Fort, very wet. I was somewhat surprised to see him, as he was down a few days previous; and when, I sent up to Coloma a number of teams with provisions, mill irons, etc., etc. He told me then that he had some important and interesting news which he wished to communicate secretly to me, and wished me to go with him to a place where we should not be disturbed, and where no listeners could come and hear what we had to say. I went with him to my private rooms; he requested me to lock the door; I complied, but I told him at the same time that nobody was in the house except the clerk, who was in his office in a different part of the house; after requesting of me something which he wanted, which my servants brought and then left the room, I forgot to lock the doors, and it happened that the door was opened by the clerk just at the moment when Marshall took a rag from his pocket, showing me the yellow metal: he had about two ounces of it; but how quick Mr. M. put the yellow metal in his pocket again can hardly be described. The clerk came to see me on business, and excused himself for interrupting me, and as soon as he had left I was told, "now lock the doors; didn't I tell you that we might have listeners?" I told him that he need fear nothing about that, as it was not the habit of this gentleman; but I could hardly convince him that he need not to be suspicious. Then Mr. M. began to show me this metal, which consisted of small pieces and specimens, some of them worth a few dollars; he told me that he had expressed his opinion to the laborers at the mill, that this might be gold; but some of them were laughing at him and called him a crazy man, and could not believe such a thing.

SUTTER'S FORT IN 1848..

After having proved the metal with aqua fortis, which I found in my apothecary shop, likewise with other experiments, and read the long article "gold" in the Encyclopedia Americana, I declared this to be gold of the finest quality, of at least 23 carats. After this Mr. M. had no more rest nor patience, and wanted me to start with him immediately for Coloma; but I told him I could not leave, as it was late in the evening and nearly supper time, and that it would be better for him to remain with me till the next morning, and I would travel with him, but this would not do: he asked me only "will you come to-morrow morning?" I told him yes, and off he started for Coloma in the heaviest rain, although already very wet, taking nothing to eat. I took this news very easy, like all other occurrences good or bad, but thought a great deal during the night about the consequences which might follow such a discovery. I gave all my necessary orders to my numerous laborers, and left the next morning at 7 o'clock, accompanied by an Indian soldier, and vaquero, in a heavy rain, for Coloma. About half way on the road I saw at a distance a human being crawling out from the brushwood. I asked the Indian who it was: he told me "the same man who was with you last evening." When I came nearer I found it was Marshall, very wet; I told him that he would have done better to remain with me at the fort than to pass such an ugly night here; but he told me that he went up to Coloma, (54 miles) took his other horse and came half way to meet me; then we rode up to the new Eldorado. In the afternoon the weather was clearing up, and we made a prospecting promenade. The next morning we went to the tail-race of the mill, through which the water was running during the night, to clean out the gravel which had been made loose, for the purpose of widening the race; and after the water was out of the race we went in to search for gold. This was done every morning: small pieces of gold could be seen remaining on the bottom of the clean washed bed rock. I went in the race and picked up several pieces of this gold, several of the laborers gave me some which they had picked up, and from Marshall I received a part. I told them that I would get a ring made of this gold as soon as it could be done in California; and I have had a heavy ring made, with my family's coat of arms engraved on the outside, and on the inside of the ring is engraved, "The first gold, discovered in January, 1848." Now if Mrs. Wimmer possesses a piece which has been found earlier than mine Mr. Marshall can tell,* as it was probably received from him. I think Mr. Marshall could have hardly known himself which was exactly the first little piece, among the whole.

The next day I went with Mr. M. on a prospecting tour in the vicinity of Coloma, and the following morning I left for Sacramento. Before my departure I had a conversation with all hands: I told them that I would consider it as a great favor if they would keep this discovery secret only for six weeks, so that I could finish my large flour mill at Brighton, (with four run of stones,) which had cost me already about from 24 to 25,000 dollars—the people up there promised to keep it secret so long. On my way home, instead of feeling happy and contented, I was very unhappy, and could not see that it would benefit me much, and I was perfectly right in thinking so; as it came just precisely as I expected. I thought at the same time that it could hardly be kept secret for six weeks; and in this I was not mistaken, for about two weeks later, after my return, I sent up several teams in charge of a white man, as the teamsters were Indian boys. This man was acquainted with all hands up there, and Mrs. Wimmer told him the whole se-

cret; likewise the young sons of Mr. Wimmer told him that they had gold, and that they would let him have some too; and so he obtained a few dollars' worth of it as a present. As soon as this man arrived at the fort he went to a small store in one of my outside buildings, kept by Mr. Smith, a partner of Samuel Brannan, and asked for a bottle of brandy, for which he would pay the cash; after having the bottle he paid with these small pieces of gold. Smith was astonished and asked him if he intended to insult him; the teamster told him to go and ask me about it; Smith came in, in great haste, to see me, and I told him at once the truth—what could I do? I had to tell him all about it. He reported it to Mr. S. Brannan, who came up immediately to get all possible information, when he returned and sent up large supplies of goods, leased a larger house from me, and commenced a very large and profitable business; soon he opened a branch house of business at Mormon Island.

Mr. Brannan made a kind of claim on Mormon Island, and put a tolerably heavy tax on "The Latter Day Saints." I believe it was 30 per cent, which they paid for some time, until they got tired of it, (some of them told me that it was for the purpose of building a temple for the honor and glory of the Lord.)

So soon as the secret was out my laborers began to leave me, in small parties first, but then all left, from the clerk to the cook, and I was in great distress; only a few mechanics remained to finish some very necessary work which they had commenced, and about eight invalids, who continued slowly to work a few teams, to scrape out the mill race at Brighton. The Mormons did not like to leave my mill unfinished, but they got the gold fever like everybody else. After they had made their piles they left for the Great Salt Lake. So long as these people have been employed by me they have behaved very well, and were industrious and faithful laborers, and when settling their accounts there was not

* Mrs. Wimmer's piece weighs about five dollars and twelve cents. The *first piece*, Mr. Marshall says, weighed about fifty cents.

SUTTER'S FORT, IN 1857.

one of them who was not contented and satisfied.

Then the people commenced rushing up from San Francisco and other parts of California, in May, 1848 : in the former village only five men were left to take care of the women and children. The single men locked their doors and left for "Sutter's Fort," and from there to the Eldorado. For some time the people in Monterey and farther south would not believe the news of the gold discovery, and said that it was only a '*Ruse de Guerre*' of Sutter's, because he wanted to have neighbors in his wilderness. From this time on I got only too many neighbors, and some very bad ones among them.

What a great misfortune was this sudden gold discovery for me! It has just broken up and ruined my hard, restless, and industrious labors, connected with many dangers of life, as I had many narrow escapes before I became properly established.

From my mill buildings I reaped no benefit whatever, the mill stones even have been stolen and sold.

My tannery, which was then in a flourishing condition, and was carried on very profitably, was deserted, a large quantity of leather was left unfinished in the vats ; and a great quantity of raw hides became valueless as they could not be sold ; nobody wanted to be bothered with such trash, as it was called. So it was in all the other mechanical trades which I had carried on ; all was abandoned, and work commenced or nearly finished was all left, to an immense loss for me. Even the Indians had no more patience to work alone, in harvesting and threshing my large wheat crop out ; as the whites had all left, and other Indians had been engaged by some white men to work for them, and they commenced to have some gold for which they were buying all kinds of articles at enormous prices in the stores; which, when my Indians saw this, they wished very much to go to the mountains and dig gold. At last I consented, got a number of wagons ready, loaded them with provisions and goods of all kinds, employed a clerk, and left with about one hundred Indians, and about fifty Sandwich Islanders (Kanakas) which had joined those which I brought with me from the Islands. The first camp was about ten miles above Mormon Island, on the south fork of the American river. In a few weeks we became crowded, and it would no more pay, as my people made too many acquaintances. I broke up the camp and started on the march further south, and located my next camp on Sutter creek (now in Amador county), and thought that I should there be alone. The work was going on well for a while, until three or four traveling grog-shops surrounded me, at from one and a half to two miles distance from the camp ; then, of course, the gold was taken to these places, for drinking, gambling, etc., and then the following day they were sick and unable to work, and became deeper and more indebted to me, and particularly the Kanakas. I found that it was high time to quit this kind of business, and lose no more time and money. I therefore broke up the camp and returned to the Fort, where I disbanded nearly all the people who had worked for me in the mountains digging gold. This whole expedition proved to be a heavy loss to me.

At the same time I was engaged in a mercantile firm in Coloma, which I left in January, 1849 — likewise with many sacrifices. After this I would have nothing more to do with the gold affairs. At this time, the Fort was the great trading place where nearly all the business was transacted. I had no pleasure to remain there, and moved up to Hock Farm, with all my Indians, and who had been with me from the time they were children. The place was then in charge of a Major Domo.

It is very singular that the Indians never found a piece of gold and brought it to me, as they very often did other specimens found in the ravines. I requested them continually to bring me some curiosities from the mountains, for which I always recompensed them. I have received animals, birds, plants, young trees, wild fruits, pipe clay, stones, red ochre, etc., etc., but never a piece of gold. Mr. Dana, of the scientific corps of the expedition under Com. Wilkes' Exploring Squadron, told me that he had the strongest proof and signs of gold in the vicinity of Shasta Mountain, and further south. A short time afterwards, Doctor Sandels, a very scientific traveler, visited me, and explored a part of the country in a great hurry, as time would not permit him to make a longer stay.

He told me likewise that he found sure signs of gold, and was very sorry that he could not explore the Sierra Nevada. He did not encourage me to attempt to work and open mines, as it was uncertain how it would pay, and would probably be only profitable for a government. So I thought it more prudent to stick to the plow, notwithstanding I did know that the country was rich in gold, and other minerals. An old attached Mexican servant who followed me here from the United States, as soon as he knew that I was here, and who understood a great deal about working in placers, told me he found sure signs of gold in the mountains on Bear Creek, and that we would go right to work after returning from our campaign in 1845, but he became a victim to his patriotism and fell into the hands of the enemy near my encampment, with dispatches for me from Gen. Micheltorena, and he was hung as a spy, for which I was very sorry.

By this sudden discovery of the gold, all my great plans were destroyed. Had I succeeded with my mills and manufactories for a few years before the gold was discovered, I should have been the richest citizen on the Pacific shore; but it had to be different. Instead of being rich, I am ruined, and the cause of it is the long delay of the United States Land Commission, of the United States Courts, through the great influence of the squatter lawyers. Before my case will be decided in Washington, another year may elapse, but I hope that justice will be done me by the last tribunal — the Supreme Court of the United States. By the Land Commission and the District Court it has been decided in my favor. The Common Council of the city of Sacramento, composed partly of squatters, paid Alpheus Felch, (one of the late Land Commissioners, who was engaged by the squatters during his office), $5,000, from the fund of the city, against the will of the tax-payers, for which amount he has to try to defeat my just and old claim from the Mexican government, before the Supreme Court of the United States in Washington.

HUTCHINGS'

CALIFORNIA MAGAZINE.

Vol. IV.   FEBRUARY, 1860.   No. 8.

BLESSING THE MINE.

THE ENRIQUETA QUICKSILVER MINE, ON THE MORNING OF DEDICATION.

THE interesting dedicatory ceremonial of Blessing the Mine is a custom of long standing in many Catholic countries, where mining is carried on, especially among those people who speak the Spanish language. Without it, workmen would feel a religious dread, and consequently a timid reluctance to enter upon their daily labors, lest some accidental mishap should overtake them from such an omission. After this has been duly performed, great care is taken to erect a shrine, be it ever so rude, at some convenient point within the mine, to some favorite tutelary saint or protectress, whose benediction they evoke. Before this shrine each workman devoutly kneels, crosses himself, and repeats his Ave Maria, or Paternoster, prior to entering upon the duties and engagements of the day. At this spot candles are kept burning, both by day and night, and the place is one of sacred awe to all good Catholics. The blessing and dedication of a mine is, consequently, an era of importance, and one not to be lightly passed over, or indifferently celebrated.

On the morning of the day set apart for this ceremony, at the Enriqueta or San Antonio quicksilver mine, the Mexican and Chilian señors and señoras began to flock into the little village at the foot of the cañon, from all the surrounding country, in anticipation of a general holiday, at an early hour.

Of course, at such a time, the proprietor sends out invitations to those guests he is particularly desirous should be present to do honor to the event; but no such form is needed among the workmen and their friends or acquaintances, as they understand that the ceremony itself is a general invitation to all, and they avail themselves of it accordingly.

Arriving in procession at the entrance to the mine, Father Goetz, the Catholic curate of San Jose, performed mass, and formally blessed the mine, and all persons present, and all those who might work in it; during which service, a band of musicians was playing a number of airs. At the close, fire-crackers and the boom of a gun cut in the ground, announced the conclusion of the ceremony on the outside; when they all repaired to the inside, where the Father proceeded to sprinkle holy water, and to bless it.

These duly performed, they repaired to the village, near which is the beautiful residence of Mr. Laurencel, its proprietor, where, in a lovely grove of sycamores, several tables were erected and bounteously covered with good things for the inner man. "Here were feasted nearly two hundred guests, of both sexes, with choice viands, in magnificent profusion, while native wines, and other light potables flowed in abundance. A large number of specially invited guests were at the same time hospitably and courteously entertained within the house by Mr. Laurencel, his lady, and her household. After dinner, there was music and dancing upon the green, exhibitions of skillful horsemanship, and a variety of amusements, which were participated in by the assembled company with the utmost zest, and were kept up, we understand, until a late hour. The day chosen for this festival was the day of San Antonio, the patron saint of the mine, and the birthday of the little Enriqueta, Mr. Laurencel's daughter, the more immediate patroness of the same."

Recently, while on a visit to San Jose, I visited the newly discovered mines of quicksilver, situated about twelve miles southward from that city.

Our road led across the valley to the south, until arriving at the Los Capitancillos Creek, whence it followed that stream for the remainder of our journey. Upon the banks of this creek, we were told, a tribe of Indians flourished in the early part of this century. They were governed by three chiefs known among the Spanish as the Capitancillos, from whence the stream took its name.

From here the broad valley we had followed stretches away to the eastward, whilst that of the Capitancillos, through which our road lay, tends towards the mountains in the south, narrowing gradually, till it winds around the western extremity of the hills in which lie the three mines of Guadalupe, Enriqueta, and New Almaden. Ascending the valley of the stream, we passed the works of the Guadalupe mine, and some two miles further on arrived at the Enriqueta.

Here we were hospitably received by the enterprising director, Mr. H. Laurencel, from whom we chiefly derived the following particulars.

Veins of quicksilver were long since known to exist in these hills, but owing to the difficulty of finding sufficient quantities of ore to render mining remunerative, nothing of importance was attempted. In November last, Mr. Laurencel employed a .party of Irish and Mexican miners to prospect it more thoroughly, and several places were found to be of good promise, and opened. One was called the Providentia mine, another was placed under the protection of Saint Patrick, and at length, in January last, the present Enriqueta Mine was found and immediately opened. During the winter and spring quite a limited number of men carried on the work, but the labors of these few were sufficient to prove that there existed a large deposit. In the beginning of June the work was advanced upon a larger scale, and preparations were made to put up the proper machinery for reducing the ore. Everything was done with dispatch, and on the spot where stood a forest in June, we saw now an establishment so far advanced as to promise to go into operation, producing quicksilver, early in September; good proof of the energy and activity of our California miners.

The system adopted for the reduction of ores, is, I understand, the same that was employed by Dr. Ure, many years since, at the mines of Obermoschel, in the Bavarian Rhein Kreis, and which has proved to be much superior to the systems in practice at the Almaden Mine in Spain, and the Idria mine of Austria.

What the production of this mine will be, is impossible to foresee; but quite a little mountain of ore, already taken out, and what we saw in our descent into the mine, looks well for the future prospect. A large number of Mexican miners were at work, and as we passed their different parties, I broke from the rocky walls a number of pieces, which, on coming to the light of day, proved to be rich ore.

The location of the Enriqueta Mine is one of considerable beauty. A picturesque valley below, with the winding stream of the Capitancillos, and pleasant groves of oaks and sycamores, looks up on one hand to the hill where the mine is perched, some three hundred and forty or fifty feet above, and on the other to the rugged mountain, rising to the height of between three and four thousand feet. The mine employs about one hundred laborers of all classes; the families added would make a total population already of about four hundred persons. A little village has sprung up near the works, containing many neat cottages, a hotel, and several stores. Two lines of stages run daily between the mine and the city of San Jose.

While here I visited also another spot of considerable interest—a gigantic oak, standing upon a prominent spur of the mountains on the south. It measures some thirty-six feet in circumference, and is, I doubt not, the largest of its family in California. From its commanding position and size, it is visible at a great distance, still towering high, when all the trees around it are dwarfed into the appearance of mere underbrush.

In leaving the Enriqueta Mine, I was more than ever reminded of the immense mineral resources of our State, and of the industry of our people. The works of years of older countries were here the labor of a few short months only.

The county of Santa Clara will find in this mine a new source of wealth, and must rejoice at the diligent prosecution of an enterprise so important. As an old miner, I was gratified at what I saw. What the California miner needs is cheap quicksilver; but, as long as its supply is limited, it is kept up at exorbitant prices

With an increased production and a healthy competition, we may expect soon to see it at such a price as will render it hereafter a small item only in the working of the quartz mines, so important a source of wealth and prosperity to California.   A. E.

SCENES IN THE MINING DISTRICTS.

BY J. LAMSON.

THE HARDSCRABBLE DITCH.

The above name is no misnomer; no mere fanciful cognomen, without sense or meaning, and adopted without reflection, or consideration of its import. The beauty and euphony (!) of the word may have had, and doubtless did have its influence with the proprietors in selecting it as the title for their ditch and company, and which possesses a significance and expressiveness which every miner well understands.

The owners of this ditch have large tracts of mining claims at Emery's Crossing in Nevada County. A company was formed for the purpose of supplying these claims with water, and the owners of the claims made various proposals to take stock in that company, which were all rejected. So they resolved to construct a ditch for themselves.

It is not my present purpose to give a history of the ditch, with all the trials, vexations and difficulties encountered in its construction. Suffice it to say, that, long before the completion of the work, obstacles were continually met and resolutely overcome.

Both ditches were commenced at nearly the same time, and both were obstinarely carried forward to their completion. It was a contest, however, in which one party or the other was destined in the end to suffer a signal defeat. One ditch would supply every demand for water, and therefore both could not be supported. The former company had money at their command, while the Hardscrabble party were compelled to rely mainly on their credit, and their own bone and muscle. Their adversaries believed they must soon yield the unequal contest, and in this belief they obstinately rejected every proposal for an accommodation, and for a union of the two companies, until the Hardscrabble party found it no longer for their interest either to offer or to accept of any terms. Both ditches were completed, but as the Hardscrabble Company were the only miners to be supplied with water, the opposing ditch, as might have been easily foreseen, proved a total loss to the proprietors, and has since gone to decay. Such instances of unyielding obstinacy and wilful blindness, in the expenditure of money, are not unfrequent in the mines.

The principal proprietors of the Hardscrabble Ditch are Charles Whitticer, William Reynolds, and Robert West. They commenced their work in February, 1856, and completed it in September of the same year, at a cost of twenty thousand dollars. The ditch takes its supply of water from the Middle Yuba, four miles above Emery's Crossing, where it ends. The river here, like most of the mountain streams of California, is but a series of wild rapids in a deep cañon. In a distance of two miles, the ditch acquires an

THE FLUME OF THE HARDSCRABLE DITCH.

elevation of ninety-eight feet above the river. Here the flume, as seen in the engraving, crosses the river. It is twenty-four inches wide, twenty inches deep, and ninety-eight feet high. It is supported by a frame, the posts of which rest upon an arch of strong lattice work, one hundred and twenty-six feet long, the lower portion of which is elevated about twenty feet above the river at low water.

The figure seen upon the flume is Robert West, better known as "Bob." He is the ditch tender; that is, he has to pass and repass along the ditch every day, examine its condition, and make the necessary repairs. It is not every one who can cross that bridge without feeling a slight degree of trepidation; but Bob, having served an apprenticeship before the mast, traverses the narrow plank that covers the flume with the same feeling of security that he would tread the deck of a ship, and often carries heavy loads over it upon his shoulders. On one occasion he transported a small cooking-stove in this manner to his cabin at the head of the ditch. Crossing the river safely, he

had nearly reached his cabin, when, unfortunately coming in contact with a branch of an oak which overhung the ditch, Bob lost his balance, and was pitched headlong into a bed of rocks some six or eight feet below him. Luckily, in the fall, his head intervened between the stove and the rocks, by which the iron utensil was preserved from destruction, while the head, which seemed to have been made of india rubber, received only a slight cut, from which the blood flowed, until the application of a warm quid of tobacco, fresh from Bob's mouth, stanched the wound, and enabled him to resume his journey, which he accomplished without further mishap.

The proprietors of the Hardscrabble Ditch have reaped a very satisfactory harvest from their investment, and acquired a handsome and well deserved competency by their laborious industry, perseverance and frugality.

THE ROANOKE TUNNEL.

A large portion of the mining, in Placer county, is done in tunnel diggings.

ROANOKE TUNNEL, PLACER COUNTY.

At Iowa Hill, Roach Hill, Monona Flat, and many other localities, the hill sides are perforated in all directions. Occasionally, the tunnels are run so near the surface, and in such numbers, as to render it unsafe to build a house of brick, or other heavy material, over them, from its liability to sink and fall to destruction.

On exploring a tunnel at Roach Hill, the Roanoke, in company with J. W. Myrick, one of the proprietors, I discovered a peculiarity which I had not observed elsewhere, though it may often occur. Having passed in about twelve hundred feet, we came to a perpendicular passage, sixty or seventy feet high, at the head of which the lead was struck, and followed by horizontal drifts. A portion of the passage was occupied by a ladder, for the use of the workmen; the other part was boarded up, in the shape of a long box, to receive the dirt, which is brought to it in cars, upon a rude railway. This box is called a mill. A space is left beneath the box of a sufficient height to run a car under, and a gate is raised, by means of a bar, when the dirt runs down, and the car is loaded with very little labor. The gate is then shut, and the car is run down the inclined plane to the end of the track, at the mouth of the tunnel, and "dumped" into a heap below. A reservoir, supplied by a ditch, furnishes water to wash the dirt. The water is applied by means of a hose, and the heap of dirt is gradually washed away, and carried down a long sluice, in which the particles of gold are retained, while the earth passes off.

When the car was loaded, Myrick and I placed ourselves on a step in the rear, and crouching down, in order to avoid contact with the roof of the tunnel, which varied from four to six feet in height, we held, or rather hung, by the back of the car, when Myric loosened the brake and we started off. The inclination of the track was so great, that we went onward with great velocity. In less than two minutes we passed out of the tunnel to the end of the track, and discharged the load. These journeys are not wholly without danger; for, should an axle break, or a wheel run off the track, as often happens, the consequences might be fatal, and are always serious.

HUTCHINGS'
CALIFORNIA MAGAZINE.

VOL. I.   SEPTEMBER, 1856.   NO. III.

METAL YARD AND ENTRANCE TO THE MINE.

THE QUICKSILVER MINE OF NEW ALMADEN.

Sixty-five miles south of San Francisco, near the head of the beautiful and fertile valley of San Jose, and in an eastern spur of the coast range of mountains, is the quicksilver mine of New Almaden.

With your permission, kind reader, we will enter the stage as it waits on the Plaza, and as the clock strikes eight, start at once on our journey. Lucky for us, it is a fine brght morning, as the fog has cleared off and left us, (on a dew-making excursion no doubt, up the country) and as we are to be fellow travellers—at least in imagination—and wish to enjoy ourselves; while the stage rattles over the pavement, and rumbles on the wood planking of the streets, let us say "good bye" to our cares, as we did to our friends, and leave them with the city—behind us.

How refreshing to the brow is the breeze, and grateful to the eye is the beautiful green of the gardens, as we pass them on our way. Even the hills in the distance now so barren and drear, are dotted with the dark green of the live oaks, and are beautifnl by contrast.

On, on we go, rolling over hills, traveling in the valley, passing farms and wayside houses; now watering horses here, then changing horses there, and dropping mail bags yonder, until we reach the flourishing old Mission of Santa Clara. Here, we long to linger, and as we look upon the orchards now laden with their fruit, we almost wish to bribe the coachman to wait while we buy, beg, or steal, those cherry-cheeked and luscious looking pears; or take a walk amid the shadows of the Old Mission church; but, the signal " all aboard," hurries us to our seats, and we soon enter an avenue of old willow and poplar trees, that extends from Santa Clara to San Jose, a distance of three miles, and which was planted by and for the convenience of the two Missions. On either side of this avenue at intervals, there are tasteful cottages, flourishing farms, nurseries, and gardens, which are well supplied with water from artesian wells.

Arriving in San Jose you find a neat and pleasant agricultural city, with all the temptations of fruit and flowers in great variety; and but for a partial failure of the crops this year from drouth, there would have been a brisk business activity observable in each department of business. One thing impressed us unfavorably here,

the large number (thirty-seven, we believe) of members of the legal profession, in so small a city, we thought of

AN OLD SAW.

An upper mill, and lower mill,
　Fell out about the water;
To war they went, that is to law,
　Resolved to give no quarter.

A lawyer was by each engaged,
　And hotly they contended;
When fees grew scant, the war they waged
　They judged, twere better ended.

The heavy costs remaining still,
　Were settled without pother;—
One lawyer took the upper mill,
　The lower mill the other.

and it set us to ruminating. But, let us jump on the box of Baker's easy coach, and we shall forget all that, and have a very pleasant ride of fourteen miles upon a good road through an ever green grove of live oaks, and past the broad shading branches of the sycamore trees, and in a couple of hours find ourselves drinking heartily of the delicious waters of the fine cool soda spring at the romantic village of New Almaden. As we have passed through enough for one day, let us wait until morning before climbing the hill to examine the mines.

This mine has been known for ages by the Indians who worked it for the vermillion paint that it contained, with which they ornamented their persons, and on that account had become a valuable article of exchange with other Indians from the Gulf of California to the Columbia river. Its existence was also known among the early settlers of California, although none could estimate the character or value of the metal.

In 1845 a captain of cavalry in the

GENERAL VIEW OF THE WORKS.

Mexican service, named Castillero, having met a tribe of Indians near Bodega, and seeing their faces painted with vermillion, obtained from them for a reward, the necessary information of its locality, when he visited it, and having made many very interesting experiments, and determined the character of the metal, he registered it in accordance with the Mexican custom, about the close of that year.

A company was immediately formed and the mine divided into twenty-four shares, when the company immediately commenced working it on a small scale; but, being unable to carry it on for want of capital, in 1846 it was leased out to an English and Mexican company for the term of sixteen years; the original company to receive one-quarter of the gross products for that time. In March, 1847, the new company commenced operations on a large scale, but finding that to pay one-fourth of the proceeds, and yet bear all the expenses of working the mine, would incur a cousiderable loss, they eventually purchased out most of the original shareholders.

In June, 1850, this company had expended *three hundred and eighty-seven thousand eight hundred dollars* over and above all their receipts. During that year a new process of smelting the ore was introduced by a blacksmith named Baker, which succeeded so well that fourteen smelting furnaces have been erected by the company upon the same principle.

The process of extracting the quicksilver from the cinnabar is very simple. The *ore chamber* B is filled with cinnabar, and covered securely up; a fire is then kindled in the furnace at A, from which, through a perforated wall of brick, the heat enters the ore chamber and permeates the mass of ore, from which arises the quicksilver, in the shape of vapor, and, passing through the perforated wall on the opposite side, enters the condensing chambers at C, rising to the top of one and falling to the bottom of the other, as indicated by the arrows, and as it passes through the condensing chambers — thirteen in number — it cools and becomes quicksilver. Should any vapor escape the last condensing chamber, it passes over a cistern of cold water at D, where from an enclosed pipe, water is scattered over a seive and falls upon and cools the vapor as it passes into the chimney or funnel chamber at E.

The quicksilver then runs to the lower end of each condensing chamber, thence through a small pipe into a trough that extends

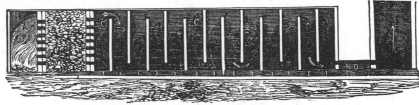

SECTION OF THE SMELTING FURNACE.

from one end of the building to the other, where it enters a large circular caldron, from which it is weighed into flasks, in quantities of seventy-five pounds. To save time, one set of furnaces is generally cooling and being filled, while the other is burning.

Now, let us gradually ascend to the *patio* or yard in front of the mine, a visit to which has been so truthfully and beautifully described by Mrs. S. A. Downer, that we are tempted to introduce the reader to such good company.

"At the right was a deep ravine, through which flowed a brook, supplied by springs in the mountains, and which, in places, was completely hid by tangled masses of wild-wood, among which we discerned willows along its edge, with oak, sycamore and buckeye. Although late in the summer, roses and convolvuli, with several varieties of floss, were in blossom; with sweet-brier, honeysuckle, and various plants, many of which were unknown to us, not then in bloom, and which Nature, with prodigal hand, has strewn in bounteous profusion over every acre of the land. To the left of the mountain side, the wild gooseberry grows in abundance. The fruit is large and of good flavor, though of rough exterior. Wild oats, diversified with shrubs and live-oak, spread around us, till we reach the *patio*, nine hundred and forty feet above the base of the mountain. The road is something over a mile, although there are few persons who have traveled it on foot under a burning sun, but would be willing to make their affidavits it was near five.

"Let us pause and look around us. For a distance of many miles, nothing is seen but the tops of successive mountains; then appears the beautiful valley of San Juan, while the Coast Range is lost in distance. The *patio* is an area of more than an acre in extent; and still above us, but not directly in view, is a Mexican settlement, composed of the families and lodging-cabins of the miners. There is a store, and provisions are carried up on pack-mules, for retail among the miners who may truly be said to live from hand to mouth. This point had been the resort of the aborigines not only of this State, but from as far as the Columbia river, to obtaint the paint (vermilion) found in the cinnabar, and which they used in the decoration of their person. How long this had been known to them cannot be ascertained; probably a long time, for they had worked into the mountain some fifty or sixty feet, with what implements can only be conjectured. A quantity of round stones, evidently from the brook, was found in a passage with a number of skeletons; the destruction of life having been caused, undoubtedly, by a sudden caving in of the earth, burying the unskilled savages in the midst of their labors. It had been supposed for some time that the ore possibly contained the precious metals, but no regular assay was made till in '45; a gentleman now largely interested, procured a a retort, not doubting that gold, or at least silver, would crown his efforts. Its real character was made known by its pernicious effects upon the system of the experimenter. The discovery was instantly communicated to a brother, a member of a wealthy firm in Mexico, who with others purchased the property, consisting of two leagues, held under a Spanish title, of the original owner. For some years but little was done. The ore proved both abundant and rich, but required the outlay of a vast amount of capital to be worked to advantage; and, while Nature with more than her usual liberality had furnished in the mountain itself all the accessories for the successful prosecution of her favors, man was too timid to avail himself of her gifts. In 1850,

the present company was formed. With untiring energy, guided by a liberal and enlightened policy, they proceeded with vigor, and at this time, the works being nearly completed, the extraction of the mercury proceeds without interruption.

"In 1850 a tunnel was commenced in the side of the mountain in a line with the *patio*, and which has already been carried to the distance of 1100 feet by ten feet wide, and ten feet high to the crown of the arch, which is strongly roofed with heavy timber throughout its whole length. Through this the rail-track passes; the car receiving the ore as it is brought on the backs of the carriers, (*tenateros*) from

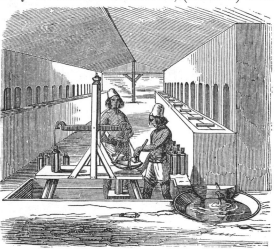

MEXICANS WEIGHING QUICKSILVER.

the depths below, or from the heights above, The track being free, we will now take a seat on the car, and enter the dark space. Not an object is visible, save the faint torch-light at the extreme end; and a chilling dampness seizes on the frame, so suddenly bereft of warmth and sunshine. This sensation does not continue as we descend into the subteranean caverns below; and now commence the wonders, as well as the dangers of the undertaking. By the light of a torch we pass through a damp passage of some length, a sudden turn bringing us into a sort of vestibule, where, in a niche at one side, is placed a rude shrine of the tutelary saint, or protectress of the mine — *Nuestra Señora de Guadalupe,* before

BUTLER

SHRINE OF SENORA DE GUADALUPE.

which lighted candles are kept constantly burning, and before entering upon the labors of the day or night each man visits this shrine in devotion. You descend a perpendicular ladder formed by notches cut into a solid log. You go down, perhaps twelve feet; you turn and pass a narrow corner, where a frightful gulf seems yawning to receive you. Carefully threading your way over the very narrowest of footholds, you turn into another passage black as night, to descend into a flight of steps formed in the side of the cave, tread over some loose stones, turn around, step over arches, down into another passage, that leads into many dark and intricate windings and descendings, or chambers supported but by a column of earth — now stepping this way, then that, twisting and turning, all tending down, down to where, through the darkness of midnight one can discern the faint glimmer, which shines like Shakspeare's "good deed in a naughty world," and

which it seems impossible one can ever reach. We were shown a map giving the subterranean topography of this mine; and truly, the crossings and re-crossings, the windings and intricacies of the labyrinthine passages could only be compared to the streets of a dense city, while nothing short of the clue, furnished Theseus by Ariadne, would insure the safe return into day, of the unfortunate pilgrim who should enter without a guide.

The miners have named the different passages after their saints, and run them off as readily as we do the streets of a city; and after exhausting the names of all the saints in the calendar, have commenced on different animals, one of which is not inaptly called *El elefante.* Some idea of the extent and number of these passages may be formed, when we state that sixty pounds of candles are used by the workmen in the twenty-four hours. Another turn brings us upon some men at work. One stands upon a single plank placed high above us in an arch, and he is drilling into the rock above him for the purpose of placing a charge of powder. It appears very dangerous, yet we are told that no lives have ever been lost, and no more serious accidents have occurred than the bruising of a hand or limb, from carelessness in blasting. How he can maintain his equilibrium is a mystery to us, while with every thrust of the drill his strong chest heaves, and he gives utterance to a sound something between a grunt and a groan, which is supposed by them to facilitate their labor. Some six or eight men working in one spot, each keeping up his agonizing sound, awaken a keen sympathy. Were it only a cheerful sing-song, one could stand it; but in that dismal place, their wizzard-like forms and appearance, relieved but by the light of a single tallow candle stuck in the side of the rock, just sufficient to make "darkness visible," is like opening to us the shades of Tartarus; and the throes elicited from overwrought human bone and muscle, sound like the anguish wrung from infernal spirits, who hope for no escape.

These men work in companies, one set by night, another by day, alternating week about. We inquired the average duration of life of the men who work under ground, and found that it did not exceed that of forty-five years, and the diseases to which they are mostly subject are those of the chest; showing conclusively how essential light and air are to animal, as well as vegetable life. With a sigh and a shudder, we step aside to allow another set of laborers to pass. There they come; up, and up, from almost interminable depths; each one as he passes, panting, puffing and wheezing, like a high pressure steamboat, as with straining nerve and quivering muscle, he staggers under the load, which nearly bends him double. These are the *tenateros*, carry-

Mineros AT WORK IN THE MINE.

ing the ore from the mine to deposit it in the cars; and like the miners they are burdened by no superfluous clothing. A shirt and trowsers, or, the trowsers without a shirt; a pair of leathern sandals fastened at the ankle, with a felt cap, or the crown of an old hat, completes their costume.

"The ore is placed in a flat leather bag, (*talégo*) with a band two inches wide that passes around the forehead, the weight resting along the shoulders and spine. Two hundred pounds of rough ore are thus borne up, flight after flight, of perpendicular steps; now winding through deep caverns, or threading the most tortuous passages; again ascending over earth and loose

stones, and up places that have not even an apology for steps, all the while lost in Cimmerian darkness, but for a torch borne aloft, which flings its sickly rays over the dismal abysm, showing that one unwary step would plunge him beyond any possibility of human aid or succor. Not always, however, do they ascend; they sometimes come from above; yet we should judge the toil and danger to be nearly as great in one case as in the other. Thirty trips will these men make in one day, from the lowest depths.

For once we were disposed to quarrel with the long, loose skirts, that not only impeded our progress, but prevented our attempt to ascend to the summit, and enjoy from thence a prospect of great beauty and extent. But one woman, we believe, has ever accomplished this feat, which severely tasks the strength of manhood.

We will now follow the *tenateros*, as they load the car with the contents of their sacks, and run after it into the open air. There they go, with shouts of laughter, and really, as one emerges into the warm sunshine, the change is most inspiriting. They have reached the end of the track, and throw off the great lumps of ore, without an effort, as if they were mere cabbages. What capacious chests, and how gaily they work! Such gleeful activity we never before beheld. The large lumps deposited, they now seize shovels and jumping on the cars, the small lumps mixed with earth are cleared off with the most astonishing celerity. Do but behold that fellow of Doric build, with brawny muscles, and who is a perfect *fac simile* of Hercules, as he stood engraved with his club, as we remember him in Bell or Tooke's Pantheon!

The ore deposited on the *patio*, another set of laborers engage in separating the large lumps and reducing them to the size of common paving stones, which are placed by themselves. The smaller pieces are put in a separate pile, while the earth *(tierra)* is sifted through coarse sieves for the purpose of being made into *adobes*. There is also a blacksmith's shop for making and repairing implements. The miner is not paid by the day, but receives pay for the ore he extracts. They usually work in parties of from two to ten; half the number work during the day, the other half by night, and in this manner serve as checks upon each other. Should a drone get into the number, complaint is made to the engineer, who has to settle such matters, which he generally does by placing him with a set nearer his capacity, or sometimes by a discharge. The price of the ore is settled by agreement for each

Tenateros CARRYING THE ORE FROM THE MINE.

week. Should the passage be more than commonly laborious, they do not earn much; or if, on the contrary, it proves to be easy and of great richness, the gain is theirs; it being not infrequent for them to make from thirty to forty dollars a week a piece, and seldom less than fifteen. In those parts of the mine where the ore is worthless, but still has to be extracted in order to reach that which will pay, or to promote ventilation, they are paid by the *vara*,* at a stipulated price. They do nothing with getting the ore to the *patio;* this is done by the *tenateros* at the company's expense, as is also the separating, sifting, and weighing. Each party have their ore kept separate; it is weighed twice a week and an account taken. They select one of their

* A *vara* is two feet nine inches.

party who receives the pay and divides it among his fellows.

The *tenateros* receive three dollars per diém; the sifters and weighers, two dollars and a half; blacksmiths and bricklayers, five and six; while carpenters are paid the city price of eight dollars a day. These wages seem to be very just and liberal, yet such is their improvidence that no matter how much they earn, the miners are not one *peso* better off at the end of the month than they were at its beginning. No provision being made for sickness or age, when that time comes, as come it will, there is nothing for them to do but, like some worn out old charger, lie down and die. This has reference exclusively to the Mexicans; and it is a pity that a Savings Bank could not be established, and made popular among them. They number between two and three hundred in all; but they are, perhaps, the most impracticable people in the world, going on as their fathers did before them, firmly believing in the axiom, that sufficient unto the day is the evil thereof.

THE GUADALUPE QUICKSILVER MINE

Is the name of a newly opened quicksilver mine, situated in a beautiful and romantic valley on Guadalupe Creek, at the extreme western point of the same range of hills as that of New Almaden, and about four and a half miles from it. This mine was discovered in 1847, but was not attempted to be worked till 1850, when a company was formed and operations commenced; but, owing to the high price of labor and supplies, and the company running short of funds, after a few months were suspended. In 1855, a new company was formed and incorporated by charter, from the Legislature of Maryland, under the title of the "*Santa Clara Mining Association, of Balti-*more," with a sufficient working capital to open the mine, erect the necessary smelting works and carry them on. These being now nearly completed, the company expect, in a few weeks, to send their first samples of quicksilver to market; and, as large deposits of cinnabar have already been discovered, the prospects are peculiarly encouraging to the owners.

Without omitting a farewell visit and a last drink at the soda springs, we leave this singular spot for San Jose; and the following morning, after passing the Old Mission and the flourishing farms along the valley, arrived in Oakland just in time to be too late for the ferry boat at noon; but patience being a virtue, as we could do nothing else for three long hours, we quietly cultivated it and reached San Francisco to — practice it.

EPITAPH ON A PATRIOT SOLDIER.

Light be the earth that lies on his breast,
  Green be the sod that covers his grave,
Hallow'd the song bird, untouch'd in its nest,
  In the ever-green laurels that over it wave.

Be honor'd the sword that he gallantly bore,
  Immortal the spot where he gloriously fell,
Be chaunted his fame on ev'ry free shore,—
  On Time's latest record his memory dwell.

Exalted his name in the land of his birth,
  Envy'd his fate by the sons of the brave,
Wide his example shall spread round the earth,
  Till it ceases to bear on its bosom a slave.

Peace everlasting dwell in his soul,
  Be welcom'd its entrance to regions of bliss,
While patriot-heroes, his name here enrol,
  The reward of the brave, there ever be his.
                                    DELIA.

WE open the hearts of others when we open our own.

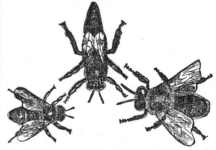

PART III

OUTINGS & OBSERVATIONS

THE PIONEER

One of nature's noblemen; lord of circumstances; master over exigencies; conqueror of the wilds; tiller of the forest; tamer of nature; provider for the needy; leader of the pathless wild; pilot of the trackless ocean.

OUTINGS & OBSERVATIONS

The first article in the first number of *Hutchings' California Magazine* was titled "The Yo-ham-i-te Valley," and its opening words were, "There are but few lands that possess more of the beautiful and picturesque than California." In the succeeding months and years the description of California's scenery, of its flora and fauna, remained one of the principal missions of the magazine, and the promotion of Yosemite the particular and ever-growing enthusiasm of its editor.

Natural history was a subject that was very much "alive" in J. M. Hutchings' time. The atmosphere of discovery was still about, and science had not reached that point where technical observations were beyond the grasp of the average reader — or writer. In the California of the 1850's so much was new that it was not overly difficult for an author or editor to tread the line between popularization and pedantry. Indeed, Hutchings could point out that science was popular, and that some of the most technical articles in his magazine had gained the distinction of being widely pirated by his journalistic readers throughout the state or even in the East.

Hutchings published so much about the natural history and the record of so many trips about the state that not all of the more interesting articles could be contained in this volume. His greatest love, Yosemite, is represented by only one of five major articles. The one chosen tells of the trip into the valley, which is that part of the extensive description that we felt might be of most interest to readers who have likely seen the valley itself with their own eyes.

The roads to Yosemite became familiar paths to J. M. Hutchings in the forty years following his retirement from the magazine. He brought his wife to the valley and built his first house there in 1862. His daughters were born — and one of them died — in Yosemite. The young John Muir hiked into the valley one day in 1868; he built a sawmill for Hutchings to get lumber out of windfall trees and lived in a roost adjoining the mill. As the children grew up they were sent off to San Francisco for schooling in the winter; in the summer they returned to Cedar Cottage, where each year they saw an increasing tide of visitors — scientists, travelers, and the merely curious. Hutchings never flagged in his efforts to publicize Yosemite, and as years went by he got more and more help. Before he had lived in the valley for long, Yosemite was known as "Hutchings' Place" to nearby residents. Still, by 1902, when J. M. Hutchings died at the gateway to his valley, he had made the name "Yosemite" known around the world.

HUTCHINGS'

CALIFORNIA MAGAZINE.

Vol. III.   MARCH, 1859.   No. 9.

THE MAMMOTH TREES OF CALIFORNIA.

BUTT AND SECTION OF THE MAMMOTH TREE TRUNK,

In the spring of 1852, Mr. A. T. Dowd, one of the "Nimrods" of Calaveras county, was employed by the Union Water Company of Murphy's Camp, to supply the workmen engaged in the construction of their canal with fresh meat from the vast quantities of game to be found in that vicinity.

Having wounded a large bear while engaged in this occupation, he industriously followed in pursuit; when to his momentary confusion, and astonishment his eyes looked for the first time upon one of those magnificent giants that have since become so famous throughout the world. All thoughts of hunting, or bear pursuing, were forgotten, or absorbed and lost in the surprising admiration which he felt.

Surely, he mused, it must be a dream, but no, the great realities were before him.

Filled with thoughts inspired by what he had seen, he returned to camp, and there related the story of the wonders he had discovered. His companions laughed; and doubted his usually reliable veracity. He re-affirmed his statement; but still they would not believe it to be true; nor would they consent to accompany him; thinking that he was about to perpetrate some practical first of April joke upon them.

For a day or two he allowed the matter to rest; submitting with chuckling satisfaction to the occasional jocular allusions to "his big tree yarn," and continued his hunting as formerly. On the Sunday morning following he went out as usual, and returned in haste, evidently excited by some event. "Boys," he exclaimed, "I have killed the largest grizzly bear that I ever saw in my life. While I am getting a little something to eat you make preparations to bring him in. All had better go that can possibly be spared, as their assistance will be needed."

As the big tree story was now almost forgotten, or by common consent laid aside as a subject of conversation; and, moreover, as Sunday was a leisure day—and one that generally hangs the heaviest of the seven, on those who are shut out from social intercourse with friends—the tidings were gladly welcomed; especially as the proposition was suggestive of a day's excitement.

Nothing loath, they were soon ready for the start. The camp was almost deserted. On, on, they hurried, with Dowd as their guide, through thickets and pine groves; crossing ridges and cañons, flats

and ravines, each relating in turn the adventures experienced, or heard of from companions, with grizzly bears; until their leader came to a dead halt at the foot of the tree he had seen, and to them had related the size. Pointing to the immense trunk and lofty top, he cried out, "now, boys, do you believe my big tree story? That is the large grizzly I wanted you to see. Do you still think it a yarn." Thus convinced, their doubts were changed to amazement, and their conversation from bears to trees; afterwards confessing that, although they had been caught by a ruse of their leader, they were abundantly rewarded by the gratifying sight they had witnessed: and as other trees were found equally as large, they became willing witnesses, not only of Mr. Dowd's account, but to the fact that, like the confession of a certain Persian queen concerning the wisdom of Solomon, the half had not been told them.

Mr. Lewis, one of the party above alluded to, after seeing these gigantic forest patriarchs, conceived the idea of removing the bark from one of the trees, and of taking it to the Atlantic cities for exhibition, and invited Dowd to join him in the enterprise. This was declined; but while Mr. L. was engaged in obtaining a suitable partner, some one from Murphy's Camp to whom he had confided his intentions, and made known his plans, took up a quarter section of the ground and with a party of men commenced the removal of the bark; after attempting to dissuade Lewis from the undertaking.* This underhanded proceeding induced Lewis to visit the large tree at Santa Cruz, discovered by Fremont; for the purpose of competing, if possible, with his *quondam friend*; but finding that tree, although large, only 19 feet in diameter,

*In the winter of 1854 we met Mr. Lewis in Yreka, and from his own lips received this account; and we think it no more than simple justice to him here to make a record of the fact, that such an unfair and ungentlemanly violation of confidence may be both known and censured as it well deserves to be

and 286 feet in height, while that in Calaveras county was 30 feet in diameter, and 302 feet in height, he turned his steps to some trees, then reputed to be the largest in the state, growing near Trinidad, Klamath county ; but the largest of these he found only to measure about 24 feet in diameter, and 279 feet in height ; consequently, he eventually abandoned his undertaking.

But a short time was allowed to elapse after the discovery of this remarkable grove, before the trumpet-tongued press proclaimed the wonder to all sections of the State, and to all parts of the world,

and the lovers of the marvelous began first to doubt, then to believe, and afterwards to flock from the various districts of California, that they might see with their own eyes the objects of which they had heard so much.

No pilgrims to Mohamed's tomb at Mecca ; or to the reputed vestment of our Savior at Treves ; or to the Juggernaut of Hindostan, ever manifested more interest in the superstitious objects of their veneration, than the intelligent and devout worshippers of the wonderful in nature, and science, of our own country, in their visit to the Mammoth Tree Grove

VIEW OF THE BIG TREE COTTAGE.

of Calaveras Co., high up in the Sierras.

Murphy's Camp, then known as an obscure, though excellent, mining district, was lifted into notoriety by its proximity to, and as the starting point for, the Big Tree Grove, and consequently was the centre of considerable attraction to visitors.

As the reader may desire to gratify his

curiosity by a visit—at least in imagination—with his permission we will consent to act as guide for the occasion, and proceed at once upon our journey.

Well mounted—this is an important auxiliary to a day of pleasure—we cross Murphy's Flat, and about half a mile from town proceed up a narrow cañon, upon a carriage road, now upon this side

WORKMEN ENGAGED IN FELLING THE MAMMOTH TREE.

of the stream, and now on that, as the hills proved favorable or otherwise for the construction of a good road. If our visit is supposed to be in spring or early summer, every mountain side, even to the tops of the ridges, is covered with flowers and flowering shrubs of great variety and beauty ; while, on either hand, groves of oaks and pines stand as shade-giving guardians of personal comfort to the traveler on a sunny day.

As we continue our ascent for a few miles, the road becomes more undulating and gradual, and lying for the most part on the top or gently sloping sides of a dividing ridge; often through dense forests of tall, magnificent pines, that are from one hundred and seventy to two hundred and twenty feet in height, slender and straight as an arrow. We measured one that had fallen, that was twenty inches in diameter at the base, and fourteen and a half inches in diameter at the distance of one hundred and twenty-five feet from the base. The ridges being nearly clear of an undergrowth of shrubbery, and the trunks of the trees for fifty feet upwards or more, entirely clear of branches, the eye of the traveler can wander, delightedly, for a long distance among the captivating scenes of the forest.

At different distances upon the route, the canal of the Union Water Company winds its sinuous way on the top or around the sides of the ridge ; or its sparkling contents rush impetuously down the water-furrowed center of a ravine. Here and there an aqueduct, or cabin, or saw-mill, gives variety to an ever changing landscape.

When within about four and a half miles of the Mammoth Tree Grove, the surrounding mountain peaks and ridges are boldly visible. Looking south, the bare head of Bald Mountain silently announces its solitude and distinctiveness: west, the "the Bear Mountain range" forms a continuous girdle to the horizon, extending to the north and east, where the snowy tops of the Sierras form a magnificent back-ground to the glorious picture.

While we have been thus riding and admiring, and talking, and wondering, and musing, concerning the beautiful scenes we have witnessed; the deepening shadows of the densely timbered forest we are entering, by the awe they inspire—at first gently, and imperceptibly, then rapidly, and almost to be felt—prepare our minds to appreciate the imposing grandeur of the objects we are about to see; just as—

"Coming events cast their shadows before."

The gracefully curling smoke from the chimneys of the Big Tree Cottage, that is now visible; the inviting refreshment of the inner man; the luxurious feeling arising from bathing the hands and temples in cold clear water—especially after a ride or walk—are alike disregarded. One thought, one feeling, one emotion; that of vastness, sublimity, profoundness, pervades the whole soul; for there—*

The giant trees in silent majesty
Like pillars stand 'neath Heaven's mighty dome,
'Twould seem that perch'd upon their topmost branch,
With outstretched finger man might touch the stars;
Yet could he gain that height, the boundless sky
Were still as far beyond his utmost reach,
As from the burrowing toilers in a mine.
Their age unknown, into what depths of time
Might Fancy wander sportively, and deem
Some Monarch-Father of this grove set forth
His tiny shoot when the primeval flood
Receded from the old and changed earth:
Perhaps coeval with Assyrian kings
His branches in dominion spread; from age
To age, his sapling heirs with empires grew.
When Time those patriarchs' leafy tresses strewed
Upon the earth, while Art and Science slept,
And ruthless hordes drove back Improvement's
        stream,
Their sturdy oaklings throve, and in their turn
Rose when Columbus gave to Spain a world.
How many races, savage or refined,
Have dwelt beneath their shelter! Who shall say,
(If hands irreverent molest them not,)
But they may shadow mighty cities, reared
E'en at their roots, in centuries to come,
Till with the "Everlasting Hills" they bow,
When "Time shall be no longer!"

Before wandering further amid the wild secluded depths of this forest, it will be well that the horse and his rider should partake of some good and substantial repast—such as he will here find provided—inasmuch as it is not al-

* Extract from Mrs. Conner's forthcoming play of "The Three Brothers; or, the Mammoth Grove of Calaveras: a Legend of California.

A COTILLION PARTY OF THIRTY-TWO PERSONS DANCING ON THE STUMP OF THE MAMMOTH TREE.

ways wisest, or best, to explore the wonderful, or look upon the beautiful, with an empty stomach, especially after a bracing and appetitive ride of fifteen miles. While thus engaged let us explain some matters that we have reserved for this occasion.

VIEW OF DOUBLE BOWLING ALLEY ON TRUNK OF BIG TREE.

The Mammoth Tree Grove, then, is situated in a gently sloping, and, as you have seen, heavily timbered valley, on the divide, or ridge, between the San Antonio branch of the Calaveras river, and the north fork of the Stanislaus river; in lat. 38° north; long. 120° 10′ west; at an elevation of 2,300 feet above Murphy's Camp, and 4,370 feet above the level of the sea; at a distance of 97 miles from Sacramento city, and 87 from Stockton.

When specimens of this tree, with its cones and foliage, were sent to England for examination, Prof. Lindley, an eminent English botanist, considered it as forming a new genus; and, accordingly named it (doubtless with the best intentions, but still unfairly) "Wellingtonea gigantea;" but through the examinations of Mr. Lobb, a gentleman of rare botanical attainments, who has spent several years in California, devoting himself to this interesting and to him favorite branch of study, it is decided to belong to the Taxodium family, and must be referred

to the old genus *Sequoia sempervirens;* and consequently as it is not a new genus, and as it has been properly examined and classified, it is now known only among scientific men as the *Sequoia gigantea* (sempervirens)—and not "Wellingtonia" or as some good and laudably patriotic souls would have it, to prevent the English from stealing American thunder, "Washingtonia Gigantea."

Within an area of fifty acres there are 103 trees of a goodly size; twenty of which exceed 25 feet in diameter at the base, and consequently are about 75 feet in circumference!

But, the repast over, let us first walk upon the "Big Tree Stump," adjoining the cottage. You see it is perfectly smooth, sound, and level. Upon this stump, however incredible it may seem, on the 4th of July, 32 persons were engaged in dancing four sets of cotillions at one time, without suffering any inconvenience whatever; and, besides these, there were musicians and lookers on. Across the solid wood of this stump, five and a half feet from the ground, (now the bark is removed, which was from 15 to 18 inches in thickness) it measures twenty-five feet, and with the bark twenty-eight feet. Think for a moment; the stump of a tree exceeding nine yards in diameter, and sound to the very center.

This tree employed five men for twenty-five days in falling it—not by chopping it down, but by boring it off with pump augers. After the stem was fairly severed from the stump, the uprightness of the tree, and breadth of its base, sustained it from falling over. To accomplish this, about two and a half days of the twenty-five were spent in inserting wedges, and

SHOWING THE CONE AND FOLIAGE OF THE MAMMOTH TREES—FULL SIZE.

then driving them in with the buts of trees, until, at last, the noble monarch of the forest was forced to tremble and then to fall, after braving " the battle and the breeze " of nearly three thousand winters. In our estimation it was a sacrilegous act; although it is possible that the exhibition of its bark among the unbelievers of the eastern part of our continent, and of Europe, may have convinced all the " Thomases " living, that we have great facts in California that must be believed, sooner or later. This is the only paliating consideration with us in this act of desecration. This noble tree was 302 feet in height, and 96 feet in circumference, at the ground. Upon the upper part of the prostrate trunk is constructed a long double bowling alley.

Now let us walk among the giant shadows of the forest to another of these wonders — the largest tree now standing— which from its immense size, two breastlike protuberances on one side, and the number of small trees of the same class adjacent, has been named "The Mother of the Forest." In the summer of 1854 the bark was stripped from this tree by Mr. George Gale, for purposes of exhibition in the east, to the height of 116 feet; and now measures in circumference without the bark, at the base, 84 feet; twenty feet from base, 69 feet; seventy feet from base, 43 feet 6 inches; one hundred and sixteen feet from base, and up to the bark 39 feet 6 inches. The full circumference at base, including bark, was 90 feet.

Its height is 321 feet. The average thickness of bark was 11 inches, although in places it was about two feet. This tree is estimated to contain 537,000 feet of sound inch lumber. To the first branch it is 137 feet. The small black marks upon the tree indicate points where $2\frac{1}{2}$ in. auger holes were bored, into which rounds were inserted, by which to ascend and descend while removing the bark. At different distances upward, especially at the top, numerous dates, and names of visitors, have been cut. It is contemplated to construct a circular stairway around this tree. While the bark was being removed a young man fell from the scaffolding— or rather out of a descending noose— at a distance of 79 feet from the ground, and escaped with a broken limb. We were within a few yards of him when he fell, and were agreeably surprised to discover that he had not broken his neck.

A short distance from the above lies the prostrate and majestic body of the "Father of the Forest," the largest tree of the entire group, half buried in the soil. This tree measures in circumference at the roots, 110 feet. It is 200 feet to the first branch, the whole of which is hollow, and through which a person can walk erect. By the trees that were bro

VIEW OF THE "FATHER OF THE FOREST."

ken off when this tree bowed its proud head, in its fall, it is estimated that when standing it could not be less than 435 feet in height. 300 feet from the roots, and

where it was broken off by striking against another large tree, it is eighteen feet in diameter. Around this tree stand the graceful yet giant trunks of numerous other trees, which form a family circle and make this the most imposing scene in the whole grove. From its immense size, and the number of trees near, doubtless originated the name. Near its base is a never failing spring of cold and delicious water.

Let us not linger here too long but pass on to "The Husband and Wife," a graceful pair of trees that are leaning with apparent affection against each other. Both of these are of the same size, and measure in circumference, at the base, about 60 feet; and in height are about 252 feet.

A short distance further is "The Burnt tree," which is prostrate and hollow from numerous burnings, in which a person can ride on horseback for 60 feet. The estimated height of this tree when standing was 330 feet, and its circumference 97 feet. It now measures across the roots 39 feet, 6 inches.

"Hercules," another of these giants, is 95 feet in circumference and 320 feet high. On the trunk of this tree is cut the name of *I. M. Wooster, June,* 1850, so that it is possible this person may some day claim precedence to Mr. Dowd in this great discovery; at all events it was through the latter named that the world became acquainted with the grove.

There are many other trees of this grove that claim a passing notice; but inasmuch as they very much resemble each other we shall only mention them briefly.

The "Hermit," a lonely old fellow, is 318 feet in height and 60 feet in circum-

THE "THREE GRACES."

ference; exceedingly straight and well formed.

The "Old Maid," a stooping, broken topped, and forlorn looking spinster of the big tree family, is 261 feet in height, and 59 feet in circumference.

As a fit companion to the above, though at a respectful distance from it, stands the dejected-looking "Old Bachelor." This tree, as lonely and as solitary as the former, is one of the roughest, bark-rent specimens of the big trees to be found. In size it rather has the advantage of the "Old Maid," being about 298 feet in height, and 60 feet in circumference.

Near to the "Old Bachelor" is the "Pioneer's Cabin," the top of which is broken off about 150 feet from the ground. This tree measures 33 feet in diameter; but as it is hollow, and uneven in its circumference, its average will not be quite equal to that.

The "Siamese Twins," as their name-indicates, with one large stem at the ground, form a double tree about forty-one feet upwards. These are each 300 feet in height.

Near to them stands the "Guardian," a fine-looking old tree, 320 feet in height, by 81 feet in circumference.

The "Mother and Son" form another beautiful sight, as side by side they stand. The former is 315 feet in height, and the latter 302 feet. Unitedly, their circumference is 93 feet.

The "Horseback Ride" is an old, broken, and long prostrate trunk, 150 feet in length, hollow from one end to the other, and in which, to the distance of 72 feet, a person can ride on horseback. At the narrowest place inside, this tree is 12 feet high.

"Uncle Tom's Cabin" is another fanciful name, given to a tree that is hollow, and in which twenty-five persons can be seated comfortably, (not, as a friend at our elbow suggests, in each others laps, perhaps!) This tree is 305 feet in height, and 91 feet in circumference.

The "Pride of the Forest" is one of the most beautiful trees of this wonderful grove. It is well-shaped, straight, and sound; and, although not quite as large as some of the others, it is nevertheless a noble-looking member of the grove, 275 feet in height, and 60 feet in circumference.

The "Beauty of the Forest" is similar in shape to the above, and measures 307 feet in height, and 65 feet in circumference.

The "Two Guardsmen" stand by the roadside at the entrance of the "clearing," and near the cottage. They seem to be the sentinels of the valley. In height, these are 300 feet; and in circumference, one is 65 feet, and the other 69 feet.

Next, though last in being mentioned, not least in gracefulness and beauty, stand the "Three Sisters"—by some called the "Three Graces"—one of the most beautiful groups (if not *the* most beautiful,) of the whole grove. Together, at their base, they measure in circumference 92 feet, and in height they are equal, and each measure nearly 295 feet.

By permission of the gifted authoress of the new play to which we have before referred, we make the following quotation:—

SEMANTHE—*Speaking to* AGNES.

Thy brothers oft remind me
Of those three trees in that stupendous grove
On which we gazed in wonder; three, alike
In height, bulk, form—symmetrical and tall.
Their stems, unsinuous, rise aloft towards Heaven,
And pierce the font-like clouds that shower down
Nature's baptismal blessing on the earth,
As if to gaze upon the dwelling place
Of Him who bade them grow as witnesses
Of His creative glory. And the three,
Alike protecting, shade the tender plants,
That nestle at their base :—like thee, dear Agnes.

Many of the largest of these trees have been deformed and otherwise injured, by the numerous and large fires that have swept with desolating fury over this forest, at different periods. But a small portion of decayed timber, of the Taxodium genus, can be seen. Like other varieties of the same species, it is less subject to decay, even when fallen and dead, than other woods.

Respecting the age of this grove there has been but one opinion among the best informed botanists, which is this—that each concentric circle is the growth of one year; and as nearly three thousand concentric circles can be counted in the stump of the fallen tree, it is correct to conclude that these trees are nearly three thousand years old. "This," says the *Gardener's Calendar,* "may very well be true, if it does not grow above two inches in diameter in twenty years, which we believe to be the fact."

Could those magnificent and venerable forest giants of Calaveras county be gifted with a descriptive historical tongue, we could doubtless learn of many wonderful changes that have taken place in California within the last 3,000 years!

THE MAMMOTH TREE "MOTHER OF THE FOREST."

Until the fall of 1855, the grove we have just described was considered the only one to be found in the State, of the same variety ; but, at the time alluded to, Mr. J. E. Clayton, while running the survey of a canal for Col. Fremont, discovered another grove of mammoth trees; and which, in 1857, were visited, and described in the following manner, by Colonel Warren, of the "California Farmer" :—

The first tree we measured was "Rambler," and measuring it three and a half feet from the ground, found it eighty feet in circumference; close at the ground, one hundred and two feet, and, carefully surveyed, two hundred and fifty feet high. Tree No. 2, nearly fifty feet in circumference. No. 3, (at the spring,) ninety feet, three and a half feet from the ground, one hundred and two at the ground, and three hundred feet high. Nos. 4 and 5 we call the sisters, measuring eighty-two and eighty-seven feet in circumference, and two hundred and twenty-five feet high. Many of the trees had lost portions of their tops by the storms that had swept over them. After measuring the first five trees, we divided our company, two taking the southeast direction, and two with myself the northerly, and keeping record of each tree measured, which resulted as follows :—

The whole number measured was one hundred and fifty-five, and these comprise but about half the group, which we estimate cover about two to three hundred acres, and lie in a triangular form. Some of the trees first meet your view in the vale of the mountain ; thence rise south-easterly and north-westerly, till you find yourself gazing upon the neighboring points, some ten miles from you, whose tops are still covered with their winter snows. The following are the numbers and measurement of the trees,

1 tree, 102 feet in circumference ; 1 tree 97 feet ; 1 tree, 92 feet ; 3 trees, each 76 feet ; 1 tree, 72 feet ; 3 trees, each 70 feet ; 1 tree 68 feet ; 1 tree, 66 feet ; 1 tree, 63 feet ; 3 trees, each 63 feet ; 2 trees, each 60 feet ; 1 tree, 59 feet ; 1 tree, 58 feet ; 3 trees, each 57 feet ; 1 tree, 56 feet ; 3 trees, each 55 feet ; 2 trees, each 54 feet ; 1 tree, 53 feet ; 1 tree, 51 feet ; 4 trees, each 50 feet ; 6 trees, each 49 feet ; 5 trees, each 48 feet ; 2 trees, each 47 feet ; 3 trees, each 46 feet ; 2 trees, each 45 feet ; 1 tree, 44 feet ; 2 trees, each 43 feet ; 2 trees, each 42 ft : 1 tree, 40 ft ; 1 tree, 35 ft ; 2 trees, each 36 ft ; 2 trees, each 32 ft ; 1 tree, 28 ft ; 2 trees, each 100 feet ; 1 tree, 82 feet ; 1 tree, 80 feet ; 2 trees, each 77 feet ; 1 tree, 76 feet ; 3 trees, each 75 feet ; 1 tree, 64 feet ; 4 trees, each 65 feet ; 2 trees, each 63 feet ; 1 tree, 61 feet ; 10 trees, each 60 feet; 3 trees, each 59 feet ; 1 tree each from 58 down to 52 feet ; 2 trees, each 51 feet ; 6 trees, each 50 feet ; 1 tree, 49 feet : 1 tree, 47 feet ; 1 tree, 46 feet ; 2 trees, each 45 feet ; 1 tree, 43 feet ; 7 trees, each 44 feet ; 4 trees, each 42 feet ; 3 trees, each 41 feet ; 8 trees, each 40 feet,

Some of these were in groups of three, four, and even five, seeming to spring from the seeds of one cone.

Several of these glorious trees we have, in association with our friend, named. The one near the spring we call the Fountain Tree, as it is used as the source of the refreshment. Two trees measuring ninety and ninety-seven feet in circumference, were named the Two Friends.

The groups of trees which we measured consisted of many of peculiar beauty and interest. One of those which measured one hundred feet in circumference, was of exceeding gigantic proportions, and towering up three hundred feet, and yet a portion of its top, where it apparently measured ten feet in diameter, had been swept off by storms. While we were measuring this tree, a large eagle came and perched upon it, emblematical of the grandeur of this forest as well as that of our country. The cones that lay in masses beneath this tree were twelve and eighteen inches long,[!] and some of them longer. Near by it stood a smaller tree that seemed a child to it, yet it measured forty-seven feet in circumference. Not far from it was a group of four splendid trees, 250 feet high, which we named the Four Pillars, each over fifty feet in circumference. Two gigantic trees, measuring seventy-five and seventy-seven feet, were named Washington and Lafayette; these were noble trees. Another group of these we called The Graces, from their peculiar beauty. One mighty tree that had fallen by fire and burned out, and into which we walked for a long distance, we found to be the abode of the grizzly ; there he had made his nest, and it excited the nerves to enter so dark an abode. Yet it was a fitting place for a grizzly.

Another tree, measuring eighty feet, and standing aloof, was called the Lone Giant; It went heavenward some three hundred feet. Another monster tree that had fallen and been burned out hollow has been recently tried, by a party of our friends, just riding, as they fashionably do in the saddle, through the tunnel of the tree. These friends rode through this tree, a distance of 153 feet, and the same feat can be done now. The tree has been long fallen, and measured, ere its bark was gone, and its sides charred, over a hundred feet in circumference, and probably 350 feet in height.

The mightiest tree that has yet been found, now lies upon the ground, and fallen as it lies, it is a wonder still; it is charred, and time has stripped it of its heavy bark, and yet as we measured it across the butt of the tree as it lay upturned, it measured thirty-three feet without its bark, and there can be no question that in its vigor, with its bark on and upright, it measured forty feet in diameter, or one hundred and twenty feet in circumference. Only about one hundred and fifty feet of the trunk remains, yet the cavity where it fell, is still a large hollow beyond the portion burned off; and upon pacing it, measuring from the root 120 paces, and estimating the branches, this tree must have been four hundred feet high. This tree we believe to be the largest tree yet discovered, and this forest we claim as the *Parent Forest of the World.*

No description we can give could convey to our readers the wonder and awe with which one is impressed, when standing beneath these giant trees; a feeling creeps upon you of inexpressible reverence for these trees, and one does not wish to speak aloud, but rather be silent and think. Man here feels his own nothingness, and his soul, unbidden, breaths that hymn—"Be thou O God exalted high,"—and praise rises from the heart to the lips spontaneously. No one, it seems to us, can enter this grove and not acknowledge the Deity and do him reverence. Would we had time and space to speak more of this wonderful Forest. We do not wish to take aught from our Calaveras friends, but if they will go and see this, they will cheerfully yield the palm, both in size and numbers.

Kneel at this simple altar, and the God,
Who hath the living waters, shall be there.

N. P. WILLIS.

A LARGE PEAR.

It must ever be a source of astonishment and gratification to Californians, that the prolific production of our soil is such as almost to challenge the world. Who could ever dream that in a country comparatively new, so much perfection has already been attained in the culture and growth of fruits, flowers and vegetables, as to give us, in a few brief years, advantages that are as yet unpossessed by older States. Where, but in California, for instance, has there ever grown a pear of such proportions as that on an opposite page?—its natural size, from a photograph taken by Mr. Carden, of Bradley's Daguerrean Gallery, near our office, and kindly loaned us for the purpose by Mrs. E. J. Weaver, of the Washington Market—weighing, as it does, two pounds twelve ounces avoirdupois, and is one of five, all nearly as large, from a very young tree in the orchard of Mr. Beard, Mission of San Jose; and gathered, too, before they were ripe, to be exhibited at the State Fair at San Jose, and were the largest offered for exhibition.

Next month we shall find room for a more extended notice of some of the vegetable wonders that we have seen —the products of California soil.

THE FARMER.

Who makes the barren earth
  A paradise of wealth,
And fills each humble hearth
  With plenty, life and health?
Oh, I would have you know
  They are the men of toil—
The men who reap and sow—
  The tillers of the soil.

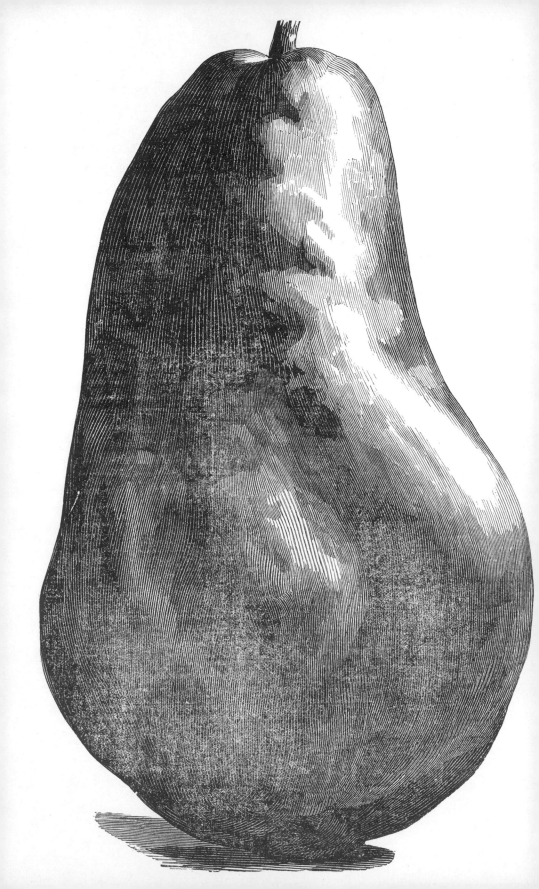

HUTCHINGS'

CALIFORNIA MAGAZINE.

VOL. V.   DECEMBER, 1860.   No. 6.

THE ALABASTER CAVE, OF EL DORADO, CO., CAL'A.

THE PULPIT.

HENEVER nature steps out of her usual course to make anything very beautiful or very wonderful, it is not unreasonable to expect that men and women, generally, will be gratefully willing to go out of their way to see it. It is true that many men love money, more than they love nature, and will not go; others, love nature more than money, and yet often feel too poor, almost, to gratify that love; and yet another class have become so much habituated to the same stool in the counting-house, the same old chair in the office, the same familiar standing-place in the store, and the same spot in the workshop, mine, or field; that nothing short of an earthquake or revolution, could induce them to turn aside from the well-worn highways of business habit, to see anything beyond themselves, and their business routine. In their eyes it is the Alpha and Omega of life, the beginning and end of all things, yea, life itself—But unfortunately—or fortunately!—hab. it unfits them for anything beyond the machine—man. The blue sky, the bright sunshine, the flower-carpeted earth, the foliage-clothed trees, the moss-grown cavern, the mighty hills, or the forest-formed harps touched by the fingers of the wind, and playing their grand old anthems of praise have no inviting and suggestive voice, that "man was made for enjoyment as well as duty—for happiness as well as business" and that the probability is apparent, that the God-like faculties bestowed upon him, enabling him, if cultivated, to hold communion with the beautiful, the enobling, the sublime, or wonderful, would not have been if man were not expected to be something loftier than a mere hum-drum business machine.

Nature sometimes turns over some new and wonderful pages in her glorious old volume, and discovers to men such marvels as the Groves of Mammoth trees, the Yo-semite valley, the Geysers, the natural bridges, and caves, and recently the Alabaster cave of El Dorado county. At such times there are many persons who will find time to open their sight-seeing eyes, and take a glimpse, if only to say, that "they have seen them," lest they should be deemed behind the age or out of the fashion. But there are others again, and their name is legion, in this new State, who adore, yea almost worship, the beautiful, the grand, the astonishing; from the handful of soil, that gives out so many varieties of rare and fragrant flowers, and luscious fruits, to the vast cathedral-formed arches and intricate draperies of stone, produced by chemical agencies and mystical combinations in one or more of nature's great laboratories beneath the surface of the earth.

With the latter class it is always a pleasure to be in company; as a pleasure shared is always doubled; besides, kindred spirits have a happy faculty of reproduction, denied to others.

A ledge of limestone rock, resembling marble in appearance, cropped out by the side of the El Dorado valley turnpike road, which, after testing, was found to be capable of producing an excellent quality of lime. Early in the present year Mr. William Gwynn employed a number of men to quarry this rock, and build a kiln. To these works he gave the name of "Alabaster Lime Quarry, and Kiln."

On the 18th of April last, two workmen, George S. Halterman and John Harris, were quarrying limestone from this ledge, when, upon the removal of a piece of rock, a dark aperture was visible, which upon being enlarged enabled them to enter. The flood of light pouring in through the opening made, enabled them to proceed some fifty feet. Before venturing further they threw a stone forward, which, falling into water, determined them to procure lights before advancing farther.

At this juncture, Mr. Gwynn came up, and, upon being informed of the discovery, sent for candles, to enable them to further prosecute their explorations. Mr. Swan of Placerville by chance making his appearance they all entered together. The result of this, after several hours spent, cannot be better given than in Mr. Gwynn's own language, from a letter addressed to Mr. Holmes, a gentleman friend of his, residing in Sacramento City, and afterwards published in the Sacramento *Bee*, dated April 19th, 1860:

DEAR HARRY :—Wonders will never cease. On yesterday, we in quarrying rock, made an opening to the most beautiful cave you ever beheld. On our first entrance, we descended about fifteen feet, gradually, to the center of the room, which is one hundred by thirty feet. At the northend there is a most magnificent pulpit, in the Episcopal church style, that man ever has seen. It seems that it is, and should be called, the "Holy of Holies." It is completed with the most beautiful drapery of alabaster sterites of all colors, varying from white to pink-red, all overhanging the beholder. Immediately under the pulpit. there is a beautiful lake of water, extending to an unknown distance. We thought this all, but, to our great admiration, on arriving at the center of the first room, we saw an entrance to an inner chamber, still more splendid, two hundred by one hundred feet, with the most beautiful alabaster overhanging in every possible shape of drapery. Here stands magnitude, giving the instant impression of a power above man ; grandeur, that defies decay ; antiquity, that tells of ages unnumbered; beauty, that the touch of time makes more beautiful; use, exhaustless for the service of men ; strength, imperishable as the globe, the monument of eternity —the truest earthly emblem of that everlasting and unchangeable, irresistible majesty by whom and for whom all things were made. WM. GWYNN.

As soon as this interesting announcement was noised abroad, hundreds of people flocked to see the newly discovered wonder from all the surrounding mining settlements of Whiskey Bar, Wild Goose Flat, Rattlesnake Bar, Pilot Hill, (Centreville,) and other places, so that within the first six days, it was visited by upwards of four hundred persons ; many of whom, we regret to say, possessed a larger organ of acquisitiveness than of veneration, and laid vandal hands on some of the most beautiful portions within reach, near the entrance. This determined the proprietor to close it until arrangements could be made for its protection and systematic illumination, the better to see and not to touch the specimens.

At this time Mr. Gwynn leased the cave to Messrs. Smith & Halterman, who immediately began to prepare it for the reception of the public by erecting barricades, platforms, etcetera ; and placing a large number of coal oil lamps at favorable points, for the better inspection of the different chambers.

The discovery being made in the spring, considerable water was standing in some of the deepest of the chambers; but signs were already visible of its recession at the rate of nearly six inches per day, and, in a few weeks, it entirely disappeared, leaving the cave perfectly dry. This afforded opportunities for further explorations ; when it was found that a more convenient entrance could be made, with but little labor, from an unimportant room within a few feet of the road. This was accordingly made, and which, in addition to convenience, allows of the free circulation of pure air. Having thus given an historical sketch of the discovery, with other matters connected with its preservation and management, we shall now endeavor to take the reader with us—at least in imagination—in describing

OUR VISIT.

We had grown tired of looking, month after month, upon the same sanctum walls ; of being a mere pen-driving machine from week beginning to week ending; and, consequently, felt ready for anything that offered a change. It is true the flowers, for the most part, had dried up and departed; that the grass had grown withered and sere, and that dust, in all kinds of cloudy sportiveness, had given intimations of a readiness to powder hair—and clothes, too, for that matter—to any extent, free of charge. Besides, knowing—or at least believing —that our "peck of dust," allowed by (no one can tell how ancient a) tradition to every person! had, years ago, followed the fortunes and destinies of our meals, and had quietly been disposed of without visible injury, we were prepared to receive any new instalments of the article in store, on our own account, or on that of anybody else.

Therefore, nothing daunted, we elbowed our way aboard the new and convenient California built steamboat, the Chrysopolis—or, as a merry friend of ours calls it, (we think in sportive derision of the name,) the "Erysipelas"—we arrived in Sacramento shortly after midnight; remained on board until daylight; at half-past six o'clock, A. M., took the cars of the Sacramento Valley Railroad for Folsom, and arrived there at a quarter to eight, making the distance of 22¾ miles, within an hour and a quarter.

Folsom is a perfect stage coach Babel, where stages from all points of the central mines connect with that terminus; but, as we shall have something to say about this in a future number, we will leave the subject for the present, and make our way for that quiet-looking, open-faced (and hearted,) middle-aged man, who is patiently sitting on the box of his stage, his good-natured countenance invitingly saying, "If there are any ladies and gentlemen who wish a pleasant ride to-day, to "Alabaster Cave," it shall not be my fault if it is

not one of the most agreeable they ever took." That gentleman is Capt. Nye.

We ask, somewhat hurriedly, if his is the conveyance for the Cave, when a bluff and kindly response is, "Yes, sir; but don't hurry yourself, I shall not start for a few minutes, and the day is before us." It may not be amiss here to remark that the Alabaster Cave is located on Kidd's ravine, almost three quarters of a mile from its debouchment in the north fork of the American river; ten miles from Folsom, by the "Whiskey Bar" road; and thirteen miles by "Shaws" road, known as the El Dorado Valley Turnpike.

As our coachman cries "all aboard," and as he has way-passengers on the latter route and none on the former, we, of course, give it the preference.

From Folsom, then, our course lay over gently rolling hills, with here and there an occasional bush or tree, to Mormon Island. Here peach orchards and well-cultivated gardens offered a grateful relief to the dry and somewhat dusty road.

Crossing the south fork of the American by a long, high, and well-built suspension bridge, we ascended, on an easy grade, to a mining camp, named Negro Hill. Threading our way among mining claims, miners, and ditches, we passed through this latter town into the open country, where buckeye bushes, now scantily clad in dry brown leaves that bespeak the approach of autumn—the nut pine, and the dark, rich foliage of white oaks, dotted the landscape.

Presidently, we reached the foot of a long hill covered with a dense growth of chapparel, composed mostly of chemisal bushes. As we ascended, we felt the advantage of having an intelligent and agreeable coachman, who explained the localities visible from the road. From the summit of Chapparel Hill, we had a glorious prospect of the country for many miles.

There, is "Monte Diablo," sleeping in the purple distance; yonder, "Sutter's Buttes," which bespeak, at once, their prominence and altitude; while the rich valley, and the bright silvery sheen of the Sacramento, and tributaries, are spread out in beauty before us. The descent to the cave is very picturesque and beautiful, from the shadowy grandeur of the groups of hills seen in the distance.

Arriving at the cave, or rather at the "Alabaster Hotel," we had an excellent appetite for a good dinner, and soon found enough to satisfy it. Indeed, we were much indebted to Mr. Holmes, the proprietor of the hotel, for the many attentions extended to us by him during our stay. This will also, with great justice, extend to the gentlemanly lessees of the cave, who, with prompt pleasure, gave us all the information, and pointed out wonders, that might have been overlooked in the multitude of attractions found.

Here let us give a table of distances to Alabaster Cave, from

Rattlesnake Bar,	1½	miles.
Pilot Hill,	4	"
Gold Hill, Placer Co	6	"
Mormon Island,	6½	"
Auburn,	8	"
Negro Hill,	6	"
Greenwood Valley,	9	"
Lincoln,	9	"
Folsom,	10 and 13	"
Uniontown and Coloma,	16	"
Georgetown, El Dorado Co.,	18	"
Diamond Sp's. & El Dorado City,	20	"
Iowa Hill, Placer Co.,	20	"
Forrest Hill,	20	"
Placerville,	23	"
Grass Valley,	30	"
Sacramento,	32	"
Nevada,	34	"
Marysville,	36	"

Dinner being quietly over, let us take a good rest before presuming to look upon the marvels we have come to see;

for too many do injustice to themselves, and the sights to be seen by attempting to see them hurriedly, or where the body is fatigued.

On leaving the hotel, it is but a short and pleasant walk to the cave. At our right hand, a few steps before reaching it, there is a lime-kiln—a perpetual lime-kiln—which, being interpreted, means one in which the article in question, can be continually made, without the necessity of cooling off, as under the old method. Here a large portion of the lime consumed in San Francisco, is manufactured. It is hauled down to Folsom or Sacramento in wagons, as return freight, and from thence transported below. To see this kiln at night, in full blast, as we did, is a sight which alone would almost repay the trouble of a visit. The red-hot doors at the base, with the light flashing on the faces of the men as they stir the fire, or wood-up; with the flames escaping out from the top; and when to this is added the deep ravine, darkened by tall, overhanging, and large-topped tree, and shrubs; while high aloft sails the moon, throwing her silvery scintillations on every object around, from the foliage-draped hill, to the bright little rivulet that murmurs by.

At these works, there are forty barrels of lime manufactured every twenty-four hours. To produce these, three and a half cords of wood are consumed, costing, for cutting only, $1 75 per cord. To haul this to the works, requires a man and team constantly. Two men are employed to excavate the rock, and two more to attend to the burning—relieving each other, at the furnace, every twelve hours; from morn to midnight.

The rock, as will be seen in the engraving, is supplied from the top, and is drawn from the bottom every six hours, both day and night.

When entering the cave from the road, which is directly in front of the aperture,

ALABASTER LIME KILN, BEYOND WHICH IS THE ENTRANCE TO THE CAVE.

we descend some three or four steps to a board floor. Here is a door that is always carefully locked when no visitors are within. Passing on, we reach a chamber about twenty-five feet in length by seventeen feet in width, and from five feet to twelve feet six inches in height. This is somewhat curious, although very plain and uneven at both roof and sides.

Here is a desk, on which is a book, inscribed, "Coral Cave Register." This book was presented by some gentlemen, who believed that "Coral Cave" would be the most appropriate name. The impression produced on our mind at the first walk through it, was that "Alabaster Cave" would be equally as good a name; but, when examining it more thoroughly, afterwards, we thought that

a greater proportion of the ornaments at the root of the stalactites, being like beautifully frozen mosses, or very fine coral; and the long icicle-looking pendants, being more like alabaster, the former name was to be preferred. But, as the name of "Alabaster" had been given to the works by Mr. Gwynn, on account of the purity and whiteness of the limestone found, even before the cave was discovered, we cheerfully acquiesce in the nomenclature given. The register was opened April 24th, 1860, and, on our visit, September 30th, ensuing, 2721 names had been entered. Some three or four hundred persons visited it before a register was thought of, and many more declined entering their names; so that the number of persons who have already visited this cave, must have exceeded three thousand. Advancing along another passage, or room, several notices attract our eye, such as, "Please not touch the specimens," "No smoking allowed," "Hands and feet off," (with *feet* scratched out)—amputation of those members not intended, we believe! The low shelving roof, at the left and near the end of the passage, is covered with coral-like excrescences, resembling bunches of coarse rock-moss. This brings us to the second doorway.

Here is the entrance to the real wonders of the cave. Before us is a broad, oddly-shaped, and low-roofed chamber, about one hundred and twenty feet in length by seventy feet in breadth, and rangeing from four to twenty feet in height.

Bright coral-like stalactites hang down in irregular rows, and in almost every variety of shape and shade, from milk-white to cream color, and stand in inviting relief to the dark arches above and frowning buttresses on either hand. While low-browed ridges, some almost black, others of a reddish-brown, stretch from either side, between which the space is ornamented with a peculiar coloring that resembles a grotesque kind of graining.

Descending towards the left, we approach one of the most beautiful stalactitic groups in this apartment. Some of these fine pendants are no larger than pipe stems, tubular, and from two to five feet in length. Three or four there were, over eight feet long; but the early admitted vandals destroyed or carried them off. Others resemble the ears of white elephants, (if such an animal could be known to natural history,) while others, again, present the appearance of long and slender cones inverted.

By examining this and other groups more closely, we ascertain that, at their base, are numerous coral-like excrescences of great beauty; here, like petrified moss, brilliant and almost transparent; there, a pretty fungus, tipped with diamonds; yonder, like miniature pine trees, which, to accommodate themselves to circumstances, have grown with their tops downwards. In other places, are apparent fleeces of the finest Merino wool, or floss silk.

Leaving these by turning to the right, we can ascend a ladder and see other combinations of such mysterious beauty as highly to gratify and repay. Here is the highest part of this chamber.

Leaving this, you arrive at a large stalagmite that resembles a tieing post for horses, and which has been dignified —or mystified—by such names as "Lot's wife," (if so, she was a very dwarf of a woman, as its altitude is but four feet three inches, and its circumference, at the base, three feet one inch,) "Hercules' Club," "Brobdignag's Fore-finger," etcetrea.

Passing on, over a small rise of an apparently snow-congealed, or petrified floor, we look down into an immense cavernous depth, whose roof is covered with icicles and coral, and whose sides are draped with jet. In one of these awe-giving solitudes is suspended a heart, that, from its size, might be imagined to belong to one of a race of giants.

On one side of this, is an elevated and nearly level natural floor, upon which a table, and seats, have been temporarily erected, for the convenience of choristers, or for public worship. It would have gratified us beyond measure to have heard these "vaulted hills" resound the symphonies of some grand anthem from Mozart, or Hayden, or Mendelssohn. Many of the pendant harps would have echoed them in delicious harmonies from chamber to chamber, and carried them around from roof to wall, throughout the whole of these rock-formed vistas.

We must not linger here too long, but,

THE CRYSTAL CHAPEL.

on our way to the Crystal Chapel, enter other little chambers, in whose roofs are formations that resemble streams of water that had been arrested in their flow, and turned to ice. In another, a perfectly formed beet, from one point of view; and, from another, the front of a small elephant's head. A beautiful, bell-shaped, hollow near here is called "Julia's Bower!"

Advancing along a narrow, low-roofed passage, we emerge into the most beauti-ful chamber of the whole suite, entitled the "Crystal Chapel." It is impossible to find suitable language or comparisons to describe this magnificent spot. From the beginning, we have felt that we were almost presumtuous in attempting to portray these wonderful scenes; but, in the hope of inducing others to see, with their natural eyes, the sights that we have seen, and enjoy the pleasure that we have enjoyed, we entered upon the task, even though inadequately, of giving an outline—nothing more. Here, however, we confess ourselves entirely at a loss.

Miss Maude Neeham, a young lady visitor from Yreka, has succeeded in giving an admirable idea of this sublime sight, in some excellent drawings, made upon the spot; two of which we have engraved, and herewith present to the reader.

The sublime grandeur of this imposing sight fills the soul with astonishment, that wells up from within as though its purpose was to make the beholder speechless—the language of silence being the most fitting and impressive, when puny man treads the great halls of nature , the more surely to lead him, humbly, from these, to the untold glory of the Infinite One, who devised the laws and superintended the processes that brought such wonders into being.

After the mind seems prepared to examine this gorgeous spectacle, somewhat in detail, we look upon the ceiling—if we may so speak—which is entirely covered with myriads of the most beautiful of stone icicles, long, large, and brilliant; between these, are squares, or panels; the mullions or bars of which seem to be formed of diamonds; while the panels themselves resemble the frosting upon windows in the very depth of winter; and even these are of many colors; that most prevailing being of a light pinkish-cream. Moss, coral, floss, wool, trees, and many other forms adorn the interstices between the larger of the stalactites. At the farther end, is one vast mass of rock, resembling congealed water, apparently formed into many folds, and little hillocks; in many instances connected by pillars with the roof above. Deep down, and underneath this, is the entrance by which we reached this chamber.

At our right stands a large stalagmite, dome-shaped at the top, and covered with beautifully undulating and wavy folds. Every imaginary gracefulness possible

to the most curiously arranged drapery, is here visible, " carved in alabaster " by the Great Architect of the universe.

In order to examine this object with more minuteness, a temporary platform has been erected, which, although detractive of the general effect, in our opinion, affords a nearer and better view of all these remarkable objects in detail.

As this spectacle, as well as the others, is brilliantly illuminated, the scene is very imposing, and reminds one of those highly-wrought pictures of the imagination, painted in such charming language, and with such good effect, in such works as the " Ara-bian Nights."

Other apartments, known as the " Picture Gallery," etc., might detain us longer; but, as they bear a striking resemblance, in many respects, to other scenes already described, we must take our leave, in the hope that we have said enough to enlist an increased attention in favor of this new California wonder.

As the ride is agreeable; the fare cheap; the coachman obliging; the guides attentive; and the spectacle one of the most singular and imposing in the State, we say to every one, by all means, *go and see it.*

INTERESTING INCIDENT.—A little girl with bright eyes and gentle countenance, was a daily visitor at the San Francisco Washington Market, for the purpose of picking up any cast-away flowers she could find. A lady, seeing her thus employed, who had noticed the punctuality of her morning visits, ventured to ask—"Jenny, what do you do with the beautiful boquets, which you daily gather and arrange here?" "Oh, ma'm," she replied, "I once had a little sister, who is an angel now, and when she was dying she said to me, 'Jenny, will you please put flowers on my grave when I am dead?' and I said 'Yes, Lela, I will.' So I gather up such a nice boquet, and every morning I place it on her grave."

CALIFORNIA FLOWERS.

BY A. KELLOGG.

In the foregoing beautiful group of California flowers, executed by Mr. Nahl, from our drawings from nature, No. 1 represents the largest and most common Iris of this coast—*Iris longipetala;* the flowers pale blue, or whitish, with deep blue veins. There are many species of the Fleur de Lis found here, some of which may prove to be new. No. 2 is the Western or Pacific (False) Honey-suckle, *Azalea occidentalis.* The flowers are perfectly white, except the lower division of its border, which is creamy, or ochreous yellowish. Some specimens we have seen with pink flowers; others of a beautiful yellow color. These plants vary much in form; but, when properly studied, we are satisfied that several distinct species may be identified.

This most ornamental under-shrub of the American forests "brings the light of other days around us," and our affections still linger fondly in the pictured past, when we searched the wild woodlands and the shady swamps for the Swamp Apple, or Honeysuckle Apple, as we designated a kind of delicious excrescence found upon them.

After the June shower, what inspirations of fragrance did we then enjoy! Hark! do you not hear celestial melody in the rolling numbers of the sweet Swamp Robin? Heaven has blest us with the sweet hermit of the grove, and the song and the flower are wreathed around our hearts in a melodious garland.

No. 3, the Rice Root of the miners, wild Guinea Hen Flower, Checkered Lily, &c. *Fritillaria mutica.* A dark brown or purplish chekered, nodding liliaceous flower; plant about two feet in height, with four to eight, or even as high as twenty, flowers. The glandular and beautifully crenulated margins are not noticed in the descrsptions. A very common bulbous plant of California. The single radicle fleshy leaf, as large as the palm of one's hand, is absent when flowering.

No. 4, *Œnothera arcuata*, (Kellogg.) Sickle-Leaf Primrose.

No. 5, *Anemopsis Californica.* A beautiful scarlet flower, found in wet places.

No. 6, Downing's Beauty—*Downingia pulchella.* In honor of the late A. J. Downing, Esq., well known to horticultural and rural fame.

No. 7, *Specularia,* a species of Venus' Looking-glass.

Vol. III.   JULY, 1858.   No. 1.

CALIFORNIA ANIMALS.

SEA LIONS.

The wonders of California extend beyond her rich gold fields, mammoth trees, towering mountains, beautiful valleys, and her delicious fruits and huge vegetables. The strange variety of animals found within her borders, form not the least remarkable and interesting portion of her history. An enthusiastic admirer of our astonishing products has said that "California is the whole world, on a small scale;" and that that which, in days past, was only secured after long and perilous voyages from one country to another, is found here, without difficulty, "all in a heap." That there is much truth in this assertion, no one who is posted will deny.

In previous numbers, as our readers will remember, our artist has furnished us with some very correct engravings of California wonders and curiosities. We have also given the more beautiful and remarkable Birds. The great interest taken in the subject induced us to send our artist among the wild animals; and the result of his visit will be found in the present issue. We think he has succeeded to a charm. The first in the list,

which forms a sort of frontispiece to the gallery of sketches, [see first page] is the far-famed "Sea Lion" of California. This is, indeed, a strange work of nature. Great numbers of them are to be found, almost at any time during a clear, warm day, upon the rocks adjacent to the sea, where they keep up a clatter not at all pleasant to hear. They manifest the fondest regard for their young calves, over which they keep the closest guard. Some of the older ones appear, at first, to be very brave, and often, when teased, make towards you with open mouths, displaying at the same time their tusks. But we have discovered them to be, as a general thing, great cowards. The simple wave of your hand will often make them "take water." Still, should they be so pressed as to render a fight inevitable, they would, in our opinion, prove very ugly customers to handle. We for one would not care to come in too close contact with them under such "pressing" circumstances. It is said, by those well acquainted with their habits, that they fight like tigers among themselves.

THE CAYOTE.

This animal is, it is claimed by some, peculiar to California, and not found in any other country. Of this we have our doubts. It may exist elsewhere—possibly in Mexico—yet on this point we cannot speak knowingly. One thing, however, we do very well know: It is the most thieving thing that walks on four legs. Our artist has, we think, displayed his genius, and taste in the manner in which he presents this strange animal to our view. It will be observed that the rascal is feasting on the bone of some poor victim which he has evidently pounced upon in an unguarded moment, during a dark night, (Cayotes seldom leave their holes during the day,) while his sneaking attitude and villainous expression of eye plainly indicate his general disposition. Our excellent Governor, during the political campaign which ended in his election to his present position, made allusion to this animal, in the course of a speech, which is still fresh in our memory. The Governor had been accused by his opponents of doing something very mean on a certain occasion, and was replying, in most vigorous and effective style to the charges. Said he: "Fellow citizens, I would rather be a Coyote, and sneak about your hen-roosts for a living, than be guilty of such an act as *that*." Certainly, the Governor could not have selected an illustration which would convey a greater abhorrence of the charges in question. It is, perhaps, unnecessary to add that, after that speech, the "mean charge" fell to the ground. Those who know anything about the Coyote will, we think, agree with us, that the engraving furnished by our artist is "to the very life."

THE WOLF.

The California Wolf, unlike those found elsewhere, is of a gray color, slightly mixed with black. It is also larger and more dangerous. It boldly attacks cattle, and its power of muscle in the neck is so great that it can gather up a calf or sheep and easily run off with it. Its scent is quite remarkable. It is said that it scarcely ever fails to reach its object, when once on the track. In the winter season it ventures very near the towns and villages, and creates considerable excitement: It never attacks horses or cattle in the rear, from the fact, probably, that the latter use their heels to too much advantage. It, however, pounces upon them in front, and generally conquers them. When suffering from hunger, it will, it is said, eat the flesh from its own bones.

THE FOX.

If there is any one animal, in the list furnished by our artist, that will be admired more than another, it is the Fox. There he is, in all the beauty of life. For swiftness of foot, and shrewdness, the California Fox is said to surpass those of any other country. Isn't he a beautiful fellow?

THE RACCOON.

It is not claimed that the above is any relation to that "same old coon" about which we have heard so much in other days. It is a native of California, and, upon examination, will be found to be different in many respects from the Coon of other States. The drawing is perfect, and is so taken as to enable the reader to view the animal in all its points. We are informed that, at certain seasons of the year, these Coons are to be found in great numbers along the upper Sacramento. We presume, however, they are confined to no particular section of the State. The California Coon is a beautiful animal, and we do not see how we could have got along without it in our series of sketches. In the above engraving we have secured it in the happiest style.

C. NAHL.   O. VAN VLECK SC.

THE GRIZZLY BEAR.

The Grizzly Bear of California is so well known, that we do not deem a description necessary to introduce it to our readers. The above engraving is a most truthful representation of this remarkable animal, as competent judges will readily admit. It appears almost as natural as when roaming at large through the mountains, and we dare say there are many of our early pioneers who, while marking out trails, or hunting for the precious metal, have seen some "just like him." The California Grizzly is unlike those of his species found in most other countries. It is exceedingly ferocious, and powerful; and, unless treated to a deadly bullet, is a hard customer to manage in an encounter. It fights with great desperation, and never yields while the least spark of life remains.

C. NAHL

THE LYNX.

The Lynx is of a reddish color, with dark brown spots on the end of the tail. In size they measure from three to four feet in length. They are exceedingly blood-thirsty, often pouncing upon more victims than they can devour at one time. They have been known to kill as many as thirty sheep in one night. They are the terror of young cattle — though the deer, it appears, is their principal food. They lie upon the branch of a tree, like a cat, and leap upon their unsuspecting victim from a distance of twelve or fourteen feet. Immediately upon grasping a sheep, they kill it by opening the veins of the throat, and then drink the blood. They then eat the intestines, head and shoulders, and leave the remainder. Singular to relate, after having killed more sheep than is required at one meal, they remove them to some secure place, and spread them out carefully in the air. They then leave for two or three days, and if, upon their return, they find the meat tainted, it is deserted for something more fresh. We have this interesting fact from old mountaineers who are well acquainted with the habits of the animal. The eyes of the Lynx are very large, full and piercing, and of a bright yellow color. The Lynx has a beautiful skin, and its meat is pronounced by those who pretend to be well posted, a rare and delcate morsel. The engraving furnished by our artist may be relied upon as entirely correct.

THE CALIFORNIA DEER.

We give above a very correct drawing of the California Deer — by many called the Elk. We are at a loss to conceive how this beautiful animal should be confounded with the clumsy, ill-shaped Elk. It differs from the Elk in a great many respects, especially in its most striking features. The Elk, besides the great hump on the neck, has a much longer head and ears, and heavier horns. The nostrils of the Elk also resemble those of the horse; while those of the Deer, as will be observed, bear no resemblance to the horse. A most striking peculiarity of the California Bucks, and one which has doubtless been observed by hunters, is their savage disposition after being wounded. After being pursued for hours, and arrested at length by a bullet, they turn suddenly upon their pursuers, and make desperate battle. This movement on their part, as may be imagined, generally creates considerable excitement; still as it is never resorted to until a leaden messenger has been felt, the gallant bearing of the animal is of but short duration. The venison of California is pronounced the finest in the world.

THE LION.

With all her wonders, there are few persons at a distance who will be willing to believe that California produces an animal like that represented in the above engraving; yet, strange and remarkable as it may appear, it is true. A veritable *Lion*, of which the above is a correct sketch, is found within the limits of our State. Hence, we choose to refer to it as the *California Lion.* We have seen one of them, and a splendid fellow he was, too. In point of size, strength, or beauty, we hesitate not to pronounce the California Lion equal, if not superior, to any that we have ever met in the famous menageries of the Atlantic States. It will be observed that they differ greatly in appearance from the Lions of other countries, resembling more the ferocious tiger of the old world.

A gentleman who passed through the northern portion of the State in the fall of '50, describes a fight which he witnessed between a Grizzly Bear and Lion. Upon facing each other, the Bear showed signs of distress, and commenced "backing out." The Lion at the same time drew himself forward very cautiously, until within ten or fifteen feet of his adversary, when coiling his tail under his body, he made a spring, with a hissing noise. He missed his object, but suddenly gathering his energies, he made a second leap, landing full upon the Bear's back. The result of the struggle soon became apparent. The Bear fought with desperation, but was finally compelled to yield beneath the huge jaws of his antagonist. The fight lasted about half an hour. The Lion was considerably bruised.

A STAGE INCIDENT.

BY DOINGS.

SOME two or more summers ago, being in Placerville and wishing to see Sacramento, I engaged stage passage, and retired in pleased expectation of a good time on the morrow—for I do love to be on the move. I was particular in engaging an outside seat, but in some unaccountable manner, neglected to mention the one desired, consequently, on the morning following, quite elated with a hot breakfast and one of those articles known in the mountains as *Regalias.* I walked up to the coach for the purpose of occupying the spoken-for-seat, and to my utter astonishment, found the outside *seats* taken, and your unfortunate friend was directed to climb on top of the stage and ride on the battens. I had nothing to say, I felt that I, and I alone was to blame ; so, without threatening to whip all the agents and everybody-else connected with the concern, I peacefully mounted, congratulating myself, that even battens were preferable to an inside seat on a hot summer day—but alas ! my judgement was not founded upon experience. Did you ever ride on the battens ? No ! well, never try it. Take the benefit of my experience and don't do it—lay over a day—eschew battens as you would a lumber wagon over a corduroy road.

The coach, inside, contained seven women, one man, five children in and out of arms. Outside, three unhappy gentlemen had the pleasure of dangling their legs over the boot, receiving the full benefit of the dust, seven or eight others hung theirs over the sides, while I with several others fixed ourselves *Turk fashion* upon the top. On the seat with the driver, sat two gentlemen who appeared remarkably well pleased with themselves, and whose looks seemed to say : we are sorry for you fellows up there—but "you wa'nt smart." On the

seat back of the drivers, there were three, the one on the right was an elderly gentleman, short and thick in stature, with a very grey head, and who wore gold-rimmed spectacles—he appeared to be good-natured, but extremely nervous. On the left, sat one who sported a light colored moustache, and who I tho't was a German. The middle of the seat was occupied by a musician, who carried under one arm an immense brass horn tied up in a green bag, and beneath the other several framed sketches—and for the articles manifested great care—especially for the horn, which he asserted time and time again, was presented to him by the band, and he would'nt have it injured for a thousand dollars. When the little nervous gray-headed man, by the rolling of the coach was thrown against him, he would exclaim : "look out ! look out sir ! you'll mash my horn ;" or, "there sir, you're on my horn again." The little man would generally reply with, " confound your horn ;" or, "you've no business to carry a horn up here. On one occasion, he deliberately took from the pocket of his coat-tail, a soda bottle and drawing the cork, applied the neck—with the bulk of the bottle slightly elevated—to his lips, and after giving his head a jerk or two backwards, removed it, replaced the cork, and peeping over his specks at the horn-blower, said, "that's the sort of a *horn* sir, to travel with," and then with a deeply satisfactory a-a-hem, returned the soda bottle from whence it was taken.—This same little man would often nervously express it as his opinion, that the coach was top heavy, and he would'nt be surprised if it turned over, "and what a nice fix you'd be in," said he to the musical man, as we were going slowly along upon a side hill, where the traveled road appeared to be in fine order, but below us the descent of the hill was rapid. Hardly had the little man uttered those words when the off wheels ran into one of those dust holes not uncommon in the summer season, and sure enough over we did go. The writer remembers very distinctly of rolling down hill in company with divers and sundry bandboxes and small packages, also something in *a long green bag*, and that he brought up by the side of a cluster of bushes, and that after a minute examination of his person, which proved that he was perfectly sound, he gathered up such of the articles as lay about him and hurried back to the scene of the disaster, where he arrived in season to assist one or two females and their offspring out of the wreck. Fortunately, no one was severely injured; but the coach was so disabled, that the driver declared it impossible to proceed, and informed us that we must walk on to the next "change," about six miles—so, off we started, all in good humor, and proceeded nearly two miles, when the musician, who was plodding along a little in advance with horn in hand and sketches under his arms, suddenly halted with an exclamation, he appeared much as a person would with a severe pain in the stomach, and to our earnest enquiry of, "what's the matter?" he yelled out in agonizing tones, "MY HORN'S MASHED!" The strings of that bag were instantly loosened, and the oddest looking thing taken out that ever any one did see of the horn kind—'twas too bad, but we laughed, we could'nt help it, 'twas so ridiculous, the idea of his having carried that treasure, the idol of his heart, that HORN, two miles, and only then discovered it to be injured—rejoiced at his own escape, that valuable instrument under the law of preservation became secondary—we laughed, aye, roared, sympathy found no chance for expression, and the little man laughed louder than all, his body bobbed up and down, his sides shook, straggling tears came to his eyes,

and his face became purple and scarlet by turns—suddenly, a change came over him, he thrust one hand into his coat tail pocket, his little body straightened up almost backward, his features became serious and almost fearful as he withdrew the hand and holding the upper portion of the soda bottle before us exclaimed, "gentlemen, 'tis no laughing matter! *my horn is also mashed!*"

FOREVER?

I.

The soft west wind comes stealing o'er
   Pacific's listening wave;
The ripples glide along the shore,
   And naiads stoop to lave
Their fairy forms within the ray
That lingers where the zephyrs play.

II.

Upon the lonely beach I stand
   And watch the waning light,
Receding from the ocean strand,
   But lingering on the height
Of yon blue mountain, in the west,
Tinging with golden hues its crest.

III.

One moment more, and softly dies
   The last faint tint away;
A sombre shadow in the skies
   Proclaims departed day;
And nature, pulseless, seems to mourn
Another sun forever gone.

IV.

Forever? No! for see! he sends
   A thousand gems of light—
Bright, sparkling stars, whose soft light blends
   Upon the brow of night;
They whisper 'long the arching skies,
"The sun—our lord—again shall rise."

HUTCHINGS'

CALIFORNIA MAGAZINE.

VOL I.   MAY, 1857.   NO. XI.

WAYSIDE WATERING PLACES.

Reader, were you ever an inside passen ger of a California stage coach, when there was just a round dozen of fellow-travelers, and who, with one exception—yourself— were all smokers, (we of course presume that no lady was of the number, as no GENTLEMAN would thus forget himself, by smoking in a lady's presence,) and being of different tastes, if not of different countries, each one smoked a cigar or cigarita, of different quality and kind? and that too, in the scorching months of summer, after the usual morning breeze had died away; and when the horses and stage were enveloped in clouds of oppressive and cough-producing dust, and which came rolling and curling in upon every passenger, with a "don't care who you are" indifference to his taste or wishes; not only half-choking him, but changing the color of his clothing and complexion, not even omitting his whiskers—that is, if he *cultivated* the last named "article?" Were you, permit us again to ask, ever a passenger at such a time?

If, with almost a shudder at the remembrance, you reply in the affirmative, you will recollect with what pleasure you welcomed the wayside house, as the stage halted to "water," or "change horses"— and how readily you jumped out to try the effect of alternate doses of dust and water,

WAY-SIDE SHADE AND WATERING PLACE.

or soda-water—with or without "suthin" in it.

Now we do not say that upon every road and at every watering place, there will be found such an inviting "shade" as the one represented in the engraving above; but, they are to be found on several of the roads leading to the mining towns, and especially, near the cities of Sacramento, Marysville, and Stockton, where the teamster, the pleasure rider, and the traveler, halts to water his stock, or "take a drink."

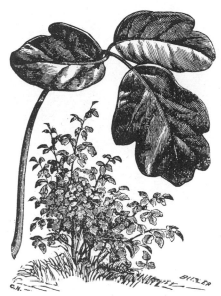

THE POISON OAK.

THE POISON OAK.

This subject has elicited more attention, and invited more examination than we supposed it probable, when the first article appeared upon it, in this Magazine. Letters upon letters, of inquiry, and for information have poured in upon us; some telling us of its inconvenient and painful effects with its accompanying symptoms; others relating the particular kinds of treatment, which have been successful to them, individually, with a variety of questions as to what it is? how to avoid it? what is a certain cure for it? etc., etc.

To satisfy these inquiries, in some measure, we renew the subject, giving some illustrations of the shrub, and its

effects, in hopes that, although we do not profess to be physician extraordinary, to this class of persons and cases, we may nevertheless diffuse information of value to those affected by it.

For ourselves we may say that we can handle it, and even eat it, with impunity, as it produces no effect whatever upon us; but we regret to say it is not thus with all.

In the early part of last month, we saw a person almost blind from its effects, and with his entire face, and portions of his body, very much discolored and swollen. In this condition he was recommended the "sweating" process, adopted and practiced by Dr. Bourne, the Water Cure physician of this city. The following statement, from Mr. M. Fisher, will distinctly explain itself.

I was poisoned by contact with Poison Oak, February 22d, 1857, at three o'clock, P. M. At ten o'clock, P. M., 24th, my condition was very distressing as shown by the *first* portrait, then taken, when I was rapidly becoming blind. The *second* portrait shows my improved state *two and a half* to *three hours later, after a thorough sweating.* The *third* portrait was taken at forty-eight hours later than the first one, and now I am entirely cured of a very severe affection which was rapidly getting worse, and exhibiting its effects all over my person; *without* medicine or any other than the mode above stated, only three baths. During the year 1853, the Poison Oak caused me partial blindness nearly one month; and total blindness for several days, with much suffering.

Now we give the above, simply to show

EFFECTS OF THE POISON OAK.

that a good sweating, and the drinking freely of cold water, with the application of cloths, saturated with warm water, to the head and face, can be practiced by any one with the greatest safety and efficiency.

"Any mode (says the *Alta*) of taking a vapor bath will do, either by means of steam admitted to a tight box, or by placing the patient under blankets, and heating the water with hot stones; or other convenient plan, so that it be effectual, and allow the patient's head to be exposed to the air, avoiding the necessity of breathing the hot and vitiated steam.

"From having witnessed its effects, we recommend the foregoing as a simple and efficient process for overcoming this troublesome disorder, to all such as may unfortunately require its aid.

There are some afflicted so severely, as to induce protracted illness, often blindness, and sometimes even death. We have frequently known it to baffle the treatment of physicians for weeks and months, subjecting the patient meantime, to great inconvenience and suffering. We have, therefore, thought it worth while to give the

AFTER A BATH OF THREE HOURS.

public the benefit of a mode of cure, applied in a case that recently came under our own observation; and which seems alike simple, speedy and efficacious."

Some have used gunpowder with effect,—others alchohol,—others strong ley—and who have become cured by rubbing the parts affected, although the "sweating" process seems to us, the most natural.

"I suggest a remedy for the pustular eruption," writes a gentleman from Umpqua City, Oregon, "produced by the poison oak:—take sulphate of iron, ten grains; laudanum, half an ounce; water, one ounce—mix and apply to the diseased surface, constantly, by means of soft linen, saturated with the solution. If the eruption is persistent, with sympathetic fever, take salts in aperient doses, and one grain of sulphate of iron, internally."

Too much care cannot be used when riding or walking near this poisonous shrub, especially by those persons who are most easily affected. It is also very desirable that a remedy should be applied as speedily as possible after its effects are first felt,—thus saving much annoyance and inconvenience.

CURED.

HUTCHINGS'

CALIFORNIA MAGAZINE.

Vol. III.　　OCTOBER, 1858.　　No. 4.

REMINISCENCES OF MENDOCINO.

THE HEADQUARTERS OF THE MENDOCINO RESERVATION.　　DISTRIBUTION OF
RATIONS TO THE INDIANS.

REMINISCENCES OF MENDOCINO.

Extracts from a Manuscript in German, entitled "TEN DAYS IN MENDOCINO."

> On the mountains is freedom! the breath of decay
> Never sullies the fresh flowing air;
> Oh! Nature is perfect wherever we stray;
> 'Tis man that deforms it with care.
>
> [SCHILLER's *Bride of Messina*.]

PART I.—TRIP FROM PETALUMA TO THE COAST STATION OF THE INDIAN RESERVATION.

In the early part of 1852, three friends, visiting Clear Lake Valley, had an opportunity of becoming acquainted with the beauty of the country north of the Bay of San Francisco.

They would have found sufficient inducement for a second excursion in their impressions of the first trip; all that they had enjoyed of nature in its silent grandeur and charming contrast; the picturesque character of the mountain region, crowned by Mount St. Helen, (on the summit of which stands a cross of bronze, erected there by a Russian surveying party from Bodegas); but more especially the sudden transition from the volcanic chaos of the declivities of Black Mountain to the park-like Eden of the shores of the Lake yet lying in almost the same quiet repose as in the early days of the Spanish conquest, when it was known to but a few as the "Laguna Grande de Napa;" but, moreover, the exciting adventures connected with the first visit; the acquaintance formed with several of the Nimrods of that mountain region and their glowing descriptions of the hidden beauties of the adjacent country and the abundance of game, proved irresistible to the early visitors and several other friends, to escape at least once a year from the wearing excitement of a business life in San Francisco, and to dedicate a couple of weeks to the further exploration of that region.

As the country around Clear Lake had lost all charms of a *terra incognita*, since it had become peopled by settlers attracted from all parts by its advantages for farming, it served but as a place of rendezvous for wider excursions; for the delights of the wilderness had to be sought in other directions, more remote from civilized life, even in the almost inaccessible haunts of the Red man himself.

Mendocino, the mountainous region south of the cape of that name, discovered in 1543 by Juan Rodriguez Cabrillo, and by him named after Don Antonio de Mendoza, then Viceroy of Mexico, was the rallying cry of the hunting party of 1857.

The trio of horsemen who first threaded their way through the mountain passes to Clear Lake, had annually gained in number, until the present company amounted to fifteen persons, but mostly comprising employees of the federal government and members of the bar. Three or four of the party, either from changes incident to life in America, or by their own roving dispositions, were enthusiastic amateurs of the noble art of woodcraft; and some had passed a great portion of their lives in the solitudes of the Rocky Mountains. Though so many professional men were of the party, and there was no lack of varied knowledge, yet there was no pretension whatever to scientific pre-eminence.

In point of practical aptitude and complete provision for improvement and enjoyment both mental and bodily, the party could not easily be surpassed. Mons. Edouart, the artist, had with him his sketch-book; several amateurs brought with them their musical instruments, which, as an orchestra to the merry choruses, tended not a little to increase the conviviality of the party.

All being animated by the resolve to forget for a while the cares of existence, everything was left to the star of good luck; trusting to the good understanding between the members and that festive humor which is sure to develop itself in the happy freedom of the mountains.

As the present excursion, planned for a wider circuit, would require at least three weeks, I was forced, though reluctantly, to decline a friendly invitation extended to me. However, when the day of departure had arrived, I could not refrain from accompanying the party for a few days, at least, at their outset. I was thereby made a participator in some very amusing events.

The subjoined sketches of what came under my own observation may give some little idea of the enjoyment of my more fortunate companions after they reached the distant hunting grounds.

On looking back to the few days passed in such happy companionship, each member must consider it as one of great satisfaction. The invigorating effect of the mountain air and scenery tended so to refresh the energies of the mind and body, that all returned to their occupations and duties with redoubled power and cheerfulness.

The groupings of the several camping grounds, offering the richest variety of the attractions of nature, furnished subject for the artist, seldom, if ever surpassed: Now in some secluded valley on the banks of a murmuring brook, surrounded by grotesque rocks; now on the green sward of some splendid forest, under the protection of a lofty pine or wide spreading oak; now on the shores of the Pacific, whose waves, with mysterious and never-ceasing music, lulled to a repose as quiet and refreshing, as could have been obtained on beds of softest down. Sometimes it chanced that the party should be suddenly overtaken by night. Then camp would be made at the first spot affording water and pasture to the animals, and to the men sufficient space to stretch their limbs.

PAECHTEL'S FARM, AT THE HEAD OF LITTLE LAKE VALLEY.

At the various camps frequent visits were received from the hardy pioneers of those regions. Shouldering their rifles, they would accompany the party a day or two for the purpose of pointing out spots where game was abundant and of enjoying the conviviality of the camp-fire. By a recital of their adventures with that mingling of romance and reality for which mountain men are famous, they would add greatly to the general entertainment.

The Indians, too, with whom we chanced to meet, were always ready to become our followers. They considered themselves amply repaid for any drudgery they might undergo by receiving the cast-off clothing of the members of the party, and a liberal supply of substantial food, to them an unaccustomed luxury.

Bountifully provided as were the party with a variety of good things from the city, and almost daily receiving a fresh supply of game, fish and other luxuries of the wilderness, "Plenty" was the prevailing feature of our camp. Although vieing in keenness of appetite with the mountaineers themselves, there was always a sufficiency to satisfy all. No one was called upon to test his powers of abstinence in the way of eating or drinking.

The outfit was excellent—probably a little too complete—requiring, as it did, the use of a number of pack animals, which often delayed our progress. However, viewed in the light of a running pic-nic, all was marvelously well arranged. Besides, while traveling through a region yet so little known, there was pleasure in the novelty of exploration; and delays, which might otherwise have

VIEW OF CAPE MENDOCINO.—THE CAPE ROCK, INDIAN FISHING CAMP.

proved vexatious, afforded opportunities of indulging in predilections for natural study, richly compensated by a variety of objects, and especially the floral beauties of the hills.

The incidents relating to one night's resting place deserve more than a general notice, on account of the hospitable reception given to a portion of the party— a reception as unexpected as it was welcome.

On the way out of what is called Ukiah Valley, owing to some detention of the pack-animals, the party became separated. The greater portion took a trail leading to a high range of mountains on the right. The remainder, some half-dozen in number, deceived by numerous tracks, took a trail leading in a different direction. The latter, supposing their companions to be ahead, hastened forward to overtake them and reach the place appointed for that night's rendezvous, before dark. After following the tracks for some distance, they found that they were becoming fewer and fainter. At last, nothing was left to guide them but the general direction of the ridge, which ran towards the valley they were anxious to reach.

Twilight was fast yielding to the deeper shades of night, when, hearing the crack of a rifle near at hand, they felt confident that at last they had reached their companions. But for some time no living soul was met; and it was long after dark that, descrying a bright light and hastening forward, they soon reached a large log-house. The brothers Paechtel, the owners, attracted by the noise of arrival, welcomed the weary travelers with all the heartiness characteristic of mountain settlers.

The genuine spirit of hospitality, which is the never-failing accompaniment of true independence, is sure to make a stopping place in the mountains one of the most pleasing recollections of a man's life.

On the borders of the wilderness the tourist has the best opportunity of enjoying hospitality in the fullest acceptation of the word. This virtue exists, no doubt, among the farming class in the valleys; but, as the settlements increase, inns and places of refreshment are opened, with all the accompaniments of traffic and travel. Genuine hospitality, then, retires modestly to the log-cabin of the pioneer, in the more remote districts.

The brothers Paechtel, three in number, are of German descent. They are in the prime of life, with intelligent and interesting features, and, as yet, unmarried. By dint of industry and economy, they have built up quite a snug establishment. A comfortable, spacious log-house, surrounded by several out-houses, serves as a dwelling for themselves and accommodation for their help. Although devoting considerable attention to agriculture, their main object is the raising of cattle. Having the advantage of an extensive range and abundant pasturage all the year, their stock, of which they have several hundred head, is in excellent condition.

On returning to the house, after providing for the horses in an excellent pasture, well enclosed, we met a relative of the Paechtels, who had just come in from his evening hunt. It was then ascertained that it was the report of his rifle that had been heard in the early part of the evening. As a trophy, he had with him the quarter of a fine, fat buck—leaving the balance to be brought in by the Indians.

Ablutions in the neighboring brook having greatly tended to our comfort, seats were taken at a bountifully-spread board. The abundant supply of warm bread, (made by one of the brothers himself,) broiled venison, fresh milk and butter, disappeared almost as rapidly as it was provided.

After satisfying our almost ravenous appetites, pipes were lighted and seats taken around the huge fire-place. A number of large logs had been brought in, and soon a bright fire was burning, which added not only to the cheerfulness, but also to the comfort. The company gave themselves up to social converse, alternately listening to and recounting whatever of interest or excitement occurred to each one.

The groupings of the party, with the addition of the dusky Indian attendants, lighted up by the glare of the blazing fire, formed a picture as original as it was complete.

Some cattle-dealers arriving in the early part of the evening, had been received with the same hospitable welcome as was the lot of the later guests. To them had been assigned all the regular sleeping accommodations of the house. Not at all at a loss, however, the worthy entertainers, bringing from the storeroom a bale of new blankets, opened and spread them upon the floor.

The party would have been in a sorry

plight to camp out that night, having left everything on the pack-horses. The idea of being separated from them never once entered the mind of any one. At last Morpheus claimed his votaries. One by one emptying his pipe, retired to their blankets. The large room, occasionally illuminated by the rekindling flame, offered a tableau of a within doors camp.

To one of the party the balsamic mountain air had become a luxury, nay, almost necessity; so, arranging his bed a short distance from the house, he slept soundly in single blessedness 'till dawn. A motion at his side having awakened him, on looking up, he found himself surrounded by the three dogs of the farm, having unconsciously enjoyed their company during the night. On seeing the lonely sleeper, imitating the hospitality

AROUND THE CAMP FIRE. CAMP BELL, MATOMKA VALLEY.

of their owners, they had undertaken the friendly task of watching over his safety and warming themselves at the same time. Had he been at all susceptible to visions, he might have imagined a visit from three young bears; and with as much reason, too, as one of the prominent members of the party thought he had been bitten by a rattlesnake, a few nights previous—his faithful dog, induced by the chilliness of the night, having crept between the blankets of his master, and applied his cold nose to some uncovered part of his person, which invited that canine homage. Being much startled,

he jumped up with a shout, supposing that he had been bitten by a rattlesnake; notwithstanding the precaution he had taken of surrounding his couch with a rope of hair, as the most effective scarecrow to the reptile.

The following morning, while at breakfast, the remainder of the party made their appearance. It was then learned that they had camped several miles back on a plateau on the mountains. They, of course, were well provided with everything to make themselves comfortable, having with them all the camp equipage.

At sunrise, from their lofty resting

place, they were regaled by a magnificent panorama, extending from their feet as far as the eye could reach.

Next morning, about breakfast time, the cavalcade of our companions having come up, all were in high glee to avail themselves of the kind invitation of the Paechtels, who, to do honor to the chief personages of our party, readily consented to make a holiday, in order to accompany us to a famous hunting ground, which, by general selection, was to be our halting place for several days.

We had an agreeable ride of a few hours, chiefly through underwood, interspersed with the manzanita tree, and alternately through chapparal of miles in extent, a favorite resort of bears; though, notwithstanding abundant evidence of bruins' proximity, we only caught sight of two, of a cinnamon color, far beyond rifle-shot distance.

Traversing a ridge, we descended into a deep valley, literally studded with isolated rocks. Several of these rocks, towering above the rest, vied in elevation with the sides of the cañon itself, their lofty pyramidical peaks emerging from the wilderness of exuberant vegetation, which covered the whole bottom of this ravine, forming a dense dome of verdure beneath the shade of which a brook of clear mountain water, leaping from basin to basin and bordered with green sward, seemed to invite us to a real hunter's paradise.

But our prospective resting place was a few miles higher up on the opposite ridge. Pursuing our course in that direction we entered a magnificent forest of noble oaks, intermixed with pine and fir; the luxuriant growth of underwood rivaling the former in beauty and variety.

Here we halted and selected a spot unobstructed by bushes for our camping ground for several days. Our pack train had come up, thanks to the good care of our excellent Chileno, in spite of impro-

vised roads; in less than a quarter of an hour the kitchen apparatus was set up, the kettle on the fire and our black cook in a state of bustling activity. At a short distance from the fire, each one, following his fancy, selected the foot of some lofty tree for his anchoring place. Our animals, as if aware of the prospective rest and leisure, scampered off briskly to the neighboring glade; a few of them only were staked out on long ropes, so as to afford a kind of rallying point for the rest, who were soon enjoying unbounded freedom and all of them luxuriating in the waving sea of wild oats. With the help of so many hands all arrangements were soon completed. No one was more indefatigable than the Paechtels themselves, who, in order to come to the aid of our committee for firewood, with the help of their reatas and the combined strength of their horses brought branches and limbs of an immense size in sufficient quantity not only to provide us for several days, but also to surround us on the windward with a huge rampart of logs, affording us a most comfortable shelter.

It being yet early, there was for us ample scope for roving about, which all of us availed ourselves of, especially the hunters, who soon gave evidence of their pursuits by the report of their rifles. As to myself, taking the course of a ridge, I enjoyed a beautiful panorama of the surrounding valleys. On returning to camp I found all in bustle and high glee. The game brought in by the hunters was made over to the cook and the gentlemen who volunteered to assist him; and soon, in the midst of the plates and covers laid on the green sward, the most delicious meal was spread that ever tempted sharpened appetites. It is superfluous to mention that our cooking committee were gratified in finding love's labor *not* lost on this occasion, and that there seemed no end to new editions.

We were yet in the midst of our social meal (and what more delicious morsel can there be than venison broiled after the fashion of California hunters!) when three dusky figures, enthusiastically welcomed, made their appearance. It was easy to see that this welcome was tendered to personages of mountain celebrity, who had left impressions not easily to be forgotten; the intrepid Ben, chieftain of the Shewallapanees, one of the wild mountain tribes, known to all who had been there before as the redoubted bear-killer, whose last victory had been purchased with the loss of his left eye—the right one being also distorted, and his face lacerated to an extent that hardly permitted any recognition of the features of the human race. Though welcomed at once by half a dozen of our company, (for strangers must be shocked by his appearance,) he never for a mo-

SHERWOOD VALLEY.   THE HUNTING PARTY EN ROUTE.

ment lost the calm and dignified manner that characterizes an Indian Chief. He had returned only three days previous from the war-path against the Kameloponees, with whom there existed a feud since the assault and murder of several of his tribe. With the moderation for which he was proverbial, he left them the choice between contest and an amicable settlement, which latter was accepted on conditions to offer "compensation for the past and guarantees for the future."

To our party the apparition of Ben and his followers was welcome also in point of information with regard to game in the mountains; as to myself it offered a welcome opportunity, through recommendation of Tobin, to obtain one of his Indians as guide; and furthermore, it was Ben's fertility of invention that provided bearers for our dogs—the poor animals being by this time so thoroughly exhausted, that they must have been left behind, had we not been able to find people to carry them.

While Ben and his people were extremely reserved in demonstrations of enthusiasm, they were by no means backward in availing themselves of the good success of our hunters, leaving nothing but skin and bone of all the venison they found on hand.

It was in this night's camp, for the first time since starting from San Francisco, that the true spirit of conviviality broke forth, which, during the first few days' marches find a drawback from the fatigue of some members of the company. By this time every one seemed to have awoke to the true independence and freedom of the mountains. A couple of violins and a flute were started from their cases, and soon all was set into electric movement; and with music and dancing, choruses and burlesque speeches, a couple of hours passed pleasantly before any one bethought himself of retiring; then a few at a time, grouped by predilection or the promptings of the moment, retired to the quiet of their lairs in that abandon of conversation which is never to be found in towns, and which inadvertantly gleans, even from the most reserved, occasional retrospective glimpses, such as afford the most racy reminiscences of these bivouacs.

The life of men like Jack Hays and Caperton, who have gone through the most daring tasks as well in guerilla war as in difficult reconnoissances, proving their valor on the field of battle as well as in the most desperate conflicts of the wilderness, but whose modesty and un-pretending manner is the very stamp of true merit—is a living book, that, however, only opens under congenial circumstances.

Besides, there was abundance of topic for interesting discussion, an inexhaustible source of material, which, under the clever polemic and acumen of our legal stars could not fail to create enthusiasm; albeit, their discussions never suffered by pedantic display, and the material for such rhetoric generally obtained healthy nourishment from the immediate accompaniments of scenery, groupings, etc.

For me this was the greatest attraction of those evenings under the starry canopy of heaven; and often, after having for a while enjoyed the conversation of my friends, on retiring to my couch, a world of reminiscences of the past rose up to commingle with the rich impressions of the day's journey.

On that evening there was certainly enough in the natural excitement of the scene to keep my thoughts riveted to our entourage. The effect of the camp-fire—which, to enliven the banquet, was fed with huge logs—was splendid. Obscured for a while, whenever a fresh supply of trees and branches subdued the glare and circumscribed it to the immediate group of our bivouac, the flames broke forth again with redoubled force, and illumined the lofty dome of branches over us, enabling us to trace out each branch and cluster of foliage; and sending its lightening flashes far into the labyrinth of reddened colonades, whose magic effect filled our minds with the interminable extent of the virgin forest.

At length quiet prevailed, and the crackling of the charred trunks and rustling of the wind in the lofty crowns of trees were the only sounds which disturbed that majestic solitude.

From Sherwood Valley, the scene of Mr. Edouart's spirited tableau, we gained the first view of Bald Mountain, towering over the coast range, which has to be traversed to enter the district along the sea-coast forming the Mendocino Reservation.

When, after a toilsome ascent of a couple of hours, we reached the summit, a panorama burst upon our view, which every one of our party must ever remember as an object of sublime grandeur.

Our range of view over a vast segment of the Pacific Ocean, and a corresponding extent of some fifty or sixty miles of seacoast before us, considering the distance yet separating us from it, must have comprised an area of at least 1,000 to 1,200 square miles; and yet, as far as the eye could reach, a seemingly interminable forest lay at our feet. A forest covering ridges and valleys in all the natural undulations of that mountain region, and receiving from the inequalities of the ground such lights and shades that, agitated by the breeze, it seemed a sea of foliage, and contrasted beautifully with the deep blue ocean fringed with its silvery surf.

Each and every one of us was impressed with the grandeur of this scene; and yet only a part—a very small part—of the Mendocino Coast Range lay before

VIEW OF THE COAST RANGE, FROM THE SUMMIT OF BALD MOUNTAIN.

us. It was sufficient to convince me that California will for centuries have virgin forests, perhaps to the end of Time!

An Indian trail, the only practicable path, follows the course of a mountain ridge running west, over gently undulating, yet never broken ground, though deep ravines lay on either side. Wherever the position of the trees offers an opening there are magnificent views, with sea and forest as the only object for the eye to rest on; scenes comparing in extent with that of the sandy desert, only that inexhaustibleness of matter is here combined with richness in form and color.

These Redwoods of themselves are a fit subject for contemplation: trees of immense size that, combining strength and elegance, rise to the skies; and some of which rival the cedars of Calaveras in age, attaining, when full grown, an elevation of three hundred feet, and a diameter of twelve to fifteen feet near the root.

The base of most of these trees show the effects of the conflagrations which year after year devastate the undergrowth of these forests, and to which one of these giants occasionally falls a victim; but many, in spite of large excavations in the trunks, capable of affording shelter to a horse and his rider, stretch their victorious crowns to the clouds, and in others the reproductive power of nature has obliterated all traces of such fires by reclothing them with rind. Here and there the offshoots of trees (fallen centuries ago) have formed a rotunda or colonade of eight or ten independent trees round the centre of the old root, each of them of full height; and the space in the centre is wide enough to serve as encampment to a caravan. Among the many bushes that form the undergrowth there are ferns of gigantic size; one species, by its overhanging wings, reminding one of the palm of the tropics, luxuriates profusely on the Medusa heads of the roots of up-torn trees. Owing to an optical deception not unusual in mountain scenery, it seemed as if we were advancing on a parallel with the sea-coast instead of traversing the intervening ridges; although gaining a free view, I could not doubt our progress—the sea being nearer —and we seemed to be equally surrounded by forest in advance as well as in the rear.

A deep gully of barely sufficient capacity to afford passage to Ten Mile River, separated us from the next ridge, which, by an ascent of similar steepness, receives the continuation of this trail. This is Strawberry Valley, if a ravine deserves the name of a valley. The stream glides in crystal clearness over a bed of pebbles clothed in delicious *clair obscure* by the overhanging branches, which only permit access to the meridian sun. A number of dead giant trees of sufficient circumference to appear like the ruins of some antique castle, stand as remains of by-gone ages in the depth of this gully, forming a venerable contrast with the exuberant growth of the new generation, by which both walls of this secluded spot are covered from the depths to the very summit.

About sundown we reached a small valley in the shape of a delta, with fine bottom land; the first clear spot this side of the coast range, and the only place since leaving Sherwoods, that exhibited any signs of cultivation.

Here we halted for the night; and all of us, overwhelmed by the grandeur of the scenery we had passed, as well as satisfied with the exercise of the day, were glad to stretch our wearied limbs upon the green sward. We enjoyed an unbroken rest in anticipation of a pleasant morning ride, to take us to the Mendocino Reservation.

PART II.—INDIAN RESERVATIONS AND THE MENDOCINO RESERVATION.

The term " *U. S. Reservation*" (Government Reservation) applies, in the United States of America, to tracts of land selected from the general mass of the domain and set apart for special purposes by the administration; all the land not covered by private claims, and therefore called " public land," remains open to settlers, at fixed prices, under the Pre-emption Law.

Indian Reservations are districts by act of Congress made over to the Department of Indian affairs, for the carrying out of special purposes, more fully explained in the following pages.

The system of these institutions, under the direct control of the Federal Government, and managed by U. S. officers, under the denomination of Indian Agents or Superintendents, is highly praiseworthy, and based on principles as humane as they are liberal. It is intended to accomplish a double purpose: to assist the growing requirements of the steadily progressing colonization, by removing the Indians from those districts where the white settlements have already increased to such an extent as to make the presence of the Aborigines a serious drawback and an increasing source of annoyance; and to concentrate in other remoter districts, best suited to their wants, the straggling tribes, already greatly reduced in numbers, to make for them a new home, where the natural elements of their subsistence are sufficiently abundant to ensure to them, under moderate labor, a maintenance from the farming establishments formed for that purpose, and liberally aided on the part of Government. The Indians are thus protected and provided for within the limits assigned to them, under a salutary control, while, by their removal, the white settlers, secured from their incursions, have free scope for extending their improvements. Thus have favorable results been generally obtained in the Atlantic States; and though, with the exception, perhaps, of the Cherokees, (where, by the mixing of races, a prosperous nation of agricultural half-breeds has sprung up,) I know of no instance of the difficult problem of conservation and civilization of the red men having been solved; their lot, considering the circumstances, has been very much alleviated, and their transition to a kind of industrial existence has stayed the annihilation of the race.

THE FISHING STATION ON THE RIVER NOYO, MENDOCINO.

The system, in itself, is comprehensive and highly beneficial; though it has been asserted in this respect, as in other branches of public service, that practice falls short of theory, and that the Indian appointments, through the management of Uncle Sam's farms, are some of the richest morsels in the gift of the leading party, to reward political merit. It is to this source (the envy arising from such assertions) that most of the invectives, and even vile aspersions, are to be attributed which repeatedly have been heaped upon Indian Agents.

Considering the remoteness of the field of action, the large contracts to be carried out for supplies of every kind to large communities, at first wholly dependent on them; the management of rations; the providing materials for buildings, bridges, and unlooked-for emergencies; the position of an Indian Agent certainly embraces a large scope for action and power, in which control is almost impossible; the more acknowledgement is due to the faithful fulfillment of the arduous duties in this particular branch of the public service. For the welfare or suffering, the comfort or misery of this mute community, as well as the preservation of the stations themselves, depend entirely on the aptitude and trustworthiness of the Indian Agents; and the fulfillment of so important a trust requires a great capacity for business, a thorough knowledge of details, untiring activity, disregarding fatigue and danger, and, above all, moderation and self-command, the indispensable qualifications for managing the rude elements of a settlement in the wilderness.

The doom of the red man is once for all irrevocably sealed, as soon as the white pioneer sets foot upon his hunting grounds. And it is difficult to say, with regard to California, whether more victims have fallen to the barbarous, half-fanatic, half-military expeditions of the Californians during the Mexican times, (to subdue certain tribes, and capture their women and children for menial service, under the pretext of Christianization,) or to the irresistible wedge of the American settler who, impatient of restraint, in his contempt for other races, remorselessly scatters all that stands in his way; or, lastly, whether deeper injury has not resulted from apparently friendly intercourse, which has introduced to the tribes the evils of intoxication, small pox, and many other diseases previously unknown to them. Compared with the misery and abjection into which most of them have sunk, by being deprived of or disturbed in their hunting and fishing grounds, and even made dependent upon their ruthless intruders, by wants they have introduced and accustomed them to, their removal to the protection and discipline of the Reservations is to be considered a great blessing!

The system is not one of compulsory labor, nor forcible conversion; and there is little if any restraint as to the exercise of their primitive rites; but the most stringent measures are taken against intoxication. The able-bodied men are kept to regular employment, while provision is made for instructing the rising generation. A small military force, to represent the mighty arm of the Federal Government, is sufficient to protect the establishment and to avoid conflicts, which, left to the workings of human passions, would, as they have done in other parts, involve whole districts in devastating warfare.

The institution of the Reservations seems to be the best mitigation under existing evils. It provides a refuge for the hunted-down sons of the wilderness; and if a prosperous future cannot be built up for them, their actual wants are at least provided for. But, within half a century, the existence of the red race will be reduced to an object of historical retrospect!

THE MENDOCINO RESERVATION.

This Indian Reservation, the largest of California, fully deserves a circumstantial description. Its principal station is on the sea-coast, near the river Noyo, which, for the first few miles from its mouth, is navigable for small craft. The outlet of this river presents a double harbor. The outer one is sufficiently sheltered, during the greater part of the year, by almost parallel promontories, projecting on both sides. Above it, a sandy spit of land, extending from the north bank nearly to the opposite shore, leaves a narrow entrance to the inner harbor, which is the usual place of anchorage for the little schooner belonging to the station. This schooner serves for fishing, and for communication with the harbor of Big River, situated about ten miles to the south.

The buildings of the station stand on a slightly elevated plain, about a mile from the sea, and nearly the same distance from the mouth of the Noyo; they consist of a spacious store-house, offices and mess-rooms, the dwelling of the Agent and some smaller cottages for the employees. There is also a physician's and apothecary's department, and a number of work-shops, The Indians regularly employed, together with their families, live close by in block-houses, arranged in an open square. In the midst of this rises what seems to be a large mound. It is a mud-plastered roof, covering a round excavation, and the whole is a good specimen, though on a very large scale, of the usual Digger Indian style of architecture. On one side is a small hole, for entrance; and another hole in the roof serves for a chimney. The Indians use this wigwam as a Temascal or sweat-bath, in which they shut up their sick to pass through an ordeal of heat and smoke, sometimes for hours on a stretch. It also serves as a council-chamber and as a banquet-hall, and for the performance of their religious rites. In it the bodies of the dead are reduced to ashes, the whole community keeping up a most doleful howling meanwhile.

Not far from the buildings, on the edge of the woods, are the Rancherias of those tribes which still live in their primitive condition. Each tribe has a separate camp, and some of their wigwams are so hidden in the bushes, that their whereabouts is only betrayed by the smoke.

Two miles further on is an outpost of about 20 soldiers, whose duty it is to aid the Agent in maintaining order. They would have an easy life of it, indeed, if they had nothing else to do. But, unfortunately, their services are very frequently required to protect the Indians against the cruelty and oppression of the white men who have settled on the outskirts of the Reservation.

The Indian tribes of the Reservation chiefly belong to those generally known in California as "Diggers." They lead a roaming life, and their temporary dwellings are circular excavations, covered with a roof of rushes, plastered over with mud — the whole looking like a hillock.

In disposition they are more peaceable than warlike, although petty feuds are continually kept up between the tribes, and they have their fighting-men and war-chieftains. They subsist chiefly on roots, acorns, seeds, grass, earth-worms, ants and grasshoppers, according to the season; but their principal food is fish from the sea or rivers. They are good fishermen, very expert in the use of spears, nets and fishing-baskets.

Their arms are too imperfect to allow them to kill game, except at a short distance; this is therefore only an accidental source of support. The mountain tribes, however, taking advantage of ravines and gullies, sometimes manage to drive a large quantity of game into some corner, from which there is no escape, and thus slaughter great numbers, and for a while revel in abundance. But the supply does not last long, as the power of the Indians to dispose of meat and to gorge themselves is truly astonishing.

The Indians, when brought into the Reservation, deliver up their arms, and they are not allowed to carry any, except when on a temporary furlough in the mountains.

The tribes of the valleys of Sonoma and Napa, and those who lived near Clear Lake, have held intercourse with the settlers for the last thirty years, or since the first settlements sprung up north of the Bay of San Francisco. Food and covering was a sufficient inducement for them to help the Spaniards during harvest. An imperfect knowledge of the Spanish language is therefore common among them, though, latterly, English has begun to take its place with those who have come in contact with American settlers.

Among the tribes of the North, which have had but little intercourse with the whites, the number of idioms is very great, and the diversity is such as to preclude almost entirely all verbal communication. But it has been proven by the philological investigations of the Jesuits in Lower California, that the divers manners of speech of the Indians were nothing more than dialects of a few stock-languages, and it is therefore a fair inference that the same will be found to be the case in the northern part of the State, though it would require laborious research to prove the fact.

The tribes living on the borders of Oregon are more athletic and warlike, a fact which they have proved on several occasions, when their resentment has been provoked by outrages committed on them by the white settlers.

Hitherto, the Reservation has received only peaceable tribes, and those which were closely pressed upon by the advance of civilization; but all the tribes now living in the north of California will, sooner or later, be induced to seek refuge under its protection.

The Mendocino Reservation, favored in many respects by nature, possesses abundant elements for the maintenance of the Indian tribes. Two other stations exist in the interior and further to the north—Nome Lakee and Nome Cult—which I purpose to visit at some future time.

The latter possesses excellent pasture land, and a stock of cattle has already been placed on it. The usual rate of increase in California is such that it will soon furnish beef cattle enough for all the stations of Mendocino—thus affording one of the principal means of supporting the Indians.

Game, though abundant, cannot be relied upon as a means of subsistence. A single hunter, roaming through the woods with his rifle, can live on the fat of the land. But a wider tract of country has to be scoured to furnish a large settled community with game; the transporta-

tion becomes onerous, and the thing is found to be impracticable.

The Reservations mainly depend for subsistence upon agriculture. The rolling lands between the coast and the mountains are covered by an abundance of wild oats, beans, clover and other nutritious grains, affording excellent pasture.

The bottom lands, along the watercourses of the valleys, are eminently adapted for cultivation. The working force of the station, under judicious direction, will soon bring out the producing qualities of these lands, which have an advantage over the heavy clay soils bordering the Bay of San Francisco, in so far that they can be ploughed at almost any season. Large tracts are already prepared for sowing. Potatoes yield abundantly, and are one of their principal resources.

The sea-fishery furnishes another main element of support. Every morning the schooner is sent out with an Indian crew, commanded by an employee. It returns towards noon with several tons of cod, rock fish, etc., together with a number of nondescript fishes—strange, uncouth denizens of the deep. The river also affords its quota as well as the sea.

The Indians are very dexterous in fishing with nets within the bar, so that the supply of fish never fails.

Our bivouac at Ten Mile River was shared by Col. Henley, the Indian Superintendent, by Lieut. Gibson, Commander of the post, by several attaches of the Reservation and by some hunters who had determined to join our party. A strong fog came in from the sea, and the atmosphere was by no means as agreeable as the balmy air of the mountains; but a good fire, aided by inward applications of "anti-fogmatics," enabled us to forget the chilliness of the nights. We had become accustomed to exercise in the open air, and, in a measure, indifferent to changes of temperature. An hour's ride in the morning was sufficient to drive away any feeling of stiffness.

While at the Reservation, we enjoyed the warm hospitality of Col. Henley, who, as far as his manifold occupations permitted, made our stay very agreeable. He gave us a hearty welcome, and afterwards, in his turn, called at our camp to participate in our convivialities.

Curiosity attracted many of the Indians from their wigwams, and the groupings of their dusky forms afforded a novel and interesting back-ground to the tableau of our camp.

The number of Indians on the Reservation is about 4,000, but, at the time of our visit, it was considerably reduced. It was their harvest season, and most of the able-bodied men had received leave of absence to collect seeds and to gather their crops, while others had gone on fishing expeditions. In this manner, by allowing them, occasionally, to return to their old mode of life, they feel less sensibly the subordination and restraint under which they necessarily live on the Reservation, and they also, without perceiving it, contribute to lessen the burden of the administration.

The many camp-fires we passed in the mountains bore evidence of the temporary scattering of the Indians.

The Reservation was, therefore, not as animated as it is usually, but there was still evidence enough to show the improvements which the Indians have received. There is a striking contrast between their former rude and almost animal state and their present improved condition. Instead of roaming about, listlessly, in the woods, and eking out a precarious life, they are now occupied in agricultural pursuits—have become acquainted with many of the usages and objects of civilized life, and no longer depend for sustenance on the uncertain results of the chase or on the scanty produce of the wild vegetation of the mountains.

The guide I had brought from the mountains could not converse with the Indians of the station; his native language was entirely different. As a free and independent son of the wilderness, he looked somewhat supercilioulsy at the doings on the Reservation. I had promised him a shirt and a blanket, as a reward for his services, and he was only waiting for them to return to his brother, the bear-fighter, Ben, in Matompka Valley. His aged father now made his appearance, and he was soon put in good humor by partaking of some of the good things at our camp. Standing upon the stump of a tree, he began talking to the winds, and gave us a specimen of Indian speech-making. He was asked to give an Indian name to the several members of our party; complying, without hesitation, he began the distribution of names, all expressive of some peculiarity of dress, voice, appearance or manner, which he caught with wonderful readiness. Some of them were translated to us, and they were appropriate and droll enough to afford us amusement at the expense of the recipients of this gratuitous baptism. He was rewarded with a black dress coat for himself, and a pair of kid gloves for his son, the bear-fighter, and perfectly satisfied with this compensation for the trouble of two days' march. An Indian will at no time shun fatigue, if it enables him to partake of the game and receive some of the cast-off clothes of the white men.

A fine specimen of the Indian was old Antonio, chief of one of the half-domesticated Bodega tribes. His four daughters —very fair specimens of young squaws— had all formed alliances with white men, and the old chief appeared to be very proud of their exalted fortunes, and to discern in perspective the perpetration of his race in a long succession of half-breeds.

HUTCHINGS'

CALIFORNIA MAGAZINE.

| Vol. II. | DECEMBER, 1857. | No 6. |

THE CALIFORNIA QUAIL.

CALIFORNIA QUAIL—MALE AND FEMALE.

This beautiful bird, the *Perdix California*, abounds throughout nearly the whole of California, if we except the more open country, entirely destitute of forest or shrubbery, and the mountain- ous districts above the line of the winter's snows.

It is a little larger than the quail of the northern and western States; but as a tit-bit for the epicure, is not its equal; its habits making it a bird of harder and tougher flesh.

Its flight is always vigorous, and often

protracted, and it moves more rapidly on foot; indeed, it seldom takes cover to lie close, like the eastern bird, but rises or runs at the first approach of danger; and though usually seeking perfect cover even at the expense of a long flight, it seldom stops but for a moment, and will then continue to run as long as pursued, or make another flight longer than before; making it a more difficult bird to sport; and yet, from its great plentifulness in many districts, there is no difficulty in procuring them in large numbers for the markets of our cities.

They are birds that can be partially tamed, or to that degree, that when kept in capacious cages, or inclosures where they can get to the ground, they will lay eggs and rear their young, like domestic fowls.

Their fecundity is truly remarkable. As an instance, a single female in the possession of Mr. John McCraith, residing at the corner of Hyde Street and Broadway, San Francisco, has laid during the past summer the astonishing number of seventy-nine eggs. She is, moreover, very tame, and will eat from

EGGS OF THE CALIFORNIA QUAIL—NATURAL SIZE.

the hand of her mistress, although rather shy towards strangers. Sometimes the male is very pugnacious to her ladyship for several days together, when she has to take refuge in a corner, or seek the protection of the tea-saucer from which they are daily fed.

This quail must not be confounded with another variety known as the mountain quail, which is about one-third larger than this, and differing in many particulars; or with another variety known in California as the large mountain quail, or grouse—the latter being a much larger bird, and far more rarely met with than either of the others, and is quite different from the partridge, pheasant, or common grouse.

The California quail is also abundant in all the northern and middle portions of Mexico—although differing slightly in the color of their plumage—and is there known as the blue quail, from the

general color of their plumage, which is for the greater part, except upon the back and wings, of a leaden or bluish colored tint.

In autumn they become gregarious to a much greater extent than is usual for its prototype in the east; as numerous distinct flocks or families unite, the aggregate of which often amounts to several hundreds; although even then, as in the spring-time, they always go in pairs. The California quail, moreover, differs from a similar variety in the east, in having a beautiful top-knot, or cluster of feathers, on the head—generally about six in number, yet appearing like a single feather—and drooping forward; while the eastern quail has no such ornament; and in the California mountain quail, instead of these hanging forward like those here represented, they are much longer and larger, and fall in a backward direction.

HUTCHINGS'
CALIFORNIA MAGAZINE.

Vol. IV.   JANUARY, 1860.   No. 7.

A TRIP TO THE CALIFORNIA GEYSERS.

BY PANORAMICS.

THE WITCH'S CAULDRON.

S THE fine little steamer "Rambler" was sounding her last whistle, the writer received a parting injunction, from a friend on the wharf, "to keep well aft," and stepped on board.

It was one of the chilliest, dreariest, most disagreeable of San Francisco's summer mornings. A dense fog, fresh from the great factory out on the Pacific, was rolling in over the hills at the back of the city, and hurrying across the bay, before a stiff northwest wind. The waves, as they rolled along the sides of the shipping, or splashed among the piles, seemed to be playing a most melancholy march, to which the great army of fog-clouds moved across the cheerless water; and their commanding officer—the wind—seemed to be continually saying "forward," as it whistled through the rigging of the ships.

The individual who is always just too late, made his appearance, as usual, as the steamer's fasts were cast off, and her wheels commenced their lively though monotonous ditty in the water.

Two or three Whitehall boatmen, who were lying off the wharf, evidently expecting such a "fare," gave their lazily playing skulls a vigorous pull, which sent their beautiful little craft darting in to the wharf. The boy with the basket of oranges hastened to offer the would be traveler "three for two bits," by way of consolation; and as he slowly proceeded up the dock again, the other boy with the papers and magazines called his attention to the last "Harper's," or "Hutchings," I could'nt distinguish clearly which.

The ten thousand voices of the city became blended into a continuous roar, as we glided out into the stream; the long drawn "go-o-o ahead," or "hi-i-gh," of the stevedores at their work discharging the stately clippers, being about the only intelligible sound to be distinguished above the mass.

Soon the outermost ship, on board of which a disconsolate looking "jolly tar" was riding down one of the head stays, giving it a "lick" of tar as he went, was passed, and we struck the strong current of wind which was blowing in at the Golden Gate, (carelessly left open, as usual.) The young giant of a city had become swallowed up in the gloom of the fog, and its thousands of busy people ceased to exist, except in our imaginations. After passing Angel Island, the fog began to lift; we were approaching the edge of the bank; and soon the sun appeared, hard at work at his apparently hopeless task of devouring the intruding fog, which had dared to interpose its cold billows between him and the bay, upon which he loves to shine.

The course of the boat was along the western side of Pablo Bay, close enough to the shore to give the passengers a fine view of it, as well as of the inland country, and the more distant mountains of the coast range. Large masses of misty clouds, which had become detached from the main fog bank, still partially obscured the sunlight, casting enormous shadows along the hill sides and across the plains; heightening, by contrast, the golden tinge of the wild oats, and giving additional beauty to the varied tints of the cultivated fields. Beyond, Tamal Pais, and the lesser peaks of the coast range, piled their wealth of purple light and misty shadows against the brightness of the western sky.

I wonder that our artists in their search for the picturesque, have overlooked the splendid scene which Tamal Pais and the adjacent mountains presents from the vicinity of Red Rock, or from the eastern shore of the straits. It is certainly one of the most picturesque scenes any where in the vicinity of San Francisco; especially towards sunset, when the long streaks of sunlight come streaming down the ravines, piercing with their golden light the hazy mystery which envelops the mountains, and brilliantly illuminating the intervening plains and hill sides. From the familiarity of the view, a good picture would, without doubt, be much sought after.

The seamanship of the pilot was much exercised while navigating the Rambler up Petaluma Creek. The creek is merely a long, narrow, ditch-like indentation, which makes up into the flat tule plains at the northern side of Pablo Bay, and into which the tide ebbs and flows. Its course very much resembles the track of a man who has spent half an hour hunting for a lost pocket-book in a field. If,

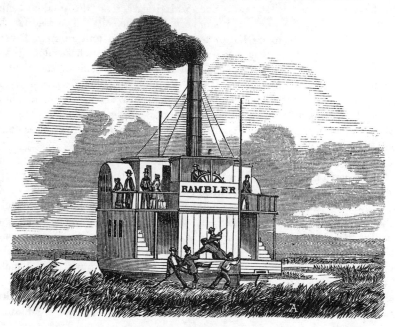

NAVIGATION OF PETALUMA CREEK.

after gazing awhile at the creek, the eye should be suddenly turned to a ram's horn or a manzanita stick, the latter would appear perfectly straight, by comparison. First we would go towards the north star awhile, then we would come to a short bend where an immense amount of backing and stopping and going ahead would occur, which all resulted in running the boat hard and fast ashore. Then the pilot, perspiring freely from his violent exertions at the wheel, would thrust his head out of the window, and, after taking a survey of the state of affairs, would set himself to ringing the signal bells again. Then the crew would get out a long pole, and planting one end in the bank, would apply their united strength to the other. No movement! Then the captain would heroically rush ashore in the mud and tules, and call for volunteers to help him push. Human strength and steam would triumph in the end, and the "Rambler," with one side all besmeared with mud, would go paddling off towards Cape Horn. After

going a short distance in this direction, another bend would be reached, when more superhuman exertion on the part of the pilot would ensue, and plump we would go ashore again! The captain would give utterance to a vigorous exclamation, (but as the expletive did no good, it is hardly necessary to repeat it here), and then he would jump into the mud again. Half the passengers would follow suit, the crew would go through with their pole exercise, pilot would play another tune on the bells, engineer would get bothered, and finally off we would start in the direction of Japan, leaving the captain and his shore party standing in the mud. Upon backing up for them to get on board, the boat would become fast again. This is a fair specimen of the navigation of Petaluma Creek above the city, (of one house,) called the Haystack.

Before reaching Petaluma, we met a little steamer coming down with a load of wood. She resembled an immense pile of wood with a smoke-stack in the centre, floating down the stream. She appeared to take up the whole width of the creek, and our passengers began to wonder how we were to get by. It was a tight fit. There was not room enough left between the two boats to insert this sheet of paper. The "Rambler" puffed, and from the depths of the wood pile was heard a sort of wheezing, as if half a dozen people with bad colds were down there somewhere, all coughing at once. The captain gave utterance to a few more expletives, as the rough ends of the wood defaced the new paint on our boat; but the skipper of the wood pile only laughed, yet as the Rambler, in passing, scraped off two or three cords of his cargo, it then became our turn to laugh.

Petaluma was reached at last, and the passengers for Healdsburg found a stage in waiting. Jumping in, we were soon whizzing across the plains behind a couple of fine colts. The road lay directly up Petaluma and Russian River valleys. Past the ranches—along the sides of interminable fields of corn and grain —through the splendid park-like groves —sometimes across the open plain, at others winding around the base of the hills which make up from the eastern side of the valley.

Santa Rosa, was reached by sunset. Our arrival was hailed by the ringing of a great number and variety of bells. How singular it is that the arrival of a stage-coach in a country town always sets the dinner bells to ringing, especially if the occurrence happens about meal time.

By the time supper was dispatched, and a pair of sober old stagers put to in the place of our frisky young colts, the moon had risen over the mountains, and

"WELL, YOU NEEDN'T QUARREL ABOUT IT."

was flooding the valley with her glorious sheen, tipping the fine old oaks with a silvery fringe of light, and laying their solemn shadows along the grass and across the road. A pleasant ride of two hours carried us to the end of our first day's journey, Healdsburg.

On the following morning, I was recommended to apply at the stable opposite the hotel for a horse. Having selected one warranted not to kick up nor stand on his hind legs, nor jump stiff-legged, nor play any other pranks, "Old Peter" was saddled and bridled; my portfolio, (which for want of a better covering, was carried in an old barley sack,) was slung on one side, and my wardrobe, (consisting of one article, which it is hardly necessary to specify,) depended at the other. A whip was added to complete the outfit, accompanied by the observation that as "Old Pete" was apt to "soger," "I might find it useful."

Then the stable man attempted to describe the road to Ray's ranch.

WHICH WAY NOW, I WONDER?

First I would come to a bridge; a mile beyond that I would see a house, which I was to pay no attention to, but look out for a haystack. Having found the haystack, I was to turn to the left, and would soon come to a long lane, which would lead me to another house, where I was either to turn to the right or keep straight ahead, he had forgotten which. At this point of the description, a bystander interposed that I must turn to the left, and upon this an argument sprung up between the two which nearly led to a fight.

Finding that there was not much information to be elicited from those witnesses, I gave "Old Pete" a touch and started, with my head buzzing with right and left hand roads, while a regiment of ranches, lanes and haystacks, seemed to be "a bobbing 'round" just ahead of the horse's nose. I found the bridge, and saw the house (which I was to pay no attention to;) there was no need of looking out for *a* haystack, for a dozen were in sight; so, selecting the biggest one, I turned to the left, according to the chart.

Rode along about a mile, and came to a fence which barred any further progress in that direction. Kept along the fence until I came to a lane which took me to a pair of bars. Let down the obstruction, traversed another lane, and at the end of it, found myself in somebody's dooryard. It was evident that I had taken the wrong road. I obtained fresh directions at the farm house, but as three or four attempted at the same time to tell me the way, all talking at once, and each insisting upon his favorite route, I speedily became mixed up again with another labyrinth of fences, lanes and haystacks. I began to doubt the existence of such a place as "Ray's Ranch." It seemed forever retreating as I advanced, like the mythical crock of gold, buried at the foot of a rainbow, which I remember starting in search of once, when a youngster.

But the ranch was found at last, and a very fine one it is, too. The house is situated a little way up in the foot-hills, and commands a splendid view of Russian River Valley, the Coast Range, Mount St. Helens, &c. The ranch itself, garden, orchards, and fields of wheat and corn, is situated in a valley, just below the house, which makes up between the steep mountain sides. A brook winds through the whole length of the little valley, affording capital facilities for irrigation.

I had the good luck here to fall in with Mr. G——, one of the proprietors of the Geysers, who was also on the way up. From the accounts which have been published, I expected to find the road from here a rough one. But it is nothing of the sort. It is a very good mountain trail, wide enough for a wagon to pass along its whole length. Buggies have been clear through, and could go again, were a few days' work to be expended upon the trail. It is quite steep, in many places, as a matter of course; but from the fact that Mr. G—— (who was mounted upon a young colt, that had never before been ridden, and had simply a piece of rope by way of bridle) *trotted* down

most of the declivities, the reader may iafer that the grade is not so very steep. I must say, though, that "old Pete" didn't exactly relish the idea of being in such a hurry.

The first three or four miles beyond Ray's, to the summit of the fisrt ridge, is all up hill; nearly 1700 feet in altitude being gained in that distance, or 2268 feet above the level of the sea, Ray's being 617.

There are few places in all California, where a more magnificent view can be obtained, than the one seen from this ridge. The whole valley of Russian River lies like a map at your feet, extending from the southeast and sonth, where it joins Petaluma valley, clear round to the northwest. The course of the river can be traced for miles, far

RAY'S RANCH AND RUSSIAN RIVER VALLEY.

away; alternately sweeping its great curves of rippling silver out into the opening plain, or disappearing behind the dark masses of timber. From one end of the valley to the other, the golden yellow of the plain is diversified by the darker tints of the noble oaks. In some places they stand in great crowds; then an open space will occur, with perhaps a few scattered trees, which serve to conduct the eye to where a long line of them appears, like an army drawn up for review, with a few single trees in front by

way of officers; and in the rear, a confused crowd of stragglers, to represent the baggage train and camp followers. Here and there, among the oaks, the vivid green foliage, and bright red stems of the graceful madrone, can be seen; and on the banks of the river, the silvery willows and the dusky sycamores.

The beauty of the plain is still more enhanced, by the numerous ranches, with their widely extending fields of ripe grain and verdant corn.

Beyond the valley, is the long extending line of the coast mountains. The slanting rays of the declining sun was overspreading the mysterious blue and purple of their shadowy sides, with a glorious golden haze, through whose gauzy splendor could be traced the summits, only, of the different ranges—towering one above the other, each succeeding one fainter than the last, until the indescribably fine outline of the highest peaks, but one remove, in color, from the sky itself, bounded the prospect.

Towards the southeast, we could see Mount Saint Helen's, and the upper part of Napa Valley. Saint Helen's is certainly the most beautiful mountain in California. It is far from being as lofty as its more pretentious brethren of the Sierra Nevada, and by the side of the great Shasta Butte it would be dwarfed to a mole hill; but its chaste and graceful outline is the very ideal of mountain form. There is said to be a copper plate, bearing an inscription, on the summit of this mountain, placed there by the Russians many years ago.

Away off, towards the south, we could discern that same old fog, still resting, like a huge incubus, upon San Francisco bay. Its fleecy billows were constantly in motion, now obscuring, now revealing the summits of different peaks, which rose like islands out of the sea of clouds. Above, and far beyond the fog, the view terminated with the long, level line of the blue Pacific, sixty or seventy miles distant.

From the point where we have stopped to take this extended view, (too much extended, on paper, perhaps the reader will think), the horses climbed slowly up the steep ascent, leading to a plateau, on the northern side of a mountain, which has received no less than three different names. As it is a difficult matter, among so many titles, to fix upon the proper one, I will enumerate them all, and the reader can take his choice. The mountain was first called "Godwin's Peak," in honor of——there, G——, the cat's out of the bag! your name has got into print, in spite of my endeavor to keep it out. With characteristic modesty, Mr. G—— declined the honor which the name conferred upon him, and it was changed by somebody or other to "Geyser Peak;" but, for some unknown reason, this name also failed to stick, and somebody else came along and called it "Sulphur Peak." Both the latter names are inappropriate, for there are no Geysers nor no sulphur within five miles of the mountain. G., I am afraid you will have to endure your honors, and stand god-father to it.

The "Peak" rises to the height of 3471 feet above the level of the sea, and its sides are covered, clear to the summit, with a thick growth of tangled chaporal. From here, the trail runs along the narrow ridge of the mountains, forming the divide between "Sulphur Creek, (an odious name for a beautiful trout stream,) and Pluton River. The ridge is called the "Hog's Back"—still another name, as inappropriate as it is homely. The ridge much more resembles the back of a horse which has just crossed the plains, or has dieted for some time on shavings, than that of a plump porker. From the end of this ridge the trail is quite level, as far as the top of the hill, which pitches sharply down to the river, and at the foot of which the Geysers are situated.

When about two-thirds of the way down the hill, the rushing noise of the escaping steam of the Great Geyser can be heard; but, unless the stranger's attention was called to it, he would mistake the sound for the roaring of the river. About this time, too, is recognized the sulphurous smell with which the air is impregnated.

Just as the traveler begins seriously to think that the hill has no bottom, the white gable end of the hotel, looking strangely out of place among its wild

GEYSER SPRINGS HOTEL.

surroundings, comes unexpectedly into sight, and his trip is ended.

Upon awakening, on the following morning, it was a difficult matter to convince myself that I had not been transported, while asleep, to the close vicinity of some of the wharves in San Francisco —there was such a *powerful* smell of what seemed to be ancient dock mud. It was the sulphur. The smell is a trifle unpleasant at first, but one soon becomes accustomed to it, and rather likes it than otherwise.

The view of the Geysers, from the hotel, is a very striking one, more especially in the morning, when the steam can be plainly seen, issuing from the earth in a hundred different places; the numerous columns uniting at some distance above the earth, and forming an immense cloud, which overhangs the whole cañon.

As the sun advances above the hills, This cloud is speedily "eaten up," and the different columns of steam, with the exception of those from the Steamboat Geyser, the Witches' Cauldron, and a few others, become invisible, being evaporated as fast as they issue from the ground.

Breakfast disposed of, Mr. G. kindly offered to conduct me to the different springs. The trail descends abruptly from the house, among the tangled undergrowth of the steep mountain side, to the river, some ninety feet below. We passed on the way the long row of bathing-houses, the water for which is conveyed across the river in a lead pipe, from a hot sulphur-spring on the opposite side.

The unearthly looking cañon, in which most of the springs are situated, makes up into the mountains directly from the river. A small stream of water, which rises at the head of the cañon, flows through its whole length. The stream is pure and cold at its source, but gradually

GEYSER CANON.

becomes heated, and its purity sadly sullied, as it receives the waters of the numerous springs along its banks.

Hot springs and cold springs; white, red, and black sulphur springs; iron, soda, and boiling alum springs; and the deuce only knows what other kind of springs, all pour their medicated waters into the little stream, until its once pure and limpid water,—like a human patient, made sick by over-doctoring,—becomes pale, and has a wheyish, sickly, unnatural look, as it feverishly tosses and tumbles over its rocky bed.

A short distance up the cañon, there is a deep, shady pool, which receives the united waters of all the springs above it. By the time the stream reaches here, its medicated waters become cooled to the temperature of a warm summer day, and the basin forms, perhaps, the most luxurious bath to be opened in the world. A few feet from this, there is a warm alum and iron spring, whose water is more thoroughly impregnated than any of the others.

A little way farther up, is "Proserpine's Grotto," an enchanting retreat among the wild rocks, completely surrounded and enclosed by the fantastic roots and twisted branches of the bay trees, and roofed over by their wide-spreading foliage. Glimpses of the narrow gorge above, with its numerous cascades, can be obtained through the openings of the trees; the whole forming one of the finest "little bits," as an artist would call it, to be found in the country.

As we proceeded up the cañon, the springs became more numerous. They were bubbling and boiling in every direction. I hardly dared to move, for fear of putting my foot into a spring of boiling alum, or red sulphur, or some other infernal concoction. The water of the stream, too, was now scalding hot, and the rocks, and the crumbling, porous earth, were nearly as hot as the water. I took good care to literally "follow in the footsteps of my illustrious predecessor," as he hopped about from boulder to boulder, or rambled along in (as I thought) dangerous proximity to the boiling waters. Every moment he would pick up a handfull of magnesia, or alum, or sulphur, or tartaric acid, or Epsom salts, or some other nasty stuff, plenty of which encrusted all the rocks and earth in the vicinity, and invite me to taste them. From frequent nibblings at the different deposits, my mouth became so puckered up, that all taste was lost for anything.

In addition to these strange and unnatural sights, the ear was saluted by a great variety of startling sounds. Every spring had a voice. Some hissed and sputtered like water poured upon red hot iron; others reminded one of of the singing of a tea-kettle, or the purring of a cat; and others seethed and bubbled like so many cauldrons of boiling oil. One sounded precisely like the machinery of a grist mill in motion, (it is called "The Devil's Grist Mill,") and another, like the propeller of a steamer.

High above all these sounds, was the loud roaring of the great "Steamboat Geyser."* The steam of this Geyser issues with great force from a hole about two feet in diameter, and it is so heated as to be invisible until it has risen to some height from the ground. It is highly dangerous to approach very close to it unless there is sufficient wind to blow the steam aside.

But the most startling of all the various sounds was a continuous subterranean roar, similar to that which precedes an earthquake.

I must confess, that when in the midst of all these horrible sights and sounds, I felt very much like suggesting to G—— the propriety of returning, but a fresh handfull of Epsom salts and alum, mixed, stopped my mouth, and by the time I had ceased sputtering over the puckerish compound, the "Witches Cauldron" was reached. (See Vignette.) This is a horrible place. "Mind how you step here,"

* This Geyser is shown in the view of "Geyser Canon." It is the upper large columnof steam on the left side of the canon; the one below it, and nearer the spectator, is the "Witches' Cauldron." The foreground of the view is occupied by the "Mountain of Fire," from which the stream issues by a hundred different apertures.

said G——, as we approached it; and with the utmost caution, I placed my *tens* in his tracks, that is, as much of them as I could get in.

The cauldron is a hole, sunk like a well in the precipitous side of the mountain, and is of unknown depth. It is filled to the brim with something that looks very much like burnt cork and water. (I believe the principal ingredient is black sulphur.) This liquid blackness is in constant motion, bubbling and surging from side to side, and throwing up its boiling spray to the height of three or four feet. Its vapor deposits a black sediment on all the rocks in its vicinity.

There are a great many other springs —some two hundred in number, I believe—of every gradation of temperature, from boiling hot to icy cold, and impregnated with all sorts of mineral and chemical compounds; frequently the two extremes of heat and cold are found within a few inches of each other. But as all the other springs present nearly the same characteristics as most of those already referred to, it would be but a tedious repetition to attempt to describe more. They are all wonderful. The ordinary observer can only look at them, and wonder that such things exist; but to the scientific man, one capable of divining the mysterious cause of their action, the study of them must be an exquisite delight.

It is worth the traveler's while to climb the mountains on the north side of the Pluton, for the fine view which their summits afford on every hand; towards the north, a part of Clear Lake can be seen, some fifteen miles distant. But perhaps the scene which would delight a lover of nature most, can be obtained by rising early and walking back half a mile upon the trail which descends to the hotel. It is to see the gorgeous tints of the eastern sky as the sun comes climbing up behind the distant mountains, and afterwards to watch his long slanting rays in the illuminated mist, as they come streaming down the Cañon of the Pluton, flashing on the water in dots and splashes of dazzling light, and tipping the rich shadows of the closely woven foliage with a fringe of gold.

PROSERPINE'S GROTTO.

Some people have said that California scenery is monotonous, that her mountains are all alike, and that her skies repeat each other from day to day. Believe them not, ye distant readers, to whom, as yet, our glorious California is an unknown land. The monotony is in their own narrow, unappreciative souls, not in our grand mountains, towering ridge upon ridge until the long line of the farthest peaks becomes blended with the dreamy haze that loves to linger round their summits. And the gorgeous glow of our sunrises, or the still more gorgeous green and orange, and gold and crimson,

of our sunsets, reflect their heavenly hues upon dull eyes indeed when they can see no beauty in them.

To the Homeward Bound.— Something to Remember.—Before going East be sure to subscribe for

Hutchings' California Magazine.

As the Yo-Semite Valley seems to be the great point of attraction to parties recreating, it may not be amiss to give, from the the *Mariposa Star*, the following amusing list of provisions that four persons deemed necessary on such a trip! —

A party recently left Joe's store at Mormon Bar for the Valley, and a friend of the *Star* furnishes the following statistics — showing the amount of "the necessaries of life" which is required for an eight day's trip in the mountains :

   8 ℔s potatoes.
   1 bottle whisky.
   1 bottle pepper sauce.
   1 bottle whisky.
   1 box tea.
   9 ℔s onions.
   2 bottles whisky.
   1 ham.
  11 ℔s crackers.
   1 bottle whisky.
   ½ doz. sardines.
   2 bottles brandy, (4th proof.)
   6 ℔s sugar.
   1 bottle brandy, (4th proof.)
   7 ℔s cheese.
   2 bottles brandy, (4th proof.)
   1 bottle pepper.
   5 gallons whisky.
   4 bottles whisky (old Bourbon.)
   1 small keg whisky.
   1 bottle of cocktails, (designed for a "starter.")

The party proceeded as far as Sebastapol, (about two miles,) and halted to rest under a tree. They were there met by a teamster, who took the following message to the Bar. "Tell 'Sam' that we are all right—have got all the provisions we want —our pack animals are doing well—we will return in eight days. About the sixth we will be at the South Fork, on our way home. Tell him to try and meet us there with some *whisky*, say about two gallons, just enough to last us home. One of our kegs *leaks.*"

SEA SONG.

BY MONADNOCK.

Like a thing of life
In joyous strife,
Our ship bounds light and free:—
As a sea gull springs
With snowy wings
In her course o'er the trackless sea.

Some love to dwell
In the quiet dell,
But the scene that delights my view,
Is a vessel proud,
With her canvass cloud,
As she sweeps the billows blue.

Some love to go
Where rivers flow
Through valleys green and fair ;—

I love the frown
When night comes down
'Mid the lightning's lurid glare.

Some love a sky
Like a maiden's eye
When it beams in the starlight hour :
I love the waves
When the storm king raves
And the white seas rise in power.

A home for me
On the trackless sea
In a vessel swift and free,
Where the whistling gale
In the swelling sail
Is raising its ocean glee.

San Francisco, July 23, 1856.

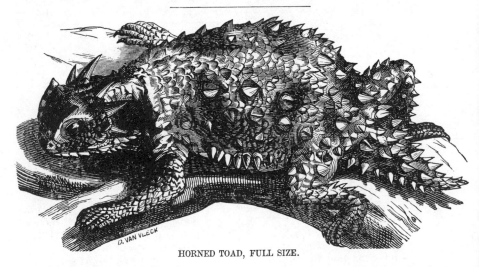

HORNED TOAD, FULL SIZE.

THE HORNED TOAD.

—

This singular little member of the lizard species is certainly a *native* Californian. Upon nearly every dry hill, or sandy plain, it is often found ; and, although in some districts of this State, it has become somewhat rare, in others it is still common. There are several varieties and sizes of it, and all perfectly harmless. It lives chiefly on flies and small insects.

The writer had a pair of these *picketed* in front of his cabin for over three months ; and, one morning, the male toad *committed suicide!* by hanging himself over a small twig, and the same day the female followed the example of the male. Upon a " *post*

mortem examination." fifteen eggs were discovered, in shape and size like those in the engraving below.

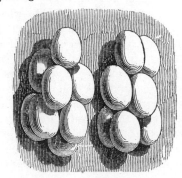

HUTCHINGS'

CALIFORNIA MAGAZINE.

Vol. IV.   OCTOBER, 1859.   No. 4.

THE GREAT YO-SEMITE VALLEY.

CHAPTER I.

How it came to be Discovered.

"I see you stand like grayhounds in
the slips,
Straining upon the start. The game 's
a foot;
Follow your spirit; and, upon this
charge,
Cry "—Ho! for the Yo-Semite!

THE early California
resident will remem-
ber that during the
spring and summer of 1850,
much dissatisfaction existed
among the white settlers and
miners on the Merced, San
Joaquin, Chowchilla, and
Frezno rivers and their tributaries, on account of the
frequent robberies committed upon them by the Chook-

THE YO-SEM-I-TE FALL, TWO THOUSAND FIVE HUNDRED FEET IN HIGHT.
[*From a Photograph by C. L. Weed.*]

chan-cie, Po-to-en-cie, Noot-cho, Po-ho-ne-chee, Ho-na-chee, Chow-chilla and other Indian tribes on the head waters of those streams. The frequent repetition of their predatory forays having been attended with complete success, without any attempted punishment on the part of the whites, the Indians began seriously to contemplate the practicability of driving out every white intruder upon their hunting and fishing grounds.

At this time, James D. Savage had two stores, or trading posts, nearly in the centre of the affected tribes; the one on Little Mariposa creek, about twenty miles south of the town of Mariposa, and near the old stone fort; and the other on Frezno river, about two miles above where John Hunt's store now is. Around these stores those Indians who were the most friendly, used to congregate; and from whom, and his two Indian wives, Eekino and Homut, Savage ascertained the state of thought and of feeling among them.

In order to avert such a calamity, and without even hinting at his motive, he invited an Indian chief, who possessed much influence with the Chow-chillas and Chook-chances, named Jose Jerez, to accompany him and his two squaws to San Francisco; hoping thereby to impress him with the wonders, numbers, and power of the whites, and through him, the various tribes that were malcontented. To this Jerez gladly assented, and they arrived in San Francisco in time to witness the first celebration of the admission of California into the Union, on the 29th of October, 1850,[*] when they put up at the Revere House, then standing on Montgomery street.

During their stay in San Francisco, and while Savage was purchasing goods for his stores in the mountains, Jose Jerez, the Indian chief, became intoxicated, and returned to the hotel about the same time as Savage, in a state of boisterous and quarrelsome excitement. In order to prevent his making a disturbance, Savage shut him up in his room, and there endeavored to soothe him, and restrain his violence by kindly words; but this he resented, and became not only troublesome, but very insulting; when, after patiently bearing it as long as he possibly could, at a time of great provocation, unhappily, was tempted to strike Jerez, and followed it up with a severe scolding. This very much exasperated the Indian, and he indulged in numerous muttered threats of what he would do when he went back among his own people. But, when sober, he concealed his angry resentment, and, Indian-like, sullenly awaited his opportunity for revenge. Simple, and apparently small, as was this circumstance, like many others equally insignificant, it led to very unfortunate results; for, no sooner had he returned to his own people, than he summoned a council of the chief men of all the surrounding tribes; and, from his influence and representations mainly, steps were then and there agreed upon to drive out or kill all the whites, and appropriate all the horses, mules, oxen, and provisions they could find.[†]

Accordingly, early one morning in the ensuing month of November, the Indians entered Savage's store on the Frezno. in their usual manner, as though on a trading expedition, when an immediate and apparently preconcerted plan of attack was made with hatchets, crow-bars, and arrows; first upon Mr. Greeley, who had charge of the store, and then upon three other white men named Canada, Stiffner,

* The news of the admission, by Congress, of California into the Union, on the 9th of Sept. 1850, was brought by the mail steamer "Oregon," which arrived in the Bay of San Francisco on the 18th of Oct. 1850, when preparations were immediately commenced for a general jubilee throughout the State on the 29th of that month.

† These facts were communicated to us by Mr. J. M. Cunningham, (now in the Yo-Semite valley,) who was then engaged as clerk for Savage, and was present during the altercation between him and the Indian.

BOATS LEAVING THE WHARF — THE ANTELOPE FOR SACRAMENTO, AND THE BRAGDON FOR STOCKTON.

and Brown, who were present. This was made so unexpectedly as to exclude time or opportunity for defence, and all were killed except Brown, whose life was saved by an Indian named "Polonio," (thus christened by the whites,) jumping between him and the attacking party, at the risk of his own personal safety, thus affording Brown a chance of escape, and which he made the best of by running all the way to Quartzburg, at the hight of his speed.

Simultaneously with this attack on the Frezno, Savage's other store and residence on the Mariposa was attacked, during his absence, by another band, and his Indian wives carried off. Similar onslaughts having been made at different points on the Merced, San Joaquin, Frezno, and Chow-chilla rivers, Savage concluded that a general Indian war was about opening, and immediately commenced raising a volunteer battalion; at the same time a requisition for men, arms, ammunition, and general stores, was made upon the Governor of the State (Gen. John McDougal,) which was promptly responded to by him, and hostilities were at once begun.

Without further entering into the details, incidents, and mishaps of this campaign—as a full account of this Indian war will make a very interesting and instructive subject of itself, for future consideration—we have thought it necessary to relate the above facts as they occurred, inasmuch as out of them originated the Mariposa Indian war, and the discovery of the great Yo-Semite valley. Therefore, with these introductory explanations, and the reader's consent, we will at once proceed upon our tour to that wonderful, mountain-bound valley of waterfalls.

CHAPTER II.
Off for the Mountains.

'Tis a dull thing to travel like a mill-horse.
QUEEN OF CORINTH.

The reader knows as well as we do that, although it may be of but little consequence in point of fact, whether a spirit of romance; the love of the grand and beautiful in scenery; the suggestions or promptings of that most loveable of all lovely objects, a fascinating woman, be she friend, sweetheart, or wife; the desire for change; the want of recreation; or the necessity of a restoration and recuperation of an over-tasked physical or mental organization, or both;— whatever may be the agent that first gives birth to the wish for, or the love of travel; when the mind is thoroughly made up, and the committee of ways and means reports itself financially prepared to undertake the pleasurable task; in order to enjoy it with luxurious zest, we must resolve upon four things—*first*, to leave the "peck of troubles," and a few thrown in, entirely behind; *second*, to have none but good, suitable, and genial-hearted companions; *third*, a sufficient supply of personal patience, good humor, forbearance, and creature comforts for all emergencies; and, *fourth*, not to be in a hurry. To these, both one and all, who have ever visited the Yo-Semite valley, we know will say—Amen.

Now as we cannot in this brief series of articles, describe all the various routes to this wonderful valley, from every village, town, and city in the State; as they are almost as numerous and as diversified as the different roads that christians seem to take for their expected heaven, and the multitudinous creeds about the way and manner of getting there, we shall content ourselves by giving the principal ones; and after we have recited the following quaint and unanswerable argument of a celebrated divine to the querulous and uncharitable members of his flock, in which we think the reader will discover a slight similarity between the position of Yo-Semite travelers, to that of the various denominations of christians; we shall then proceed to explain how and when we journied there, and who were of the party.

An aged and charitable christian minister had frequently experienced much painful annoyance from an unmistakable bitterness of feeling that existed between the members of his church and those of a different sect; and as this was contrary to the word and spirit of the Great Teacher, and a great stumbling block to the usefulness and happiness of the members of both denominations, he notified them that on a certain Sunday, he wished his brother minister to close his doors, as he wished to address the members of both churches at the same time, on a very important subject. This was accordingly granted him. When he ascended the pulpit, he looked affectionately at his hearers, and thus began — " My christian friends, there was a christian brother—a Presbyterian—who walked thoughtfully up to the gate of the New Jerusalem, and knocked for admittance, when an angel who was in charge, looked down from above and enquired what he wanted. 'To come in,' was the answer. 'Who and what are you?' 'A Presbyterian.' 'Sit on that seat there.' This was on the outside of the gate; and the good man feared that he had been refused. admittance. Presently arrived an Episcopalian, then a Baptist, then a Methodist, and so on, until a representative of every christian sect had made his appearance; and were alike ordered to take a seat outside. Before they had long been there, a loud anthem broke forth, rolling and swelling upon the air, from the choir within; when those outside immediately joined in the chorus. 'Oh!' said the angel, as he opened wide the gate, ' I did not know you by your names, but you have all learned one song, come in! come in!! The name you bear, or the way by which you came, is of little moment compared with your being able to reach it at all, or the wonders you will now behold, and the gratification you will experience.'—As you my brethren," the good man continued, "as you expect to live peaceably and lovingly together in heaven, you had better begin to practice it on earth. I have done."

As this allegorical advice needs no

THE START.

words of application either to the Yo-Semite traveler or the christian, in the hope that the latter will take the admonition of Captain Cuttle, "and make a note on't," and with an apology to the reader for the digression, we will now proceed *en route.*

The resident of San Francisco can have his choice of two ways for reaching Stockton; one, for the most part, overland by stage, as follows:—

	Miles.
F'm S. F. to Oakland, by ferry, which is	8
F'm Oakland, by stage, to San Antonio,	2
" San Leandro	7
" San Lorenzo	11
" Hayward's	13
" Alvarado, or Union City,	18
" Centreville	22
" Mission of San Jose	27
" Hart's Station	30
" Livermore's	34
" Mountain House	44
" Harland's Ferry	60
" French Camp	66
" Stockton	79

Whole distance from San Francisco to Stockton, by this route, 79 miles.

Or, making his way to Jackson street wharf, a few moments before four o'clock, he can take one of the California Steam Navigation Company's boats, and arrive in Stockton, by water,—distance 124 miles—in time for any of the stages that leave that city for the mountains. We chose the latter route; and, on the evening of the 14th of June of the present year, found ourselves on board the Helen Hensley, Captain Clark, (one of the oddest looking, and at the same time one of the most intelligent specimens of steamboat captains we ever met.)

As the steamboat Antelope, bound for Sacramento, was heavily freighted, we had the advantage of taking and keeping the lead, and arrived at Benicia at twenty minutes to seven o'clock—distance thirty miles, from San Francisco—at least half an hour ahead of her; a circumstance of very unusual occurrence, and which seemed to afford considerable satisfaction to the more enthusiastic of the passengers; for, whether a man may be riding on any four legged animal, from a donkey to a race-horse, or in any kind of vehicle, from a dog-cart to a train of cars; or in any sailing craft that floats, from a flat-bottomed scow to a leviathan steamer, such is his perverse desire to be able to crow over something or somebody, that if he breaks his neck in the attempt to pass a fellow traveler; or runs the risk of losing a wheel, or his life, while driving furiously; or takes an extra and speedy, though not always the most popular, method of elevation, upon the broken fragments of an exploded boiler, he is sure to wish for the success of that particular animal, vehicle, or craft, on which he may for the time be a passenger! We do not say that *we*, (that is, our boat), were "racing," for we were not; nor do we say that we were in any danger, for the officers of the boat—and of all these boats—were too careful to run any risks, especially as all "racing" is strictly prohibited by the Company.

The run across the straits of Carquinez, from Benicia to Martinez, three miles distant, took us just ten minutes. Then after a few moments delay, we again dashed onward; the moonlight gilding the troubled waters in the wake of our vessel, as she plowed her swift way through the bay of Suisun; and to all appearance deepened the shadows on the darker sides of Monte Diablo, by defining, with silvery clearness, the uneven ridges and summit of that solitary mountain mass.

At twenty minutes past eight, P. M., we entered the most westerly of the three mouths of the San Joaquin river, fifty-one miles from San Francisco and twenty-one above Benicia—after passing the city of New York on the Pacific, the intended "Eden" of speculators and castle-builders—without performing the fashionable courtesy of calling.

The evening being calm and sultry, it soon became evident that if it were not the hight of the mosquito season, a very numerous band were out on a free-booting excursion; and although their harvest-home song of blood was doubtless very musical, it may be matter of regret with us to confess that, in our opinion, but few persons on board appeared to have any ear for it; in order, however, that their musical efforts might not be entirely lost sight of, they took pleasure in writing and impressing their low refrain in red and embossed notes upon the foreheads of the passengers, so that he who looked might read—musquitoes! when, alas! such was the ingratitude felt for favors so voluntarily performed, that flat-handed blows were dealt out to them in impetuous haste, and blood, blood, blood, and flattened musqitoes was written in red and dark brown spots upon the smiter, and behold! the notes of those singers were heard no more "that we knows on."

While the unequal warfare is going on, and one carcass of the slain induces at least a dozen of the living to come to his funeral and avenge his death, we are sailing on, up one of the most crooked and most monotonous navigable rivers out of doors; and, as we may as well do something more than fight the little bill-presenting and tax-collecting mosquitoes, if only for variety, we will relate to the reader how, in the early spring of 1849, just before leaving our southern home on the banks of ' the mother of rivers,' 'the old Mississippi,' a gentleman arrived from northern Europe and was at once introduced a member of our little family circle. Now, however strange it may appear, our new friend had never in his life looked upon a live mosquito, or a mosquito-bar, and consequently knew nothing about the arrangements of a good *femme de charge* for passing a comfortable night, where such insects were even more numerous than oranges. In the morning he seated himself at the breakfast-table, his face nearly covered with wounds received from the enemy's proboscis, when an enquiry was made by the lady of the house, if he had passed the night pleasantly? "Yes,—yes," he replied, with some hesitation, "yes—toler-a-bly pleasant — although — a — *small* —*fly*—annoyed me—somewhat!" At this confession, we could restrain ourselves no longer, but broke out into a hearty laugh, led by our good-natured hostess, who then exclaimed: "Mosquitoes! why, I never dreamed that the marks on your face were mosquito bites. I thought they might be from a rash, or something of that kind. Why! didn't you lower down your mosquito-bars?" But as this latter appendage to a bed, on the low, alluvial lands of a southern river, was a greater stranger to him than any dead language known, the "small fly" problem had to be satisfactorily solved, and his sleep made sweet.

Perhaps it would be well here to remark, that the San Joaquin river is divided into three branches, known respectively as the west, middle, and east channels; the latter named, being not only the main stream but the one used by the steamboats and sailing vessels, bound to and from Stockton—or at least to within about four miles of that city, from which point the Stockton slough is used. The east, or main channel, is navigable for small, stern-wheel steamboats, as high as Frezno City. Besides the three main channels of the San Joaquin, before mentioned, there are numerous tributaries, the principal of which are the Moquel-

umne, Calaveras, Stanislaus, Tuolumne, and Merced rivers. An apparently interminable sea of tules extends nearly one hundred and fifty miles south, up the valley of the San Joaquin; and when these are on fire, as they not unfrequently are, during the fall and early winter months, the broad sheet of licking and leaping flame, and the vast volumes of smoke that rise, and eddy, and surge, hither and thither, present a scene of fearful grandeur, at night, that is suggestive of some earthly pandemonium.

The lumbering sound of the boat's machinery having suddenly ceased, and

BOWER CAVE.

our high-pressure motive power having descended from a regular to an occasional snorting, gave us a reminder that we had reached Stockton. Time, forty-five minutes past two o'clock, on the morning of the 15th. At day-break we were again disturbed in our fitful slumbers by the rumbling of wagons and hurrying bustle of laborers discharging cargo; and before we had scarcely turned over for another uncertain nap, the stentorian lungs of some employee of the stage companies announced that stages for Sonora, Columbia, Murphy's, Mokelumne Hill, Sacramento, Mariposa, and Coulterville, were just about starting. The moment that "Coulterville" was included in the list it recalled us to wide-awake consciousness that as we had come on purpose to go by that route, we had better be moving in the premises. Therefore, hurriedly making our toilet, and hastily going ashore, we each deposited seven dollars in the palm of the agent as our fare to the Crimea House, at which point another deposit of five dollars was to insure us safe and speedy transit in some other conveyance from that place to Coulterville.

A portion of our pleasant little party having joined us in Stockton; and, as we are now all snugly ensconced in the same stage, we will proceed to initiate the reader into the dramatis personæ of this (to us) deeply interesting performance. Rev. F. C. Ewer, and lady; (and when we mention "Rev." we hope that no one, at least in this instance, will associate it with anything prosy, or heavy, or dull, otherwise we wish at once to cut his or her acquaintance at the outset,) Miss Marianna Neill, Mr. L. C. Weed, our excellent photographer, and your humble servant, J. M. H. "All aboard!" cried the coachman; "all set," shouted somebody, in answer.

"Crack went the whip, and away went we."

There is a feeling of jovial, good-humored pleasurableness that steals insensibly over the secluded residents of cities when all the cares of a daily routine of duty are left behind, and the novelty of fresh scenes opens up new sources of enjoyment. Especially was it so with us, seated as we were, in that comfortable, old stage, with the prospect before us of witnessing one of the most wonderful sights that is to be found in any far-off country either of the old or new world. Besides, in addition to our being in the reputed position of a Frenchman with his dinner, who is said to enjoy it in three different ways; first, by anticipation; next, in action; and third, on re-

flection; we had new views perpetually breaking upon our admiring eyes.

As soon as we had passed over the best gravelled streets of any town or city in the State, without exception, we threaded our way past the beautiful suburban residences of the city of Stockton, and emerged from the shadows of the giant oaks that stand on either side the road, the deliciously cool breath of early morning, laden as it was with the fragrance of myriads of flowers and scented shrubs, was inhaled with an acme of enjoyment that contrasted inexpressibly with the stifling and unsavory warmth of a lilliputian state room on board the steamboat.

The bracing air had partially restored the loss of appetite resulting from, and almost consequent upon, the excitement created by the novel circumstances and prospects attending us, so that when we arrived at the Twelve Mile House and breakfast was announced, it was not an unwelcome sound to any one of the party. This being satisfactorily discussed, in eighteen minutes, and a fresh relay of horses provided, we were soon upon our way. At the Twenty-five Mile House we again exchanged horses. By this time the day and our travelers had both warmed up together; and before we reached Knight's Ferry, as the cooling breeze had died out, and the dust had begun to pour in, at every chink and aperture, the luxurious enjoyments of the early morning were departing by degrees—in the same way that lawyers are said to get to heaven!—and when a group of sturdy, athletic miners was seen congregated in front of the hotel, and the bell and its ringer had announced that Knight's Ferry and dinner were both at hand, it would have been the height of preposterous presumption in us to attempt to pass ourselves off for "white folks" before we had made the acquaintance of clean water and a dust-brush.

THE GREAT YO–SEMITE VALLEY.

After taking refreshments with loss of our appetites and forty-five minutes, we not only again "changed horses," but found both ourselves and our baggage changed to another stage—as the newest and best looking ones seemed to be retained for the level, and city end of the route, while the dust-covered and paint-worn are used for the mountains. As we shall probably have something to say concerning these towns on our return, we will respond to the coachman's "all aboard," by calling out "all set," and thus leave it for the present.

At the Crimea House, our bags and baggage were again set down, and after

CAMPING AT DEER FLAT — NIGHT SCENE.

a very agreeable delay of one hour, during which time the obliging landlord, Mr. Brown, informed us that errors of route and distance had been made by journalists who were not quite familiar with their subject, and by which those persons who travel in private carriages were liable to go by La Grange, some five miles out of their way.

Here a new line as well as conveyance was taken, known as the "Sonora and Coulterville," and as that had now arrived, we lost no time in obtaining possession of as good seats as we could find, and reached Don Pedro's Bar about six o'clock, P. M. But for an unusual number of passengers, we should have been here subjected to another change of stage; now, fortunately, the old and regular one would not contain us all, so that the only change made was in horses, and after a delay of twelve minutes, we were again dashing over the Tuolumne river, across a good bridge.

Now the gently rolling hills began to give way to tall mountains; and the quiet and even tenor of the landscape to change to the wild and picturesque. Up, up we toiled, many of us on foot, as our horses puffed and snorted like miniature steamboats, from hauling but little more than the empty coach. The top gained, our road was through forests of oaks and nut pines, across flats, and down the sides of ravines and gulches, until we reached Maxwell's Creek; from which point an excellent road is graded on the side of a steep mountain, to Coulterville, and all that the traveler seems to hope for, is that the stage will keep upon it, and not tip down the abyss that is yawning below. Up this mountain we again had to patronize the very independent method of going 'afoot'; and while ascending it, our party was startled by a rustling sound being heard among the bushes below the road, where shadowy human forms could be seen moving slowly towards us. Hearts beat quicker, and images of Joaquin and Tom Bell's gang rose to our active fancies. "They will rob and perhaps murder us," suggested one. "We cannot die but once," retorted another. "Oh, dear! what is going to be the matter," was sent in a loud, shrill whisper from the owner of a treble voice in the stage. "Let us all keep close together," pantomimed a fourth, an outsider. "I *shall* faint," (another sound from within.) "Please to postpone that exercise, ladies, until we reach plenty of water," respectfully and cheerfully responded a fifth, and who evidently had some particular interest in the speaker.

"That's a hard old mountain," exclaimed the ringleader of the party that had caused all our alarm, as he and his companions quietly seated themselves by the side of the road. "Good evening, gentlemen." "Good evening." Why, bless my soul, these men who have almost frightened us out of our seven senses, are nothing but fellow travelers!" "Could'nt you see that?" now valorously enquired one whose knees had knocked uncontrollably together with fear only a few moments before. At this we all had to laugh; and the driver having stopped, said, "get in, gentlemen," we had enough to talk and joke about, until we reached Coulterville, at a quarter to ten o'clock, P. M. Here, by the kindness of Mr. Coulter, (the founder of the town,) our much needed comforts were duly cared for; and, after making arrangements for an early start on the morrow, we retired for the night, well fatigued with the journey; having been upon the road fifteen and one-half hours.

As we wish to make these sketches of use to future travelers, we have been particular in noting time, cost, distance, and numerous other particulars, and as we have reached the end of our journey by stage, we append the following:

TIME AND DISTANCE TABLE FROM STOCKTON TO COULTERVILLE.

			Time made.	Miles.
Left Stockton at 1-4 past 6, A. M.				
From Stockton to 12 Mile House			1.35	12
From	"	to 25 Mile House	4.15	23
From	"	to Foot Hills	4.35	30
From	"	to Knight's Ferry	5.40	37
From	"	to Rock River House, (including detention for dinner)	7 40	44
From Stockton to Crimea House			8.40	48

Here we exchanged stages, and delayed one hour.

		Time made.	Miles.
From Stockton to Don Pedro's Bar, (including delay at Crimea House)		11.30	60
From Stockton to Coulterville, (exchanged horses and was delayed 12 min.)		15.30	71

Our first considerations the following morning were for good animals, provisions, cooking utensils, and a guide,—the former (all but the *good*) were supplied by a gentleman who rejoiced in the uncommon and somewhat ancient patronymic of Smith, at twenty-five dollars per head for the trip of eight days, almost the original cost of each animal, judging from their build and speed, so that the bill run as follows:—

5 saddle horses, one for each person,	$125
1 pack mule	25
Guide	25

We hope before the next traveling season commences that reasonable arrangements will be made for a daily line of *good* saddle animals, both here and at Mariposa, (a most excellent starting point,) for it is much to be regretted that such exorbitant charges should preclude persons of limited means from visiting this magnificent valley. For the supply of provisions and cooking utensils, Mr. Coulter and the guide relieved us of all anxiety; and, at a quarter to nine the next morning, we were in our saddles, ready for the start. How we were attired or armed; what was the impression produced upon the bystanders; or, even what was our own opinion of appearances, "deponent saith not."

CHAPTER III.

The Route to the Valley.

Life, so varied, hath more loveliness
In one brief day, than has a creeping century
Of sameness.

BAILEY'S FESTUS.

For the first three or four miles, our road lay up a rough, mountainous point, thro' dense chaparal bushes that were growing on both sides of us, to a high, bold ridge ; and from whence we obtained a splendid and comprehensive view of the foot-hills and broad valley of the San Joaquin. At this point we entered a vast forest of pines, cedars, firs, and oaks, and rode leisurely among their deep and refreshing shadows, occasionally passing saw-mills, or ox-teams that were hauling logs or lumber, until we reached "Bower Cave," at about half past one, P. M., twelve miles distant from Coulterville.

This is a singular grotto-like formation, about one hundred feet in depth, and length, and ninety feet in width, and which is entered by a passage not more than three feet six inches wide, at the northern end of an opening some seventy feet long by thirteen feet wide, nearly covered with running vines and maple trees, that grow out from within the cave ; and when these are drawn aside, you look into a deep abyss, at the bottom of which is a small sheet of water, made shadowy and mysterious by overhanging rocks and trees. On entering, you walk down a

flight of fifty-two steps, to a newly constructed wooden platform, and from whence you can either pick your way to the water below, or ascend another flight of steps to a smaller cave above. But

DESCENDING THE MOUNTAIN TO THE YO-SEMITE VALLEY.

although there is a singular charm about this spot that amply repays a visit, we must not linger too long, but pay our dollar, (fifty cents too much), and renew our journey.

As the day was hot, and the ride a novelty to most of us, we took a long siesta here, not fairly starting before a quarter to five o'clock, P. M. From this point to "Black's Ranch," our five miles' ride was delightfully cool and pleasant, and for the most part, by gradual ascent up a long gulch, shaded in places with a dense growth of timber, and occasionally across a rocky point to avoid a long detour or difficult passage. This part of our journey occupied us two hours. After a short delay, the ladies and a portion of our party started on, while Mr. Ewer and the writer having found one of the discoverers of the mammoth trees of Mariposa county, remained behind to glean some interesting facts concerning them, which will appear in due season before this series of articles is finished. While thus engaged, we had not noticed the fast gathering night shadows; and, when we made the discovery, we gave the spurs to our horses and hurried off.

On account of the steep hill-side upon which our trail now lay, and the pious habits of one of our horses, as the night had become so dark that we could scarcely see our hands before us, this ride was attended with some danger, and required that in consideration of the value, on such a trip, of a sound neck, if only for the convenience of the thing, we remembered and practiced too, the Falstaffian motto concerning discretion, and took it leisurely; arriving at Deer Flat, six miles above Black's, at a quarter past nine o'clock, P. M.

As our absence had created no little anxiety to at least one of the ladies of our party, on account of a husband being among the missing, our safe arrival in camp was welcomed with rejoicing acclamations. A good hearty meal was then discussed, and preparations made for passing the night, as comfortably as possible, in our star-roofed chamber, but on account of the novelty of our situation, to several, in camping out for the first time, it was long past midnight

"Ere slumber's spell had bound us."

Deer Flat is a beautiful green valley of about fifteen or twenty acres, surrounded by an amphitheatre of pines and oaks, and being well watered, makes a very excellent camping-ground. By the name given to this place, we thought that some game might probably reward an early morning's hunt, and accordingly, about day-break, we sallied out, prepared for dropping a good fat buck, but as no living thing larger than a dove could be started up the amount of fresh meat thus obtained was not very troublesome to carry.

A few minutes after seven o'clock on the morning of the 17th, we again started, and although not in the possession of the brightest of feelings, either mental or physical, we had no sooner become fairly upon our way than the wild and beautiful scenes on every hand made us forget the broken slumber of the night, and the unsatisfactory breakfast of the morning, as we journeyed on towards Hazel Green, which point we reached in two hours,— six miles distant from Deer Flat.

From this point the distant landscapes began to gather in interest and beauty, as we threaded our way through the magnificent forest of pine on the top of the ridge. Here, the green valley deep down on the Merced; there, the snow-clothed Sierra Nevadas, with their rugged peaks towering up; and in the sheltered hollows of the base, Nature's snow-built reservoirs, were glittering in the sun. These were glorious sights, amply sufficient in themselves to repay the fatigue and trouble of the journey without the remaining climax, to be reached when we entered the wondrous valley.

At ten minutes to eleven o'clock, A. M. we reached Crane Flat, six miles from Hazel Green; where, as there was plenty of

DISTANT VIEW OF THE "POHONO," (INDIAN NAME,) OR BRIDAL VEIL WATERFALL.
[*From a Photograph by C. L. Weed.*]

grass and water, we took lunch and a rest of about two hours.

From this point parties visit the small grove of mammoth trees, to be seen on this route, but as our party was too anxious to look upon the great valley of waterfalls, we did not go down to see them; at our request, however, Rev. J. C. Holbrook has kindly favored us with the following extract from his note-book, which may happily supply the omission: —

"From Crane Flat we made a little detour to the right of about a mile and a half, to see some "Big Trees." We found them to consist of a little cluster on the side of a deep cañon, of the same species of cedar as those which form the celebrated grove in Calaveras county. They are monsters, and of almost incredible size. Two of them grow from the same root, and are united near the base, and hence we call them the "Siamese Twins." They are virtually one tree, being nourished by the same roots. We paced the distance *around* them at the bottom, close to the bark, and found it to be thirty-eight paces, or one hundred and fourteen feet, which would give as the *diameter* of both, thirty-eight feet!

The bark on one side has been cut into, and it measures twenty inches in thickness. At a few rods distance, interspersed among other trees, are four or five others of these monarchs of the forest, of which two or three are twenty-six paces each in circumference, or seventy-eight feet, with a diameter of twenty-six feet. They are perfectly straight, and tower up heavenward from 150 to 200 feet.

These trees are well worth visiting by

any one who has not seen the groves in Calaveras and Mariposa counties. Such dimensions seem almost too marvelous for belief to persons at a distance. I sent the above statement to a daily paper in a western city, and in publishing it, the editor said: "We call particular attention to the statement relative to California forest trees. It *would be accounted apocryphal had it a less reliable source.*" The trail is very plain from Crane Flat to these trees, although the descent and ascent to and from them is rather laborious, especially on a day as intensely hot as was that on which I visited them."

It is difficult to say whether the exciting pleasures of anticipation had quickened our pulses to the more vigorous use of our spurs, or that the horses had already smelled, in imagination at least, the luxuriant patches of grass in the great valley, or that the road was better than it had been before, certain it is, from whatever cause, we traveled faster and easier than at any previous time, and came in sight of the haze-draped summits of the mountain-walls that girdle the Yo-Semite Valley, in a couple of hours after leaving Crane Flat—distance nine miles.

Now, it may so happen that the reader entertains the idea that if he could just look upon a wonderful or an impressive scene, he could fully and accurately describe it. If so, we gratefully tender to him the use of our chair; for, we candidly confess, that we can not. The truth is, the first view of this convulsion-rent valley, with its perpendicular mountain cliffs, deep gorges, and awful chasms, spread out before us like a mysterious scroll, took away the power of thinking, much less of clothing thoughts with suitable language.

And I beheld when he had opened the sixth seal, and, lo, there was a great earthquake; and the sun became black as sackcloth of hair, and the moon became as blood,

and the stars of heaven fell unto the earth, even as a fig tree casteth her untimely figs; when she is shaken of a mighty wind.

And the heaven departed as a scroll when it is rolled together; and every mountain and island were moved out of their places.

And the kings of the earth, and the great men, and the rich men, and the chief captains, and mighty men, and every bondman, and every freeman, hid themselves in the dens and in the rocks of the mountains; and said to the mountains and rocks, Fall on us, and hide us from the face of him that sitteth on the throne, and from the wrath of the Lamb: for the great day of his wrath is come; and who shall be able to stand?

These words from Holy Writ will the better convey the impression, not of the thought, so much, but of the profound feeling inspired by that scene.

"This verily is the stand-point of silence," at length escaped in whispering huskiness from the lips of one of our number, Mr. Ewer. Let us name this spot "The Stand-point of Silence." And so let it be written in the note-book of every tourist, as it will be in his inmost soul when he looks at the appalling grandeur of the Yo-Semite valley from this spot.

We would here suggest, that if any visitor wishes to see this valley in all its awe-inspiring glory, let him go down the outside of the ridge for a quarter of a mile and then descend the eastern side of it for three or four hundred feet, as from this point a high wall of rock, at your right hand, stands on the opposite side of the river, that adds much to the depth, and consequently to the hight of the mountains.

When the inexpressible "first impression" had been overcome and human tongues had regained the power of speech, such exclamations as the following were uttered—"Oh! now let me die, for I am happy." "Did mortal eyes ever behold such a scene in any other land?" "The half had not been told us." "My heart is full to overflowing with emotion at the sight of so much appalling grandeur in

RIVER SCENE IN THE YO-SEMITE VALLEY, NEAR THE FOOT OF THE TRAIL.
[From a Photograph by C. L. Weed,]

the glorious works of God!" "I am satisfied." "This sight is worth ten years of labor," &c., &c.

A young man, named Wadilove, who had fallen sick with fever at Coulterville, and who, consequently, had to remain behind his party, became a member of ours; and on the morning of the second day out, experiencing a relapse, he requested us to leave him behind; but, as we expressed our determination to do nothing of the kind, at great inconvenience to himself, he continued to ride slowly along. When at Hazel Green, he quietly murmured, "I would not have started on this trip, and suffer as much as I have done this day, for ten thousand dollars." But when he arrived at this point, and looked upon the glorious wonders presented to his view, he exclaimed, 'I am a hundred times repaid now for

all I have this day suffered, and I would gladly undergo a thousand times as much, could I endure it, and be able to look upon another such a scene."

Admonished by our excellent guide, (whom everybody called "Sam,") we were soon in our saddles, and again on our way, never dreaming that we had spent more than a few brief minutes here, although our time-pieces told us that we had delayed forty-five, but which ought to have been prolonged to at least one day.

About a mile further on, we reached that point where the descent of the mountain commences; and where our guide required us to dismount, while he arranged the saddle blankets and cruppers, and straightened the saddle girths. Some were for walking down this precipitous trail to the valley, but as the guide informed such that it was nearly seven miles to the foot of the mountain, the desire, for the time being, was overcome; yet, in some of the steepest portions of the trail one or two of the party dismounted, neither of whom, we are proud to say, was a lady.

About two miles from the "Stand-Point of Silence," while descending the mountain, we arrived at a rapid and beautiful cascade, across which was a bridge, and here we quenched our thirst with its delicious water. Here we will mention that there is an ample supply of excellent cool water, at convenient distances, the entire length of the route, whether by Coulterville or Mariposa.

Soon, another cascade was reached and crossed, and its rushing heedlessness of course among rocks, now leaping over this, and past that; here giving a seething, there a roaring sound; now bubbling, and gurgling here; and smoking and frothing there, kept some of us looking and lingering until another admonition of our guide broke the charm and hurried us away.

The picturesque wildness of the scene on every hand; the exciting wonders of so romantic a journey; the difficulties surmounted; the dangers braved, and overcome; put us in posession of one unanimous feeling of unalloyed delight; so that when we reached the foot of the mountain, and rode side by side among the shadows of the spreading oaks and lofty pines in the smooth valley, we congratulated each other upon looking the very picture of happiness personified.

But as the sun had set, and a ride of six miles was yet before us ere we reached the upper hotel (Hite's) to which we were going, we quickened our speed, and reached the ferry. Here a new difficulty presented itself, inasmuch as the ferryman had left it for the night, and lived nearly half a mile above. This however, was overcome, by bringing a fowling-

piece into excellent play, (nearly the only one called for on the entire route,) on account of the scarcity of game, and after a delay of nearly one hour we were ferried across, at the rate of thirty-seven and a half cents per head, for men as well as animals, and at half-past nine o'clock, P. M., we arrived at the end of our day's journey. We feel confident that we express the sentiment of each when we say that this day will be remembered among the most delightful of our lives.

TABLE OF DISTANCES, AND TIME OCCUPIED BY OUR PARTY IN GOING TO THE VALLEY.

	Time of travel. h. m.	Rest'g & camp'g. h. m.	Dist. miles.
From Coulterville to Bower Cave,	4 25		12
Rested at the Cave,		3 40	
From the Cave to Black's Inn,	2 00		5
Rested at Black's		20	
From Black's to Deer Flat,	1 45		6
Camped for the night at Deer Flat, from 9 p. m. till 5 min. of 7 a. m.,		9 55	
From Deer Flat to Hazel Green,	2 00		6
Rested at Hazel Green,		10	
From Hazel Green to Crane Flat,	1 30		6
Rested and lunched at C. Flat,		2 15	
From Crane Flat to "Stand-point of Silence,"	2 10		9
Stopped at "Stand-Point of Silence,"		45	
From Stand-Point of Silence to 2d Cascade Bridge,			2
From 2d Cascade to foot of Trail, into Valley.,			5
From foot of Trail to upper Hotel,			6
From Stand-Point of Silence to Upper Hotel,	5 15		
Total time of Travel,	19 5	17 5	
Total time of resting and camping,	17 5		
Total time from Coulterville to Hotel in Valley,	36 10		
Total distance,			57

In our next number we shall continue this series of articles on the Yo-Semite Valley, and present some of the most skilfully drawn and finely executed engravings of all its most remarkable scenes that have ever appeared in this work, from photographs and sketches taken from nature.

Near View of the YO-SEMITE FALLS,
2,500 FEET IN HEIGHT.

[*From a Photograph by* C. L. WEED.]

GENERAL VIEW OF THE YO-SEMITE VALLEY,

From Open-eta-noo-ah,—Inspiration Point,—on the Mariposa Trail.

THE ROAD-RUNNER OF CALIFORNIA.

THE "ROAD-RUNNER."

This very strange and rare bird, called, in Spanish, *Courier del Camino* or *Piasano*, is peculiar to California and some portions of Mexico. So far as I am acquainted, it has not been described by any ornithologist, and still remains a distinct and isolated species from all other birds, roaming about over barren plains and hills, in search of lizards, snakes, and other reptiles, upon which it preys.

It is always seen upon the ground when first discovered, and instantly runs off, with remarkable fleetness, to the nearest thicket or hill, where it generally escapes from its pursuers either by hiding or sailing from one hill to another. It is very quick in its motions—active and vigilant; indeed, its remarkable swiftness enables it to outstrip a good horse.

At first sight, one would suppose it to be a species of Pheasant, or belonging to the ambulatory or galinaceous class of birds; but when examined more closely, it resembles them in no particular.

The most remarkable feature about it is its feet, these being more like those of clinging birds, such as the woodpecker or parrot, having two toes behind and two before, armed with sharp claws. Its legs being strong and muscular, make it well adapted for running.

Its plumage is rather coarse and rough, of a dusky hue, marked with white and brownish specks on the neck and upper parts, while its under parts are of a dirty white. The tail is long; the bill is strong and slightly curved; eyes of a greyish brown, the pupil encircled with a light colored ring. A bare space extends from the eye to the back of the neck, of a pale blueish color, tinged with red.

At times it utters a harsh note, not unlike the sudden twirl of a watchman's rattle.

The Road-Runner is seldom seen on trees, unless pursued very closely, when it has been seen to spring from the ground to the branches, at a height of ten or fifteen feet at a single bound; but it prefers running along a road or path, from whence it derives its name.

THE MALE CALIFORNIA CONDOR, ON THE WING.

A TRIP TO WALKER'S RIVER AND CARSON VALLEY.

by *. *. *.

To the mountains! Ho for the mountains, was my joyous and almost involuntary exclamation, as I waved an adieu to a bevy of friends who had gathered on the stoops of two little cottages that stood side by side, just at the margin of the blackened space that now marked where, but a few days before, stood Columbia, that beautiful but ill-fated mountain city, then little else than a mass of mouldering ruins, and turned my horses head towards the bold range of mountains that rises immediately to the eastward, accompanied by three pleasant companions, all accoutred and provisioned for a journey of adventure and, mayhap, discovery, to the little known, though much talked of, Walker's River. Though an invalid myself, with scarcely more than sufficient strength to enable me to crawl into my saddle, yet I felt a thrill of joy and a wild enthusiasm at the thought of casting aside, for a season, all cares of business, and of being soon enabled to snuff the pure mountain air, unalloyed by the sickening vapor, and, more than all, the health-destroying dust that ever hovers about the area of civilization in California. Ye who have never felt the palsying grasp of a subtle disease that is drawing the pale of oblivion, slowly but surely, over the vital organs, shrouding the soul with its dark shadows, mayhap to make the vision of an hereafter more bright and glorious, know not the wild, yet mournful enthusiasm of the weary invalid, as he recedes from the busy haunts of man, and penetrates deeper and deeper into the mountain solitudes, where his fevered brow may be cooled by the refreshing breeze that is purified by the limpid snow, and perfumed by the uncultured flowers—for, as he rises higher and higher, each new feature of wild grandeur that presents itself to his sensitive gaze, forces upon his susceptible reason new proofs, as it were, of a Divine Omnipotence, and he seems, as he stands on some lofty peak or overhanging crag, far removed from the busy world below, in closer communion with Him who doeth all things well, and though the cheek may bear the hectic blush and the eye the warning glow of death, yet the spirit of the soul is calm, for it feels that Immortality is real.

The day of our departure had been big with annoyances and hindrances incident to all parties bent upon like excursions. In the first place, one who was to have been of the party was prevented from going, or, rather, did not appear at the appointed time, and another had to be sought to fill his place—a matter which, however, was very easily accomplished Then a pistol had been left behind, and another gun was needed. One pack animal that we had relied upon could not be had, and another one must be hunted up; however, one was soon secured, (all but the secured,) for, after having engaged a mule, it could nowhere be found. Every nook and corner of the district was searched, but that "mula" was missing. It always had been just at hand, but, as a matter of course, now that it was wanted immediately, it took this particular apportunity to step out, and it was only after several hours' *buscaring* that it turned up.

All was now ready to commence packing, which task was soon accomplished, for though the day was far spent, we determined to make a start, in strict accordance with prior arrangements; and as the weather was exceedingly hot, we thought a few miles travel by moonlight would be even more pleasant than by the light of a scorching sun; and, accordingly, at 5 o'clock, P. M., on the third day of September, we were *en route*, with two pack animals, one month's provisions and the necessary accompaniments for rough camp-life; together with tools for prospecting, guns for hunting, fishing-tackle for fishing, and, in fact, fully prepared for a good time generally—with two dogs, as body guards.

At sunset we were at the Mountain House, situated at the top of the high ridge that rises immediately above Columbia. It was a calm and beautiful sunset; the tinge of the western horizon was peculiarly soft and mellow, which, together with our elevated position, made our spirits light and buoyant, for we were now fairly started upon our adventurous journey, and were even so soon almost at the verge of civilization, for low down in the valley we had just left, we could discern the blue, smoky vapor rising above Columbia, while immediately below us, at the base of the ridge, nestled he quiet little camp of Yankee Hill; beyond which, to the eastward, there are only a few ranches, together with the numerous lumber mills that are scattered through the vast tract of timber country, for a distance of fifteen miles.

Washing the dust from our throats with a cool beverage proffered us by the generous host of the Mountain House, Mr. Northey, we again set out for our destination for the night, eighth miles further on. The full moon shone out with all its splendor, and the cool breeze that swept over the ridge over which lay our road, made our jaunt for that evening a pleasant one. At 10 o'clock we reached ———— saw-mill, aroused the occupants to procure feed for our animals, which was kindly furnished us; and, for ourselves, we broached a box of sardines,

which, with a biscuit and a cup of water, sufficed for our supper; after which, we spread our blankets on the stoop of the dwelling, and, though the bed was somewhat less soft than the one we had of late been accustomed to, yet the fatigue of the day caused us to sleep soundly and sweetly.

At early dawn we arose and made our breakfast after the style of our supper, with the addition of a cup of tea, and were soon moving again. Our road now for some twenty-five miles lay through the section of country situated between the south fork of the Stanislaus and the north fork of the Tuolumne. It is marked by nothing of interest, except being that through which run the monster ditches of the Tuolumne County and the Columbia and Stanislaus River Water Companies, and its vast products of lumber from which Tuolumne county is almost wholly supplied.

At 12 o'clock we arrived at a meadow, where we halted for a little while to rest. Here we watered our animals and quenched our own thirst at an ice-cold spring. We drank long and deeply, for we knew that our road to Strawberry Flat, a distance of thirteen miles, lay for the most part upon the high ridge that separates the two rivers, and without water for the entire distance, and as the sun was pouring down his rays upon us without his ever taking this fact into consideration, we might well expect to suffer somewhat; which anticipation was fully realized, for as we descended at 5 o'clock into that beautiful and romantic little valley, our lips were parched and voices husky, and to the limpid water of the little stream that meandered through it, the north fork of the Tuolumne, we paid an homage almost akin to that of the Arab to the Spring of the Desert.

Throwing the packs from our animals, we soon had them picketed in the luxuriant grass that covered the flat; a merry fire soon blazed up beside a cedar log hard by, and in a very short time a cup of tea—tin-cup, we mean—and a warm biscuit were placed at our service by our expert companion P., which, together with a slice of pork held for a moment to the blaze on the end of a stick, made us a glorious supper, however much it may have been in contrast to the usual suppers in our respective boarding-houses. For this particular time I speak for my companions and for myself generally; for now I paid little respect to our festive board. I was an invalid at starting, and this day's journey, under a scorching suu, had nearly prostrated me, and at early twilight I spread my blankets close by the fire and rolled myself up in them; treating the proposition of Judge ——, for an early start on the morrow, rather coldly.

The morning found us less nimble than we had anticipated the evening previous. For my own part, I could hardly rise from my blankets; nor was I alone, now, in my tribulation, for the Judge's feet refused to stand the pressure of a boot—one ankle and five toes were blistered—and C. uttered several decisive grunts as he came out of his blankets; the cords of his legs had been put to too great a strain in climbing those tedious hills and in applying the boot somewhat freely to "mula," who, by the way, fully sustained her character as a mule, by "acting up" whenever opportunity offered. P. was the only sound man in the party, not even *excepting the dogs!* for they were foot-sore, and as he was not particular, we soon decided to lay by a day and recruit—a conclusion very easily arrived at, for, in addition to the reasons already given, we wished to visit one of the large reservoirs of the Tuolumne County Water Co., situated at the northern extremity of the valley, and distant about two miles from our camp; and then, too, we had noticed in the deep holes of the little branch just at hand, an abundance of mountain trout, which our judgment of

what constituted good living made us desire to transfer to our spacious fry-pan.

Our morning meal dispatched, we turned our first attention to the trout, and invited them to partake of a grasshopper delicately tendered them on the point of a hook, but lo! they did not appreciate our generosity, but on the other hand, rather insulted us for our kind attentions by eyeing the shining bait askant, giving apparently a dainty snuff and then turning lazily away in seeming disgust, while we peeped shyly over a projecting rock, or through a screening bush, with watery mouths in anticipation of fried trout. This caused us to scratch our heads in perplexity, but we soon hit upon a plan which "sort o' got 'em" in every sense of the word, by bringing our pick, shovel and pan into requisition, and draining and bailing out their holes, leaving them high and dry.

It was now proposed to visit the reservoir. For my own part, I felt hardly able to mount my horse, which my companions had kindly saddled for me, but finally summoned the necessary resolution and started, accompanied by the Judge and C., P. having volunteered to stay in camp. A half-hour's ride through a dense growth of pine, cedar and fir trees brought us to the margin of the beautiful sheet of water, formed by a monster dam thrown across the south fork of the Stanislaus by that energetic and pioneer of water companies, the Tuolumne County Water Co.

This reservoir, which is one of four which that enterprising company has constructed in the last two years, under the superintendence of the indefatigable —— Holton, and at a cost of about $135,-000; it covers an area of about one mile in length by one-third to one-half mile in width, with an average depth, when full, of thirty feet. The dam is sixty feet high in the centre from the bed of the river, with a span of two hundred and fifty feet, and is built of heavy barked timber, plat-

RESERVOIR OF THE TUOLUMNE COUNTY WATER COMPANY, AT STRAWBERRY FLAT.

ted and graveled, with an inclination of about thirty-eight degrees, so that the heavier the pressure of water, the firmer it is pressed down to its foundation. It is thrown across the mouth of a rugged cañon with solid granite for either abutment, and is, truly, a stupendous piece of work, reflecting much credit both upon the company and the superintendent. Since its completion it requires the attention of only two men, who gauge the water and repair leakages, and who live in a cabin near the dam.

On the north and east of the reservoir the mountains rise abruptly from the water to the height of many hundred feet, and are almost one solid mass of light granite, sparsely covered with stunted pine and cedar, and for the most part almost inaccessible. The view from the dam in this direction is grand and picturesque, and especially when the sun has just sunk behind the western ridge, and these hoary hills cast their dark shadows in the calm and placid water,

which reflects, at the same time, all the tints of the mellow evening sky, the whole scene is one of rare romantic beauty.

The only approach to the dam is by a rugged and circuitous trail over a rocky point that makes out to the flat some third of a mile from the dam. Judge and C. being desirous of visiting it, started up the trail; while I, feeling in no way improved by my ride, lay down to rest in the shade of a little cedar, just at the water's edge, and at the termination of the rocky point. After the lapse of an hour I was aroused by the splash of an oar, and, on looking up, saw my companions just rounding the rocky point with a clumsy skiff, or raft, made of a dry cedar log, halved and the two parts fastened together, with the ends sharpened. They brought me an invitation from the gentlemanly occupant of the cabin at the dam—for at this time only one man was there—to come down and remain with him for the night, which I very willingly accepted, feeling that in my present condition, a comfortable bunk would be preferable to the turf at our camp. Taking a little turn over the reservoir in search of a duck that they had been told was hovering about it—and which we found, but did not succeed in killing—my companions landed me at the cabin, and then returned to camp. At dusk Mr. C. returned again, to remain with me, bringing my rifle, and being determined, he said, to capture the duck in the morning.

I turned out the next morning, feeling considerably improved, but not sufficiently so to risk starting on our journey, and C., answering for our other two companions, kindly consented to abide my time; and, after breakfast, proposed to look out for the duck that we had seen the evening previous, volunteering to row me to a rocky point, where I might lie in wait, while he started the game. Getting on board the raft he soon set me down on one of the little rocky mounds that rise out of the water near the upper end of the reservoir ; and very soon, to my agreeable surprise, he drove the duck towards me; when, fortunately, I made a lucky shot and killed it. Returning to the dam we took dinner with our host, and thanking him for his kind attentions, returned to camp. Dressing our duck, we perched it upon a willow stick over our fire and watching the process of its roasting with watery mouths—little dreaming we had caught something that might be called a wolf in sheep's clothing, and but for its feathers gathered around it when done—with tender solicitude. A single bite at a side bone was sufficient for me, the rank, fishy odor that ascended my nostrils caused me to hurl it away in disgust. P. followed suit—Judge and C. forced down a couple of mouthfuls, when all agreed in the propriety of consigning it to the dogs, and even they, after a snuff or two, turned away from it with an air of offended dignity, and we ex-claimed with the poet—deviating slightly in the application :—

Nature never made but one such duck,
And broke the die (or certainly ought so to have done,) in getting this one up.

On the following morning, I rolled out from my blankets, feeling much better, when preparations were made for an immediate start, and as the sun peeped over the eastern ridge, we were again, *en route*. A little distance from our camp, we struck into the old Emigrant road of 1852, bearing due East, and immediately commenced the ascent of the first ridge. Four miles of constant rise, brought us to what are known as Bill's Meadows. The air now began to be cool and bracing, and I fancied that I could feel additional improvements at each succeeding mile. From the Meadows, our trail took a Northeasterly direction, along a high ridge of gradual, but easy ascent, for some five or six miles, when we rose an abrupt and rugged point, where a view presented itself of the wildest grandeur, causing us to halt for a while to satisfy our gaze. The trail here lay upon the very verge of a giddy precipice, facing the Northwest, at the base of which, lay heavy banks of snow; and below this, was a succession of little basins of water fed by the slow melting of the snow-drifts ; their margins carpeted with beautiful green, presenting a truly romantic picture. Below, at the left, was the deep gorge through which runs the south fork of the Stanislaus, and still lower down, at a distance of some two miles, yet apparently almost at our very feet, was visible a portion of the great upper reservoir of the Tuolumne County Water Co.,—nine miles above the one at Strawberry Flat,—while beyond, to the west, rose a ridge, composed of one solid mass of bleached granite, without a single tree or shrub to relieve it, of its barren and dreary aspect ; while to the right, a little farther on, and looking to the north, rose in bold relief, those novel peaks of valcanic formation, called the "Tooth-picks."

Our trail from this, lay upon an entirely granite formation, and threaded among the rocks, leading us to all points of the compass, the marks of the passage of the Emigrant wagons, were still plainly visible, and now, at every few rods, pieces of their wrecks were yet to be seen. At 4 o'clock, we descended abruptly into a valley of considerable extent, but, for which we know no name. Here was excellent grass and several little minature lakes ; and, as the margin of one of which attracted our special attention, we concluded to pitch our camp.

It was a thing of rare beauty—a basin scooped out of the solid granite, which here presented a horizontal face of one or two acres, and at the elevation of several feet above the surrounding valley, without inlet or outlet, and with a depth of some three feet, its water cool and clear as crystal. On the east side, was a little plat of grass, and here we picketed our horses, while for ourselves, we selected a cosy little nook just a few rods to the south, where we built a cheerful fire and spread our blankets with a breastwork of rock on either side.

The next morning found us early a-stir and all feeling much better than any previous day. For my own part, I was mending fast, being now able to consume my ration of pork and bread, to the entire satisfaction of the party.

Leaving this valley we rose a low granite ridge, and in a quarter of an hour descended into another of greater extent, but presenting, for the most part, a barren appearance, and through which our trail wound circuitously for some three miles, when we found ourselves on the ridge which lies immediately on the west side of the middle fork of the Tuolumne, and near its source. We now bore directly north, our road being somewhat rugged, yet not very difficult, and

at 2 o'clock descended into what is known as Relief Valley. This valley takes its very appropriate name from the fact that it was here that relief was brought to the emigrants in their almost starving condition, from the generous-hearted citizens of Sonora and Columbia—among whom was my present companion, Judge C. The passage of this emigrant train, which forced its way through this almost impassable section of the Sierra Nevadas in 1852, was one of peculiar hardship and suffering—excelled in this respect, perhaps, only by the ill-fated one of '46, that starved on the Truckee. They followed the ill-judged advice of a few persons from Tuolumne county, who went out and met them at the sink of the Humboldt, and at the junction of the old emigrant road with Carson river, thirty-five miles west of the Desert, a large train with a vast amount of stock struck off to the south, following up Walker's river, and crossed the mountains at the source of its western branch. Much of their road, after getting into the mountains, they were compelled to make, hauling their wagons up some of the steeps by means of ropes, while their stock died at a fearful rate. At one place, a few miles to the east of the Summit, they were forced to drain down some three or four feet of a small lake to enable them to ford it on one side—it being utterly impossible to go around it; and such was the nature of their trials for near one hundred miles, occupying so much time that their provisions gave out, when they sent an express through to Columbia and Sonora for relief, and a pack-train was immediately fitted out, which, as we have shown, reached them in this valley, the recollection of which, I doubt not, is, and ever will remain fresh in the minds of those who were of the unfortunate party. The bleached bones of many, many animals are still to be seen scattered over it, as, in fact, they are on either side of the trail for a distance of more than a hundred and fifty miles, and now, in many places where all signs of the trail were obliterated, we took our course by the whitened bones alone. The valley is shut in by high barren mountains, and at the base of the ridge that bounds it on the northeast, courses in a direction bearing northwest the middle or main fork of the Stanislaus. The valley slopes gently to the north and east, and about midway of it our trail "run blind," there being a mirey strip running nearly across the entire flat. Here we came to a "standstill," but not until we were well in the mire, not daring to take our animals across until we had found the trail beyond, being, as yet, entirely at a loss at what part of the valley we would make our egress.

I dismounted and stood upon an elevated sod, while my horse was half leg deep in the mud. P., with one of the pack animals, was in a like position, while Judge reversed the position with the amiable mule, for he stood in the mire nearly to the tops of his boots, while mula "humped" herself and gathered all four feet on a little grass sod and stood high and dry. C. forced his way across, a distance of some two hundred yards, to search for the trail, and directly came to a halt and commenced searching among some low bushes. Soon Judge became impatient and halloed, asking if he had found the trail.

"Never saw huckleberries so thick in my life," was the response.

"Well, but have you found the trail?"

"Be blow'd if ever I saw them plentier in the States."

"D—n the huckleberries," responded Judge; and letting go the rein to the mule, struck out to search for the trail himself, and very soon apprised us that it was found, when we again pushed on, not stopping to gather the berries, though they were plenty and of excellent flavor.

Our road now, contrary to our expectations, bore southeast, and across the river, when we commenced a sudden ascent,

difficult and almost dangerous. In about an hour we struck the extreme eastern branch of the main river, and following it up for a half hour we again pitched our camp for the night, in a grove of cedar near a little bar, which afforded just sufficient grass for our animals for the night. We were now in a truly wild spot, and the mountains on each side of us presented a curious picture, from the fact of their being of such entire opposite formations, and at the same time in such proximity. To our right, and rising abruptly from the branch, the mountain was one unbroken mass of bare granite, its depressions still containing masses of snow, to which Judge and C. climbed and could almost have thrown a snowball into our camp-fire. To the left the ridge was of volcanic formation, and at a distance of three hundred yards from the stream, presented a perpendicular face to the height of twelve hundred feet from the river bed.

This night we suffered somewhat from cold, for we had attained a great altitude, and a chilly wind sucked down the gorge, but the next morning all of us were feeling exceedingly well, notwithstanding. We were now six miles from the Summit, and making an early start, wishing to pass as far beyond it as possible this day, we began to be sensible that our blankets were insufficient for the climate we were entering.

The trail now, for the next mile, became at each step more rough and difficult, and, in some places, almost dangerous. Then we descended again to the stream, and from thence on to the Summit the road was of gradual and easy ascent. As we crossed the stream we passed into a grove of poplar and cedar, when "Miss Kit," one of our pack animals—a frivolous little mustang—took upon herself the responsibility of a stampede and scattered the various articles that composed her pack pretty considerably. She struck out up the flat like a flying arrow to the distance of a hundred and fifty yards, when she suddenly wheeled and took a bee line for my honest old horse, with the evident intention of upsetting his pack, viz: myself. Anticipating her design, I drove the spurs into my horse and took cover behind a large cedar just in time to retain my equilibrium, and directly a sudden sheer brought her up "all standing" against a low-spreading poplar, when C. caught her bridle-rein and administered a few lusty kicks, which had the salutary effect of making her "behave herself" for the balance of the day. "Mula" during this time, contrary to our expectations, carried herself very decorously, for, instead of joining in the "lark," made quickly for a clump of willows on the bank of the creek, with one ear cocked forward and the other back, showing that she was looking at least two ways for Sunday, and backed up into them, evidently to keep out of harm's way, presenting a comical though very sensible appearance.

We now began to feel the cold very sensibly as we neared the Summit—the wind blowing from the southeast was raw and cutting, causing me to button closely my "roundabout" and bring into requisition my buck-skin gloves. It grew colder and colder, and, as we rose to the Summit, my teeth chattered and limbs quaked, and, as a last resort, I donned a heavy overcoat that C. had tied upon my saddle, and even then shook like one in an "ager fit." My companions being on foot, suffered less, yet their heavy coats were anything but burdensome now. Heavy banks of snow lay on either side of our trail, though exposed to the sun at least eight hours in the day.

The scene that presented itself as we stood upon the dividing ridge was wild and picturesque, yet dreary and cheerless—we could not well fancy one more so. The sky was partly overcast with low, scudding clouds and the sun looked pale and cold. The low points that rose on either hand were barren and dreary, and those at the south and east were more generally covered with snow. A little below us, looking southeast, and across which lay our trail, was a flat, or valley, of considerable extent, in the centre of which was a little lake of a few acres; which, however, only added to the dreariness of the scene, for the cutting blast swept across it, driving it into little angry waves, and as we threaded our way in gloomy silence along its margin, we realized to the fullest extent our previous anticipations in regard to finding a cooler climate. The raw wind cut and chapped the tender skin of our faces, so suddenly boosted up from a more congenial atmosphere, while the water from our eyes almost frosted on our cheeks, causing us to hold in tender regard all warm places, though perhaps 'twould be better to make *one* exception. A few dwarfish cedars only six or eight feet high, constituted all the timber or shrubbery within our view. Nothing of any description appeared to claim residence here but the little chipping squirrel, and he seemed to gain but a meagre subsistence, judging from his puny appearance—not even a raven hovered about to breathe the gloomy silence with his ominous croak—all was dreary and cheerless, and we hastened our steps onward to find a more congenial scene.

An hour's travel carried us across the Summit plain, when we began to descend the eastern slope, and three miles further on, struck the first considerable branch of Walker's river, down which we continued our course, crossing it many times, the road, meanwhile, becoming more and more rugged, while pieces of wagons were to be met with at every few steps.

(*Concluded in our next.*)

Never be ashamed of confessing your ignorance; for the wisest man upon earth is ignorant of many things, inasmuch as that which he knows is a mere nothing in comparison with what he does not know.

HUTCHINGS'
CALIFORNIA MAGAZINE.

VOL. II.   JUNE, 1858.   No. 12.

FARM HOUSE IN CARSON VALLEY.   SCENE NEAR GENOA.

A TRIP TO WALKER'S RIVER AND
CARSON VALLEY.

BY *. *. *.

(*Concluded.*)

At 3 o'clock, P. M., we came to a lake, partially drained by the emigrants, to make it more easily forded, and which, like them, we were compelled to ford. The road from this point to the place of our encampment three miles below, beg-gars all description.   How an emigrant train could ever get over it with their wagons, was, to us, almost a problem. In this short distance we passed the wrecks of about twenty wagons, some of them still in a tolerable state of preservation, while the bones of cattle were thick-ly strewn on either side; a sad memorial of the hardship of the passage.   In many places, had our animals made a misstep, they would have been hurled into a yawning gulf below. I was compelled to ride from my utter inability to walk, excepting down some of the roughest descents, and then I clung to my horse with suspended breath as he clambered up the rocky steeps.

Just before sunset we descended to the river again, which was here a great deal larger than where we last crossed it, three miles above, showing that some considerable branch from the east had formed a junction with it, as we were still on the west side. On a little grassy flat, we pitched our camp, tired and exhausted, each entertaining a vague hope that we might not be obliged to retraverse the road we had just passed.

We were now twelve miles from the Summit and in a somewhat milder climate, yet our cheerful fire imparted a pleasing sensation to our still shivering bodies.

Anxious to get out of this inhospitable region, we made an early start on the following morning. In the first half mile we crossed the river three times; then, for a mile, our trail was as rugged and difficult as it was the evening previous, when we descended suddenly into a large and beautiful valley, and through which wound the river, now quiet and noiseless, and we felt assured, from the appearance of the country to the north and east, that we were now out of the rugged hills, and that our road henceforward would be comparatively easy. Here we met the U. S. Surveying party of Von Schmidt, on its way to the west side of the mountains, having closed its labors for the season. This party had been running the eastern boundary line of the State, having been out since February. The party numbered some ten men and as many animals. Von Schmidt himself was not with them, he having returned by one of the southern routes.

We detained the party a few moments in making inquiries respecting the country beyond and the trail to Carson Valley, but of this latter they could tell us nothing. Their last camp, from whence they started the day before, was in the vicinity of Mono Lake and distant some thirty-five miles, and on or near the extreme eastern branch of Walker's river, and we hastily came to the conclusion to follow their trail to that point. We inquired respecting the mining in that region, for just previous to our starting on our journey we had read glowing accounts of successful mining on the east fork of Walker's river, but they informed us that these reports were mere fabrications, for they had known of but one prospecting party having penetrated that section—that they "raised the color," but nothing more, and very soon left. To our inquiries respecting Indians they told us that they had seen none, excepting a small party of Monos that hovered about their last camping place, but that the evening before they saw fires, indicating that there were some around. Bidding them a hasty good morning, with an injunction to report us to our friends in Sonora and Columbia, we passed on across the river and over the low ridge to the east, and in a half hour we descended into the valley where the surveying party had camped the night previous—the smoke still curling up from their camp fire.

This little valley, or basin, was one of the few truly beautiful spots in this wild region, containing perhaps thirty or forty acres, and at the northern extremity a little miniature lake, the water cool and clear as crystal, and floating upon its surface was a little flock of ducks, which gave life to the picture. On the south and east, and rising abruptly from the little grassy meadow, were high barren peaks, while on the west was a low sandy ridge, over which lay our trail.

One mile further on and gradually descending, we came to another valley, larger but less romantic and beautiful; then the trail bore more to the east, and a little way beyond we rose a sandy ridge, when we overlooked still another little basin and lake quite similar to the one just described, lying a little to the left of the trail, and in the pond a flock of canvass backs, which we at once resolved to attack. Just as we came to this conclusion we descried a smoke curling up from behind a low ridge a little beyond the valley we had just crossed, and directly, a little more to the north, though at a greater distance, another and more suspicious smoke rose suddenly, leaving us no longer in doubt of our proximity to Indians. We felt thankful for so much good luck, for this was the first game of any description since that memorable duck of Strawberry Flat.

We now resumed our journey, and one mile further on we came to another lake of the same beautiful nature, but considerably larger than the last two. A large flock of ducks were occupying this also, but our efforts to get a shot were unavailing. Passing on two or three miles further we descended to a fourth and larger valley, and here we discovered in the trail fresh Indian footprints, made since the passing of the surveying party the evening previous, which fully confirmed our suspicions of their being around us, and we doubted not that even then they were watching our movements from behind some screening rock on the adjoining ridges.

About midway the valley the trail ran blind, and we spent more than an hour in searching for its place of egress, and finally struck off to the northwest, regardless of it, and about two miles further on, struck another large fork of the river coming in from the southeast, and here again found the trail. There was excellent grass on either side of the stream, and this being the first consideration in selecting a camping place, we crossed over and concluded to end this day's journey here.

The country now immediately around us began to indicate the existence of gold, and P. resolved to make here his first prospect, and, accordingly, unbundled his pick and shovel and struck into a little bar a few yards below, and his first pan prospected a color, as did also two or three succeeding ones, but nothing more. This, however, he got in the loose gravel high up from the ledge. What a more thorough prospect might develop we are unable to say. That gold exists in this locality is certain, but we doubt if it does so to any considerable extent.

This night we used more than ordinary caution in our camping arrangements, taking our animals close in beside us and letting our fire go down early, lest it might more readily expose our position to the Indians should they entertain hostile designs towards us, but the morning found us all right, as usual. The night was cold and chilly, the white frost gathering thick on our blankets and water froze in our cups; but, nevertheless, we passed it very comfortably under the lee of the thick willows that lined the bank of the stream.

From this point we took a direction due east; saw a sandy table land a few hundred yards from our camp, and now our trail lay for a mile and a half over a sandy plain, when a slight descent brought us into a lovely little valley running east and west, at the far end of which we observed a curious mist rising, and as we entered the meadow we discovered a beautiful and limpid little streamlet silently coursing through the tall rich grass which lopped over and so nearly concealed it that we were not aware of its presence until my horse was about to stumble into it. Our trail lay along the northern margin of the valley, and as we approached its eastern end, we discovered the origin of the mist or steam. Here was a large and beautiful hot soda spring, from which flowed the stream that ran through the meadow. The spring boils up from the level ground just above a rocky point that makes out into the valley from the low ridge on the north, making a noise like that of a boiling cauldron, and presenting a novel and beautiful appearance. Its temperature was equal to boiling water, and what appeared to us very curious, not more than twenty feet above it was another spring, though very small, the water of which was almost ice cold. The hot spring yields about forty or fifty inches of water, and just below the rocky point it has formed a large body several feet in depth, of what appears to be decayed soda, while here the pure, fresh soda, like a heavy white frost, borders each side of the stream, and more singular than all, only four hundred yards below the spring the stream is literally alive with little fish, which we ascertained to be suckers.

VALLEY OF THE HOT SODA SPRINGS, TWO MILES EAST OF WALKER'S RIVER.

About three hundred yards below the spring the soda mound terminates abruptly, making a little fall, or rapid, over which a small portion of the stream ripples, while the main body of the water sinks a few yards above, and again gushes out at the base of the mound, forming a kind of natural bathing tub, in which we luxuriated—for it was indeed a luxury compared to any other bath. The temperature of the water here was just as high as our bodies could bear, and as we lay with the swift soft current passing over us, our heads a little elevated by making a pillow of a rock, we could gaze upon the heavy banks of snow that lay on the lofty peaks to the west, and set at naught the chilly air that wafted down from them.

The next morning we were off early. About one mile from the spring a high ridge of ragged granite, intermixed with the conglomerate rock, intersected our trail, but through which there is a natural pass, the cliffs rising almost perpendicularly on each side, while the little space between of a few yards in width, across which lay our trail, was smooth and level and carpeted with rich grass, while underneath the cliff to the right was a little grove of a dozen poplars, making it, altogether, a romantic spot, and we named it "The Portal."

Beyond this pass we entered another valley of some three miles in length by a half mile in width, with a gentle inclination to the east, and bound on the north and south by high ridges, their bases well timbered with pine and cedar. Passing this we descended suddenly into another valley larger but less beautiful, stretching away to the south, and through which ran a beautiful stream, one of the tributaries of the middle eastern fork of Walk-

THE PORTAL.

er's river. This valley was some six miles in length, but far less fertile than those through which we had just passed, being for the most part a barren, sandy waste, corresponding with the hills surrounding it.

Following the trail of the surveying party we passed the entire length of this valley, and down the stream for about two miles beyond, when we suddenly emerged into another valley that far excelled in extent and fertility any that we had yet seen, being, as we judged, fifteen or twenty miles in length by five or six in width, and coursing through it to the north runs the middle east fork of Walker's river. The tall rank grass, as I rode through it, reached nearly to my knees, and at a distance, as the wind waved it, it presented the appearance of a vast field of grain. To the east of the valley rose a low, barren ridge, apparently that which separated this from the extreme eastern branch of the river. We called the valley the Big Mono, from the fact of our finding here a small party of Mono Indians.

The trail for the first few miles was dim and difficult to follow, running entirely blind in some places, causing us to pick our way cautiously, but presently it became more broad and beaten, showing the recent footprints of Indians, which induced us to believe that we should come out somewhere, at least, and probably at some large rancheria; but this mattered little to us, since it kept a course agreeable to our notions of the locality of Carson Valley. It lay through a country rough, wild and barren, with not a single valley for a distance of twenty-five miles to relieve it of its desolate appearance, yet, agreeable to our expectations of it as an Indian trail, it was comparatively easy. It crossed one deep gorge or chasm through which bubbled a limpid stream which run to the west and emptied into the river. The ground on either side, to the very brink of the chasm was nearly level, it being here a kind of table land lying between the high ridge to the right and the river low down to the left, and it seemed that the ground had some time been opened here by some terrible convulsion of nature. It was little more than an easy rifle shot across it, and yet it was not less than three hundred feet to the bed of the stream. We had to lead our animals down the zigzag trail with the greatest care, and in ascending the opposite side, I was obliged to pass my rifle to my companions and give all my attention to the guiding and clinging to my horse, now swerving to one side to avoid some sharp jagged rock, then lying forward on the neck of my horse to keep my head from coming in contact with some overhanging trees, for though I was much improved in health, yet it would have been impossible for me to have ascended this steep on foot, and as my kind and faithful horse rose to the plain above he trembled in every limb. From this place on for five or six miles our trail was again easy, when the ridge over which it lay terminated abruptly in a rugged granite range which stretched across the country from east to west, and pitching to the north, and here again, for a short distance, we found a rough trail. As we turned a sharp point of rock an extensive valley suddenly burst in view far down below, but apparently within an hour's travel, and though it was now only about 3 o'clock, yet it was near sunset ere we fairly struck into it, and descending rapidly all the while. Such is the delusion of vision in this region. Distances that seemed only three or four miles generally proved to be twice and even thrice that number.

We designated this the Big Pyutt Valley. It is some fifteen miles in length by four in width. The main chain of the Sierras rises abruptly from the valley on the west, and near the base is sparsely covered with pine and cedar, while on the east rises a low ridge almost entirely without tree or bush, while to the south the mountains rise suddenly to a great height and are a succession of sharp peaks. The western fork of Walker's river, with all its tributaries concentrated, traverses its entire length near the base of the western ridge and passes out to the northeast. The northern portion of the valley in the immediate vicinity of the river is rich alluvial soil, but by far the greater part of it is a sandy desert.

In the afternoon I proposed to C. to take a little *pasea* down the valley, and, accordingly, we mounted our animals and

PYUTT INDIANS FISHING IN WALKER'S RIVER.

proceeded down the river about two miles, when we crossed over and came up the opposite side. As we rounded a little knoll we discovered what appeared to be nearly the entire rancheria of Indians in a bend of the river making preparations to catch fish, and we at once rode down

to witness the sport, which proved to be a novel scene. Stretching nearly across the stream was a rocky bar, over which a very little of the water rippled, while the main body of it made a sudden bend around, keeping close to the opposite bank. Just above the bar was a deep eddy, and above this the stream was broad, shallow and rapid, and skirted on each side with a thick growth of low, withy willow. Here of this willow the Indians made a drag about two feet in diameter and in length sufficient to reach across the stream. On the bar they had built a slight wall of the small rock in the form of a half circle, at the lower side of which was a willow fish-trap, the water being only a few inches or a foot deep inside the circle. When all was ready they swung the drag out across the stream and let it sweep down to the eddy when they all gathered in above it and keeping it near the bottom swept it through to the shallow bar, bringing the two ends to join the wall, when they had all the fish "corraled" within the circle, then pressing their knees upon the drag to keep it firmly to the bottom, they commenced the exciting sport of pulling out the fish, which as a matter of course endeavored to find a place of egress at the upper side, The suckers, which constituted a greater portion of the fish, were easily taken in this way; but the trout, more wily, flipped lightly over the drag and away up stream again. The scene they presented as they knelt over the drag, men and squaws, old and young mixed up indiscriminately, and carried the fish to their mouths as they caught them to bite their heads, frequently holding them in their teeth for some minutes, the poor suckers twisting themselves spasmodically in their death agonies, was truly ludicrous and amusing. A few of the fish entered the trap, and at the last, one big fellow seemed to have got an idea of the danger that awaited him on either hand, and flipped about in the centre of the pool, foiling for a long time all their efforts to catch him, they in the meantime getting highly excited, but finally a squaw pounced upon him and held him up in triumph.

These Indians were of the Pyutt tribe, and this range of country was evidently their summer hunting ground. They were very friendly, but a little shy, and the information that we desired respecting the locality of Carson Valley they would not or could not give us.

The next morning we made an early start. We had discovered the emigrant trail on the west side of the river, and crossed over immediately at our camp. It was rather a cool, frosty morning, and none of us relished the idea of wading the stream; so we spliced two of our trail ropes, and attaching one end to the neck of the little mustang, C. rode her over, then P. hauled her back, by which means he too got over with dry feet; but Judge becoming a little impatient at the time which this course occupied, pulled off his boots, and rolling up his pants, started across on his own hook, with his boots slung over his shoulder and the shovel for a staff, presenting a very apt illustration of Pilgrim's Progress.

We soon came to where the valley narrowed up and the river made out to the east, our trail now lying along its bank, occasionally bearing out over the little rolling knolls to the right. An hour's travel brought us to where the river made into a wild gorge, the hills rising abruptly on either side, and here we halted for a few minutes to water our animals and rest our own weary limbs. We felt the importance of getting through this pass before nightfall, knowing that our safety for that night depended upon our camping in an advantageous position, and we very soon pushed on again. The trail entered the gorge, and in the next mile and a half crossed the river four times; and here along the banks of the stream was growing in considerable numbers the tree known as the Balm of Gilead—a fact that we consider worthy of mention.

The valley that we were now entering was after the style of the last, being, for the most part, a sandy waste, and skirted on the east by a range of barren hills.

The river, after making into it, turns suddenly and runs north about four or five miles, and then takes a course directly east and passes out through the ridge. The trail, after leaving our camp, for a mile was broad and well defined, and then made into a grassy bottom, where all traces of it were obliterated. We searched a while for it and then halted for a consultation. To the north we observed a low pass in the mountain, and we judged the trail must pass out there, and we accordingly crossed the river and struck out for it.

Keeping down the river for about a mile and a half we struck a broad Indian trail bearing off to the northeast, and at once resolved to pursue it. An hour's travel brought us on to the ridge, when we entered the gap into which it made, and then descended rapidly down a rocky gorge, and in a half hour more emerged into another extensive valley, which we called the Pyutt Desert, and through which coursed Walker's river, with all its tributaries concentrated.

Being now all anxious to return to our respective homes, and feeling also the necessity of "hurrying up" on account of the shabby condition of our purses, we determined, as the sun was yet near two hours high, to prosecute our journey a little further still, and accordingly started on again, accompanied by one of the guides, who now took it on foot, leaving his pony with his companion. We pro-

FORDING WALKER'S RIVER.

ceeded up the river a short distance and crossed over to the north side and very soon struck into the emigrant road, that great highway between the Mississippi and the broad Pacific. We passed on about five miles and camped just at sunset on the bend of the river, and in close proximity to a small party of emigrants.

We started the next morning at an early hour and at noon arrived at the trading post, a little bush concern, the proprietor's stock of trading material consisting of a very few drygoods and a good deal of whisky. Here we got some butter to go with our bread, making us what we then termed an excellent din-ner, which having dispatched, we then proceeded to dress up our Indian guide.

This night we reached Gold Cañon, crossed the river and camped on the opposite side in order to find grass for our animals. At this place we found about twenty American miners and some forty or fifty Chinese, and from the man who kept the little trading post here we learned that the diggings prospected well, and that a company of men were about conducting water in by a ditch about four or five miles long. From where we first struck the road to this place it had kept along the bank of the river, which was skirted by thrifty cottonwoods; but from here on to Eagle Valley, it lay across what is termed the Nine Mile Desert, when it again struck the river, and then again bore off across a rolling country and came into Carson Valley at Silver Creek, leaving Eagle Valley to the northwest.

We had been told that the Mormons were in encampment at Eagle Valley just preparatory to their exodus, and C. and myself rode around to look at them, while Judge and P. took the direct road to Carson Valley. We saw probably a hundred wagons drawn up in a half circle, and in an enclosed field, containing many hundred acres, were several hundred head of mules and horses, while the saints themselves were loitering idly about, evidently ready to move at a day's notice. Having satisfied our curiosity we put our horses into a smart gallop across the rolling sandy plain to the south, in order to come up with our companions, for we had traveled out of our direct course some four or five miles, and in a half hour came into Carson Valley at Silver Creek, and again joining our companions pushed on to Genoa, better known, however, as the Mormon Station, where we arrived a little before night, and adding a little to our stock of provisions—or rather to our stock of flour, for a few pounds of that article constituted all we had—we moved on two miles further, and camped near a farm-house.

Genoa is a little village containing, in all, about twenty-five buildings, among which there is one store, one hotel, a billiard saloon and blacksmith shop, and it presented, at this time, a very lively appearance, from the fact probably of the great number of emigrants that were recruiting in the valley. Its location is pleasant and romantic withal, for it stands upon a little slope at the very base of the mountains, which rise abruptly from the valley to a great elevation, the northern sides of their bold sharp peaks still glistening with snow.

It commands a view of almost the entire valley, which is here some fifteen miles broad, and is shut in on the east by a lower range of mountains and the prospect is really beautiful, for the serpentine course of Carson river can be traced by the willows that border its either bank, while thousands of cattle may be seen scattered over its entire surface. Altogether, it is a pleasant place.

We next came to Carson Cañon, entered it and camped on a little flat about a mile from its mouth, in company with five emigrants, with whom we had traveled most of the day. This cañon, through which Carson river leaps and foams, is a wild rocky gorge, six miles in length, and opens into Hope Valley, when the road forks—that to the right leading to Placerville, and the left to Murphy's, by the Big Tree Grove. The next day we passed through the cañon, and taking the Big Tree road, accompanied by several emigrants, we camped that night one mile to the west of the Summit. The road thus far from the cañon far exceeded in excellence all that we had previously anticipated of it, presenting a strange contrast with that over which we passed in our outward journey, and which, we will venture to assert, will hold true also in regard to any other road over the Sierra Nevadas, and we predict that when its superior excellence is more generally known, almost the entire overland emigration to our State will pass over this road, notwithstanding the powerful influence that is constantly kept at work in Carson Valley by the people of the northern districts to turn the emigration that way. We amused ourselves somewhat while passing through the valley in testing the truthfulness of this northern influence, for our companion C. had twice passed over both the Placerville and Big Tree roads, and mixed up as we were with the emigrants, and presenting an exterior, from our long journey, essentially the same, to our inquiries we received the same recommendations of the northern routes, and the same derogatory opinions of the Big Tree road that was dealt out to the luckless emigrant.

The next morning we rose from our blankets at an earlier hour than usual, from the fact of our suffering somewhat with cold. As we gathered around our cheerful fire it occurred to us that this was the Sabbath, and as the sun shot in upon us his genial rays through the tall junipers that grew on either hand, we felt, standing as we were almost on the very summit of the "snowy mountains," with the broad view of the receding hills, even to the valley of the San Joaquin, before us, a thrill of devotion and a higher conception of Him who teacheth us wisdom in the simplest of His works, and speaketh to us in the thunder of the elements.

Passing on over a road equally as easy as that from the Cañon to the Summit, we camped at night within three miles of the Big Tree Grove. The next morning, having resolved to take breakfast at the Big Tree, we started unusually early, and before the inmates of the Big Tree House were astir we reined our horses up before it; the thought of the excellent table that was sure to be spread before us having doubtless accelerated our steps. Ordering our meal, we occupied the intervening time in scrubbing our grim and sunburnt faces and clearing the dust from our swollen eyes.

Our breakfast over—and it took no little time to get over it, either, considering its excellence together with the length and breadth of our stomachs—we took a hasty glance at the sights—their worldwide celebrity leaving it unnecessary for us to enter into the description in regard to them. For my own part I climbed, by means of a ladder, on to the section of the tree lying near the house, rolled a game of tenpins on one of the two alleys on the log, and danced a single-handed

schottische to music of my own making on the stump; then, jumping on my horse, galloped out into the grove and rode my horse, sitting nearly erect in my saddle, through a section of some thirty feet of one of the old fallen trees, and returning to the house we again resumed our journey, and at 1 o'clock entered Murphy's, where, to my companions, Judge and C., the journey was ended. Taking a social dinner at Sperry's excellent hotel, we separated, P. and ourself to return to our respective homes at Sonora and Columbia, where our friends met us with some doubts as to our identity, so disguised were we under our sunburnt skins and tattered habiliments; and on comparing dates we found that we had been absent twenty-seven days, and had traveled in that time four hundred and fifty miles.

A CALIFORNIA GRAPE.

The above engraving represents the natural size of a grape, of the Muscat of Alexandria variety, plucked from one of many bunches, each bunch weighing from three to four and a half pounds, from the ranch of Capt. Macondray, at San Mateo. If the illustration given were but a trifle smaller it would then be the average size of every grape grown on that vine during the past summer.

HUTCHINGS'

CALIFORNIA MAGAZINE.

VOL. IV.   APRIL, 1860.   No. 10.

NOTES AND SKETCHES OF THE WASHOE COUNTRY.

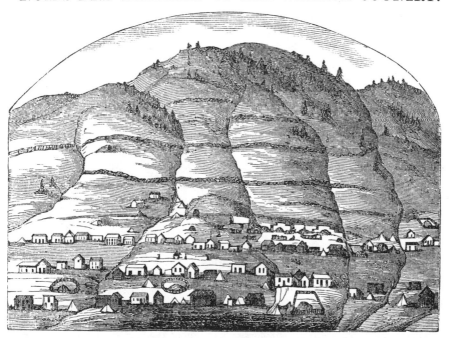

VIRGINIA CITY AND THE COMSTOCK LEAD.

VAILING ourselves of the topographic knowledge and artistic skill of a gentleman recently returned from the rich silver mines, east of the Sierra Nevada, we present the patrons of our magazine with a life-like view of several important localities in that region. The first of these is a sketch of the celebrated Comstock lead, with the adjacent mining hamlet of Virginia City. This lead, at the point exhibited in our cut, being that at which the rich silver ore was first struck, is about fifteen miles in a direct line north of Carson City;

and nearly twenty miles, going by the wagon road. It is situated nearly half-way up the eastern slope of a mountain spur branching off from the Sierra, near Carson City, and running north to the Truckee river. This spur has since been very appropriately named the Silver Range. It is about 2,500 feet high, and separates the main Carson from Washoe Valley. It is almost entirely destitute of vegetation, there being but little grass and only a few stunted pines and cedars scattered over it, with a small grove of tall trees at two or three points along its summit.

Running along its sides are numerous ledges of quartz rock, cropping out in places for a considerable distance. Some of these are much decomposed on the surface, and by being worked, either by means of washing or crushing, yield various amounts of the precious metals, being a mixture of gold and silver. It was while working one of these veins, last spring, that James Finney, better known as "old Virginia," came upon the rich silver ore which has since been taken out in such large quantities and rendered the Comstock lead so famous. Finney worked the vein as a placer claim, taking out a species of gold dust depreciated with silver, and making twenty or thirty dollars a day to the hand. But, coming at length upon the worthless *blue stuff*, as he termed it, but in reality the rich sulphurets, he became disgusted with his luck, and not being longer able to make whiskey money, parted with his claim, selling it to five men, named Comstock, Penrod, Corey, Reilly and McLaughlin, the consideration being an ancient horse, with thin flesh and a short dock. Most of these men with hardly a better appreciation of the property they had acquired than the original vendor, shortly after parted with their interests in it for a mere nominal consideration. McLaughlin, who sold to Hearst and Morrison, getting

$3,500; Penrod and Comstock, who sold to Walsh, getting the former $5,000 and the latter $6,000; and Corey, who sold to Beard & Co., getting $7,000 for his share. Reilly, who did not sell until five months after, got $40,000, besides his share of the ore previously taken out. The entire claim of these parties as it originally existed, was eighteen hundred feet long and one hundred feet wide — being fifty feet on each side the vein, and running downward as far as it extended, or they might choose to go. This claim was afterwards reduced to fourteen hundred feet, so that they conveyed at the time of selling, two hundred and thirty-three and one-third feet a piece; of that portion parted with prior to the sale, one hundred feet was given to Comstock and Penrod, as their exclusive property, in exchange for a small water privilege owned by them and necessary to the working of their united claim by the Company. This one hundred feet, situated four or five rods north of the excavation from which the rich ore was first taken, was afterwards sold to some Mexicans, and was thenceforth known as the Mexican or Meldenado claim. It has since proved exceedingly valuable, and being in a more satisfactory condition as to title and possession, commands a higher price in the market than any other portion of this lead. It is the most northerly point on the Comstock vein, at which the rich sulphurets have been struck in any quantity, though about one-half of this claim lies beyond it.

Going south, we have next to the Mexican, the Ophir Company — two hundred feet, about the center of which the first discovery of silver was made; next the Central Company, one hundred and fifty feet; then fifty feet, a part of the original Corey claim, and finally the California Company's Claim of two hundred and fifty feet, which disposes of the Comstock Claim as it originally existed; though the same vein has since been traced some distance, both north and south, and a great number of claims have been located on this supposed extension thereof. For more than a mile towards the south, the Comstock lead can be easily traced and identified, both by its continuity and the rich character of the rock. Beyond the California Claim, in this direction, very valuable outcroppings have been met with at several points, more especially on what is known as the Gould and Curry, and on the Hale and Norcross Claims. Here better surface rock has been obtained than was first met with on the Comstock Claim itself. In consequence of these discoveries, the prices of these claims have gone up to enormous figures —even so high, it is said as $700 per foot.

Not only has this wonderful silver lode been found to extend itself longitudinally, but parallel veins have been formed in close proximity, proving that the argentiferous deposits of this locality spread in every direction. Amongst these lateral veins, the Grass Valley, Winnemucca, Sacramento, Bryan, Hagen, &c., are reported valuable; the four last mentioned showing every evidence of being genuine silver lodes, of a similar character to the Comstock vein. That they possess substantial merit, is shown by the high prices they readily command in the market; some of them selling for more than the Comstock claim, for a period of several months after it had been opened and the quality of its ores determined. The belt of these rich parallel veins does not seem to be confined to the immediate vicinity of the Comstock lead; on the Rogers vein, several miles to the east, the rich sulphurets have been struck and traced south across Six Mile Canon into the Yankee claim, where they reappear in all their richness. At other points in the neighborhood, and at those still more remote, not simply traces of silver, but ore assaying hundreds of dollars to the ton has been met with. There is therefore good reason to believe that this entire portion of western Utah abounds in argentiferous deposits, many of which will be brought to light the present season, others perhaps being reserved for future exploration.

The mining hamlet seen in our cut, and ridiculously called Virginia City, as if in derision of the man whose ill-luck it seems designed to perpetuate, sprang up during the past summer, but grew slowly, owing in part to its unfavorable situation, and still more to the difficulty of getting lumber for building. It is expected to grow more rapidly this spring, though the entire absence of wood, and water fit for drinking, in the neighborhood, will operate as a great drawback on its prosperity. It is also, owing to its elevation and exposure, an exceedingly cold and dreary place during the winter. With water, and fuel, for reducing the ores, this could hardly fail to become a town of some magnitude. As it is, it would be difficult to say much about its future. It at present contains about a dozen stone houses, two or three times as many built of wood, of every size and description, with a number of tents, shanties, and other temporary abodes. Owing to the scarcity of lumber, and the difficulty of hauling stones, not a few, on the approach of cold weather, dug excavations in the side hill and, covering them with earth, passed the winter there.

In front of the rich mining claims are arastras, at work crushing the decomposed quartz and the poorer class of silver ore, that will not pay to be sent to San Francisco. Here, also, are to be seen workmen wheeling out, through the open cuts made at the top, the refuse rock, earth, quartz, and the rich sulphurets; the latter of which are boxed up, preparatory to transportation. Scattered about the place are the usual paraphernalia of a mining camp, while at various points in the vicinity, are to be seen prospecting tunnels, open-cuts and shafts, nearly every important claim having had some work of this kind performed upon it. Cropping out along the hills are numerous quartz ledges, some of them so prominent as to be seen for several miles, others barely coming to the surface and showing themselves only at intervals. The famous Comstock lead is of the latter class, and is made conspicuous in our picture only because of its great intrinsic value.

About four miles south of Virginia City, is another locality, of such striking characteristics that our artist has thought worth while bringing it into notice. This place is known as the "Devil's Gate," being a pass in Go^{ld} Cañon, about twenty feet wide, with perpendicular rocky walls, running to a great height. Thro' this the toll road leads, and besides being noticable for its striking and rugged features, it has other, and, to the utilitarian, greater attractions, as the center of an extended district rich in auriferous quartz In the immediate vicinity of the "Gate" are several veins of well known value, prominent among which are the "Twin Lead," the "Bench," the "Badger," &c. A few rods below the "Gate" a town has recently been laid out, called "Silver City." It now contains a dozen or two houses, of a temporary character, the growth of the place having been retarded, as have all the towns in this region, from scarcity of building material. It is situated on both sides of the ravine known as Gold Cañon, which is here narrow, affording but little room for a town, unless it be carried up against the adjacent hill sides. Several arastras have been introduced into the cut, these being in constant use for working up the rotten quartz, found in most of the surrounding claims, and frequently yielding large amounts of deteriorated gold. A great

number of tunnels are being run into the hills, hereabout, some of which have already struck rich quartz, and the others are going on with good prospects of success. Standing below the "Gate," and looking west up the cañon, a great number of parallel knolls run north, forming the base of a rugged mountain in that direction. Running horizontally over these are numerous quartz ledges, all taken up and held at high prices, since nearly all have exhibited more or less gold. In the back ground, to the west, we get a glimpse of the "Silver Range," the base about three, and the summit five miles distant. It is a bold and barren chain of hills, about 2,500 feet above the level of Carson Valley, which it separates from Washoe Valley, lying along the western base of this "Range." On the left, stretching south from the "Gate," are two bluff mountains, between which runs the west branch of Gold Cañon. The lower, and more prominent of these, rises to a height of near 2,000 feet, and having been called by some Mexicans, prospecting about it, the "Cerro Alto," it still bears that name. About half way up it, on the side next Gold Cañon, is a "bench," or table, across which runs a quartz lead, which, having been taken up, it was afterwards called the "Bench Claim."

It is a singular circumstance, that two brothers, Englishmen, having gotten the idea that silver existed at this spot, proceeeed there some three or four years ago, sunk a shaft on this "bench," and erected a small furnace for smelting the ore. One of the brothers dying, the other, disheartened, left the place after filling up the shaft they had dug, by placing timbers transversely across it about twelve feet below the mouth, and covering them with earth. This would seem to have been done that their labors, should they ever be discovered, might not give the impression that they had gone far down.

Their furnace, a rude affair, probably at best, had also been demolished, and when the writer visited the spot last summer, nothing bnt a heap of stones and some fragments of charcoal remained of these pioneer silver works, thus erected by these ill-fated brothers, so far beyond the confines of civilization. The grave of him who perished, is still to be seen by a cedar on the hill side, all trace of the surviver having been lost; nor would it ever have been known whose work this was, but for this faint tradition, known only to a few of the older residents in these

THE "DEVIL'S GATE."

parts. That any one should have went there at that early day in search of silver, seems strange enough, when taken in connection with the little that was then known of that remote region, and with the astounding discoveries of that metal that have lately been made so near by. Whence these brothers got their notion of silver at that point, what discoveries they may have made, or why nothing further was ever known of them or their labors, remains, as it no doubt ever will, a mystery. The most likely solution of it is, that they derived the idea from one of those legendary tales of mineral wealth, so often heard and so little heeded, though not always devoid of some foundation in fact; while, as to the brother who came away, he may have since followed his kins man to the unknown land; or surviving, have left the country, and perhaps never yet so much as heard of the fabulous treasures since, found fast by his mountain home.

The next place exhibited by our artist is *Carson City;* a town that, having wholly grown up within the past year, has already attained a very respectable magnitude; not only eclipsing its older and politically more favored rival, Genoa, but advanced rapidly towards the position it must hereafter hold, as the great central depot, and distributing point of Western Utah. This beautifully located and promising town is situated on the west side of Eagle Valley, about eighteen miles south of Virginia City, and twelve north of Genoa. It stands immediately at the foot of the Sierra, which rises behind it to a height of more than three thousand feet, being covered with pine forests from its base to its summit. Coming down from the mountain, and crossing the valley below, are numerous rivulets of pure cold water, which, with the springs found on the margin of the plain, afford ample supplies for the use of the town, (through which it courses in channels dug for the purpose,) as well as for irrigation.

Eagle Valley, containing an area of nearly one hundred square miles, is itself one of the most beautiful in a long series of mountain vales that skirt the eastern base of the Sierra. Watered by the Carson River on the one hand, and by the many rills mentioned on the other, with numerous springs, hot and cold, pure and mineral, scattered over its surface; covered with green sward along its western margin, and environed by hills, it seems the perfection of landscape scenery, and every way fitted for the abode of man. Nature, in fact, seems to have destined this for an important point in the future of this country. Here, by the configuration she has impressed upon the country, all the great highways seem compelled to center. Standing at the gateways of the Sierra, and on the threshold of the Desert, Carson City commands the passage, trade and travel of both; while her central position as to the mines makes her the supplying agent for them; leaving her future growth to be determined only by that of the mineral districts around her. Which way soever we would proceed from this point, a comparatively good natural way opens itself to us. Westward, leading out toward Placerville, a good route is found by the old Johnson Trail, over which a wagon road, much shorter and better than that now traveled by way of Genoa,

could easily be opened. Going northward through Washoe, Steamboat and Truckee Valleys, by the Henness Pass, into the populous mining counties of California, we follow nearly all the way along a natural depression with a smooth surface, and even surmount the Sierra, scarcely being conscious of the rise. This town is also on the great Emigrant Trail across the Plains; while southward it communicates with Carson Valley, the Walker River and Mono districts, by means of roads, over which, with very trifling expense, heavily laden teams might be made to pass.

Here, also, the entire country to the east, and for some distance north, must come for lumber, this being the nearest point from which supplies of this indispensable material can be drawn. Intervening between the country along the Lower Carson, including most of the mineral region, so far as discovered, and the Sierra Nevada, on which alone trees suitable for lumber abound, is the Silver Range, a rugged chain, destitute of timber.

Carson City is laid out in regular squares, the streets being straight and wide; and, as the surface is perfectly level, no grading or other labor is required to prepare the lots for building. The soil about it is of such a nature that neither the mud or dust become excessively troublesome at any season of the year. Water of the best quality is abundant, running through the town in small ditches dug for the purpose. It is procured both from the springs adjacent, and the streams coming down from the mountains, which never fail, winter or summer. There were but two or three houses on this spot, one year ago; now there are over one hundred, and there would have been more than double that number, had lumber been plenty, even at the high prices men were willing to pay for it. Some of the houses are built of adobe, several of them large and sub-

CARSON CITY.

stantial; suitable material for making these, as well as brick, being abundant in the neighborhood. Several kilns of brick were burnt within a mile of the city last summer. Most of the houses, however, are of wood, and some few of even less durable substances. The permanent and floating population of this place reaches from ten to fifteen hundred, and is rapidly on the increase. Property has also advanced at a corresponding rate, but is still far from having reached such a figure as the situation and prospects of the town seem to justify. It would of course be too much to affirm that this must positively become a large and opulent city; but it may safely be said, if any town of magnitude is to spring up in this transmontane region, nature, as well as the mineral developments being made, clearly indicate this as the site of it.

In a ravine two miles west of the town,

in the midst of fine timber, a steam saw-mill was erected last fall, but it could not supply one tithe of the demands made upon it, being of only moderate capacity, and not kept constantly running at that. Other mills of like kind are about being put up, and the prospect is that lumber will be both cheap and plentiful before the summer is far advanced. When this shall be the case, aided by brick, sand-stone and adobe, with not only lime-rock, but a species of natural cement near at hand; with improved roads, and the prospect of a heavy immigration meeting here next season, and a rich mineral district unfolding itself all around her, Carson City must become a large and thriving City, if there is to be any such within the limits of Western Utah; and everything considered, it may justly be said to have a promising future before it.

The next and last place depicted by our artist is Genoa, the oldest, and until

GENOA.

recently the largest, town in Western Utah. It was first settled by the Mormons; who, as early as 1850, erected some cabins here, and afterwards more substantial houses, mills, &c. It is handsomely located on the west side of Carson Valley, right under the Sierra, which rises abruptly over it, being covered from top to bottom with pine trees, not very large or suitable for lumber, yet, being the best to be had, they are made to answer every purpose. Genoa, like Carson City, is well watered, by a number of rills coming from the mountains and flowing through the streets. One of these is made to drive both a flour and saw-mill, situated in the edge of the town, as seen in our picture.

Genoa contains about fifty houses, mostly frame, a few being of logs or adobe. At the time Carson County was organized, Genoa was made the county seat, which it has continued to be nominally ever since. The U. S. District Court was also held here last fall by Judge Cradlebaugh; but there is a talk of all these courts, as well as the other offices, whether territorial or belonging to the general government, being removed to Carson City on the opening of spring. Property has recently advanced somewhat in this place, but not at such a rate as in its more fortunate and progressive rival.

Genoa has a resident population of about 200. Amongst these are a number of Mormon families, some of whom have never left since their first settlement here; others are a part of those who having repaired to Salt Lake, at the time of the calling in of the Saints, and becoming disgusted with their experience there, returned to their old homes, much poorer, but hardly wiser for their melancholy journey. Adhering to their peculiar notions, and still cherishing in secret the fatal dogmas of their religion, they do not readily affiliate with the Gentiles around them, nor is there a likelihood of any cordial feeling ever existing between the two classes.

HUTCHINGS'

CALIFORNIA MAGAZINE.

VOL. I.   **JUNE, 1857.**   NO. XII.

WATER-FALL ON THE MAIN NORTH FORK OF FEATHER RIVER.

A JAUNT TO HONEY LAKE VALLEY AND NOBLE'S PASS.

Late in the month of November, 1854, a party of three—only *one* of whom was a horseman—left the fertile and well settled American Valley, Plumas county, on a jaunt towards the then comparatively unknown country, lying on both sides of the Sierra Nevada range, in the vicinity of Noble's Pass : and as neither of the party was rich—except in prospect—(a very doubtful one at that) we adopted the primitive and independent method of " footing it," (with the exception mentioned) taking a horse with us to save the necessity of becoming our own pack animals.

After we had fairly left the settlements,

however, one of our party made a double discovery—one part of which was, that he, unfortunately, was "born tired," or, in other words, believed himself in every way capable of enduring a great amount of ease;—the other part being, that a few blankets, cooking utensils and something to cook, were but a very poor load for a horse—scarcely enough for ballast—and that by sitting upon the aforesaid blankets, and utensils, and articles to be cooked, so great an oversight might be entirely remedied; and as we thought the proposition was somewhat original, and in favor perhaps of the man, if not of the horse, the experiment was assented to, with what success these pages may occasionally relate.

Now we think that all will admit, that often in the dim and shadowy depths of an unknown country, or future, the adventurous spirit feels a peculiar charm; and in which there is a wondering yearning after its mysteries; with a speculative wish to fathom its untold secrets, and know of its unrevealed peculiarities, which nerves him against fatigue, exposure, and even danger; in which comfort and safety are for the time forgotten or overlooked.

It was with a feeling akin to this, that a party of three persons left the pleasant associations of American valley, and, after passing Judkins' Saw Mill, commenced ascending a good mountain trail, running in an east-of-north course, towards Indian Valley. Upon the top of the ridge, about two miles west of the trail, is a very beautiful, clear, and rock-bound lake, from whence a fine view can be obtained of the valley below.

The first point reached in Indian valley, was the ranch of Mr. Job Taylor, (the first settler in the valley,) about eleven miles from the American ranch, American valley. Here we not only saw some very fine wheat —grown on Mr. T.'s ranch—but partook of some good bread made from the same stock of wheat; and the finest flavored butter, without exception, that we have yet tasted in California.

This valley is beautifully picturesque and fertile, and about twenty-three miles in length—including the arms—by six in its greatest width; being about fifteen miles southwest of the great Sierra Nevada chain; and, (like most of these valleys,) runs nearly east and west. Surrounded, as it is, by high, bold, and pine covered mountains of irregular granite, over thirteen hundred feet in height from the valley; and which on the south side are nearly perpendicular. This valley is well sheltered, and is said to be several hundred feet less in altitude than the American, although many miles nearer the main chain.

Leaving these good things, we crossed to the north side of the valley, which at this point is about one and a half miles wide; then, turning northward, kept up it, by the banks of a beautiful stream, to the residence and ranch of Judge Ward, distant from Taylors, about seven miles.

Here we were kindly welcomed and hospitably entertained by Mr. Ward and his amiable and pleasant family—a treat we did not dream could be in store for us, so far away, and almost on the very tops of the Sierras. As long as memory remains we shall treasure up the many kindnesses shown us during that visit.

At their fireside too, we met an intelligent Russian, named Isadore, who had been the frequent companion of Peter Lassen—now a resident in this valley—in his many rambles among the mountains, and to whom we were indebted for much interesting information concerning the country we were now about to visit.

Our good friends, believing it to be very desirable that we should here obtain a guide, in company with Isadore, we made our way to a group of Indians, which had formed at the corner of the corral, and who, evidently awaited with some anxiety, the cutting up of a beef, which had been killed that morning.

"Doctor," said Isadore, in the Indian dialect, as he put his hand familiarly upon the shoulder of an old weather-beaten In-

THE INDIANS "GUIDE" US.

dian, "these men want you to guide them to Honey Lake Valley, by the Big Meadows; do you understand?"

The old Indian looked at us, and then at the beef, and shrugging up his shoulders, drawled out, "See—me sabe."

"Well, what say you, Doctor, will you go with them, to show them the way?" He still kept his eyes upon the inside portions of the beef, which were now being taken out, without giving an answer.

"What say you Doctor, I ask—will you go? These men will give you plenty of meat; plenty for your wife and children, and plenty for you to eat all the way to Honey Lake Valley, and back again; now, what say you Doctor?"

At the mention of so many good things the old man turned gradually round, and looking thoughtfully about him, by way of reply said—

"Pikas no good Indian—Pikas no good," and then renewed his longing look at those portions of the beef so soon to be thrown away.

It appears that in the fall of 1851, the Pitt River Indians—called by these Indians "Pikas,"—made up a war party against the Indian Valley Indians, for the purpose of obtaining their squaws—the possession of the women being the only motive for the war—and the latter being by far the weaker party, lost a large number of their men in killed, and their women as prisoners.

When the news of this slaughter reached the whites who had made settlements in this valley; and who felt that these Indians were somewhat under their protection, they made up a party, thirteen in number, for the purpose of assisting the Indian Valley Indians in chastising the Pitt River Indians. This party, under the old pioneer Peter Lassen, left Indian valley, accompanied by all the able bodied Indians that could be found.

After being out a couple of days, according to his usual custom, "Old Peter," (as Mr. Lassen is familiarly called) awoke at daybreak, and was sitting quietly upon the ground smoking his pipe, when he saw Indians, with stealthy steps passing among the trees, and entirely away from his own party; quietly taking up his faithful rifle, he, with unerring aim, shot one of the Indians in the head, muttering as he again reloaded his "old shooting iron :" "There's one wiped out." He again fired; "down he comes," said he, as he again quickly began reloading. "That fetches him," as a third fell, never to rise again. "This was but the work of a minute," said Isadore, as he related the narrative, "Old Peter shot down three of the Indians, without taking his pipe from his mouth."

By this time the whole camp was in motion; and, with this beginning, they eagerly followed up the advantage gained; and when "Old Peter" gave the characteristic order—"Pitch in Blueskins"—to the Indians, they, in company with their thirteen white friends, made sad havoc that day among their enemies, the Pikas, completely routing and conquering them.

This was the last time the Pitt Rivers' ever troubled the Indian Valley Indians; although the latter are ever in perpetual dread of the former.

This explains somewhat the cause of the old man's remark—"Pikas no good Indian —Pikas no good."

Promises of protection being given by Isadore, on our behalf, the "Doctor" reluctantly consented to guide us, on the twofold consideration of allowing another Indian to accompany him, and both being well fed and protected on the journey. This being satisfactorily arranged, and a liberal quantity of beef having been carried by the Indian to his family, after much delay, we left the kindly hospitalities of our pleasant host, on our somewhat perilous jaunt.

Making our way up the valley, in the direction of Lassen's Big Meadows, (which lie about fifteen miles, a little north of west, from Judge Ward's) the Indians *guided us* by remaining about one hundred yards behind, for about three miles; when on turning round we saw them rapidly disappearing among the trees. The louder we called for them to return, the faster they ran in the opposite direction, until they were entirely lost sight of among the bushes·

At first we thought that perhaps they had forgotten something which they wished to take with them, or to their families, and would soon return to us; but, although we went slowly on, we never saw the weatherbeaten faces of our blue-skinned guides any more.

A SHORT VOYAGE IS UNDERTAKEN IN AN INDIAN CANOE.

Being thus left, we had either to return and procure other guides — which perhaps might prove to be equally valuable — or guide ourselves. — Two chances, however were open to us ; Peter Lassen had left Indian Valley for the Big Meadows, with a two-horse team, for the purpose of obtaining some old iron, and we *might* meet with him ; who, "would very willingly guide us all through that country." The other chance was in meeting with some Indians to guide us who were not afraid of "Pikas," — both very doubtful chances, truly.

We came in sight of those broad and beautiful "Meadows," just as the sun was

A SLIGHT BACK-SET TO PRESENT COMFORT,

sinking below the dark belt of pines which girdles them in, and as we descended the gently sloping hills, to the edge of the valley, we saw the smoke of an Indian encampment curling up from among the willows of the river ; so, considering that

"He is thrice armed who hath his quarrel just,"

we made boldly towards it. As we approached we discovered that the encampment was on the opposite side of a deep, clear stream—the eastern or main branch of Feather river—fortunately however, we saw an Indian coming rapidly down the river in his canoe, when we immediately hailed him ; and he, without hesitation, made straight towards us, politely—for an Indian—proffering us the use of his canoe, in which to cross the stream if we wished.

Two of us at once availed ourselves of the offer, but as this craft was not sufficiently commodious to accommodate a horse, he was necessarily taken by our ease-enduring hero to a more suitable crossing below.

Here however the thoughtful animal— perhaps foreseeing the probable result, or from some conscientious scruples lest he might accidentally, and unintentionally, be the cause of drowning himself and his rider, refused to enter the water until he had dismounted ; and even then, was so unreasonable as to require the gentle coaxing of a small oak tree upon his back and sides, before showing any willingness to "take to the water." A reluctance afterwards appreciated by our hero when the stream was discovered to be too deep for the animal's crossing without swimming ; thinking it

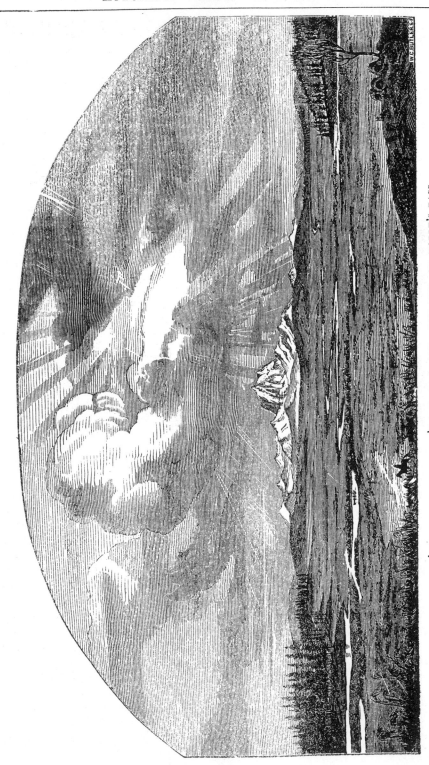

LASSEN'S BUTTE, FROM LASSEN'S MEADOWS, AND WEST END OF NOBLE'S PASS.

safer for himself, and quite as pleasant, to cross in an Indian canoe.

This task being accomplished, we pressed a dollar on the palm of the Indian, who not only seemed to know what it was for, but was almost beside himself with excitement as he opened and closed his hand again and again to take a peep at it, and be sure that it was a reality, and not the phantom of some tormenting dream!

As it was now nearly dark, we turned across a heavily timbered point towards the sheltered margin of the northwest branch of North Feather—and which is much lower, and much smaller than the one we had just left behind us. Here we found an excellent camping place for ourselves, and plenty of feed for our animal. Our evening meal being prepared and eaten, we spread our blankets beneath the outspreading branches of a lofty pine, and lay gazing upward at our gorgeous and star-lighted chamber, listening to the music of the evening breeze as it swelled and swept among the swaying tops of the surrounding forest pines, and were soon lulled by its soothing melody to sleep—sleep that was sweet, deep and refreshing.

About daybreak the following morning, the hoarse howling of a wolf, and the loud snapping and whining bark of some coyotes awoke us. Before us lay the broad Lassen's Meadows, entirely surrounded by low timbered ridges ; and in the distance, bold, grand, and cold, towered Lassen's Butte ; but, when the sun arose and gilded it with rosy, golden sun-light, it was gorgeous— it was magnificent.

A glance at the sketch of Lassen's Butte (from Lassen's Meadows) and west end of Noble's Pass on another page, will give the reader an accurate idea of this section of country. It is nearly level. There is scarcely a ridge between these many valleys, where a wagon would not almost remain without being locked, after the animals had been removed ; and that too without ever being touched by the hand of man.

HONEY LAKE VALLEY, AND EAST END OF NOBLE'S PASS.

THE LAST FLAPJACK FRIED.

Being anxious to know about the depth of snow which falls here during a severe winter, we conversed with several of the most intelligent of the Indians, and the greatest depth given by them for several years past, was three feet and six inches,—and some winters it has not been over two feet in depth ; and this is in valleys among the very tops of the Sierras.

About a quarter of a mile below the point seen in the left corner of the view mentioned, just above the forks of the river and on the east or main branch of the stream, there is a beautiful waterfall of about thirty five feet in height, and sixty feet in width, which would not only enable settlers to drain the whole valley—nearly thirty square miles in extent—but give the finest water-power in the world, and timber sufficient for the entire length of a railway from the Missouri to the Sacramento river. Indeed we wonder that these innumerable advantages are so generally unknown or almost entirely overlooked.

Lest we might weary the reader by relating the adventures and experiences of sev-

eral days spent among the valleys and low hills between here and Honey Lake Valley, we will ask him, if he pleases, to accompany us to the shores of that lake. (See page 535.) It is a beautiful sheet of water, is it not ?

It is said to be twenty miles in length by sixteen in width. The hills on the opposite, or northern side, are entirely without trees. To the right of the highest hill seen in the distance, are several large boiling springs, one of which is nearly two feet in diameter, and flows into the lake. Susan river, and several smaller streams, also empty into the lake, and either sink or evaporate.

In the summer of 1856, a company of men built a small boat for pleasure excursions, and on their first trip six of them were drowned ;—one, unfortunately, being our good friend Isadore. Alas ! Isadore, for thy gentleness and kindness, many loved thee, and for thy true-hearted manliness many respected thee ; and—as always when the good die—Isadore, many mourn thy departure.

But a very limited and indefinite impression of the extent, or fertility, or even beauty of this valley can be formed by the view from the south shore of the lake, looking north, for while the hills in front are low and without timber of any kind, those behind you are high and bold, and covered to their summit with a dense growth of excellent timber. The hill to the west, being nearly in the center of the valley, including the lake, shuts out the most fertile portion of the valley.

Within the past two years a band of settlers have taken up the principal part of this valley, of whom Mr. I. Roop was the pioneer, and have put it under cultivation, and this spring Mr. Roop, in company with others, has taken there the necessary machinery for the erection of a saw and flouring mill.

Being without the limits of the State of California, a public meeting of the settlers of the entire district was convened, when it was unanimously voted to be called the Territory of Natauque.

Most persons are well aware that the emigration on what is known as Noble's Route—(Peter Lassen however it is claimed by the old settlers in Indian Valley, is entitled to that honor, having known it long before Mr. Noble ever saw it, and moreover was his guide all through this route, Mr. N. being entirely unacquainted with it. This Mr. Lassen himself solemnly affirmed in our hearing, and to us; and we make mention of it now that honor may be given where honor is most due.) Most persons, we repeat, are well aware that the emigration on what is known as "Noble's Route," enters the northern side of Honey Lake Valley, about three miles west of the lake (which, being shut out by the hill before mentioned, is not often seen by the

WE HAVE SEEN OUR COURSE.

emigrant, from the road,) and after traveling up this valley for about fifteen miles,
enters Noble's Pass, and crosses the Sierra
Nevadas almost without knowing it. This
low ridge, known as the " Pass," is one continuous forest of magnificent pines the
whole distance through it, and so level that
one is puzzled to know whether it is up or
down.

We have crossed the Sierra Nevadas in
seven different places, and we unhesitatingly affirm, that this is the only good
natural pass that we have yet seen. Indeed,
from the top of " Pilot Peak," or " Slate
Creek Point," the whole country both
north and south of this pass, can be seen to
descend gradually towards it.

This route, we believe, can be traveled at
any and all seasons of the year, by the
locomotive, without the least serious
obstruction from the depth of snow, should
such a boon ever be conferred upon California, and upon the Union.

Having seen all that we deemed desirable, (the provisions becoming low,) we
determined on crossing the high mountainous ridge on the southern side of the
valley, and thus strike Indian Valley in a
direct line if possible : especially as black
and heavy masses of clouds were gathering
around the higher peaks of this mountain
range, threatening to give us a little more
moisture than we needed, just then.

Making our way up an arm of the valley towards the apparently lowest portion
of the mountain, now lying between us
and the goal of our present wishes, we met
with a mishap—(at least our equestrian
traveling companion did)—in the following
manner : We (the pedestrians) had crossed
a narrow and deep ravine and reached the
hill beyond it, when suddenly we heard a
splash and a struggling noise, and looking
round found that the whole bank for several feet had given away, and "the horse
with his rider had both gone below."

Of course it never does to desert a friend
when in difficulties, and consequently we
ran to his assistance, and are therefore
happy in being able to say that by dint of
patience, coupled with perseverance, he
was "considerably dipped," but was not
drowned. This somewhat dampened his
clothes, while it fired his courage, and
after some delay, and the use of several
short, but very emphatic words, not generally expressed in saying one's prayers, he
again mounted, and we resumed our journey.

Just after reaching the summit, snow
commenced falling in large wide flakes,
admonishing us to make all possible haste
to some place of safety—an admonition
most scrupulously regarded. The remembrance of the fate of the Donner party of
emigrants, so many of whom perished but
a few miles southeast of our present position, in 1846, did not decrease our desire to
avoid a similar end.

In this dilemma night overtook us—night
with its darkness, uncertainty, and storm.
No cheering star to light and guide us ; no
well-worn road or trail by which we might,
though slowly, grope our way amid the
darkness, to some brightly glowing fireside
in the most humble cabin.

Our position was no way improved by a
knowledge of the fact that, in making our
way among the bushes, we had lost our
only compass. Not being able to do otherwise, we came to the praiseworthy conclusion to camp—if we could find a place
level enough to sleep, without standing
up ; and were soon well (!) "accommo-
dated," among some rocks by the side of a
stream.

Having but little food left, the cooking
of our supper was not the most difficult
task ever accomplished. Our only duties
therefore consisted in cutting bunch grass
from among the bushes, by firelight, for our
horse, and making the best of our circumstances by forgetting them in sleep.

Early the following morning we awoke ;
and as we fried our last " flapjack," we
watched for the day—hoping that one sight
of its first gray dawn would lift the clouds
of doubt and uncertainty from our minds,

by indicating the course we must that day pursue, to reach Indian Valley.

At last day came, cloudy and heavy, casting no light, mentally, on our dubious way. We might be right, and, by the same rule, we might be wrong. Usually on such occasions, each individual member of a party holds a different opinion to the other. This rule was not departed from at this important juncture of our affairs, for being only three in number we had but three opinions. These however we agreed individually to hold, without remaining in camp, foodless, to debate them; consequently, we made our way onward as best we could, among snow, rocks, trees, and dense chapparal, when to our great joy a gleam of sunlight, (the only one we saw throughout the day, and only for a moment,) fell upon a tree, but, casting a shadow, *it told us our course.*

Now we have often been benighted, and as often, when we saw a distant light or camp-fire twinkling, though dimly, in the distance, we have been rejoiced—but now a thrill of wild delight electrified our hearts, such as we never felt before, or since.

How forcibly does this teach us, gentle reader, that however dark and doubtful may be our prospect now, that some welcome and long looked and perhaps prayed for ray of sunlight, may cast a guiding shadow upon our path, at a time too when it is most needed, and which, while it brightens and gladdens the present, may perhaps, determine a long and prosperous future. Therefore we say *Hope* and *Strive* ever—always.

Our course now being plain, we lost no time in taking advantage of the knowledge so providentially obtained, and before midnight we were striving to forget our long fast, and our many troubles, at the well furnished table and pleasant fireside of our amiable and hospitable friend, Judge Ward. The agreeable associations, pleasant converse, and sweet songs of that amiable family, and happy mountain home, will ever linger upon the heart, and be treasured among the most pleasant recollections of a jaunt to Honey Lake Valley.

The following description of the country and road from the Humboldt river to the Sacramento Valley, by Honey Lake Valley and Noble's Pass, from the pen of Mr. John A. Dreibelbis, who passed over the route several times during the summer and fall of 1853, will be read with interest, especially at the present time :

" *From the Humboldt to Cold Springs,* 14 *miles.*

Course west, road level ; water sufficient for one hundred and fifty head of stock at a time ; good bunch grass on the hill-sides and heads of cañons. Thence, to—

Rabbit Hole Springs, 18 *miles.*

Course north of west ; road ascending about two miles, through a low gap of mountain range, then descending slightly eight miles ; the rest nearly level to Rabbit Hole : bunch grass south east and south west for three miles ; on left hand in ravine is water sufficient for from one to two hundred animals : Thence, to—

Black Rock Springs, 24 *miles.*

Course north west ; road for the first eight miles has a few gulches, the remainder is then an entire desert, perfectly level and hard ; very little of anything growing upon it ; some good feed about the Spring, but not extensive ; water hot, but cools somewhat in running off, and is healthy for animals ; rye and salt grass in abundance one and a half miles north : Thence, to—

Granite Creek, 22 *miles.*

Course south of south west ; road excellent over a perfect desert, as smooth as a planed floor and nearly as hard, and not a vestige of vegetation on it for twenty-two miles. This stream comes out of a notch of the mountain range on the right hand, pretty well at the end. Leave the desert by turning into this gap half a mile to camp ; bunch grass on the foot hills. It will be readily seen that between this point and Rabbit Hole, a material cut-off could be effected, so that forty-six miles might be made in thirty, with fully as good road, but no water ; the cut-off, however, would be but six miles longer than from Black Rock to Rabbit Hole. Thence, to—

Hot Spring Point, 3 *miles.*

Course south of south-west, road level, distance three miles ; grass all along on the left; boiling springs scattered all through which makes it dangerous to let stock range upon it. Thence, to—

Deep Springs, 7 miles.

Course north-west, road level. Here you double the extreme south end of mountain range; grass and water in abundance, of the very best quality; this is a good place to lie over a day or two. Thence, to—

Buffalo Springs, 16 miles.

Course west, road level. Directly after leaving the Springs, you enter a desert; after passing eight miles over an arm of it, then eight miles through sage, you come to the bed of a large dry creek, its banks covered with dry grass for some distance; some water in holes that will do no injury to stock; one half mile beyond this and about two hundred paces on the right hand, are the Springs. Thence, to—

Smoke Creek Meadows, 13 miles.

Course west six miles, level ground; then four miles over low hills to creek; thence up creek, along the cañon, three miles to camp. Here is an extensive valley, from three hundred yards to two miles wide; its length is not ascertained. This valley produces clover, bunch grass, &c., of the most luxuriant growth. Thence, to—

Mud Springs, 9 miles.

Course west: You travel up Smoke Creek Meadows two miles; then over the point of a low ridge into Rush Valley. This valley is two miles long, by half a mile wide, excellent grass and water. The road here is on table land, fifty to seventy-five feet above the level of the plains or desert, and is perfectly level. Thence, to—

Susan River, 9 miles.

Course west, six miles south-west, and three miles west, to camp. Emigrants should start early from Mud Springs, as the road is covered with cobble stones, which makes it slow and tedious; it is nearly level till you descend slightly to the valley of the stream, [known as Honey Lake Valley.] This is a delightful valley, its soil of the most productive kind, and is from five to seven miles wide, and covered with clover, blue-joint, red-top, and bunch grass, in great abundance. The stream abounds in mountain trout, which are easily taken with hook and line. Thence, to—

Head of this Valley, 14 miles.

Course west: You cross Willow Creek two miles after leaving camp on Susan River. This stream rises in the west, runs east out of the Sierra Nevada, into the val-

ley, and about twenty or twenty-five miles down it, to Honey Lake. Thence, to—

Summit Springs, 18 miles.

Immediately after leaving the valley, you enter open, but heavy pine woods—not unwelcome to the sun-scorched emigrant—and commence ascending the Sierra Nevada gradually: Water four miles on the right, and some grass; and again five miles on the left, but no grass; the road somewhat stony in places; the ascent is so gradual that on slight observation it seems as much down as up; in fact, a great part is level, and enough timber on one mile on each side of the road, from the valley to the summit, to build a double railway track to the Missouri River. Course west, grass and water. Thence, to—

Pine Creek, 8 miles.

Course, north west, to avoid a cluster of buttes; road level, grass and water;—thence to—

Black Butte Creek, 12 miles.

Course, north-west four miles; then turning west to south-west; grass and water; road level. The country here, and for twenty miles back, must be considered the summit, as it is impossible to ascertain the precise place, owing to the flatness of the country. The small streams that rise on the buttes around and run down their sides, all sink, or form small lakes and marshes, there not being slope sufficient to run off their waters. Thence to—

Black Butte, 6 miles.

Course, south-west; road, heavy sand; thence to—

Pine Meadows, 4 miles.

Course, west; road level and good; water and grass. Thence to—

Hat Creek, 4 miles.

Course north-west; road gradually sloping; only about one hundred feet where a wagon wheel need be locked. Thence, to—

Lost Creek, 2 miles.

Course west, road nearly level. Thence, to—

John Hill's Ranch on Deer Flat, 14 miles.

Course west; the two first miles slightly up hill, fifty or sixty feet only of which is steep; after a distance of forty miles, embracing the entire western slope of the Sierra Nevada, it is almost a perfect grade to the Sacramento River. Thence, to—

McCumber's Mills, 8 miles; Shingle Town, 3 miles; Charley's Ranch, 4 miles; Payne and Smith's 6 miles; Dr. Bakers, on Bear

Creek, 7 *miles; Fort Reading on Cow Creek,* 4 *miles; Sacramento River* 3 *miles.*"

This estimate of distances, the whole route through, overrun those of Mr. Kleiser's, as measured by his road-ometer, about the same time.

THE MINERS' DEATH.

In a glen of the Sierras, where a rapid river rolled,
From the wild Nevada's summits, with offerings of gold—
On the banks where he had toiled for many a weary day,
Parched with a burning fever, a dying miner lay.

"Come closer to me, mother, put your hand upon my brow;
As you kissed me when we parted, my mother, kiss me now—
Life's dream is almost over, it shall waken soon in joy—
My mother, bless me softly, as you blessed me when a boy."

He died alone and friendless : but in his fevered dream
A mother, like an angel, came beside that golden stream ;
But the hands of thoughtless strangers, as the sun sank in the west,
Without a tear, without a prayer, consigned him to his rest.

Wherever, in this western land, has rolled the living tide
Of emigrants with golden dreams, the mounds lie side by side—
In Nevada's rugged gorges, in every mountain glen—
On hill side and by river, are the graves of noble men.

The wild flowers bloom above them, in beauty, every spring—
Sweet offerings of nature's hand, which friends may never bring ;
But far away, in other lands, fond eyes grow dim with tears,
And vainly wait the coming of the loved of other years.

The stars drift up the mountains into depths of azure skies,
And gaze upon the lonely graves like watchful spirit eyes ;
But far away, in eastern lands, the bright stars beaming there,
Look down on faces, watching in tearful, midnight prayer.

In the western El Dorado, beside the mountain streams,
The hearts of weary men, at night, turn homeward in their dreams ;
But far away, across the sea, how many hearts are breaking,
For those who sleep beisde these streams, the sleep that knows no waking.

S.

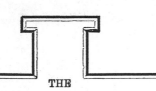

CHARLES F. ROBBINS,
EXECUTES EVERY DESCRIPTION OF
BOOK, CARD AND JOB

PRINTING

111 CLAY STREET.

111 CLAY STREET.

TYPE, PRESSES AND PRINTERS' MATERIAL,
FOR SALE AT REDUCED RATES.

☞ Orders from the Country respectfully solicited. ☜

PART IV

ODDS & ENDS

CHILEANS

"I am perfectly satisfied with my condition as a woman, with my cigarita in one hand, and my other hand and arm where it should be. . . ."

ODDS & ENDS

It is not the purpose of our selection from *Hutchings' California Magazine* to present a balanced image of the nature of the journal, any more than it was J. M. Hutchings' purpose to draw a complete picture of life in California. Both of us have selected what seemed to us best and most interesting. If the sections in this volume on the mining regions and the natural wonders of California illustrate the recurrent *theme* of the magazine, the following unrelated pieces better demonstrate its *flavor*.

Lack of space prevented us from presenting a fair sampling of the generally atrocious fiction which forms a scrubby background to the California articles: hence, we have left it all out. Hutchings frequently complained in his remarks to contributors of the dearth of fiction which was genuinely Californian. He was more than justified, for the typical product published in his magazine leaves one with the impression that the author (prudently anonymous in most cases) might have been torn between setting his story in Scotland or Sardinia, but finally chose California because he knew that Hutchings was such a crank on the subject.

Some notion of the quality of the fiction in *Hutchings'* may be gained from the offering in the "Juvenile Department" which appears on the following pages; it is one of numerous exhortations on the theme of death designed to frighten good manners into little children. The youth of California was blessed by the early disappearance of the "Juvenile Department"—though it certainly did not founder because local writers had lost their taste for the grotesque. A somewhat sounder feature, the "Editor's Table," appeared continuously after the first few numbers, and "Our Social Chair" spans the history of the magazine. Both are expressions of Hutchings' sometimes rambling and usually benign views of the times.

J. M. Hutchings' editorial opinions were hardly designed to induce fervor or inspire retaliation. The editorial on "The Iron Horse" in this section is of unusual vigor; in it he favors the construction of a transcontinental railroad. On the other hand, Hutchings was opposed to the extortionate practices of the current transportation monopolies, the Pacific Mail Steamship Company and the California Steam Navigation Company, and he occasionally hurled a blunt barb in their direction. WATER was a recurrent editorial theme: the state did not need greater population or more capital, it needed more water for the diggings. Hutchings seems to have been as blind to the obvious ill effects of hydraulic mining as he was to the less savory possibilities inherent in a transcontinental railroad.

Insight and analysis obviously were not Hutchings' bent. But in "outsight" and description his tastes ranged wide. We have omitted many articles that illustrate this range (from the burial customs of the Chinese Empire to the several extensive discursions on the sagacity of animals) in favor of the California material. A notable exception is the article on the nefarious deed of the Mormons at Mountain Meadows: confronted by the spectre of Brigham Young, whom he describes elsewhere as a cunning hypocrite possessed of an unusually foreshortened brainpan, J. M. Hutchings could show some real spleen.

HUTCHINGS'

CALIFORNIA MAGAZINE.

Vol. V.   NOVEMBER, 1860.   No. 5.

THE BACTRIAN CAMEL.

THE BACTRIAN CAMEL IN CALIFORNIA.

HE Bactrian camels, fifteen in number, which reached San Francisco in July last per schooner Caroline E. Foote, from the Amoor river, and which still remain in our neighborhood, deserve much more attention than they have as yet received. Not so much because they come from the far interior of Asia, and are curiosities in themselves, are they entitled to consideration; but we think that the animal will yet be acclimated in America, and that the present importation is only the first of a series of private ventures, which will eventually result in giving to the United States a domestic animal of great value and importance. It was supposed by Mr. Otto Esche, the importer of the present herd, that they were well adapted for the transportation of goods from point to point in the mining regions, or, if not there, certainly on the sandy plains which are found between the Sierra Nevada and Salt Lake, and on the desert wastes which make up the southern portions of the United States territories from San Bernardino across to El Paso. It seems, indeed, to have been the intention of establishing a Camel Express from California to Salt Lake, and, if the animals were found well adapted to the country, to extend it as far east as Missouri. Hitherto, however, no trial has been made of the animals, and with the exception of a few days of exhibition for the benefit of the German Benevolent Society, they have attracted but little public attention.

Owing to the want of proper accommodations on the vessel, the animals reached San Francisco in very poor condition, lean, meagre, and with their double humps shriveled down to mere skinny sacks, which hung in flabby ugliness over their sides. Even when in the best condition, the camel can not be called a beautiful animal; but it is doubly or trebly ugly, when in ill condition. An attempt is now being made to bring them back to their pristine vigor and health by sending them out to pasture near the Mission Dolores; but what effect the unaccustomed Californian diet will produce, and what the final result of the camel enterprise as a whole will be, remains to be seen. Enough, however, has been done, and the interests of the country are sufficiently at stake, to justify us in taking a Californian interest in the welfare and general prospects of the distinguished strangers. We have therefore presented above the portrait of one of our Camel Pioneers, confident, or at least hoping, that the picture as we give it, with Californian surroundings, will not be an unfrequent one in future views of our State.

The Bactrian or two-humped camel differs in various respects from the Arabian or one-humped camel, numbers of which were imported by the Government from Smyrna in Asia Minor a few years ago, and which have attracted much national attention. There were, among the Government importations, several Bactrians; but they were lost, and we believe that these now Californian specimens are the only ones in America. They are much more heavily built, of stouter limbs and much stronger animals than the Arabian camels. Their usefulness as beasts of burden, is generally regarded as limited, on account of the difficulty of loading them, but this can easily be overcome by Yankee ingenuity. They can, moreover, be used with much success as draught animals; and owing to their great powers of endurance and peculiar adaptation to desert countries, would without doubt be found of great value in those sections of our country for which they were intended. If the Government or some public spirited institution could but devote the proper care to the subject, we have every reason to believe that the importation of camels into America would lead to results second only to the importation of horses and cattle, neither of which, it is to be recollected, were native to the western hemisphere. We can see no good reason why the camel, which is quite as useful in its place as the horse or the cow, can not be naturalized, quite as well as they.

Much of the information given about the camel in the early books on natural history is incorrect; and if we trust entirely to the reading of our boyhood we will have very erroneous ideas in regard to the character and peculiarities of the animal. It is not, as is generally supposed, peculiarly adapted to the torrid zone; but on the contrary it suffers quite as much from great heat as it does from intense cold. It is truly better calculated for deserts and level countries; but it can very successfully cross ranges of mountains even when they are covered with snow and ice. Its feet, which are generally supposed to be soft and velvety, fitted only for sandy traveling, are clothed with thick and leathery skin, as tough as horn, and calculated quite as well for sharp stones and flinty ground as for the sandy wastes of the desert. It moves with embarrassment in wet and slippery places; and frequently, when driven over such spots, if not hoppled, the poor animal is made to split up, by the straddling of its hind legs. The Bactrian, however, is much better calculated to cross such places than its cousin of Arabia.

The speed of the camel has been generally overestimated. The dromedary, a "fast" variety of the Arabian camel, can indeed travel a hundred miles in a day on an emergency; but the ordinary rate does not exceed fifty miles. Loaded camels do not usually travel more than thirty miles a day; and loads "tell upon them" quite as much as upon other animals. The ordinary load of a strong camel does not exceed 600 pounds; but for a short distance, say a mile or two a very strong camel will carry from 1,000 to 1,200 pounds; but the fast dromedary will not carry over 300 pounds. The gait depends, almost as much as that of the horse, upon training; and to make a good rider much care and attention are necessary.

The great advantages in using camels in certain portions of our country are their adaptability for making long journeys and passing over wide tracts of desert, where there is a scarcity of food and water; the cheapness of keeping them, and the length of time for which they are serviceable. At four years of age they can commence carrying loads, and they continue of use till twenty or twenty five; but they may be said to be in their prime only from their fifth to their tenth or twelfth year. They eat and thrive upon almost every kind of vegetation that grows. They like to gather their own food, and will eat almost anything, thistles, prickly pear leaves and thorny weeds, which are too dry and useless for any other land but a desert. A very little also goes a great distance, and owing to the hump, which may be pronounced one of the greatest "institutions" in the animal creation, the camel is enabled to lay up an ample supply of food at the start, to last a long time. This hump, together with the water reservoir of the stomach, justifies the use of the term often given to the camel, of being "the ship of the desert," carrying as it does stores of food and drink for use on the journey. The hump is composed of gelatinous fat, very plump when the animal is in good condition, and seems to be intended for no other purpose than to supply food, by reabsorption, when other sustenance fails. It is not necessary to the animal's vitality: on the contrary it is said to have been often opened and large portions of the fat cut away, without in any manner injuring or affecting the general health of the animal. The condition of the camel is judged from the appearance of the hump: and in the case of the Bactrians, which arrived here in July, the most casual observer could observe by looking at the lean and shriveled humps that they were in very bad plight. After long and painful journeys, it is not unusual to see a camel with very little or no appearance of a hump or humps. The water reservoir is a peculiar sack of cavities or cells, which contain some twenty or more pints of water, or of a pure and drinkable secretion resembling it.

The camel is a chewer of the cud; its flesh resembles beef but is more tender; and its milk can hardly be distinguished either in color or taste from cow's milk. It is subject to very nearly the same diseases as cattle, and it is supposed that a good cow-doctor would be able to prescribe successfully for camels.

Much amusement has been afforded late students of natural history by a curious discussion which was once carried on in relation to the seven callosities, which are seen upon the camel, and upon which it rests when lying down. One party seriously contended that they were not natural, but had been produced by ill treatment and hard usage through a series of ages; while the other party considered it necessary to quite as zealously and warmly argue the contrary. The callosities were given to the camel from the time of its original creation quite as certainly as was its hump, its stomach, its split nose, and the curious power it has of closing its nostrils.

In character the camel is generally gentle, submissive and patient to the will of man; but sometimes more or less "stubborn." Some are even trained for the arena or prize-ring. Their contests, however, are rather amusing than dangerous; though sometimes they break each other's legs. Fighting, indeed, is not unnatural to them, for when two strange males meet, where there are females, they wrestle for the supremacy; and the conquered one ever afterwards acknowledges his inferiority by not so much as daring to look at a female.

It remains for actual experiment to determine which of the two species of camels is best adapted to the United States. Very likely one species will be found best for one region or one kind of service and another for another; and the mule camel or hybrid cross of the Bactrian male upon the Arabian female may just as well combine the power of the former, with the one hump and quicker movement of the latter in America as in Asia. For crossing the plains the Arabian would perhaps be best; for the hilly regions of California, probably the larger and hardier Bactrian, whose ordinary size is about seven feet and a half high, ten feet long and nine or ten feet around the body over the front hump. The weight of the animals is about two thousand pounds. Much valuable information concerning the camel and the history of the camel enterprise by the United States Government is to be found scattered through the reports to the Secretary of War on the subject, printed in 1857, to which we are in part indebted for the information herein given.

———————

SUBTERRANEAN HEAT.—The *Los Angeles Star* relates that the sulphur springs at Temascal have undergone a change of late, which, if taken in connection with the disappearance of other springs in that vicinity, would seem to indicate some subterranean disturbance. The great spring, used for bathing, has become much hotter, with a greatly increased volume; while a small spring, a few yards distant, has not only increased, but becomes occasionally hot—it being formerly icy cold.

C. NAHL

QUEEN EMMA.   PRINCESS VICTORIA.   QUEEN DOWAGER.   MAID OF HONOR.
          KING KAMEHAMEHA IV.   PRINCE LOT KAMEHAMEHA.

THE ROYAL FAMILY OF HAWAII.

SAW MILL RAILROAD ON THE NORTH FORK OF THE COSUMNES RIVER.

The illustration above, representing a Saw Mill Railroad, constructed on the side of a steep mountain, on the north fork of the Cosumnes river, near Sly Park, shews what is and can be done to accomplish a given purpose, when it is required. In the summer of 1852 this railroad and a saw mill were erected in this wildly romantic spot, under the superintendence of Dr. Bradley of the corporation of Bradley, Berdan & Co., for the purpose of sawing the lumber required in the construction of their large canal, from this stream to the mining towns of Ringgold, Weberville, Diamond Springs, Missouri Flat, El Dorado City, (then called Mud Springs,) Logtown, and several other mining localities in the southern portion of El Dorado county, to supply those districts with water for mining.

This railroad is built upon an inclined plane, at the (often quoted) angle of forty-five degrees, for the purpose of lowering saw-logs to the mill. The car descends with its load, and being attached by a rope thro' a pulley at the top to the empty car, the weight descending causes the empty car to ascend; and by which contrivance the necessity of any other kind of machinery for that purpose is obviated.

We happened to be one of a very agreeable little party to visit this singular place, and could the reader have seen us—ladies and gentlemen, cold chickens and sandwiches, boiled ham and water melons, blankets and daguerrean instruments—all snugly stowed away in that coach, and then have heard the jokes and fun going on, if he had not been envious of our enjoyment, we know he would like to have been of the party,—that is, if he liked pleasant company.

Now it so happened that we all endorsed the opinion that frolic was better than pills; and pure mountain air than powders; and open-hearted, jovial, and unrestrained laughter, better than medicine of any kind; however, it seemed to be well understood, that care was to be left behind. It is pleasant to forget care for at least one day, is it not reader? Perhaps, though—we say perhaps—you may belong to those long-faced, slab-sided, door-post-built, cold-and-immovable countenanced kind of folks, who don't believe in fun, and certainly not in pic-nic parties. Well then, we pity you; no we don't either, for you don't deserve it—you

don't. You may be like a friend of ours who is always thinking that things in general—just now—look remarkably blue; and things in particular, particularly black—not a bright, but a *dull* black. If he has just come out of a good speculation, (for he is generally successful,) he hangs his face in elongated mourning, lest he should go in on the next. When he is well—which is very seldom—he looks daily forward, with agonizing anxiety to the day when he may become sick—and the moment he begins to feel unwell, he has day visions of Death, with his scythe and hour glass at his side; and although he dislikes the thought of him exceedingly, he will keep him in imagination by his bed—no doubt wishing (just for the looks of the thing, and to oblige him,) that he would put those weapons of his in the cupboard, or leave them at the foot of the stairs!

Now, if you claim any sympathy or relationship with this eminent friend, we are glad that you were not of the party, simply because we don't like sour faces. They don't look right, well enough no doubt in the curd and cheese business, but not good for pic-nics.

On, on, we go, as merry as crickets; now passing through long forests of trees; now ascending or descending a gently roll'ng hill; then taking alternates doses of dust and soda water—jokes and cakes—until we arrived at the top of a hill overlooking a cañon. Here, on looking down, we saw something resembling two long lengths of broad ribbon with bars across, lying on the side of the hill. When the question was asked, "What is that?" it was answered with "that is a railway, and we take all our logs down that rail to the mill—that dark spot down yonder; and we have all to take a ride on it to the mill."

"I never *can* ride down there!" cries a lady.

"O, yes," urges a gentleman.

"Why that railway is nearly upright?" queries a second lady.

"Oh, dear!" sighs a third.

" Never mind," soothingly suggests a second gentleman.

" I never can !" objects another lady.

" If the rope should break !" suggests a fifth.

" Why, really there is no danger," cries gentleman number three, " for altogether we are not as heavy as a green pine log, and *that* never broke it."

After some hesitation and delay, one gent seats himself in the car, (fitted up with seats for the occasion,) and with sundry questions and entreaties, and sighs and oh dears, the whole party join him, and at last we are all safely seated ; while beneath the seats are the water-melons and blankets, cold fowl and daguerrean instruments, cakes and shawls, pies and over-coats. Now off we go!

" Oh, do stop ! stop ! oh do !" cries a lady.

" *I will* get out !" exclaims another.

But one and all affirm *that* to be next to impossible.

" It is too steep ever to reach the river on foot."

" Let me try," beseeches a lady.

" Then—if you *will*," answers a gent, " I will assist you."

And she *did* try, and the gent *did* assist her to the bottom ; but oh ! ye tall pines and spreading oaks, what a time they had of it !

Slowly again we started, and with many heart flutterings and tremblings, fears and exclamations, on, on, we go, until the anticipated danger over, we all stand in safety at the bottom of the railway ; and then we calmly looked our enemy in the face and took courage.

" Bless me !"

" Catch me on that again !"

" Who'd have thought it ?"

" How steep it looks !"

" Oh dear me !"

" Well, I never !"

" No you don't—if I know myself !" with sundry other remarks of surprise and consolation, were interrupted by our guide and host, Dr. B., who informed us that the perpendicular height of the hill from where we stood to the top, was seven hundred feet, and the length of the railway on the steep side of the hill, was only one thousand feet in length.

" You saw the building on the top, where the logs lie ?" he continued.

" Yes."

" That is called by the workmen the ' hypo,' and the mill down here where we stand, they call the ' depot.' Just look around."

We did look around, but what a wild, craggy place for a mill, that itself was built upon rocks ; the fire-place, hearth and chimney in the kitchen were all natural formations of the rock. A flume which has been constructed, is built, or rather hung upon rocks ; a prop here, a packing there, and a brace yonder ; here, a tree cut off, formed a post ; there, a rock formed a stay ; while the water rushed and leaped on, on, down the steep rocky bed of the river, as though it cared for nothing and no one.

Friend B. we give you credit for your undaunted perseverance. This work, with many others, shews what can be accomplished by patient, unswerving determination and skill. If at any time a miner should, for a moment, be disposed to think lightly of water companies, we wish him to visit the upper end of most of our canals, there to witness the expense, labor and energy expended on them. At this mill was sawed all the lumber needed in the construction of the flume ; besides supplying many thousands of feet of lumber, for sluice making and other purposes, in the settlements below.

It is a magnificent sight to see the stately pine and venerable oak, growing upon and among vast piles of rocks ; in some instances a large overhanging tree growing in the seam, or between two rocks, as though it were a lever placed there by nature to overturn portions of the mountain above, adding wildness, boldness, beauty and sublimity to the beautiful landscape.

After enjoying the good things provided by our worthy host, and all the pleasant and exhilerating recreations of fun and frolic, we wended our way along a plank on the top of a serpent-like flume, until it intersected the road below, (as none cared to ascend that railway again,) where our coach had been sent to meet us, and soon we were " all aboard," and on our way homeward, indulging in the reminiscences and enjoyments the trip had afforded us. Should any of our readers ever go upon a jaunt of this kind, they have our best wishes that an equal amount of pleasant and sunny gladness may keep them company on the way, and then we know that they will say, " Yes, we enjoyed it," when the journey is ended.

———

" WELL, let us go, as it is about time all honest folks were in bed."

Ah ! yes—then *I* had better be off—but *you* need'nt hurry on that account !

———

" I see better without wine and spectacles than when I use both," said Sidney Smith.

HUTCHINGS'

CALIFORNIA MAGAZINE.

Vol. III.   APRIL, 1859.   No. 10.

SCENES AMONG THE INDIANS OF CALIFORNIA.

THE BARGAIN.

ALMOST every Californian, who has passed the precincts of any commercial city of the State, is more or less familiar with the manners, habits, customs, and peculiarities of the California Indians, especially in particular sections; but as these differ in form and character, among the different groups of tribes, even in districts adjoining each other, we may, perhaps, present several interesting facts, which, although known by some, are not known by others; and which, in either case, will be at once recognized as faithful pictures of Indian life around us.

As these Indians are simply men and women, and without doubt the lowest in morality and intellectual ability on this continent, the generous reader, however philanthropical in his intentions and benevolent in his wishes, must not expect us to paint them as heroes, or portray them as angels, for they are neither. Yet, without the prejudice arising from an unfavorable first impression and confirmed by the observation of years, we shall endeavor to be just; allowing the reader to be the judge, when we have finished our task.

According to the report of Col. T. J. Henley, Superintendent of Indian affairs for California, from the most reliable information that could be obtained, the number of Indians in the various counties of the State is as follows: in San Diego and San Bernardino, 8,000; in Los Angeles, Santa Barbara, San Luis Obispo, Monterey, Santa Clara, and Santa Cruz, 2,000; in Tulare and Mariposa, 2,500; in Tuolumne, Calaveras, San Joaquin, Alameda, and Contra Costa, 4,100; in Sacramento, El Dorado, and Placer, 3,500; in Sutter, Yuba, Nevada, and Sierra, 3,500; in Butte, Shasta, and Siskiyou, 5,500; in Klamath, Humboldt, and Trinity, 6,500; in Mendocino, Colusi, Yolo, Napa, Sonoma, and Marin, 15,000. In addition to those mentioned, the number of Indians collected and now residing upon the Reservations, is: Klamath, 2,500; Nome Lackee, 2,000; Mendocino, 500; Fresno, 900; Tejon, 700; Nome Cult Valley, (attached to Nome Lackee,) 3,000; King's River, (attached to Fresno,) 400. Making the total number of Indians in California, about 60,600.

By those who are the best informed concerning them, an opinion has been expressed that, since the discovery of gold, the Indians in this State have been almost decimated; as, unfortunately, they have cultivated all the vices, and become possessed of many of the diseases, without practicing any of the virtues of the whites. Lewdness and liquor have been the destroying angels of the race; and the cause, with but one or two exceptions, of all the Indian wars that have been known here. We speak not at random, however much it is to be deplored, for we have the facts before us.

With all their failings, it cannot be denied that the California Indians are an interesting people. Their appearance, even, next to the feeling of pity or disgust, is provocative of mirth. Who, for instance, can meet an Indian in the public street, or by the way-side, habited as he generally is in the cast-off garments of the whites, without a smile of mirth imperceptibly stealing across the countenance. Perhaps his brawny and chocolate colored body is covered with a solitary white shirt, (or chemise, as they are not very particular); and his matted and heavy black hair is surmounted by a somewhat dilapidated though fashionably built hat; these two articles constituting his "full dress." Clad in a greasy old silk dress, or dirty cotton gown, by his side walks his squaw—an equally interesting object with himself—to whose face and arms soap and water appear to have long been alienated. Then, to "cap the climax" of the picture, a youthful scion of the pair, who is a subject of equal cleanliness with his mother, and dressed like his father—minus the hat and shirt—carries a miniature bow and arrows. Who that can witness such a sight, even though they pity, and resist a smile?

The amount of comfort the males are capable of enduring, very naturally allows the females the opportunity of performing all the labor of the camp, field, or foraging excursions, or of its going unperformed; for although their liege lords may be by their side, or within call, their natural gallantry is no obstacle whatever to such an arrangement being perfectly satisfactory; and in case of refusal on her part, the commencement of warlike demonstrations on his, is generally productive of acquiescence. This, however, is not always the case, as the following narrative will show:

One bright May morning, when on a visit to Placerville, El Dorado county, an old friend enquired if we would not like to witness an Indian mourning scene. Of course the reply was in the affirmative, and in a few minutes we were on the ground. As we drew near the spot, we could hear the mournful wailing cry, as it rose upon the air. Groups of Indians were scattered around, some sitting, others walking, and one party of females were engaged in cooking.

In an inclosure, formed of bushes on one side and the rude habitations of the Indians on the other, were from forty to fifty men and women. Here, three or four were sitting in a group; there, a similar number were standing up or moving about, with arms held up, now on this side, and now on that, and sometimes stamping with their feet; the faces of nearly all were hideously painted (black); but as the paint was mixed with water, when a tear rolled down, it left a lighter streak behind. All were wailing and weeping, because sickness and death were desolating their tribes, and making their camp-fires sorrowful and lonely.

It was an affecting and melancholy scene. Outside, dogs were snarling and fighting and Indian children unconsciously at play.

While these things were going on, the arrival of three Newtown Indians—each armed with an old musket or rifle, and one of them carrying a bottle of whiskey in his hand, from which numerous drinks were taken from time to time—created an unusual stir in camp. This event, while it illustrates some traits of Indian

AN INDIAN WOMAN CARRYING ACORNS TO CAMP.

character, brings us to the *denouement* of our narrative.

The ringleader of the three, we afterwards learned, had obtained his wife from this tribe; but, as he had frequently beaten and abused her, she had lately sought the protection of her tribe, much to the annoyance of her spouse, who, after some explanation, had been allowed

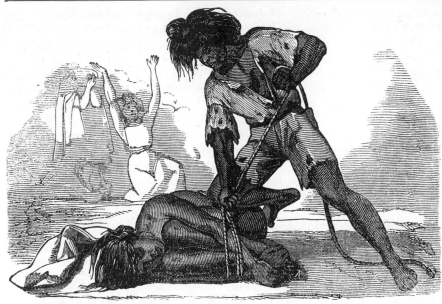

AN INDIAN BINDING THE CORPSE FOR BURNING OR BURIAL.

on all former occasions to depart with her. This time, however, as the beating had been excessive, she refused to return with him; and as her relatives had declined to interfere in the matter, and moreover had intimated their determination to resist any attempt on his part to force a compliance, in a fit of drunken madness he had paid this visit to demand his squaw, and to threaten that, if not given up quietly, he would take her by force.

Taunting and threatening words were fearlessly used on both sides, followed by the breaking up of the mourning group, and the movement from camp of all the women and children; and as the leader of the Newtown Indians grew more and more excited, cocking and uncocking his rifle while walking to and fro, matters began to grow serious; and before we were fully aware of it, the sudden discharge of a gun, and the falling of the brother of the woman, fatally wounded, announced that the work of death had begun.

In order to see the fight, and yet be in a place of safety, we ran for a large pine tree; but, in our eager curiosity to watch the progress of events, we entirely forgot to seek its protection by getting behind it. Fortunately, the showers of arrows and musket balls, that followed the retreating footsteps of the aggressors, passed by us, and we escaped uninjured. Not so the Newtown Indian; who, the moment his death-dealing weapon was discharged, had thrown it down, and ran for his life; but, with his back and side almost covered with the arrows of his pursuers, he fell to rise no more. The first and last cause of this tragedy was whisky—sold to the Indians, against all law, by————whites! Heaven save the mark.

After a number of the arrows had been removed from the corpse of the slain—some of which had entered about eight inches—we returned to the encampment, and such a sight of blood and mourning and dirty faces our eyes saw never. Women were bathing the wounds of the dying man; his mother stood wailing at the entrance to his hut; while his wives were seeking to soothe him with their affectionate caresses, and praises of his goodness and kindness. Just as evening threw its shadowy mantle on the hill-tops around the village, the loud, discordant wail that arose from the sorrowful mourners told us that he was dead, and that he too had entered the spirit-land of his fathers.

As the Newtown Indians had sent out scouts to watch the issue of this proceeding, and as these had doubtless returned and given a report of the death of one of their tribe, an attack of revenge was expected; and, to prevent a surprise, runners were sent out in every direction, and upon every prominent hill watchers were stationed. Although this was continued day and night for nearly a week, the enemy did not make his appearance.

When an Indian is known to be near his departure to the spirit-land, his head is generally pillowed in the lap of one of the nearest and dearest of his relatives, while those who stand around him almost invariably chant, in a low, monotonous tone, the virtues of the dying; and with this soothing lullaby he falls asleep in death. As soon as his heart has ceased to beat, the sad news of his demise is conveyed to all his relatives, both far and near; and the low chant is changed to loud and mournful wailings, while those who are near beat upon their chests with their clenched fists, and with tearful eyes fixed upwards, they apostrophize the spirit of the departed.

It is a singular fact, that although in some districts of the State, some Indians burn and others bury their dead, all prepare them for final disposition in the same manner, which is as follows:—A blanket being spread upon the ground, the corpse is laid upon it; when a brother, or some other relative, after folding the limbs upon the chest, with the knees towards the chin, proceeds to bind the body and limbs together as tightly as it is possible so to do. It is then wrapped in the blanket and placed upon the earth, with its face upwards and exposed. All this time the wild howling and wailing continues, until the body is ready; then for about twenty minutes or half an hour, the mourning ceases, and not a sound intrudes upon the stillness and rude solemnity of the scene. At a given signal all rise simultaneously—the women to renew their wailing, and the men to build a funeral pyre, or to prepare a grave.

If the corpse is about to be burned, when the fuel is about two feet in height, every sound again ceases, and, amid a death-like stillness, the men place the body upon the pyre. This being done,

AN INDIAN WOMAN PANNING OUT GOLD.

additional wood is piled upon it, until all but the face is completely covered. Slowly and solemnly the oldest and nearest relative advances with torch in hand, and sets the wood on fire.

As soon as the first curling cloud of smoke is seen to ascend, the discordant howling of the women becomes almost

AN INDIAN SWEAT-HOUSE.

appalling; while the men in some instances stand in sullen and unbroken silence, and in others join their notes of woe to those of the devoted women. All the relatives who are nearest and dearest to the consuming dead, with long sticks in their hands, commence a frantic dance around the burning body, occasionally turning it over and stirring it up, that it may consume the more speedily.

The motive which impels them to this, is their belief in a vast and pleasant camping ground situated in some beautiful country in the direction of the setting sun, where they again meet their relatives and friends, and live in perpetual ease and plenty together. This camping ground, they believe, is presided over and governed by a chief of great power and goodness, and about whom they need give themselves no uneasiness whatever. They also believe in an evil spirit, who is capable of doing them any amount of injury, and who is constantly upon the look-out to give them all the trouble he possibly can, and eventually to keep them away from this pleasant camping place and the society of their friends;

him they think it worth their while to conciliate or cheat, according to circumstances; and as they believe also that the heart is the immortal part, and that he is seeking to make it a prisoner, by noises and motions they try to attract his attention while the body is burning, as it is at that season the heart leaps out; and, if his attention is attracted and drawn off by their manouverings, the heart makes its escape and is eternally safe. This is the reason for the hideous noises and waving of cloths practiced during the process of burning.

Those Indians who burn their dead, believe that the evil one keeps perpetual guard over the graves of those who are buried, and when the heart would escape it is secured, and perpetually employed in giving sickness and ill luck, and other annoyances to their living relatives, out of revenge for their indifference and neglect of their future welfare.

After the body is nearly consumed, the blackened remains are taken from the fire and rolled in a cloth and blanket, to cool it a little, when his wives separate the remaining and unconsumed portions of the body, and around each piece wind a long string of beads. Every particle is then carefully placed in a basket that has been beautifully beaded and worked for such an occasion, with any other valuables that have been reserved. This being done, and the fire rebuilt, the basket and its contents are placed upon it; and while that is being consumed, cloths, blankets, dresses, beads, arrows, knives, pocket-handkerchiefs, and everything else that has been touched by the dead body, are added to the flames. When these are burned, every unconsumed log is

AN INDIAN WOMAN GATHERING ACORNS.

carefully scraped, all the ashes swept together, and the whole, with the exception of a small portion reserved for mourning, are placed in another basket, and then buried.

The reserved ashes after being mixed with pitch obtained from pine trees, is spread over the faces of the female relatives as a badge of mourning, and which, although very hideous to our sight, is sacred to theirs, is allowed to remain until it wears off, which is generally about six months.

Most of those Indians who bury their dead, although their belief in the future is similar to that of the others, have but one anxiety, and that is to put them in the ground before the coyotes cry at night, and then the heart is safe. These generally build a fire upon the grave.

All of the Indians, we believe without exception, cast the personal property of the

deceased, as well as presents of their own, into the grave, that he may want nothing when he joins his friends in the great camping-ground out west.

Several tribes hold the belief that after Indians die they lie three days in the ground and then go upward and become stars. Chiefs become "big" stars. They than go westward to the general camping ground.

If a woman dies while becoming a mother, the child, whether living or dead, is buried with its mother. When a child dies, it is completely enveloped in beads before it is buried, that it may have plenty of ornaments to play with and amuse itself in the other world.

In violent pains, of all kinds, they scarify and suck the place. A "doctor" will sometimes put a straw, or two or three grains of barley, or a small stone, into his mouth, and make the patient believe such to have been the cause of his suffering, and which he has been fortunate enough to remove. An Indian of fine stature and good disposition, who made his home with Judge Ward, in Indian Valley, Plumas county, had the misfortune to fall from a horse, and was taken up senseless. Four young Indian women immediately opened a vein in his temples and sucked out the blood until he recovered sufficiently to be removed from the house to their camp; where they tended him with the greatest care and kindness until he was convalescent, and again able to resume his usual duties about the farm.

For the cure of fevers, the Indians who live in the valleys generally enter an underground building, called the "sweathouse," constructed for the purpose, the roof of which is supported by posts, is covered with earth, and is generally water tight. A hole at the side forms the double convenience of a door and a chimney. A fire is made in the centre, or on the side nearest the patient, who reclines in a state of nudity on a shelf or bunk at the side until he is in a profuse perspiration, when he immediately leaves his underground steam-bath, and plunges into the river. This will generally cure him. If it does not, he repeats the experiment. This building is also used for the purpose of visiting in during the cold and wet days of winter.

Many of the Indians in the northern part of the State use the seed of clover grown in swampy places, as an antidote to poison oak. The "ring-worm" is cured by placing the milk of the poison oak in a circle round the affected part. But our knowledge of the practice of medicine among the Indians is exceedingly limited; and whether this arises from a neglect to enquire, or a contempt for the art; or a reluctance on their part to divulge "professional secrets," we are unable to determine.

The profession of "doctor" among them is very popular, and although their knowledge of Indian Medical science is exceedingly limited when compared with that of any of the tribes east of the rocky mountains, they sometimes perform a

INDIANS COOKING, IN FRONT OF THEIR HUTS.

AN INDIAN WOMAN GRINDING ACORNS AND SEEDS.

work; the men the eating, grumbling, and sleeping.—When a winter store of acorns is to be provided, all the women and children are sent out among the oak trees, to gather them.

A large cone-shaped basket is carried at the back by means of a band that extends across the forehead from the sides of the basket; into this they are thrown as they are picked up. They are then taken to camp and spread upon the ground to be dried by the sun; after which they are tied in cloths and stored in huts or trees,* or are ground for present use.

Seeds, next to acorns are the greatest staple they can command for winter consumption. To obtain these the women and children go into the valleys and woods and beat them into their capacious mouthed baskets, with a bush; and after taking them to camp, dry them in the same manner as the acorns; and then clean them by tossing them up from a flattish shaped basket, at the same time blowing out the chaff and dust, if the breeze is not strong enough to do it for them.

Clover forms a favorite repast in early spring, when it is young, and as this grows in great plenty by every little stream, an abundance is easily obtained. The same may be said of grass and various kinds of salads and greens.

Roots of various kinds are much prized, and which are generally dug with a pointed stick, and eaten raw like the others. From this employment, we presume, originated the name of Digger Indians.

few simple cures, and, on this account, are looked up to with considerable respect. In their charges they are very exorbitant, and as they are able to live on the fat of the land (of Diggerdom) and the life they lead is exceedingly easy; their young men are as anxious to become members of "the faculty" as our young dependent-spirited "bloods" are to become politicians.

Before the influx of the whites the Indians lived principally on acorns, roots, weed and flower seeds, clover, gnats, wild greens, sap of the white pine, mushrooms, grasshoppers, rabbits, rats, squirrels, fish, and sometimes antelope or deer; or anything else that could be easily obtained; but since the discovery of gold they will linger around cabins and slaughter houses for any refuse they can find; although they manifest no objections whatever to a well cooked meal of vegetables and meat, or any scraps they can collect from the white man's table.

As before alluded to, the women do the

*The storing of acorns in trees is now almost abandoned on account of their destruction and waste, from sheer wantonness, by thoughtless or unprincipled whites.

Grasshoppers are a great luxury, and are used as meat, and eaten in various ways. Sometimes they are caught, threaded on a string, hung over a fire until they are slightly toasted, and then eaten from the string. At others, the grass is set on fire, which both disables and cooks them, when they are picked up and eaten, or laid aside for future use. The most popular method of providing these, however, and which we have seen most frequently, is, in first digging a hole deep enough to prevent their jumping out; after which a circle is formed of Indians both old and young, and male and female, who with a bush in each hand, beat from side to side, now with the right then with the left, when the insects keep jumping toward the hole, into which they fall and are there caught. They are then gathered into a sack and saturated with salt water. A trench is then dug, and in it a fire is built, after which the ashes are cleaned out, and the grasshoppers put in, and then covered with hot rocks and earth until they are cooked. They are then taken out and eaten, in the same manner as we eat shrimps; or put away to mix with acorn or seed meal, after being ground into a pasta.

Acorns, berries and seeds of all kinds, are reduced to flour by the women, who sit upon a flattish rock and with an oblong stone weighing from six to ten pounds, grind it to powder by repeated blows.

Their process of boiling the flour thus ground, is very primitive. Bowl-shaped and water-tight baskets, holding from two to four pecks, are nearly filled with water, into which the flour or meal is stirred to make it of the consistence needed; when rocks, that have previously been heated until they are nearly red, are immersed, and the water boils. When the mush is sufficiently cooked, it is poured into smaller baskets to cool, from whence it is eaten with the two forefingers. Rabbits, rats, squirrels, with other meats, and fish, are either boiled in a similar manner, or broiled upon a stick.

Antelope and deer are generally surrounded on a rainy day, and driven into a swampy place, where they mire, and are then taken.

Hunting is too active an employment to square with their ideas of ease and comfort, and consequently is not very vigorously followed. If a deer is killed with bow and arrow, or even with an old shot gun or musket, as they have such now, it is not from any systematic purpose or plan of hunting, but simply by accident.

In the spring season, a grand fandango is given, to which all the tribes that are friendly to each other, or to which they are related by intermarriage, are invited, and which not only answers the usual purpose of such a gathering, but is about the same as a prayer meeting for plenty of all kinds of food.

To the casual observer, a fandango is a wild, careless, free-and-easy dancing and feasting party, and nothing more. To the Indians it is a friendly gathering together of the remnants of their race for the purpose of perpetuating and cementing the bonds of union more closely between each other and the various tribes around; and at the same time to transmit from generation to generation the great deeds and noble actions of their forefathers. According to our estimate of the latter named virtues, this exercise might be conducted with great brevity; but, if they can ennoble and elevate each other, by telling of some kind action, however small it might have seemed in our eyes, let us not despise it. Any particular tribe wishing to have a fandango sends messengers to all the chiefs of the surrounding tribes, to whom they give the invitation and a bundle of reeds, or sticks, to indicate the number of days to elapse before it takes place; sometimes notches are cut in a stick, or knots are tied in a string, for that purpose. Then

THE ATTACK.

the tribe giving the invitation proceeds to select a suitable spot on which to hold the fandango; the one that is most shady and pleasant, and nearest to good water and plenty of firewood, is preferred.

Extensive preparations are immediately commenced. Rabbits are snared, fish are caught, acorns are ground, panola provided, roots are dug and washed, grasshoppers taken and dried, and large pieces of firewood gathered, besides beef, flour, and other luxuries obtained from white men, in readiness for the day. It must not be supposed that the tribe giving the invitation provides everything for the occasion; by no means, as every one who attends takes something to make up the variety and quantity of the general table.

At such seasons, both male and female dress themselves according to their most extravagant notions of paint and feathers. Several weeks are frequently consumed in making head-dresses and other ornaments, of feathers, shells, and beads, in which the top-knots of quails, and scalps of the red and black headed California woodpecker, show to great advantage. These and numerous other ornaments of considerable value are prepared, and perhaps not used more than once before they become a portion of the offerings to the dead.

When the day arrives, groups of Indians may be seen wending their way to the festive scene; and, as many have to travel fifteen or twenty miles, the whole day is consumed in assembling together and conversing in groups on little family matters.

In the evening, when all are assembled, the "band," (which consists of about a dozen men, with reed whistles, and wooden castanets with which they beat time,) begins a monotonous *"feu-feu"* with their whistles; while the dancers follow their leader with the castanets, and keep time in a perpetual "*hi hah! hi hah!*" until they are out of breath, when they take their seats, to listen to a speech from their greatest chief or patriarch, in which he recounts the heroic deeds of their noble warrior ancestors!

About thirty-five or forty are dancers for the evening, while the others sit down and look on, and sometimes break into a loud laugh at some mishap or mistake of a dancer.

When the first dance is over, the feast commences, and justice is certainly done the eatables provided. It is a scene that is rich with gluttony and drollery; and once seen, the remembrance is never obliterated from the memory. The feast concluded, the dancing is renewed, and continued until morning, when they finish the provisions that were left over at supper-time, and retire to rest beneath the shelter of a tree.

These dancing parties are frequently continued for several days, and, (as at others more fashionable) many a Digger youth falls irretrievably in love with some fair (!) Digger maiden.

This being properly understood by the parties most interested, the fortunate lover gathers together such property as he possesses, and repairs to her father to strike the bargain. The old man looks surprised, hesitates, looks at the candidate for his daughter's hand, then at the amount of goods that is brought him as an equivalent for his child. The question being argued, (of course eloquently,) if the match is considered a good one, the old man's thoughtful face relaxes into a smile, the property is exchanged, he tells him to make her a good husband, and the union is complete.

With some of the tribes, when an Indian wishes to marry, the female runs and hides herself; and, if the male succeeds in finding her within a given time, they live together.

There seems to be no formal marriage ceremony among the California Indians. The wife being looked upon as a species of slave property, a trade is made and they unceremoniously live together.

Frequently when a man is hunting for a wife he plays upon a small reed whistle; and as the women understand it, he is invited to tarry for a talk, or allowed to pass on according to the estimate in which he is held by those he may visit for the purpose.

They frequently gamble away their wives just as they do any other kind of property.

Quite often a given number of Indian men agree to fight for a certain number of Indian women, on which occasion each party puts up equally. As soon as either party is victorious, the women, who have been awaiting the chances of this kind of war, arise, and go with the victors, apparently satisfied with the result.

To obtain women is a frequent and only cause of war among them. When any particular tribe runs short of squaws, it unceremoniously steals some from an adjoining tribe, which on the first favorable occasion returns the compliment—sometimes with considerable interest.

Polygamy is common. Some of the chiefs have from four to seven wives. As among the Mormons this is regulated by their ability to support them. Many of the "undistinguished diggers" have from three to five wives.

Before concluding this article we wish (with all their imperfections and obstacles, and they are many) to give our testimony in favor of the Reservations established by government to teach the Indian race the arts of agriculture, and the principles of self reliance. They are doing much to ameliorate the condition of the race, and in staying the sweeping hand of annihilation. But while we accord thus much to the system, we enter our protest to the promiscuous and libidinous intercourse allowed at these reservations by those placed in charge. In our opinion, founded upon observation, no officer should be appointed, no white man employed who has not a wife to accompany him there; and who could have as eleva-

AN INDIAN FANDANGO, AT NIGHT.

ting an influence with the females as the husband has with the males.

We would also suggest the desirability of teaching the mechanic arts, in all its various branches, to the men; and of giving some suitable and acceptable employment to the women. Active employment being as great a civilizer among men as any code of morals ever promulgated.

THE SAILOR'S DEATH.

BY A NEW CONTRIBUTOR.

"Homeward bound" a swift-winged vessel
  Sped upon her joyous way :—
One amid a group of gladness
  On a death-bed helpless lay.
Dimly rose the distant mountains
  Gladdening every sailor's eye !
"Shipmates! let me see the landmarks,
  Raise me up before I die."

"I have lived a life of peril
  Battling tempest, storm and gale,
I have mocked at death and danger
  When the bravest men grew pale !
I have lived upon the ocean,
  Let my grave be in the sea,
Let no earth clods press my bosom,
  Let no coffin fetter me."

Night had settled on the ocean,
  Thunders pealed in solemn tone'!
Nearer, from the clouds of blackness
  Came the muttering tempest's moan.
Upright rose the ghastly sailor,
  As the lightnings lit the sky,
In a desperate death struggle,
  Wildness in his glaring eye.

"Shipmates!" curses rest upon ye,"—
  Fiercely shook his bony hand,
"I will haunt your dying moments
  If ye bury me on land."
Morning broke—the smiling hill-slopes
  Spread like paintings to their view,
But the sailors sank their shipmate
  In the waters deep and blue.

THE IRON HORSE.

ELIHU BURRIT, the learned blacksmith, thus eloquently discourses upon the iron horse:

"I love to see one of those huge creatures, with sinews of brass and muscles of iron, strut forth from his smoky stable, and saluting the long train of cars with a dozen sonorous puffs from his iron nostrils, fall gently back into his harness. There he stands, chemping and foaming upon the iron track, his great heart a furnace of glowing coals; his lymphatic blood is boiling in his veins; the strength of a thousand horses is nerving his sinews—he pants to be gone. He would "snake" St. Peter across the Desert of Sahara, if he could be fairly hitched to it; but there is a little, sober-eyed tobacco-chewing man in the saddle, who holds him in with one finger, and can take away his breath in a moment, should he grow restive and vicious. I am always deeply interested in this man, for begrimmed as he may be with coal diluted in oil and steam, I regard him as the genius of the whole machinery—as the physical mind of that huge steam horse."

Now for ourselves we want to see this "iron horse" snorting and puffing through one of the many passes of the Sierra Nevada mountains, and as he rushes on, on, beneath the shadows of our densely timbered forests, or darts across or down our beautiful and fertile valleys; we don't care if all the Indians in creation lift up their hands in wonder at it, or fly with fear from before it. We want a Railroad.

What care we if this or that political party make it a hobby, jump astride it, and seek to ride into power upon it; all we say is—*give us the Railroad,* give it to us *somebody*—give it to us *anybody*—give it to us *everybody*. It is the RAILROAD that we want; and

The Pacific and Atlantic Railroad, the immediate want of the age, and of the people of the United States.

we will not quarrel about the source from whence it comes. We don't care who gives it, who pays for it, or whether it pays for itself—to us that is of lesser importance, altogether. Give us the Railroad, gentlemen senators and congressmen, and give it to us *at once.* No shirking, no shuffling, no log-rolling delay, no quibbling, no subterfuges, nor substitutes. We want *the Railroad.* Yes, we, THE PEOPLE want it, *and must have it.* And please not forget that *we want it without delay! Progress* prays for it—*Commerce* waits for it—*Peace or War* demands it. Then why not give it? Besides we want "to go a visiting 'the old folks at home,'" and as we can't afford to go one way, we want to go the other; and there are many more just like us—too many. You who live in comfort and luxury at home must not forget the "red shirts" and workers here. Certainly not. Then there are a *few* of our acquaintances east of the Rocky Mountains, yet; and they wish to have a little pleasure trip to see us—"drop in to breakfast" early some morning, and after "panning out" a little gold—just enough for a finger ring,— to say good bye, and return by way of Salt Lake City, to see the "Saints" and elders, and their wives, as well as take a peep at the little saints, just to see, you know, if they are like other little people: and what is of more importance, find out if the saints of the masculine gender are simply men, or giants, that they can manage more than *one* wife.

Then, again, we want to send our friends a basket or two of our ripe luscious peaches, and a box of our "five pound bunches" of tempting, mouth-watering grapes, and a car-load or two of our forty-five pound watermelons, and a thousand other good things that we have, for dessert.

Besides there are *one* or two articles we wish to import in quantities—and the first to be mentioned is *muslin*, with a pretty, good-tempered, loving, kind-hearted, intellectual, and contented lady-love, within it; or, if you will give us the latter we will grow all that we want of the former. Now if that one consideration is not enough to tempt you to give us the Railroad, we will talk to you about China and the East Indies, and—well, all the places and things that must come and go upon this great highway towards the setting sun, and the rising of empires on the broad and beautiful Pacific, &c., &c., &c., until you go to sleep: and, on awaking, find yourself a day behind the age. The "*Iron Horse*" gentlemen, the IRON HORSE, THE IRON HORSE—give it to us *at once,* and our consequent prosperity shall tell you how much we appreciate the gift.

"MADAM —— How is it that you are always so early at church? Because it is one part of my religion, not to interfere with the religious worship of others."

[We hope that the *gentleman* who wears creaking boots, and always enters church about the middle of the service, will, to oblige us, read the above twice over, and in future if he *will come late,* take his boots off before walking down the aisle to the farther end of the church; and when he *departs,* carry his boot-jack under his arm, in the same way he used to do his Bible!]

REMEMBER IT.—The natives upon the Isthmus of Panama have a saying concerning fruit, that it is *gold* in the morning, *silver* at noon, and *lead* at night.

Editor's Table.

THERE are times in the history of districts, as well as of nations, when passing events write their greatness and importance upon the age. It is thus with California. Ten years ago she commenced the entry of no insignificant record. Then she startled the world into a doubtful possibility that an age of gold was about to be inaugurated. Ten years ago two men were conversing together, at Coloma, upon the probability that Australia contained as vast and as rich a field of gold as California. One of those men was Marshall, the discoverer of gold in California, and the other was Hargreaves, the discoverer of gold in Australia. That conversation led to the latter result. Ten years ago, men, in respectable numbers, began to people the almost unoccupied valleys bordering the great Pacific, and began to lay that foundation upon which the present glorious superstructure of progress is gradually arising. Ten years ago, the population of California was less than twenty-seven thousand; now it is nearly six hundred thousand. Then the whole country was an uncultivated wilderness; now its valleys are gardens of loveliness. Ten years ago, not the echo of a white man's voice resounded from the mountain and pine-topped walls of the rivers; now nearly every cañon is made vocal by the hum of human voices. Ten years ago, Solitude held supreme sway in the densely-timbered forests and fastnesses of wild beasts; now the woodman's axe and miner's pick announce that Solitude is no more. Ten years ago, electricity was unknown here as a channel for human thought; now we have nearly one thousand miles of telegraph line; and, even while we are now writing, the electric current is being taught to leap the tops of the Sierras—not at random, but under the discipline of human mind. Ten years ago, the East and the West were united only by vast desert solitudes; now lines of mail stages are becoming the means of a brighter union, and their way-stations the nucleus of sundry outposts of civilization. Ten years ago, the overland emigrant required one hundred and seventy days to reach the green valleys of the Sacramento from the Mississippi; now he can accomplish it in twenty-four, and probably in eighteen days. Ten years ago, no steamship plowed the waters of the great Pacific; now there is a fleet which puts us in a communication with old homes and new ones—the great regret is that it should be controlled by a monopoly. Ten years ago, no cities· or villages, except those of the Indian, dotted the uneven landscape; now they are to be seen alike in the fertile valleys, among the rocks of the mountain streams, and on the tops of the mountains, giving out the busy hum of active life and civilization. Ten years ago, the prow of but an occasional vessel plowed the wave-crested foam of our principal harbor, San Francisco; now its annual tonnage makes it the fourth in the Union—excelled only by New York, Boston and New Orleans. Ten years ago, her exports consisted, almost exclusively, of hides and tallow, and that but in limited quantities; now her annual export of gold alone exceeds seventy millions of dollars; then add to that quicksilver, lumber, shingles, sheepskins, hides, tallow, wool, flour, oats, wheat, barley, potatoes, salmon and a hundred other articles of lesser extent and value, and we may ask, what has indeed been wrought within the last ten years? Ten years ago, but a single newspaper—and that an American (the Californian)—was published from the Gulf of California to the Polar Sea; now, in this State alone, there are nearly ninety newspapers and periodicals. Ten years ago, the only articles of manufacture, with few exceptions, were the seed-gathering and cooking baskets of the Indian; now we have nearly eight hundred saw, quartz and grist-mills; besides iron and brass foundries, machine shops, sugar refineries, a paper mill, soap, perfumery, furniture, safe, lock, broom, candle and cracker manufactories, and an untold number of others. These, and a thousand unmentioned causes, have united to assist California in writing her importance upon the ever-changing pages of history, and are suggestive of what she might be if her destiny were united to the East by that long-hoped-for, but too-long-delayed Atlantic and Pacific Railroad.

Monthly Record of Current Events.

As this was compiled, and by some oversight mislaid until it was too late for insertion this month, we are reluctantly compelled to defer its publication until next.

SANTA CLARA'S DAY.

A feeling of sadness unconsciously steals over one, as he looks upon the changes that American civilization has brought to the native Californian and Mexican resident in California, since the conquest in 1846, and the discovery of gold in 1848. Politically and socially, they had experienced many changes, anterior to the advent of so numerous a band of enterprising men as the conquerors proved. But, when they came, the world seemed to be in danger of being turned upside down to the native residents; and to the prejudices, employments, social habits, and amusements of the former, they evidently became so. The half-dreamy and semi-religious teachings introduced and practiced being more like a compromise between the barbarian on the one hand, and ethical refinement on the other, than any particular system of theology taught elsewhere.

As in other countries, where the Spanish language is indifferently spoken, and the Roman Catholic religion in its most depraved aspect, is a branch of the national belief, both men and women attend mass on Sunday morning, and in the afternoon a bull fight, at which the priests themselves are often present. Yet this differs only in a degree with the more refined amusements of the present age, with all its pretentious religious progression; having this distinction, however, that it is not only not customary, but is unmistakably unpopular for a religious teacher to be found in the theatre, or ball-room, or engaged at a game of ball or billiards on the Sabbath day.

Now, although by an act of the State Legislature, all barbarous amusements are suppressed, and all cruel sports very justly interdicted, both on week-days and Sundays, many others of a highly exhilirating and amusing character are still permitted, and enthusiastically practiced by the Spanish-Catholic population around the old Missions, especially on feast days, in honor of their saints. Of these, Santa Clara seems to be by far the most popular of all the saints in the calendar, and consequently receives a proportionate amount of attention.

Our readers are aware that the Mission of Santa Clara, situated some forty-eight miles south of San Francisco, was dedicated to this favorite personage, who is looked up to and feted as the Patron Saint of the Mission; and although nearly all the lands that belonged to it are claimed by settlers, who have divided it up, fenced and planted it, so that waving trees, flourishing fields of grain, fruit orchards, flower gardens, and beautiful cottages, almost exclusively fill up the landscape,—there the old Mission Church still stands on the plaza, with which is connected the most flourishing educational Catholic College in the State.

At sun-rise of the day especially devoted to this favorite Saint, the matin-bell calls the dusky sons of the soil to

NATIVE CALIFORNIAN AT FULL SPEED, TAKING THE BURIED ROOSTER BY THE HEAD.

prayers. It is an interesting sight to see them issuing from their humble tile-roofed dwellings, the señoras and señoritas dressed in the brightest of all the principal colors, and with the men sauntering near them, wending their way to the house of prayer. Then with the men to enter the solemn and shadow-filled edifice devoted to supplication, and hear the low matins chanted, or watch the solemn ceremonials at the altar, and the equally solemn countenances of the worshippers, and it will carry you back, far back, into that shadowy part of their history that you cannot but remember with pity, that they have been so far distanced in the race of life by a higher civilization, with which they have had no sympathy, and are consequently left behind.

But the moment the threshold is re-crossed, and their feet tread the dusty road, or the green sward in front of the church, a change, apparently amounting to an entire transformation, is everywhere visible. The muttered response is exchanged for the merry, musical laugh, and the bent posture for a lively light-footed skip. All the plans for a day of thorough enjoyment are eagerly discussed; and all the preparations in progress for a general holiday are recounted.

Wayside stalls laden with fruits, cakes, sweetmeats, toys and refreshments of various kinds, stand here and there—all of which are well patronized by the juvenile branches of the family, and their visitors, who come in from all the surrounding ranches.

As soon as their early mid-day meal, such as we call breakfast, is over, which is generally about eleven o'clock, some introductory pastimes are indulged in by the younger pleasure seekers, and which, about one o'clock, P. M., give way to such as are most popular among the adults. As these are somewhat numerous, and would, if fully described, far exceed the limits of a magazine article, we must content ourselves by noticing only a few of the principal ones.

As every native Californian is as much at home on a horse, as a Sandwich Islander is in the sea, and as horses are their particular pride, even while they excessively abuse them, and skill in riding is esteemed as among the first of accomplishments, those sports, which afford the most favorable opportunities for their display, and the costly caparisons of the animals they ride, are by far the most attractive. One of the most popular, next to horse-racing, is the following:

The body of a live rooster is buried in the earth, with nothing but the head visible above ground, a signal is given to the horseman, who is in readiness about sixty yards distant, when by a sudden plunge of the spur the horse is rode rapidly forward, and if by a dexterous swoop the rider can stoop low enough and succeed in taking the bird by the head while the horse is at full speed, he bears off the trophy with triumph, amid the applause of the concourse assembled. But, should he fail in the effort, as frequently happens, he not only loses the favors he expected to win, but is sometimes unhorsed, with violence, and dragged in the dust, at the risk of breaking his limbs or his neck, and greeted with derisive laughter from the spectators. Horses and their trappings, and oftentimes sums of money, are staked upon the success of such an attempt.

Another source of amusement, is to place a raw-hide flat on the ground, then after riding at full speed for some distance, to rein the horse suddenly in the moment his forefeet strikes the hide; if by any possibility this is not accomplished, the rider is berated for his unskillfulness.

Cock-fighting is by no means the least attractive divertisement among the men; but as this ought to be classed among their every day pastimes, it is generally reserved for small occasions.

But the greatest of all sources of gratification to all classes and sexes, were the bull-fights, and bull and bear fights. As San Jose and her sister Mission of Santa Clara were the most flourishing of all the Missions, and as the latter was the especial favorite of all the Patron Saints, her bull-fights were the best in the country. After the discovery of gold, and before their grounds were much settled up by the Americans, they continued them with more zeal and magnitude than ever, until prevented by the town authorities in 1851, which was the last time they were permitted within the limits of the town.

On this occasion it was acknowledged to be the most extensive they had ever had; and was continued for nearly a week. Twelve bulls, two large grizzly bears, and a considerable number of Indians were engaged, at different times, for the amusement of the assembled multitude. In the second day's encounter, four Indians and one horse were killed, and several wounded by the bulls; the loss of the horse seemed to cause far more regret than did the Indians. When the latter were gored by the sharp horns of the bull, the band would strike up a lively tune to smother his cries or moans, and the people appeared to be immensely pleased at the performance.

The Padre in charge at the time was a Franciscan, and evidently enjoyed the sport, but he was removed the following year, and a Jesuit appointed in his place, who denounced all such cruel sports from the altar, to the great displeasure of the Californians generally.

Although this day is still the greatest holiday time at these two Missions, horse-racing in all its diverse maneuverings, with dancing and other harmless pastimes, are the principal methods now engaged in to spend the day pleasantly.

Santa Clara's Day, of the Franciscan Order, recurs on the 12th of August, and this is the day observed at the Mission of Santa Clara. It will be well that this distinction should be remembered, as there is another Santa Clara's Day, on the 18th August, originated by a different Order.

NATIVE CALIFORNIANS THROWING THE LASSO.

Editor's Table.

THE encouraging favors extended to our Magazine, from contributors and friendly well-wishers, leave us indebted in many grateful remembrances of their kindness; and we trust our acknowledgments will be shown in the progressive improvement of each department of our work, as experience teaches to us our wants, and kindly solicitude adds to our list of contributors and subscribers.

We can assure our friends that we are anxious to have a magazine that will reflect the thoughts and aspirations of Californians, and make a lonely hour pass off pleasantly: something, that when the miner is tired with his hard day's labor, he can peruse with pleasure: yet, something that the merchant or professional man can take up and find that his thoughts are drawn away from the business of the day, with all its cares. Something, too, that the lovers of the beautiful may delight to see, as we picture the scenery and the wonders of our magnificent State.

It is very cheering to find that from all portions of the State, we receive words of commendation and encouragement, and a steady increase in the number of subscribers. We hope our friends will continue to extend their favors; and we certainly shall our endeavors.

———

It is with great pleasure that we notice the progress of the mechanic arts in California, and the development of that mechanical skill which is a source of prosperity as well as pride to any State, and especially to a new one like ours. One of the most beautifully perfect specimens of mechanical skill that we have seen upon this coast we saw a few days ago at the office of Dr. E. K. Jenner, 108 Montgomery street, San Francisco, who although an excellent surgeon dentist, has employed his leisure time in making a highly-finished, double-barrelled, revolving rifle, entirely his own workmanship and design, even to the tools necessary to its construction. The barrels, and a revolving cylinder, containing seven chambers, are made of the finest quality of cast steel. The locks, plates, trimmings, &c., are forged from horse-shoe nails, carbonated into steel. The tube-chamber, powder-bed, bands, thumb-piece, &c. &c., are all made of gold, to prevent corrosion; and the whole are so beautifully and compactly fitted that, with a spring here and another there, pivots yonder and screws somewhere else, it operates with the ease and precision of clock-work. The cap-house, containing fifty-four caps, is fitted in the cylinder, and made to revolve at will, and entirely independent: yet, at each movement, a cap is thrown upon the tube by means of a concealed spring, and at each cocking of the hammer the cap is taken off and the tube left clear. The chambers are loaded from the muzzle, by means of an extension rod which is neatly fitted between the two barrels, and is there securely held with a spring, and can be taken out and replaced easily and speedily. The lock is so arrang'd that it can work with or without a hair-trigger. This rifle discharged a ball through a seasoned piece of redwood, sixteen inches in thickness, and afterwards struck an object at the distance of half-a-mile. Both barrels can be fired at the same time, if desired.

We should like to see the grizzly bear whose skull would turn a ball from this rifle. If the Doctor should take out a patent—as we understand he has no thought of doing—we believe such a rifle would become a great favorite with hunters, and would bring him a pecuniary reward for his mechanical genius.

We are glad to see that we have such men among us, and we shall ever be pleased to notice the progress of anything appertaining to California, and especially so perfect and beautiful a piece of workmanship as that shown to us.

SAN FRANCIS, Sept. 20, 1856.

MR. EDITUR :—My Deer Sur,—I did'nt rite to you, last munth cause I never do anything in a passhun. If I had rit then I shonld hev rit in a passhun. My blud biled all over when I seed that ere letter I sent you stuck in your Magazeen. I rit it to you privit, just to give you a little frendly device and you hev went and printed it and put my name down in full length at the bottom of it. What will my frends think of me wen they see it? I tell you what it is Mr. Editur, you hev bruised my confedenc. You thort to sell your book by xgibbiting my name as one of your distrib-iturs. You thort to make my name and my litterary reputation secure prescribers for Hutchings Callforny magazeen *without fashon plates*—I know you did. Then anuther thing, you sed you ment to onsult your Artis about sum fashon plates. Hev you ever dun it? No i'll warrent you hevent. Now I can't see no reason on airth why you should be so dif-ferent to your own good, unles you are an old bachilur and then I dont wunder at it. A marred man would know how necesary fashons are to femails and women and that a book without fashons in it is no beter than a ship is that's lost her ruder, and cant no more make hed way in socity than a woman can without cloths made in the fust stile of fashon. Yes, the more I think of it the more I'm sure of it that your Magazeen aint suted to the litterary character of our femail people nor never will be Ontill you put the fashons in it, and ef you Dont put em we dont take your book—there Now—and I shood like to know how men is going to get along without us femails, us peci-bly editurs. Youve got my dandur up, for surtin in that tother letur of mine and now you may put this un in if you like.

I meen too, to find out wether you am a bachilur or no—for if you are, you can no more make a editur than you can anything else. I dont want to speak too discuragin, because I want to see a Californy magazeen,

and as I am a littel anxus about its duing well I may try if I cant get sum rale Smart woman to marrey you, and then you and the maga-zeen will do fust rate, and I'll be bound she'll see that you'll hev the fashons.

MRS. MARY METWITH,
Mother-in-law to Gudge Swinem.

P. S. —Would you just Anser me wun questen Mistur editur About that bachilur bisness, and send it through the post directed

Mrs. MARY METWITH.

Now Mrs. M., how do you suppose we feel after that lecture? Don't you believe that at this moment we are prospecting for the smallest kind of a knot-hole, that we may creep through and be no more seen forever; but ready " to leave this world and climb a tree?" Did you intend that " shame should burn our cheeks to cinders?" " What then is man? The smallest part of nothing." And we are sorry, for we will say with Shakspeare, " He was not born to shame :
Upon his brow shame is ashamed to sit."
And we will also add, that although

" 'Tis man's pride,
His highest, worthiest, noblest boast,
To stand by helpless woman's side,"

and, we suppose, give her the fashions! yet, we must say no. Mrs. M., we cannot give you the fashions: and if we had the most coaxing and the prettiest little piece of goods in the world for a "rale smart wife," it couldn't be did. What would Godey say? Why, "Pshaw! he ought to know better." And our artist made the remark—a very beau-tiful remark it was, too—"pshaw! nonsense !" Then wife says she's going to look after you, and added something about writing to widows (she says she knows you are a widow,) through the post-office, and something about birds, and chaff; and I don't know what. We are, how-ever, sorry that we have " bruised your con-fedenc ;" but if you had instructed us not to publish your letter, why we should never have dreamed of such a thing. Now, is that explanation enough? because we must *obey* the wife about that post-office business!

ANSWERS TO CONTRIBUTORS AND CORRES-PONDENTS.

R.—We felt about seven years younger, after perusing your article. All right, old boy. " There's a good time coming," yet.

Juvenile Department.

ALWAYS BE GRATEFUL.

"How long you staid away, mother, and I am so sick; this pillow is so hard; Papa and sister don't know how to take good care of me, as you do. I wish you would never leave me again, until I get quite well."

These were the fretful words addressed by little Henry Gray to his mother, as she re-entered his room, after an absence of about half an hour.

"Do not fret, my son," said the kind mother, as she seated herself by the bedside, and gently passed her cool hands over Henry's feverish brow. "I do not like to see you indulge this fretful disposition. I fear you forget to be thankful to the good God who has given you so many blessings, and so many kind friends to love and take care of you. Look about this room, my son; is it not furnished with everything to make you happy? Is not the carpet soft and beautiful? When you look at its gay flowers you may almost think yourself in a beautiful garden. The chairs with their soft, red cushions, seem to invite you to them; the table almost groans under the weight of pretty toys and elegant books; even your little Canary, outside the window, seems to call upon you to join him in his song of thankfulness."

"I don't care for any of them, mother," replied the wayward boy; "I don't like the room, nor anything in it; I don't like to be sick, and take nasty medicine, and lie in this old bed all day."

"I know, my child, it is not pleasant to be sick, but it is sometimes necessary, and then we should try to be as patient as we can. Shall I tell you where I went when I left you this morning? You remember little Johnny Davis, whose mother died last month, and who lives in the little shanty at the end of the lane?"

"O, yes, mother, I remember."

"Well, my son, I went to see him; he is very sick, much sicker than you are, and his father is very poor so that he has to go away to work, every day, and that leaves little Johnny quite alone, all day, unless some kind neighbor happens in to see him. Poor little fellow, how glad he looked to see me this morning when I went in, and how he thanked me for an old coverlid which I took over to cover him with, for Johnny has no nice bed like yours, with soft, warm blankets to cover him, nor any nice pillow to lay his little hot and aching head upon—some coarse straw thrown loose upon the hard floor, is all the bed he has, and his little torn pants are his only pillow. The room is bare and dirty; an old box turned upside-down, answers in place of a chair; the stove is a broken, rusty, old thing, and looks as if it had not had a fire in it for many a day. That, with the pine table which his mother used to keep so nice and white, but which is now black and dirty, is all the furniture the house contains, except a few pieces of broken delf. Johnny has no kind sister to wait upon him, while his father is absent; no one to give him medicine to make him well, no kind mother to make him nice gruel, or bathe his little hot hands and face. There he lays all day, alone, neglected and very dirty; his little flaxen ringlets which used to look so nice, when his mother was alive are now a tangled mass. When I went there this morning, I took that toast which you said was not "fit to eat;" you ought to have seen how eagerly he ate it, only stopping to say "it was very good of you to bring me nice toast to eat. Dear mamma used to make me toast, but since she died I haven't had any." I took some water and washed his hands and face, and as I did so, the tears came into his eyes. he said "Oh, your hands seem so like my poor dear mamma's, but, she is dead, and can never wash her little Johnny's face and hands any more." I tried to sooth his feelings, by talking to him a few moments, promising to see him soon again, and hastened home to you, my son. Oh, what a contrast there is between your happy home, and his miserable and uncomfortable shanty. You have everything to make you happy; he has nothing, but his contented spirit and his sweet, submissive disposition."

"Mother, I see that I have been a naughty, thankless boy. I will try to be more patient, in future: and spare you often, to go and see little Johnny, and please take him some of my nice things, every time." CARRIE D.

A FAIRY WEDDING.

"O, then I see, Queen Mab hath been with you."—*Shakspeare.*

Come join your hands and hie with me,
A Fairy wedding you shall see;
Come sit ye down upon the grass,
And see the pigmy pageant pass;—
First, drink this draught, while I a spell
Will put upon this fairy dell.
Here comes my lady Emmet, gay,
Grasshoppers chaunting, line the way;
She's seated in an acorn shell,
Joined to daisy wheels so well,
And by such perfect mimic art,
No earthly genius can impart.
Her earwig steeds are swift in pace;
Her cobweb reins she holds with grace;
Her whip, a trophy of yon plain—
A spider's leg—in battle slain;
Her guards, red-coated lady birds,
Advance in order, close in herds;
Now see them how they form in lines,
And how their dotted armor shines,—
And whither does she drive away—
To yon green hillock bright and gay.
The fairies bid the zephyrs blow,
The hair-bells joining are not slow,
But merry peals ring one, two, three,
To lead the great festivity.
Meanwhile, the pigmy fairies rove,
And flit about through vale and grove;
Gathering dainties rich and rare,
To make a sumptuous bill of fare.
Under a tent-convolvulus white,
Invited to keep out of sight

The vulgar gazing of the crowd,
Who rent the air with huzzas loud;
Her carriage stops; and my lord ant,
Who waits almost with bosom faint,
Helps her alight with graceful hand;
While crickets guards, with all their band,
Strike up a merry, chirping strain,—
My lady bows and smiles again,—
Lord ant, for her, thanks them aloud,
And makes a speech above the crowd.
Now to the feast:—On mushroom's spread—
Grown in one night, where fairies tread—
A gossamer table-cloth is placed,
Whereon the fairies show their taste.
Some tiny seeds, both ripe and good,
A strawberry fresh, from neighboring wood,
A giant grain-choice of the field,
By fairy arts already peel'd;
Nectar, pressed by fairy hand
From honeysuckles of their land;
Some tiny drops of fragrant dew,
Which lillies oft display to view,
And which the fairies have distilled,
And every moss-seed-bottle filled.
Now a huge beetle from his hole,
In shining surplice black as coal,
Is summoned to perform the rite
And make them one.—A solemn sight.—
After the cloth's from table cleft,
The crowd now feast on what is left:
See how they scramble, push and crowd.
Hear how they hum and whiz aloud.
But now, a moth the signal giving,
All's hushed as though no one were living·
The happy pair ascend the car—
'Tis growing late, their home is far—
With the loud huzza, and one cheer more
Proclaims the solemn rite is o'er.
The glow-worms light them on their way,
The fairies guide 'till break of day,
And watch, until they're out of sight,
Then wish them all "good night," "good
    night."
                                MARIAN.
SAN FRANCISCO, Oct. 20th, 1856.

There are more elements of success in the single beat of a stout heart, than in all that this or the other can say or do. If you want to get along and be good-looking, smart and well off as anybody, don't be afraid.

EFFIE IS DEAD.

WORDS BY J. C. MORRILL.

MUSIC BY JAS. C. KEMP.

Moderato affetuoso con espressione.

Step lightly, breathe softly, Speak not a - loud, She lies there so

meekly in her snow-white shroud; Her eyes once so beaming their lustre have

shed; She lies as if dreaming, But O! she is dead.

We watched her while dying—
  Her pulse, faint and low,
Hung trembling a moment—
  Her life seemed to flow
Like the ebbing of waters,
  Then settled to rest,
And Effie had gone to
  The home of the blest.

Sweet music from heaven,
  When dear Effie died,
Seemed floating around her
  On every side.
The harps of the angels
  Breathed softly and low—
A grief in our gladness,
  A joy in our woe.

We decked her with flowers
  Sweet-scented and fair—
A wreath on her coffin,
  A rose in her hair;
We know that their petals
  Will shortly decay,
But Effie will float with
  Their perfume away.

Step lightly—breathe softly—
  Speak not aloud;
She lies there so meekly
  In her snow-white shroud!
Her eyes, once so beaming,
  Their lustre have shed,—
She lies as if dreaming,
  But O! she is dead!

HUTCHINGS'

CALIFORNIA MAGAZINE.

Vol. IV. SEPTEMBER, 1859. No. 3.

STATE ASYLUM FOR THE INSANE.

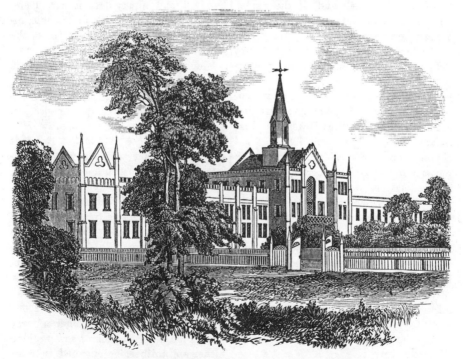

VIEW OF THE WEST FRONT OF THE STATE ASYLUM.

IF ANY person would fully realize the untold blessedness of a sound mind, let him pay at least one visit to the Asylum for the Insane. The vessel that left our port but yesterday with every timber sound, and every rope and sail in order, her captain skillful and her crew able seamen, spreads her canvas to the breeze and rides in majesty past the rocky shores of the Golden Gate, and out to sea, may, even when the pilot is at the helm, and after braving in safety many a storm, strike some unknown and unexpected reef and become a total wreck. How very often is it thus with the human mind? From sources and causes the least suspected, they strike and founder in the deep, dark sea of chaotic delirium; or, as sometimes is the case, are stranded upon the sandy shore of circumstances, for a season, until the next spring-tide of Reason lifts them up, and they are borne upon it by the favoring breezes of kind attentions, back again to the joy-welcomed haven of Consciousness, and are themselves again once more. Ah! blessed return.

A few days ago we visited the Asylum which the State has provided for the unfortunately afflicted, and, if the reader pleases, we will relate to him that which we saw and heard.

The building is situated in the suburbs of the city of Stockton, about three-quarters of a mile northeast of the steamboat landing, and which, as you approach, presents an imposing and very inviting exterior. The beautiful flowers and luxuriant foliage of its well laid out and cleanly kept grounds—the work of the patients themselves—tend very much, in our estimation, to relieve it of that repulsiveness which many very naturally feel when visiting such an institution for the first time.

We had scarcely rang the bell, and been shown into a sitting-room, on the left of the entrance, when the resident physician, Dr. Aylett, very kindly offered to escort us through its long corridors and numerous apartments, to see for ourselves the various phases of the minds diseased.

But as the Doctor has been called away for a few moments, while he is absent we will relate to the reader that Capt. C. M. Weber, of Stockton, donated one hundred acres of land to the State for this purpose, and on the 17th of May, 1854, an Act was passed, and appropriations made, by the State Legislature, establishing the Asylum for the Insane. About twenty acres, out of the one hundred, are in a high state of cultivation, and from which an ample supply of vegetables are obtained; and as there are about one thousand five hundred young and thrifty fruit trees growing, of different kinds and varieties, fruit will be obtained next year in abundance.

The buildings themselves are commodious and conveniently arranged. The main structure is seventy feet square and three stories high, to which two wings have been added, of the same hight, each of which is one hundred feet in length, making, in the aggregate, three hundred and ninety feet front. There are two large yards, male and female, inclosed by a wall twelve feet high at the lowest grade line.

The management of this Asylum is entrusted to a Board of five Trustees, appointed by the Legislature, who discharge their duties without compensation, and whose term of office expires in 1861. Dr. William D. Aylett is the Resident Physician, under whose general superintendance the institution is managed, and whose salary is $5,000 per annum. Dr. Thomas Kendall is the Visiting Physician, who attends daily and prescribes for each patient, and whose salary is $3,000 per annum. But here comes the Doctor, so let us depart with him and inspect the building and its inmates.

As we began to tread the bright, clean floors of the first story, we were somewhat at a loss to divine whether a large proportion of those men we saw walking hither and thither, or engaged in some useful employment, were patients or assistants and keepers; but our guide soon relieved us of any doubt in the premises, by informing us that they were patients, and that this division of the building was devoted to those whose cases were of a milder type. Some were reading, others were writing, in one or another of the rooms opening on the main corridor; and the rest were walking up and down, as if meditating. From here we passed into the yard, where some were sitting beneath the shade of a tree, amusing themselves with a game well known among children as "Fox and Geese"; others were looking on, or seeking the shade of the doorways and walls. Here also was a wooden tower, and a water tank capable of holding 7,000 gallons, into which water is pumped up by steam power, and from thence distributed in pipes to every part of the building. Here also is the dining-room, and hot and cold baths for the men, each one of whom is required to bathe once a week, some twice a week, and others every day, just as their case requires.

From the yard we re-entered the building, and examined the store-rooms, kitchen-range, and other apartments on the ground floor, and found them very conveniently arranged; after which, we ascended to the second story, where the corridors were divided into several compartments by a strong lattice-work, the doors of which were kept locked. As might be expected, here the countenances of the patients indicated a more malignant form of the disease; and although a few were employed in some useful or amusing occupation, a large proportion were wandering up and down, talking to themselves; others, as though glad to see strange faces, sought us for their auditors, while they descanted upon the pastimes they were about to enjoy; the vessels they owned, and hourly expected from some prosperous voyage, with very valuable cargoes; the noises they heard; the apparitions they saw, &c.; but as it would be impossible to give scarcely a brief epitome of these things in this article, we shall refer to them in some future number.

What was our astonishment here to hear our name several times pronounced by different persons, with the inquiry— "Don't you know me, Mr. ——?" and from some of those, too, whom we had known under very prosperous circumstances, several long, long years ago. How Change, Disappointment and Misfortune sometimes do their work! We noticed, too, that although their hands were extended to us in warmth and kindness, and their faces were lighted up with a gleam of brightness, it was but momentary.

From this point, we passed to the female department, and which was as cleanly kept as that of the males. Here, one woman, who had passed the prime of life, was engaged in working a sampler, on which a rude attempt was made to give it the resemblance of a planet, under which she persisted she had been born; some nodded and smiled; others looked solemn and melancholy; others, again, were sewing, and knitting, and reading.

It is a depressing sight, indeed, to witness either man or woman when reason is dethroned; but it is a wise provision of the State that such should be well cared for, and by kind and suitable treatment, both physical and mental, restored to their former sanity.

The most prolific causes of insanity, we regret to learn, are masturbation and intemperance, especially the former; next to these, want of chastity and incontinence is another very productive source of this malady; to these add physical debility, loss of property, disappointment in love, puerperal fever, spiritualism, religious excitement, epilepsy, fright, and various other evils, both mental and physical.

The number of patients now under treatment in this institution, are two hundred and eighty males, and sixty-six females, making in the aggregate three hundred and forty-six.

THE MASSACRE AT MOUNTAIN MEADOWS.

THE MOUNTAIN MEADOW MASSACRE.

It will be remembered that some of the heart-sickening details of this terrible massacre have appeared at different times in the public journals of the day. By the kindness of a friend we are enabled to place before the reader two illustrations of the scenes, and in connection therewith a brief narrative of that fearfully cold-blooded slaughter. Perhaps we ought here to remark that the numerous statements are so very conflicting that we find it next to impossible to give a succinct and reliable history of the sad event; but from the various sources from whence information has been received the following will be found nearly to approximate to correctness.

"A train of Arkansas emigrants, with some few Missourians, said to number forty men, with their families, were on their way to California, through the Territory of Utah, and had reached a series of grassy valleys, by the Mormons called the Mountain Meadows, where they remained several days recruiting their animals. On the night of September 9th, not suspecting any danger, as usual they quietly retired to rest, little dreaming of the dreadful fate awaiting and soon to overtake them. On the morning of the 10th, as with their wives and families, they stood around their camp-fires passing the congratulations of the morning, they were suddenly fired upon from an ambush, and at the first discharge fifteen of the best men are said to have fallen dead or mortally wounded. To seek the shelter of their *corral* was but the work of a moment, but there they found but limited protection.

"To enable you to appreciate fully the danger of their position, I must give a brief description of the ground. The encampment, which consisted of a number of tents, and a *corral* of forty wagons, and ambulances, lay on the west bank of, and eight or ten yards distant from, a large spring in a deep ravine running southward; another ravine, also, branching from this, and facing the camp on the southwest; overlooking them on the northwest, and within rifle-shot, rises a large mound commanding the corral, upon which parapets of stone, with loopholes, have been built. Yet another ravine, larger and deeper, faces them on the east, which could be entered without exposure from the south and far end. Having crept into these shelters during the darkness of the night, the cowardly assailants fired upon their unsuspecting victims, thus making a beginning to the most brutal butchery ever perpetrated on this continent.

" Surrounded by superior numbers, and by an unseen foe, we are told the little party stood a siege within the corral of several days, sinking their wagon-wheels in the ground, and during the darkness of night digging trenches, within which to shelter their wives and children. A large spring of cool water bubbled up from the sand a few yards from them, but deep down in the ravine, and so well protected that certain death marked the trail of all who had dared approach it. The wounded were dying of thirst; the burning brow and parched lip marked the delirium of fever; they tossed from side to side with anguish; the sweet sound of the water, as it murmured along its pebbly bed, served but to heighten their keenest suffering. But what all this to the pang of leaving to a cruel fate their helpless children? Some of the little ones, who though too young to remember in after years, tell us that they stood by their parents, and pulled the arrows from their bleeding wounds.

" Long had the brave band held together; but the cries of the wounded sufferers must prevail. For the first time, they are (by four Mormons), offered their lives if they will lay down their arms, and gladly they avail themselves of the proffered mercy. Within a few hundred yards of the corral faith is broken. Disarmed and helpless, they are fallen upon and massacred in cold blood. The savages, who had been driven to the hills, are again called down to what was denominated the 'job,' which more than savage brutality had begun.

" Women and children are now all that remain. Upon these, some of whom had been violated by the Mormon leaders, the savage expends his hoarded vengeance. By a Mormon who has now escaped the threats of the Church we are told that the helpless children clung around the knees of the savages, offering themselves as slaves; but with fiendish laughter at their cruel tortures, knives were thrust into their bodies, the scalp torn from their heads, and their throats cut from ear to ear.

"To-day, I ride by them, but no word of friendly greeting falls upon my ear, no face meets me with a smile of recognition; the empty sockets from their ghastly skulls tell me a tale of horror and of blood. On every side around me for the space of a mile lie the remains of carcasses dismembered by wild beasts; bones, left for nearly two years unburied, bleached in the elements of the mountain wilds, gnawed by the hungry wolf, broken and hardly to be recognized. Garments of babes and little ones, faded and torn, fluttering from each ragged bush, from which the warble of the songster of the desert sounds as mockery. Human hair, once falling in glossy ringlets around childhood's brow or virtue's form, now strewing the plain in masses, matted, and mingling with the musty mould. To-day in one grave, I have buried the bones and skulls of twelve women and children, pierced with the fatal ball or shattered with the axe. In another the shattered relics of eighteen men, and yet many more await their gloomy resting-place.

I have conversed with the Indians engaged in this massacre. They say that they but obeyed the command of Brigham Young, sent by letter, as soldiers obey the command of their chief; that the Mormons were not only the instigators but the most active participants in the crime; that Mormons led the attack, took possession of the spoil; that much of that spoil still remains with them; and still more, was sold at the tithing office of the church.

Such facts can and will be proved by legal testimony. Sixteen children, varying from two to nine years of age, have been recovered from the Mormons. These could not be induced to utter a word until assured that they were out of the hands of the Mormons and safe in the hands of the Americans. Then their tale is so consonant with itself that it cannot be doubted. Innocence has in truth spoken. Guilt has fled to the mountains. The time fast approaches when justice shall be laid to the line, and righteousness to the plummet."

On sending a statement to Utah Territory, in April last, Brigadier General Clarke directed the officer in command, Major J. H. Carleton, 1st Dragoons, to collect and decently to bury the remains of the victims of the Mountain Meadow Massacre.

Arriving at Mountain Meadows, Maj. Carleton found that the General's wishes had been in part anticipated by Captain R. Campbell, 2nd Dragoons, who, "on his way down," says Major Carleton, "passed this spot, and before my arrival had caused to be collected and buried the bones of twenty-six of the victims."

Major Carleton continues: "On the 20th instant, I took a wagon and a party of men and made a thorough search for others amongst the sage bushes for at least a mile back from the road that leads to Hamblin's house. Hamblin, himself, shewed Sergeant Fritz, of my party, a spot on the right hand side of the road where he had partially covered up a great many of the bones. These were collected, and a large number of others on the left hand side of the road, up the slope of the hill, and in the ravines and among the bushes. I gathered many of the disjointed bones of thirty-four persons. The number could easily be told by the number of pairs of shoulderblades, and by lower jaws, skulls, and parts of skulls, etc., etc. These, with the remains of two others, gotten in a ravine to the east spring, where they had been interred at

THE MONUMENT.

but little depth—thirty-four in all—I buried in a grave on the northern side of the ditch. Around and above this grave, I caused to be built, of loose granite stones, hauled from the neighboring hills, a rude monument, conical in form, and fifty feet in circumference at the base and twelve feet in height. This is surmounted by a cross, hewn from red cedar wood. From the ground to the top of the cross is twenty-four feet. On the transverse part of the cross, facing towards the north, is an inscription carved deeply in the wood:

"VENGENCE IS MINE: I WILL REPAY SAITH THE LORD."

"And on a rude slab of granite, set in the earth and leaning against the northern base of the monument, there are cut the following words:

HERE
120 *Men, Women, and Children,*
WERE MASSACRED IN COLD BLOOD, EARLY
IN SEPT., 1857.
They were from Arkansas.

"I observed that nearly every skull I saw, had been shot through with rifle or revolver bullets. I did not see one that had been 'broken in with stones.' Doctor Brewer showed me one, that probably of a boy of eighteen, which had been fractured and split, doubtless by two blows of a bowie knife, or other instrument of that character.

"I saw several bones of what must have been very small children. Doctor Brewer says, from what he saw, he thinks some infants were butchered. The mothers, doubtless, had these in their arms, and the same shot, or blow, may have deprived both of life.

"The scene of the massacre, even at this late day, was horrible to look upon. Women's hair, in detached locks, and in masses, hung to the sage bushes and was strewn over the ground in many places. Parts of little children's dresses, and of female costume, dangled from the shrubbery, or lay scattered about; and among these, here and there, on every hand, for at least a mile in the direction of the road, by two miles east and west, there gleamed, bleached white by the weather, the skulls and other bones of those who had suffered. A glance into the wagon, where these had been collected, revealed a sight which can never be forgotten."

The Mormons set up the plea that some of this party poisoned a spring, by which several persons and some stock fell victims. But that so large an amount of poison could be in the possession of an emigrant train is most improbable. On the other hand it seems scarcely probable that plunder alone could be a sufficient inducement to the murderers to sacrifice so great a number of human lives. Indeed, the *cause* of this wholesale slaughter is to this hour shrouded in mystery. Major Carlton most probably knows it better than any other man, and we much regret that we have not his entire and candid report. That it was committed by Mormons, aided by Indians, there can be no doubt. Judge Cradlebaugh thus brings the matter home to them in his charge to the Grand Jury of Provo City, in March last:

"I may mention to you the massacre at the Mountain Meadows. In that massacre a whole train was cut off, except a few children, who were too young to give evidence in court. It has been said that this offence was committed by the Indians. In committing such an outrage, Indians would not so discriminate as to save only such children as would be unable to give testimony of the transaction in a court of justice. In a general slaughter, if any were to be saved by Indians, they would have been most likely those persons who would give less trouble than infants. But the fact is, there were others there engaged in that horrible crime.

"A large organized body of white persons is to be seen leaving Cedar City late in the evening, all armed, traveling in wagons and on horseback, under the guidance and direction of the prominent men of that place. The object of their mission is a secret to all but those engaged in it. To all others the movement is shrouded in mystery. They are met by another organized band from the town of Harmony. The two bands are consolidated. Speeches are made to them by their desperate leaders in regard to their mission. They proceed in the direction of the Mountain Meadows. In two or three days they may be seen returning from that direction, bearing with them an immense amount of property, consisting of mules, horses, cattle and wagons, as the spoils of their nefarious expedition. Out of a train of one hundred and forty persons, fifteen infants alone remain, who are too young to tell the sad story. That Indians were engaged in it there is no doubt ; but they were incited to engage in it by white men, worse than demons.

"I might give you the names of the leading white persons engaged, but prudence dictates that I should not. It is said that the Chief Kanosh was there. If so he is amenable to law, and liable to be punished. The Indians complain that in the division of the spoils they did not get their share—that their white brothers in crime did not divide equally with them, but gave them the refuse."

CLEAR LAKE, FROM THE RIDGE NEAR THE GEYSERS.

CLEAR LAKE.

The above excellent sketch of this mountain-bound sheet of water, has been kindly furnished us by Mr. Geo. Tirrell, an artist of great merit, who has spent nearly three years in picturing on canvas the beautiful scenes of California. As we never had the pleasure of seeing this remarkable lake, and as it has been well and fully described in our cotemporary, the *Hesperian*, we take pleasure in transcribing the article entire:

This beautiful Alpine sheet of water, overshadowed and hidden, so to speak, by surrounding peaks of the coast mountain, is one of the many inviting localities of our State, and deserves, as it is destined to be, far better known than it is at present. To the tourist, in search of the picturesque and sublime, the lakes of Switzerland could not present a more attractive feature. It is about fifty miles from Napa City, in a direction a little west of north. The route from the latter place to the lake, passes over alternate ranges of mountains and intervening valleys, presenting a variety of scenery that would well repay the journey, even without the crowning view of one of the greatest natural curiosities of California. Clear Lake is an enormous fountain, having no supply tributaries, save the numerous springs, many of them boiling hot, rising on its margin and perhaps welling up from its bottom. A small river runs from it called Cache Creek, which, after pursuing a southeasterly course about fifty miles, enters the Sacramento Valley, and is lost among the lagoons that border the river. The lake is near the axis or divide of the coast mountains, on their eastern slope, and has an elevation of twelve or fourteen hundred feet above the sea level. The shape is irregular, and extends N. W. from its outlet, in length, about twenty-five miles. The breadth is variable ; in traversing the lake from the outlet of Cache Creek, the shores alternately widen and contract from one to three miles, until, at a distance of ten or twelve miles, it is suddenly narrowed to less than half a mile ; beyond this, the shores recede away from each other, to meet again in the distance, inclosing a circular basin of twelve miles in diameter ; this portion is known as Big Lake, in contradistinction to the part east of the strait, which is called "Lower Lake." On the south side of the Big Lake is Big Valley, a fertile plain of considerable extent, bounded on the south by a mountain ridge that divides it from the waters of the Pluton river, tributary to Russian river. The portion of the lake east of the straits, is crowded by the mountains, which spring up from the water's edge. Towards the eastern extremity, however, they recede, and a valley is formed that extends five or six miles beyond the lake, down Cache Creek. The peculiar, sinuous shore line, gives rise to numerous little bays and harbors, where the light canoes of the Indians are anchored, when their dusky owners rest from their work of catching fish, or killing wild fowl, with which the water abounds. Several beautiful little islands, elevated but a few feet above the water, shaded with broad-spreading, evergreen oaks—of the extent of from one to fifteen acres, add much to the picturesque effect. To these secluded spots the Indians of the neighboring valleys have retreated; and the wreck of a tribe that, but a few years ago, was counted by thousands, now finds ample room for its diminished numbers on these isolated specks of land. They are a harmless and inoffensive people, and seem to have no difficulty with the whites. They live abundantly on fish and fowl, and the only dread they seem to have, is that they may be forced to go to some Government Reservation.

On the north side the mountains rise from the immediate margin nearly the entire length of the lake, leaving only a narrow pathway near the water. A few little valley coves of exceedingly fertile soil, lie hid in the folds of the mountain, and open to the lake their only outlet. The largest of these is called "Loon Valley," and contains about fifty acres. With this exception the north shore is bold and precipitous. The water has a depth of fifty or sixty feet to within a few yards of the land, all around the northern side; towards the eastern extremity there are, however, several little bays with shelving shores and bottoms. In one of these bays, numerous springs of boiling hot water make their way up through the fissures of the smooth rock bottom, extending from the margin of the water to a distance of two or three hundred feet into the lake, spreading along the shore to twice that distance, and forming one of the most delightful bathing places imaginable. You can have a bath of almost any temperature, by getting nearer or farther from one of the hot jets. Some caution is, however, requisite, as I found to my cost, by placing my foot, when wading about, over one of these jets. Several such places are observable, where hot water, accompanied with gas, issues from round openings in the rocks. In one place in the centre of the lake, I found gas bubbles, in large quantities, constantly agitating the surface, over an extent of hundreds of acres. The water was seventy-five feet deep, and although the surface presented no increase of temperature, I imagine the bottom was a locality of hot springs, such as I observed along the shore in shallow water. Some of these springs seem to be pure water, others are highly impregnated with mineral matters. The whole neighborhood abounds with mineral springs, generally hot, and the volcanic aspect of the country gives reason to believe that subterranean fires are yet active at no great depth below.

THE CITY OF STOCKTON.

This flourishing commercial city is situated in the valley of the San Joaquin, at the head of a deep navigable slough or arm of the San Joaquin river, about three miles from its junction with that stream. The luxuriant foliage of the trees and shrubs impress the stranger with the great fertility of the soil; and the unusually large number of windmills of the manner of irrigation. So marked a feature as the latter has secured to the locality the cognomen of "the City of Windmills."

The land upon which the city stands is part of a grant made by Gov. Micheltorena to Capt. C. M. Weber and Mr. Gulnac, in 1844, and who most probably were the first white settlers in the valley of the San Joaquin; although some Canadian Frenchmen in the employ of the Hudson Bay Co. spent several hunting seasons here, commencing as early as 1834.

In 1813 an exploring expedition under Lieut. Gabriel Morago visited this valley, and gave it its present name—the former one being "Valle de los Tulares," or Valley of Rushes. At that time it was occupied by a large and formidable tribe of Indians, called the Yachicumnes, which in after times was for the most part captured and sent to the Missions Dolores and San Jose, or decimated by the small pox, and now is nearly extinct. Under the maddening influence of their losses by death from that fatal disease, they rose upon the whites, burned their buildings and killed their stock, and forced them to take shelter at the Missions.

In 1846, Mr. Weber, reinforced by a number of emigrants, renewed his efforts to form a settlement; but the war breaking out, compelled him to seek refuge in the larger settlements, until the Bear flag was hoisted, when Capt. Weber, from his knowledge of the country, and the devotedness of those who had placed themselves under his command, was able to render invaluable aid to the American cause.

When the war was concluded, in 1848, another and successful attempt was made to establish a prosperous settlement here, but upon the discovery of gold it was again nearly deserted.

Several cargoes of goods having arrived from San Francisco, for land transportation to the southern mines, were suggestive of the importance of this spot for the foundation of a city, when cloth tents and houses sprung up as if by magic. On the 23d of December, 1849, a fire broke out for the first time, and the "linen city," as it was then called, was swept away, causing a loss of about $200,000. Almost before the ruins had ceased smouldering, a new and cleaner "linen city," with a few wooden buildings, was erected in its place. In the following spring a large proportion of the cloth houses gave place to wooden structures; and, being now in steam communication with San Francisco, the new city began to grow substantially in importance.

On the 30th of March, 1850, the first weekly Stockton newspaper was published by Radcliffe and White, conducted by Mr. John White.

On the same day the first theatrical performance was given, in the Assembly Room of the Stockton House, by Messrs. Bingham and Fury.

On the 13th of May following, the first election was held—the population then numbering about 2,400.

June 26th, a Fire Department was organized, and J. E. Nuttman elected Chief Engineer.

On the 25th of the following month, an order was received from the County Court, incorporating the City of Stockton, and authorizing the election of officers. On the 1st of August, 1850, an election for municipal officers was held, when seven hundred votes were polled, with the following result: Mayor, Samuel Purdy; Recorder, C. M. Teak; City Attorney, Henry A. Crabb; Treasurer, Geo. D. Brush; Assessor, C. Edmonson; Marshal, T. S. Lubbock.

On the 6th of May, 1851, a fire broke out that nearly destroyed the whole city, at a loss of $1,500,000. After this conflagration a large number of brick buildings were erected.

In 1852, steps were taken to build a City Hall; and, about the same time, the south wing of what is now the State Asylum for the Insane, was erected as a General Hospital; but which was abolished in 1853, and the Insane Asylum formed into a distinct institution by an act of the Legislature. In 1854 the central building was added, and in 1855 the kitchen, bakery, dining-rooms and bathrooms were also added.

On the 1st of February, 1856, another

fire destroyed property to the amount of about $60,000; and on the 30th of July following, by the same cause, about $40,000 worth of property was swept away.

Of churches there is an Episcopal, Presbyterian, Methodist Episcopal, Catholic, Methodist Episcopal South, First and Second Baptist, Jewish Synagogue, German Methodist, and African Methodist.

There are two daily newspapers published here, the "San Joaquin Republican," Conley & Patrick, proprietors; and the "Stockton Daily Argus," published by Wm. Biven. Each of these issue a weekly edition.

Of Public Schools, there are four—two Grammar and two Primary—in which there are about two hundred scholars in daily attendance, and four teachers, one to each school. There are also four private Seminaries—Dr. Collins', Dr. Hunt's, Miss Bond's, and Mrs. Gates'.

Stockton can boast of having the deepest artesian well in the State, which is 1002 feet in depth, and which throws out 250 gallons of water per minute, 15,000 per hour, and 360,000 gallons every twenty-four hours, to the height of eleven feet above the plain, and nine feet above the city grade. In sinking this well, ninety-six different stratas of loam, clay, mica, green sandstone, pebbles, &c., were passed through. 340 feet from the surface, a redwood stump was found, imbedded in sand from whence a stream of water issued to the top. The temperature of the water is 77° Fahrenheit—the atmosphere there being only 60°. The cost of this well was $10,000.

Several stages leave daily for different sections in the mines.

One of the principal features connected with the commerce of this city, is the number of large freight wagons, laden for the mines; these have, not inappropriately, been denominated "Prairie Schooners," and "Steamboats of the Plains." Some of these have carried as high as 32,000 pounds of freight.

LARGE MULE TEAM, GOING OUT OF STOCKTON, OFTEN CALLED "PRAIRIE SCHOONERS."

CITY OF STOCKTON.

BRIGHAM YOUNG.

Brigham Young, Governor and ex-officio Superintendent of Indian affairs of Utah Territory,—First President, Prophet, Seer, Revelator and Translator of the Church of Jesus Christ of Latter-day Saints, commonly known as Mormons, was born in the year 1801, in the state of Vermont; the same state which gave birth to Joe Smith, the founder of Mormonism. He is about five feet eight or nine inches high; stout body, well proportioned for labor; weighs between 175 and 200 pounds; light brown sandy hair, generally worn pretty long; face shaved close; light blue eyes; Hebrew nose; long upper lip; mouth tolerably large; chin ill-defined. When his mouth is open, his long teeth, his stout and strong under jaw and bull neck indicate to the spectator a ferocious disposition. The lower portion of the face is more developed than the upper; the animal predominating. His head from front to back measures little more than six inches. His countenance is unusually changable in expression; in fact he possesses great command over it, and readily changes it from the innocent playful expression of the school-boy, to the black and blood-thirsty visage of a cunning and cowardly villain.

BRIGHAM YOUNG.

Cunning, instead of wisdom, and hypocracy, instead of candor, are leading characteristics with him.

His temperament is a mixture of the sanguine and lymphatic. The lymphatic is plainly indicated under the chin, as seen in the picture. He walks like a blustering bragadocio—undignified—rolling his shoulders or body from side to side; and bluster instead of courage marks his rule.

When dressed in a common suit of black, with dress coat, he appears as a respectable but common farmer,—with his shirt in country bumpkin style, collar turned down, wristbands turned up over his coat sleeves. Usually he wears what may be styled a morning gown, of green merino, trimmed with velvet, over his ordinary clothes, doubtless to assist in rendering his appearance more dignified, as well as indicate his degree of priesthood. For strangers observe that the three heads of the Mormon hierarchy wear similar coats, differently colored; green, purple and blue.

In warm weather Brigham usually wears lighter colored and looser clothes, rendering him more dignified in appearance. To finish his dress he wears his hat eternally on the back of his head; in the pulpit as well as in the street.

He is deficient in dignity. The moment he relaxes his grumness or suspicious reserve—sometimes mistaken for dignity—he is thoroughly common-place, and fails to command respect except that which his peculiar position compels.

He is very illiterate, and seldom looks in a book from years end to years end. A stranger once asked him in Salt Lake for his autograph and birth-place, and in the place of Vermont, he wrote Vermount.

Of his history, antecedents, and his connection with the Mormons, but little is known, even among his most devoted followers. It appears, however, that he lived in western New York about or near the time and place that Mormonism took its rise. He then had a wife and two children, girls. He was known there as a trifling, shiftless fellow, procuring a mean and scanty living, by making and selling split baskets.

By trade, however, he appears to have been a house painter; but, that, for some reason, he did not follow. It is said he exhorted occasionally among the evangelists in that locality; although he has been heard to say since, that before his connection with Mormonism, he was a disbeliever in revealed religion. This probably may have been the fact, and his exhortations hypocritical, adopted merely to aid in securing a beggarly livelihood; for charity, it is said, was commonly extended to his sickly wife and helpless children.

In the year 1832 he connected himself with the then contemptible followers of Joe Smith, the Mormon. Since then his history is the history of Mormonism.

A little before or after he joined the Mormons, his wife died; and sometime in 1832 he arrived at the Mormon head quarters at Kirtland, Ohio, with his two children. Joe Smith furnished him with some work at painting, he receiving his pay out of the common stock crib. Since this, he has ever displayed exemplary loyalty to the person and doctrine of the now immortal Joe Smith, and often boasts in his public harangues of his undeviating fidelity to what may be

styled a Yankified rehash of Jesuitism.

After settling his family at Kirtland, he married the second time a lady named Angell, who is now alive at Great Salt Lake City, by whom he has had issue—two boys, Joseph and Brigham, and a girl now married. The two daughters by his first wife are also married and living at Salt Lake; one of them to her father's brother-in-law, under the polygamic system. His son, Joe, considered by pious Mormons a drunken rowdy, when about twenty, married at Salt Lake a cigar girl who lived on Fourth street, St. Louis, and well known to the fast young men of that city as not being over discreet. Brigham however said when he heard the report of the St. Louis Mormons who arrived with her, that she was as good as Joe, so that settled the marriage.

The second son, Brigham, is also married. He is short and thick set, of rough manners, but better liked than the taller and more delicately formed Joe.

From the best data, it appears Brigham has had about sixty wives; many of these, either for want of fidelity, or because they could not feel satisfied to allow him to divide his affections with so many, have been divorced, and some have darkly hinted at the Henry VIII system. At present, between forty and fifty acknowledge him as their husband. Of this number, some six or ten are held by proxy for the notorious Joe. Smith. Smith's mantle having fallen on Brigham, he had also to attend to their temporal wants. The Mormon poetess, Eliza Snow, brother of Lorenzo Snow, one of the twelve apostles, is one of this number; a sister of Huntington, the destroying Angel, and Indian interpreter, who had first a husband in the States whom she drove off for Joe Smith, and after Smith's death attached herself to Brigham, by each of whom she has had children; a west India sea-captain's widow, who is well advanced in years, and teaches music, but who in her strange career crossed the Atlantic from

England to the West Indies some twenty times; Mrs. Cobb, a Boston lady, who left her husband and grown up family and run off with Brigham, carrying her youngest child with her, being more ambitious of Heavenly distinction than many others, got Brigham to seal her to Joe Smith, since his death. These are the most conspicuous of the proxies. The remainder of Brigham's Goddesses (married women are considered goddesses; single are angels) vary from joyous sixteen to wrinkled sixty. Beauty and education are sadly wanting in his collection; for a more common, homely-looking set were never gotten together. The only way this can be accounted for is, that when he commenced forming his harem, the doctine was very unpopular, and he was compelled to put up with the best he could get.

The green-eyed monster, jealousy, finds plenty to occupy himself with in the domestic circle. The one most noted for jealousy is a tall lady, with two interesting little children. She has threatened Brigham with death, and to leave eyeless and bald some of his favorites. Brigham, through fear, has been compelled to leave her "solitary and alone" in a small cottage near his residence. He considers her a devil. Young Brigham, when he speaks to her, calls her by the expressive names of his "father's concubine," "legs to eternity," or "legs almighty." Naturally, she is a high-spirited woman; and but for the cursed Mormon delusion might have passed through life respectably and happy. She says that she forsook her relations for Mormonism; that they now look on her as a cast-away; and that she is fully determined to remain with the Mormons, and go to hell with them. Some fourteen of Brigham's wives ride to church in a big omnibus, known as "Brigham's carriage." This she calls a "flying brothel."

Brigham's children, by his Spirituals, do not number more than thirty. Many of them are fine-looking children; and chiefly girls. He has expressed himself as determined to marry his children, one to another. This incestuous connection, he says, is according to the sacred order of the priesthood.

Brigham's house is the first, with the exception of a small shed, near the Council house, that was built in Great Salt Lake City. When the Mormons first went to Salt Lake they built an adobe fort, in the shape of a hollow square, in which the whole colony lived the first winter. In the summer following, the house represented in the picture was erected, after Brigham's second arrival in the valley. It is built, as all buildings are there, of abodes or sun-dried brick, and then stuccoed with plaster of Paris, which is abundant in Utah. It contains three or four bedrooms, a parlor, and kitchen; and has been used specially as a residence for his first wife. Neither of the spirituals have ever been received there except as visitors. A long shed, divided like stalls, stood near it, in which some eight or ten spiritual families resided. The house is situated on a little knoll on the eastern side of City Creek— a small stream of pure water, which takes its rise in the Wahoatch mountains, seen behind the house, and is now separated near Brigham's house, running in little rivulets in every street in the city, being used for domestic purposes and irrigation.

The situation was well chosen. It overlooks nearly the whole of the city— particularly the southern and eastern portions; taking in at one glance the whole of Salt Lake Valley south of the city. From it can be seen on the east the lofty and eternally snow-capped Wahoatch range stretching south to the boundary of Utah Valley, fifty miles distant; in the centre of the valley the Mormon Jordan, which takes its rise in Utah Lake South, and describes its serpentine course till it reaches Great Salt Lake, where it

RESIDENCE OF BRIGHAM YOUNG, AT SALT LAKE CITY.

loses itself on the saline flats which border the lake; in the west, Tosele mountains, twenty-three miles distant, lofty as the Wahoatch, capped with a mantle of snow and girdled with clouds—its northern extremity jutting out into Great Salt Lake, whose mirror-like bosom, studded with rugged islands, and a setting sun on the far-distant Sierras behind the lake, radiating high into the blue and cloudless heavens tall columns of light, affords the beholder one of the most enchanting and sublime pictures that human eyes ever rested on.

The building to the left is a barn. Within a little time past Brigham has erected a more spacious seraglio, immediate west of the house represented in the picture.

He has numerous blood relatives near him in Salt Lake, among whom are numbered four brothers and a sister. Joseph is a diminutive, harmless personage, with a very religious whine and most saintly countenance. He has had a difficult hand to play, in trying to induce his first wife to consent to the spiritual wife system. John is a big, fat sot, and of no account to himself or anybody else. Lorenzo is short, stout, red-haired and coarse-featured—more industrious than either of the others. He is a bishop. Phineas is the eldest. His first wife lives in the States, and will not submit to polygamy. He is a schemer, and some say worse. Mrs. Murray, a very stout old lady, with a kind heart and genial manners, is the only sister. She was, however, a spiritual of Joe Smith.

Brigham's manners has always been considered rough and repulsive to his followers. In the pulpit he speaks with a great deal of ease and fluency. Profanity and obscenity are common-places with him when preaching.

He is well known as being fond of women. He is nearly as fond of brandy and Monongahela. Occasionally he gets on midnight carousal with a favorite few; becomes gloriously oblivious, turns summersaults, and sings—

> " The Lord into his garden went,
> To see if Adam had done his stint,
> And when he found the work was done,
> He passed around the bottle of rum.''

STOCKTON.

BY S. H. S.

In the tules of the lowlands,
  Bordering the San Joaquin,
With its bridges, mills, and Islands,
  Lakes around and lakes between,
Stockton looms upon the vision,
  With her cupolas and vanes,
And the prestige of position
  As the city of the plains.

With her villas neat and pretty,
  Hemming in the busy mart—
Of the system now the city
  Seems the great commercial heart;
Arteries in all directions
  Life unto the hills convey,
Men of fair and all complexions
  Strive and labor night and day.

From the golden mountains daily
  Comes the ore beladened team;
While her port with colors gaily
  Speaks the commerce of the stream;
And her summer fields are teeming
  With the golden fruits and grains.
Thus in hopeful promise beaming,
  Blooms the city of the plains.

PETER LASSEN.

WHO has not heard of Peter Lassen? —*old* Peter Lassen, as he is often familiarly called?—one of the oldest of our old pioneers, and after whom so many localities are named. For instance, we have "Lassen's Butte," a famous landmark at the head of the Sacramento valley, and from whence the main and north forks of Feather River obtain their source. Then there is " Lassen's Pass " of the Sierras, in latitude 41° 50′, and "Lassen's Big Meadows," on the upper waters of Feather River; and others, similarly named, on the Humboldt River. Indeed, from the pioneering proclivities of old Peter, every snow-covered peak, and every green valley, and pass of the Sierras, has become as familiar to his sight as the sombre top of Monte Diablo is to the residents of San Francisco. With this introductory, we will now give a brief biography of the man.

Peter Lassen, then, is a native of Copenhagen, Denmark. He was born on the seventh of August, 1800, and is consequently now in the fifty-ninth year of his age. At the usual time of life he was apprenticed to the trade of a blacksmith, in his native city. At the age of twenty-seven, he made his master-piece. Custom there requires, that before a young man can commence business on his own account, he must be able to manufacture some article in his trade that is difficult to accomplish, or the necessary government certificate will not be granted him. When this is received, he can go to any part of the country that pleases him, and there begin for himself.

In his 29th year, he emigrated from Denmark to the United States, and arrived the same year in Boston. After several months' residence in eastern cities, following his trade for a livelihood, he removed to the west, and took up his residence at Katesville, Charlton county, Mo., where for nine years he practised the two-fold occupation of blacksmithing and farming.

In 1838, he formed a military company of seventy-five men, ready for military duty, in his adopted State.

In the spring of 1839, he left Katesville, Mo., in company with twelve others —two of whom were women, (missiona-

PETER LASSEN.
From a Photograph by R. H. Vance.

aries' wives)—to cross the Rocky Mountains into Oregon. These fell in with a train belonging to the American Fur Company, which swelled their number to twenty-seven; and all traveled in company.

After the usual mishaps and fatigues of such an undertaking—when there were no roads, and the compass was their only guide—they arrived at the Dalles, Oregon, in October of the same year, leaving the two women at Fort Hall.

From the Dalles, they proceeded down the Columbia River to Fort Vancouver—then a post of the Hudson's Bay Company, but now belonging to the United States—and thence up the Willamette to a few miles above Campouit, now Oregon City; but as his company, (now reduced to seven men,) could not settle to suit themselves, after wintering here, they prepared to start for California.

As a sufficient company could not then be raised to cross the mountains and enter California overland, they were fortunate enough to find a vessel, named the "Lospanna," ready for sailing to San Francisco, after discharging its cargo of machinery and other articles for the missionaries of this district. This vessel was twice in danger of being wrecked, before getting fairly out of the Oregon waters ; once on Tongue Point, and once on a low rock at the mouth of the Columbia River.

Several weeks thus consumed, at last in safety they reached Fort Ross—then a Russian trading post, numbering some three hundred souls—from whence they obtained a pilot to Bodega, where they landed, and, after a short stay, attended with sundry difficulties with Gen. Vallejo and other Spaniards, they left for Capt. Sutter's camp, near the mouth of the American River, since known as Sutter's Fort, where they remained some fifteen days, and then started for Yerba Buena, now San Francisco ; but, shortly afterward, Mr. Lassen went to San Jose, to winter, where he worked at his trade for a living.

In the spring of 1841, he purchased half a league of land near Santa Cruz, where he built a saw mill, which was the first one ever built and put into successful operation in the country. A sawmill had been previously commenced, and partially built, at Fort Ross ; but, having been washed away, was not again rebuilt. After cutting from forty to fifty thousand feet of lumber, he sold out his mill and ranch to Capt. Graham—who still resides there—taking one hundred mules for his pay, intending to return with them to the United States ; but not being able to raise a company, the idea was abandoned.

In the fall of 1842, he took them up into the Sacramento Valley, and ranched them near Capt. Sutter's.

About this time Gen. Micheltorena, made him a grant of land, previously selected by Lassen, on Deer Creek, to which in the fall of 1843 he removed, with but one white man for his companion ; who, some two months afterwards, became tired of the solitary life led there, and left him ; when, although alone, surrounded by many hundreds of Indians, he lived in perfect safety, and without ever seeing a white man for nearly seven months. Having worked at his trade for Capt. Sutter, and received his pay in stock ; which, with the increase, he added to his band, he was now the possessor of between two and three hundred head ; and yet, from the first hour to the last of his residence there, not one was ever disturbed by the Indians. All the labor of building his house and cultivating his farm was performed by Indians.

In the fall of 1844, a circumstance occurred which ought to be associated with the history of this State, and which is this : Some whites visited the neighborhood of Mr. Lassen's residence, for the purpose of trapping beaver, with whom was an Oregon half breed named Baptiste Chereux, who, while camping with his company on Clear Creek, found a piece of gold, in weight about half an ounce . but, thinking it some kind of brass metal, kept it in his shotpouch, never dreaming that it was gold. After the gold was discovered at Coloma, this man returned to the same spot on Clear Creek, and discovered a very rich lead.

Col. Fremont, with fifty of his men, the following spring, remained some three weeks, sharing the hospitalities of Lassen's house ; for the full account of which we must refer the reader to Col. Fremont's journal.

In April, 1846, and about eight days after Fremont had left Lassen's on his way to the Dalles, Oregon, Mr. Gillespie arrived with dispatches for Colonel F., from the U. S. Government ; when Mr. Lassen and three others. after killing meat enough for the party, started after him, and delivered the dispatches in safety. On the Klamath Lake, the Indians of that tribe made an attack upon them in the night, after previously crossing them in their canoes ; but one of Lassen's party having rode on ahead of the rest some distance, and found Col. Fremont, he returned in time to offer succor to the little party of whites.

During the war with Mexico, Mr. Lassen took an active and efficient part. When that was ended, and peace proclaimed, he and others returned to their homes, when the gold discovery was made known.

Unfortunately, old Peter took a partner about this time, who, it seems by Lassen's account, was a great rascal ; when he, with some sharper lawyers, began to relieve him of his hardly-earned riches. After several years of litigation, and its accompanying annoyances, Mr. Lassen lost his house and lands, and every head of stock that he had so industriously gathered around him ; so that, in his declining days, he was driven to poverty and the loneliness of a mountain life, and now resides in Honey Lake Valley.

All the anecdotes and hair-breadth escapes of his eventful life, would make an interesting volume. We regret that our limited space has compelled us to give so brief an outline of his history ; but which, nevertheless, we hope will be found both interesting and instructive ; especially the closing moral—*Beware of bad partners, and nine-tenths of the lawyers*—and if need be, add the other tenth, and thus eschew law and lawyers altogether.

THE HONEY BEE
OF CALIFORNIA.

In connection with the illustration which we present to our readers, of the Apiary of Harbison & Bros, we also give a statistical sketch of the rise and progress of this, now quite lucrative branch of husbandry.

During the month of February, 1853, Mr. C. A. Shelton, formerly of Galveston, Texas, started from New York with twelve swarms of bees (in which Commodore Stockton and G. W. Aspinwall were interested) and arrived in San Francisco during the month of March following, with but one live swarm: this he put on board a steamer bound for San Jose ; en route the steamer burst her boiler and, though Mr. Shelton was numbered with the dead, his bees escaped nninjured, and were taken to San Jose. Of their increase we are not fully advised. In the fall of 1854, Messrs. Buck & Appleton, of San Jose, received the next swarm which was brought to California. During the fall of 1855, Mr. J. S. Harbison, of Sacramento, who was thoroughly acquainted with the habits and treatment of the bee from an early period of his life, sent East for a swarm, which arrived in Sacramento February 1st, 1856 ; most of the bees had died during the passage. Enough, however, remained to prove that, with careful handling, they could be successfully imported and allowed to propagate in California. Having full confidence in this, he returned to the Atlantic States in the spring of 1857, and prepared for shipment, sixty-seven swarms, with which he arrived in Sacramento December 1st of the same year. By the March following, the effects of the voyage reduced them to fifty, at which time they were again reduced to thirty-four, by sale. During the ensuing summer (1858) he increased these to one hundred and twenty; and in the fall he sold all save six. Again, on the steamer of September 20th, 1858, he went East for the purpose of transporting another stock, which had been prepared for that purpose during the previous spring and summer. On the 6th of December, he sailed from New York with one hundred and fourteen colonies, and arrived in Sacramento January 1st, 1859, with one hundred and three, in a living condition. Of this importation, sixty-eight were from Centralia, Illinois—the longest distance which bees have been known to be transported — the remaining forty-six were from Lawrence county, Penn. The length of his last voyage, together with the backward and unfavorable spring of 1859, decreased the number of this importation to sixty-two : these, with the remaining six from the previous year, he increased to four hundred and twenty-two colonies; or, at an average increase to the hive of five and seven thirty-fourths. During the fall just past, he sold two hundred and eighty-four swarms. The plan for the now celebrated "Harbison Hive," was perfected by J. S. Harbison, between the 20th of December, 1857, and the 18th of January, 1858, at which time he mailed his application for the patent, which was issued January 4th, of the present year; farther improvements have since been made by him which, in due time, will be made public. From as close an estimation as can be made, by those well informed, the State now contains three thousand two hundred swarms, of which number twelve hundred are in the Harbison hive.

Of the modes of importing bees to California, the most novel was that of Mr. J. Gridley, who brought four swarms across the plains from Michigan, lashed to the back part of his wagon ; he arrived at Sacramento on the 3d of August last, and seemed much surprised on learning

THE APIARY OF J. S. & W. C. HARBISON, SACRAMENTO CITY.

the extent of their cultivation in this State.

As an instance of the growing importance of this branch of industry, it may be of interest to state that Mr. L. Warner, at Sacramento, (who is the General Agent of Mr. Harbison) has sold, since the 1st of August of this year, upwards of sixteen thousand dollars worth of bees. Mr. W. has been engaged in the business since the year 1855, and sold the first swarm of bees in the Sacramento valley.

Many of those interested in bees, have of late expressed fears lest the country would soon be overstocked: if such persons will consider for a few moments the large population of this State, and which is daily increasing, but few of whom, as yet, have *a single swarm*, (for all the bees in the State are contained in *nine* counties) and let them also consider that the people of the United States are *but just finding out how* to make bee keeping profitable, and if this will not quiet their nerves, let them make a few figures on the demand and limited supply of honey. In Germany, where the best and most scientific attention has been devoted to bee keeping, for the last *two centuries*, and whose authors have thrown more light upon the natural history of the bee, than any others in the known world, the people find the business very lucrative. To one who has not made a close calculation, it may seem a bold assertion, but it is an undeniable fact, that California can export honey and wax with profit to the New York market! The climate of California is peculiarly adapted to bee culture; for, while a swarm in the Atlantic States does well when it produces two swarms and from twenty-five to thrity pounds of honey, in the vicinity of the Sacramento river, five strong swarms can be made from the one that will yield surplus honey during the season, which may be set down as from the latter part of February to the first of November,—eight months! two-thirds of the year! And there is not a month in the year but what they may be seen out of the hive. It has been said that "the bee will cease to lay up stores for winter when it learns that forage is so easily obtained"; those who speak thus, certainly know nothing of its natural history, *for no bee* (save the queen) *ever lives over six months*, and during the height of the working season, they seldom attain the age of fifty days ; hence, if no better reason could be produced (and there can be) they would never find out the fact in time to profit by it. In any and all countries, bees *will* work, as long as they have pasturage, and room in which to store the produce of their labors.

————

The honey bee, which from the early dawn of civilization, has been the wonder of philosophers and the admiration of poets, is now attracting a degree of attention in this land of flowers, that will, in the course of a few years, enable us to speak of our State as one literally "flowing with milk and honey."

Much in regard to the habits of this interesting insect, which was formerly enveloped in profound mystery, has recently been explained, through the agency of the ingenious transparent hives that are now in common use ; and many of the facts which curiosity has discovered, have been of great pecuniary benefit to the practical apiarian.

In the family of twenty-four thousand, which compose a good swarm of bees, there are about two thousand drones and one queen. The others are called workers. The queen is a large, long, graceful insect, with a small waist and small wings ; she moves about in the hive with great rapidity, depositing her eggs in the cells prepared by the workers for that purpose, and acts as the leader in the exodus of the new swarm. She lives about three years.

The workers which, of course, compose the most of the hive, are small and compact in form, and vigorous in their movements. They are supposed to be imperfectly developed females, and are generally called neuters. They have the power of producing from the ordinary grub or egg, a queen, when, from any cause, one is required. The means by which this singular result is accomplished, is not known, but it is believed by some of those who have given the matter their careful attention, that a peculiar kind of food, which unerring instinct designates, has much to do in producing the queen!

The drones, which are the males, are considerably larger than the workers, and move about slowly, rarely leaving the interior of the hive, except in very pleasant weather. They collect no honey, and in autumn they are nearly all destroyed by the workers, to which they fall an easy prey, being destitute of stings.

Nursing the young, building the cells and collecting the honey together, with all the fighting with rival swarms, devolves upon the workers; which in industry, and in fidelity to their superiors, afford an example worthy of the imitation of rational creatures.

Volumes might be written upon the singular habits of the bee, but I propose to simply state a few practical facts in connection with bee raising in California, and to point out the great advantages it has over other localities. It has by some been sagely assumed that, on account of the mildness of our winters, bees will have no *motive* for working, and will, consequently, become "lazy"; but this belief is unfounded in philosophy or fact, for, bees work from *instinct*, and not from motive, as for the attainment of an object which reason shows to be necessary, and it is a fact that in the Red river swamps, where the climate is more mild than that of this State, bees abound in the greatest profusion, and fill the trees with vast quantities of honey which they never consume.

All things considered, California, as a honey producing State, has no equal. The climate is not so warm as to melt the combs, and so mild are our winters that the bees can work during the entire year, in the vallies. During about two months in the rainy season, they do not collect quite so much honey as they consume; but, during the remaining ten months, they are constantly accumulating a surplus.

In the Atlantic States, they produce but little honey between the last of June and the middle of September, the time at which the buckwheat fields are in bloom, when they enjoy a short season of honey-gathering, that is suddenly terminated by the frosts, which make them consumers until the blooming of orchards in the ensuing spring. In this State, at all seasons, they have access to rich honey-producing sources, among which I may mention the tule swamps, the bottom willows, the mustard fields, the numerous flower gardens, and the vast profusion of wild flowers which, during a considerable portion of the year, beautify our fertile plains, and gracefully undulating foot hills, and adorn even the lofty summits of our mountains. In the valley of the Sacramento, there is a peculiar plant or shrub which, in the dryest part of the year, affords large quantities of the finest honey.

In the valley of the San Joaquin, after the spring flowers are past, during the months of July and August, they gather mainly from the Button-bush; and from that time to the end of the year, nearly every oak tree being covered with a kind of honey dew, they gather from this their main harvest. The sap of the Osage orange is also much used. Their principal time of working is from ten to three o'clock.

From one hive, in Capt. Webber's garden, at Stockton, housed April 5th, 1857, the following quantities of honey were taken the same year: —

27th April.............18 pounds 6 ounces.
4th June................17   do
5th July................17   do   8   do
20th July..............20   do
11th August..........20   do
2d September........19   do

and during the same month, twenty lbs. more, giving a total of 132 pounds surplus honey, and one swarm of bees.

To every twenty pounds of honey, about one pound of wax is produced. Honey left for their sustenance during the winter was never touched; proving that a certain amount of honey is produced here all the year. Since then they have yielded from two to three swarms of bees per year, and when this is done, less honey is gathered and stored.

Moths, and other insects, which often prove destructive to bees in the Atlantic States, have seldom given the apiarian any trouble, except in the case of weak hives, brought from the East. The natural vigor of the bees in this country, enables them to repel all such foreign invaders.

In the Atlantic States a hive rarely swarms more than once in a season; but here, a single hive has been known to produce in one year, no less than nine healthy swarms, making, with the original, ten swarms; and, in one instance, in Sacramento county, a single hive produced eight swarms direct—two from the first new one, and two from the second—making an increase of twelve swarms in one year, which, with the original hive, yielded one hundred and twenty-five pounds of honey.

When the production of honey is the principal object, the swarms are not divided so often as when the multiplication of the number of hives is desired by the owner. Under favorable circumstances, five good swarms can yearly be produced from one, when increase in the number of hives is the main object; and, under ordinary circumstances, an increase of four per year may be put down as a moderate average. If the production of honey be the leading object, each old hive will annually yield two new swarms, and with these new swarms, furnish one hundred and fifty pounds of honey. In this State each hive will, of itself, yearly produce twice the quantity of honey which, with the same amount of attention, it would yield in the Atlantic States.

The ruling price for a full hive of bees is one hundred dollars. Eighteen months ago, a gentleman in San Jose, purchased six good hives for six hundred dollars, and since that time, he has realized from their increase alone, the snug sum (in cash) of eight thousand dollars.

Such are a few brief but significant facts concerning the culture of bees in this State. The demand for honey which, at wholesale, is worth about fifty cents per pound, is greater than the supply, and even at greatly reduced prices, bee raising must, with the facilities afforded by California, remain a safe, profitable and agreeable business.

Of the many moveable comb hives now in use, Langstroth's is considered by many practical apiarians, as one of the best; but the common bee hive answers a very good purpose, and perhaps, for those unacquainted with the bee business, they are preferable to any of the complicated patent hives.

Among the books on bee culture that may be read with profit by those interested in the further examination of this subject, I may mention Quimby on Bee Keeping, and the last edition of Langstroth on Bees. They contain much curious and valuable practical information in regard to matters pertaining to bees, and should form part of the library of every apiarian.   J. A. B.

VIEW OF D STREET, MARYSVILLE.

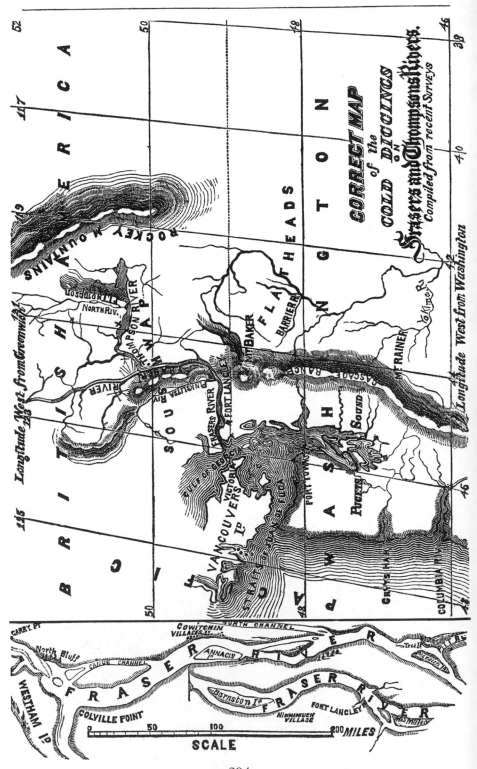

HUTCHINGS'

CALIFORNIA MAGAZINE.

Vol. 5.   APRIL, 1861.   No. 10.

THOMAS ARMSTRONG.

THOMAS ARMSTRONG.

THOMAS ARMSTRONG, the gifted engraver of a large proportion of the beautiful illustrations that have for several years embellished this magazine, has gone to the angels. At eleven o'clock, on the morning of the 21st of December last, he was at work; at half-past five, on the evening of the same day, the gravers he had so skillfully used lay untouched by his work; the hand that once grasped them was pulseless and cold with the ice of death. He died of congestion of the lungs.

Mr. Armstrong was born in the county of Northumberland, England, February, 1818, and was consequently in the 43d year of his age when he died. In early life he left his native place to seek his fortune in the great city of London, where he served his apprenticeship as an engraver. On the completion of his engagement, his services were secured in some illustrated works, then in progress; and when the Illustrated London News was first published, he executed many of its engravings. Seeing his aptitude and devotedness to business, the publishers of several standard works, such as Thos. Rymer Jones' "Natural History," "The Illustrated British Ballads," and numerous other literary productions of the first class, obtained his services.

At the age of twenty-two he was married to his first wife, by whom he had two daughters, both of whom were married and settled in California.

In 1848 he removed from London to Paris, and was an eye-witness of the stirring scenes of the French revolution of that year. In the autumn of 1848, not liking the manners and customs of the French, he left Paris with his family for Australia, where he had the misfortune to lose his amiable and excellent wife.

Hearing of the discovery of gold in California, he sailed for San Francisco, where he arrived early in 1849.

Immediately after his arrival, instead of following the eager tide of gold seekers, he devoted himself to his favorite employment, and on the 13th of October, 1849, he issued the first view ever published of the city and harbor of San Francisco. This was a large copper-plate engraving.

On the 4th of September, 1850, in company with another gentleman, Mr. Armstrong commenced the publication of the first pictorial paper of the Pacific coast, entitled "The Illustrated California News." To this he devoted himself both day and night, seldom giving himself more than from two to three hours' sleep. Owing to the all-absorbing pursuits of money-making, with the population of the new El Dorado, their enterprise was not sufficiently remunerative to warrant its continuance after the first seven numbers.

In 1855 he married his second wife, an excellent and devoted woman, by whom he had one daughter.

The earlier California resident will readily call to mind the graphic illustrations of the "Placer Times and Transcript," the "Sacramento Union," the "Golden Era," and "Wide West," with their richly embellished pictorial editions; with those of the "Miner's Progress," "Chips of the Old Block," "The Idle and Industrious Miner," and numerous other spirited engravings, nearly the whole of which were executed by the subject of this sketch. This brief outline brings us to Mr. Armstrong's connection with this magazine; and, considering its sudden and melancholy termination, the most painful part of our sad task.

The first engraving executed by him for this work was a "View from the Big Rookery" at the Farrallone Islands, page

56 of the first volume; and the last was the "Library of the What Cheer House," page 295 of the fifth volume. The latter he had just finished, when, on rising from his chair, he said, "I don't feel very well this morning; I think I will go and take a bath." Alas! we little thought he had then occupied that seat for the last time. It was the brightest day of our magazine's existence when he came to work for it, and the darkest when he was called from it by the hollow and irresistible voice of death.

The many hundreds of engravings executed for us, during a period of between four and five years, as well as for others preceding us, unanswerably attest his remarkable industry and skill—and there is not an engraver on this coast that would not cheerfully accord to him the well deserved credit of being at the head of the art in California.

Besides his peculiar talent, he was always gentlemanly, prompt, reliable, and not only honest, but honorable, in all his dealings. In his accounts we never discovered an error. An unpleasant word, or thought that we know of, never passed between us. He understood and carried out the divine rule of "As ye would that men should do unto you, do ye even so unto them." This made all business transactions with him of the pleasantest character. We would that there were more such men.

His devotedness to the fine arts caused him to do his utmost to foster, preserve and perpetuate them. This made him the life of pictorial engravings on the Pacific; and, but for him, and the gifted brothers Nahl (happily still living among us), most of rhose spirited scenes of California that have been given to the world, would have been slumbering in obscurity and comparatively unknown.

Possessing an inexhaustible fund of information, coupled with brilliancy in wit and good-humored repartee, he was remarkably good company. When in London, his evenings were frequently spent with such men as Douglas Jerrold and others of his class. His cheerful disposition, his excellent conversational and musical talents, and his warm-hearted friendship, secured to him a large and devoted circle of friends, and none more than the writer.

His bereaved family, to whom he was attached by ties of more than ordinary affection, while they mourn his sudden departure, will, we trust, feel that he is ever present among them to cheer and to bless them; and that, as their ministering spirit, he is ever watching over them with that tenderness he always cultivated on earth, to be perfected in heaven.

OUR FIRST FAMILIES.

A MEMBER OF THE FORMER F. F.'S.

LEST aspiring young Californians should, hereafter, when visiting in sister States, through the vanity natural to tender years, be tempted to boast of being allied to the first families of the Golden State, and so arouse ridicule where they wish to awaken envy, we present for their contemplation the head of a real and most respectable F. F. C., who would no doubt affectionately reciprocate claims of relationship, or dignify with the title of "Knight of the Scarlet Blanket" any one who would, in consideration, bestow on her one of those much prized and brilliant envelopes.

A MEMBER OF THE PRESENT F. F.'S.

As a contrast to the above, we place before you a likeness, the type of the nobility of our State. A representation of a hardy miner's phiz. Mark the expression of the eye and nostril. A volume of hardy experiences, of sagacity, of early reliant and lion-like prowess reveals itself in his stern glance, and in the deeply graven lines of his face. One feels like at once conceding that he is capable of that directness of aim and insight which inspires faith in a leader under difficulties, and gives assurance that he will reach the desired end by the shortest means, whether that end must be attained by tunnelling to the centre of one of the Sierras, or cutting through a mountain of interested legislation straight to the pure gold of justice it conceals. For, submit his flowing locks and beard to a skillful barber and his garb to the tailor, and lo! our miner would emerge in an hour equipped to grace any seat in the halls of State, which the choice of his confreres may confer ; and to defend their rights, or right their wrongs, unbiased by the influences that frequently bear sway in legislative halls.

The severe discipline inculcated by the exigencies of life in the mines, has developed a race of sturdy lords of the soil unrivalled by any other body of men in existence. Well may California be proud of her adopted sons, the heroes of her future bards and romancers, and who shall live to see themselves renowned as the founders of a band of States whose wealth and importance can now be but half imagined.

To those whose sympathies for the bereaved may lead them in imagination to the sad scene, the annexed touching incident, from the Tuolumne Courier, will be read with melancholy tenderness : —

When the conflagration which destroyed Murphy's Camp broke out, the mournful services of a funeral were being performed. A mother had lost her little child of some two years old. The little procession had reached the village church, and were there paying the last sad tribute of affection, when the fearful cry of fire smote upon the ear of that little group. So great was the panic, as the flames burst upon their sight through the church windows, that, involuntarily, all rushed out to render aid in staying the progress of the flames. In a moment, the poor mother found herself alone with her dead child; and, taking up the little coffin, returned to her home alone and unnoticed !

Poor lonely mother, at that moment thou must have needed the angel-ministerings of thy departed little one, to soothe and comfort thee on thy sorrowing journey of return. God help thee.

EDITOR'S NOTE: The editorial below appeared in the last number of volume 4. It is the clearest statement in *Hutchings'* pages of the difficulties in the way of continued publication of the magazine. The next year did not see improvement in the financial situation, nor did the hoped-for improvements in the magazine materialize. Rather, the numbers of the final year show retrenchment: the total number of engravings declines, and the major illustrated articles almost disappear. As J. M. Hutchings had sustained the magazine in style through four lean years already, it seems likely that the gradual failure of his health had more to do with the decline of the *California Magazine* than did money.

Editor's Table.

HE present number completes THE FOURTH VOLUME OF THE CALIFORNIA MAGAZINE. Four years, with their anxieties and gratifications, their toils and pleasures, their disappointments and hopes, their sorrows and joys, have rolled away into the irrevocable past, since its first publication. Like the miner, who year after year keeps drifting ahead in his tunnel with the hope and expectation that "pay dirt" will be found "just a little further in," have we labored unfalteringly on. Unlike many an industrious company of miners, who toil on, on, without even receiving a sufficient remuneration from the drift to pay for the mining tools, candles, blasting powder, fuse and other essential etceteras required in their work, we have met with an amount of success that has enabled us from its proceeds, to defray the cost of the materials used—*but no more.* As yet, every dollar that has been received has been paid out for engravings, composition, press-work, paper, binding, and other requisite expenses, directly incurred by the work, without allowing anything for our current personal expenses even. There are but few who prefer, even if they can afford it, to "work for nothing and board themselves," and we cannot confess to being exceptions to that rule.

This is not all, inasmuch as before the first number of this Magazine was issued we traveled from one end of the State to the other, in search of sketches and information of and about California, with which to embellish and enrich our work, so that it might be the more worthy of the great end we had in view; in which employment nearly four years of time and some six thousand dollars in money were expended, and of which no return whatever has yet been made.

The fact is we committed a financial error at the commencement of publication, in placing the subscription price of a California *illustrated* Magazine at $3 00 per year, 25 cents per single number—instead of $4 00 per year, and 37½ cents per single number. For a Magazine with the same amount of reading matter, *without illustrations,* some little profit might have been realized. The Pioneer Magazine, containing 64 pages, without illustrations, was $5 00 per year, or 50 cents per single number. The Pacific Expositor, containing about the same amount of reading matter as the CALIFORNIA MAGAZINE, without illustrations, is $3 00 per year, or 37½ cents per single number. The Pacific Medical Journal, of about the same size, without illustrations, is $5 00 per year, or 50 cents per number. The Hesperian, and California Culturist, both of which are published at an outlay not exceeding that of the CALIFORNIA MAGAZINE, are, the former at $4 00 per year, and the latter $5 00 per year. We mention this not by any means as a reflection upon those excellent journals, but to show, that, relying upon a much larger circulation, ours was commenced, and has been continued, at too low a price, for an *illustrated* California work.

With these facts before our friends, not for complaint, will they please allow us to suggest, *that each subscriber and purchaser endeavor to get at least one more to join him*, so that our circulation may be doubled—and which, while it will afford some little towards our personal expenses, will also enable us to add improvements now in contemplation.

If any of our subscribers have any numbers of this Magazine for March, 1857, which they do not intend to bind into a volume, we are authorized to offer $1 00 each for two copies of that date, or for four current numbers. It will also very much oblige us, if any persons having numbers one and nine for July, 1856, and March, 1857, if they do not require them for binding, to send them to our office, and we will forward in return two or even three of the current month, or exchange them for almost any other numbers.

SINCE our last issue, the entire State has been thrown into great excitement by the painful tidings of the massacre of several whites, at different points on the Carson River, Territory of Nevada, by the Indians, and their houses burned to the ground. As this was deemed the commencement of a protracted Indian war in that section, military companies were formed immediately and started out, one of which, numbering some 105 men, came upon the enemy near Pyramid Lake, who being well armed and in great numbers, forced the whites to retreat, with a loss of twenty-one men killed, besides others being wounded.

A number of horses, and all the supplies were taken by the Indians. As soon as this news was sent from one end of the State to the other, several military companies were called out and others formed, to march at once to the seat of war. Public meetings were convened and subscriptions raised to provide all the necessary supplies. At the request of Governor J. G. Downey, all the arms and ammunition required were placed by Gen. Clarke at the service of the State.

Each of the Washoe mining districts were declared under martial law, and all the able bodied men to be found were ready to render assistance. Fearing an attack at Virginia City, all the women and children were gathered within a fire-proof building, and defenses erected around it. Much of this alarm was altogether unnecessary, as none of the hostile Indians were found to be within fifty miles.

It would seem from the information at hand, that the Pah Utah, Pitt River, Shoshones and other Indians, to the number of about 1500, are in league together, instigated and commanded by some unprincipled whites, generally thought to be Mormons; but whether this is founded in fact or not has yet to be proved. Be that as it may, the peaceful settlements in Nevada Territory are harassed by Indian aggressions and excesses. It is rumored that a white man entered the hut of one of the principal chiefs of the Pah Utahs, and without the least provocation deliberately shot him down, and in revenge for this his people attacked the whites. We give this as rumor only, although it may be true.

IT is a humiliating fact, that nearly the entire newspaper press, not only of this State but of the United States, and Europe, for the time being, unhappily, has overlooked its great and ennobling mission of human elevation and refinement, and polluted its columns by publishing the particulars of the recent brutal encounter between two pugilists; and thus winked at, or pandered to, one of the most demoralizing exhibitions the world ever saw. Not only has the subject been forced upon the public through the journals of the day, as an item of news, but column upon column of biographical, historical and descriptive pugilism have been presented, that directly magnified its actors into great men and heroes, as when a city has been saved from destruction, or a country delivered from ruthless invasion.

Now we ask our brethren of the press, if this be right? If it is well, that such brutalizing encounters should be magnified into importance as items of news, even, outside the columns of journals devoted almost exclusively to such themes; to say nothing of "full particulars" being inconsiderately thrust into family circles, and almost necessarily made the subject of conversation at the dinner table or in the drawing-room? Are its tendencies such as will foster progress, or promote the weal of any people? Let the ebbing of this tide of demoralization, just forced to flow, but be closely watched, and it will give the answer.

WE omitted to mention, last month, that the portrait of Padre Junipero Serra, daguerreotyped from a painting in the Convent of San Fernando, city of Mexico, was obtained through the kindness of Major Wm. Rich, Secretary of Legation of the United States in Mexico in 1853, and who will please accept our thanks.

To Contributors and Correspondents.

☞ This month will complete our *Fourth Volume* — see Editor's Table. We most cordially, and with heart-feeling gratitude, return our sincere thanks to our many kind friends, who, from month to month, have sent us articles and subscriptions for our magazine during the past year. We hope they are not yet weary in well doing, but intend to continue their favors in the next, and for many years to come.

We shall be most happy at any time to receive offerings to California literature from its numerous friends, and from those, too, who have not before written for this magazine.

Any persons sending us their address with their articles, will always receive a reply by letter, with the assurance that even though their favors should prove unsuitable, their rejection will be strictly confidential.

B. T.—There is an unfairness in your arguments that precludes the acceptance of your article.

M. P.—Sunshine may be oppressive and almost unendurable, but we do not see how the same truth will apply to happiness.

D.—Yours are always welcome.

E.—We shall be pleased to receive other articles from your pen.

D. P.—If you write to the State Superintendent of Education, he will give you the information required. We cannot.

A., Oroville.—You cannot have read our notices to contributors, or you would have found that nothing which occurs of *sect* or *party* is admissible in this magazine. Scientific, historical, or descriptive matter upon California, is always acceptable.

C. B.—Send it and let us see it. Include your name and address.

G.—We cannot insert a portion until the whole is completed, and in our possession. A little reflection will satisfactorily explain the necessity for such a rule.

C.—Thank you for your many good wishes. We hope that every bucketful of pay-dirt in your claim will be spotted with gold; for such men, when rich, generally use it well. Don't let your present success make you forget your past misfortunes, or those of others whose "row of stumps" to-day are quite as hard to "hoe" as your's were six months ago.

To Everybody.—Now is a good time to subscribe. Don't forget this, as our next No. commences the *Fifth Volume* and new year of HUTCHINGS' CALIFORNIA MAGAZINE. We want to double our circulation this next year. Who will help us? Now, too, is a good time to form clubs. Begin at once, and send down your subscriptions.

PREMIUMS

— 402 —

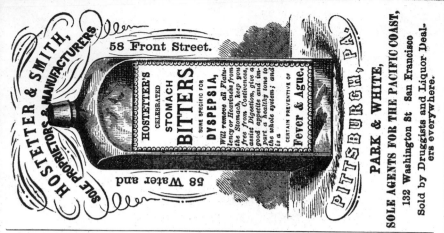

Dr. Wistar's Balsam of Wild Cherry,

FOR THE INSTANT RELIEF AND RAPID CURE OF

CONSUMPTION!

AND ALL ITS INCIPIENT SYMPTOMS, SUCH AS

Coughs, Colds, Hoarsness, Croup, Influenza, Bleeding of the Lungs, Liver Affections, Pains in the Breast and Side, Night Sweats, Phthisic. Inflammation of Lungs and Throat, Whooping Cough, Asthma, and all Bronchial affections?

☞ BEWARE OF BASE IMITATIONS!! As there are a number of *Counterfeits* bearing the name of Wistar's Balsam of Wild Cherry, purporting to be the "Genuine and Original," we therefore *caution* all persons who purchase the Balsam of Wild Cherry, to look well at the *signature* before buying. The genuine Wistar's Balsam of Wild Cherry has a FAC-SIMILE of the signature of Henry Wistar, M. D. Philadelphia, and Sanford & Park, on a steel-engraved wrapper. Therefore be cautious, as none can be genuine without the signature of Sanford & Park.

For sale by respectable Druggists.

PARK & WHITE, Sole Agents,

SAN FRANCISCO.

LYON'S MAGNETIC POWDER AND PILLS,

FOR THE DESTRUCTION OF ALL KINDS OF

Garden Insects, Ants, Bedbugs, Roaches, Ticks, Fleas, Moths, Rats and Mice, &c.

What greater trouble, in an hour of ease,
Than gnawing rats, bed bugs and fleas?

Gardens can be preserved and houses rid of these pests. It was discovered by Mr. E. Lyon, a French Chemist, in Asia, and has been patronized by all Eastern governments and colleges. Reference can be made wherever the article has been tried. *It is free from poison,* and harmless to mankind and domestic animals. Many worthless imitations are advertised. Be sure it bears the name of E. LYON. Remember—

'Tis Lyon's Powder kills insects in a trice,
While Lyon's Pills are mixed for rats and mice.

Sold by Druggists everywhere.

PARK & WHITE, Agents,

132 WASHINGTON ST., SAN FRANCISCO.

INDEX

The date of original publication of each article will be found after the title below, in cases where the date has not appeared with the article itself. Illustrations or illustrated articles are indicated by an asterisk *.

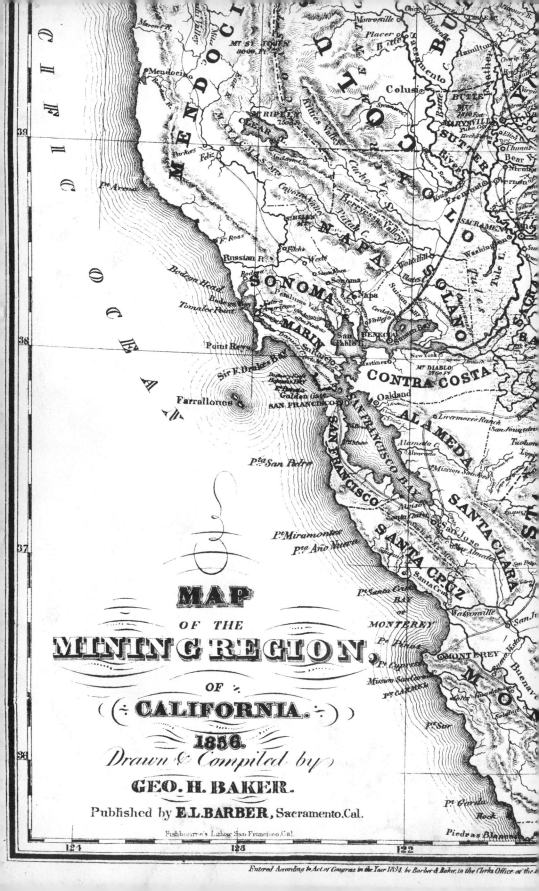

MAP
OF THE
MINING REGION,
OF
CALIFORNIA.
1856.
Drawn & Compiled by
GEO. H. BAKER.
Published by **E.L. BARBER**, Sacramento, Cal.

Fishbourne's Lithog. San Francisco, Cal.